D0860571

DATE DU

HYDROPOLITICS
of the
NILE VALLEY

Contemporary Issues in the Middle East

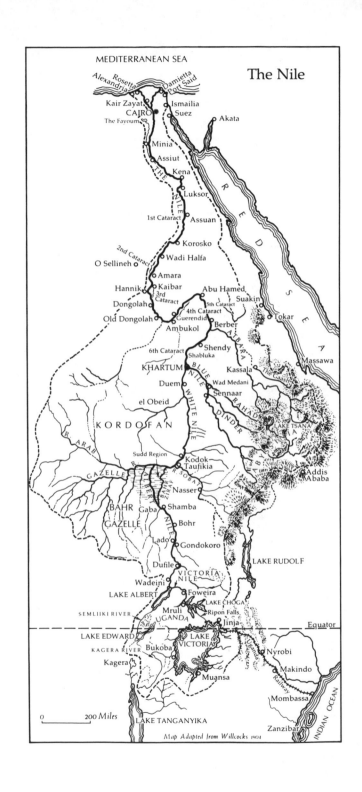

The Nile

HYDROPOLITICS
of the
NILE VALLEY

JOHN WATERBURY

SYRACUSE UNIVERSITY PRESS
1979

Library of Congress Cataloging in Publication Data

Waterbury, John.
Hydropolitics of the Nile Valley.

(Contemporary issues in the Middle East)
Bibliography: p. 273
Includes index.
1. Nile River—Regulation. 2. Nile Valley—Politics
and government. I. Title. II. Series: Contemporary
issues in the Middle East series.
TC518.N6W37   363.6'1'0962   79-16246
ISBN 0-8156-2192-2

To
Trishka

John Waterbury is Associate Professor at the Woodrow Wilson School of Public and International Affairs, Princeton University, and author of *The Commander of the Faithful: The Moroccan Political Elite* (1970), *North for the Trade: The Life and Times of a Berber Merchant* (1972), *Patrons and Clients* (1977), *The Middle East in the Coming Decade* (1978), and *Egypt: Burdens of the Past, Options for the Future* (1978).

CONTENTS

MAPS

FIGURES

TABLES

ACKNOWLEDGMENTS

THIS STUDY was made possible through the generous support of two organizations. The American Universities Field Staff sent me to Cairo as their Middle East Associate in 1971. From that time until 1977 I accumulated much of the material that has informed the following chapters. In 1976 I was the recipient of a Rockefeller Foundation grant to carry out research specifically related to the international management of the Nile River. This grant afforded me the opportunity to travel extensively in the Sudan and acted as a catalyst to the structuring of this book. Both organizations are, of course, in no way responsible for the kind of information marshalled below or for the conclusions I have drawn therefrom.

Numerous individuals have shared their expertise and insights with me over the years. Among them were Gordon McLean and Kingsly Haynes of the Ford Foundation, Cairo; Rushdy Said, Mohammed Kassas, Mustapha Gabali, Ali Fathy, Hilmy Said, Sarwat Fahmy, and Ibrahim al-Ghatwari, all well-known to those concerned with Egyptian agriculture, irrigation, and river hydrology. Likewise Christaan Gischler of UNESCO, Cairo, was unstinting in the time put at my disposal. On various occasions Minister of Land Reclamation Osman Badran, Minister of Irrigation Abd al-Azim Abu Al-Atta, and Speaker of the Parliament Sayyid Marei all found time to answer many of my questions. In the Sudan I owe a special debt of thanks to Jeswald Salacuse of the Ford Foundation, as well as to Michael Cruitt of USAID and Frederick Gerlach of the U.S. Embassy, Khartoum. Ronald Colley of Lonrho helped me become acquainted with the Kenana scheme, and William McNabb and William Evely were equally helpful in explaining to me the activities of the UNDP in the south. The HTS team at Nyala were warm and expert hosts during my sojourn in the west. Minister of Irrigation Yahya Abdel-Maguid, his successor, Saghayroun al-Zein, Minister of State for Agriculture Hussein Idris, Regional Deputy Minister for Agriculture David Basyuni, and Jonglei Commissioner Abdullahi Ibrahim were invaluable sources of information on problems of Sudanese agriculture and water resources.

Many others in Egypt, the Sudan, and elsewhere rendered me similar services in understanding the subject I chose to tackle. They are hereby gratefully albeit anonymously acknowledged and remembered.

Princeton, N.J.   JW
Spring 1979

HYDROPOLITICS
of the
NILE VALLEY

INTRODUCTION

IT HAS BECOME nearly a truism since the second World War that the nation state in many ways has outlived its usefulness. The preoccupation with frontiers, the compartmentalization of policy-making into domestic and foreign spheres, the reification of the political and economic sovereignty to which international realities give the lie seem, at a distance, outdated. Our new received wisdom stemmed first from the nature of modern weaponry in the cold war, the so-called delicate balance of terror. No nation, whatever its politics, whatever its conceptions of sovereignty, could be completely sheltered from nuclear holocaust. Subsequently attention has shifted to global interdependence in resource utilization. The "energy crisis" has brought to the fore a handful of states that control the world's supply of fossil fuels, and even the mightiest among nations must pay those states heed. Less spectacular because more gradual are other transnational resource crises: pollution of the atmosphere and the seas, destruction of forests — the world's lungs — desertification, inadequate food supplies and famine, and finally—because it is in part the concern of this study—the growing competition for fresh water.

Agriculture places far and away the heaviest demand upon fresh water supplies. If the world's growing populations, especially those of the developing countries, are to eat, let alone enter the industrial age, the pressure upon existing water resources will become much more intense. The FAO has estimated that for the Third World simply to hold its own in terms of food supply will require by the turn of the century the extension of irrigation to some 22 million hectares (1 ha. = 2.4 acres) and the delivery of an additional 440 billion m^3 of fresh water* to the new fields.[1] This water will come for the most part from rivers, or from the water tables that are fed by and feed into those rivers.

*Throughout this study m^3 will be used as the standard measure of water volume. One m^3 of water equals 1,000 kilograms (kgs) in weight or one metric ton. Billion throughout means one thousand million.

1

Rivers have a perverse habit of wandering across borders (simply by way of example, the Rhine, the Danube, the Euphrates, the Indus, the Brahmaputra, the Mekong, the Nile, the Congo, the Senegal, the Niger, the Platte, the Amazon, and the Colorado), and nation states have a perverse habit of treating whatever portion of them that flows within their borders as a national resource at their sovereign disposal. But water is ambient, and the consequences of its use or removal are felt downstream. The immediate result may be shortages and/or deteriorating quality; an ultimate result may be war. The stigma attached to tampering with water supply is ancient; it is, at whatever level of society, *casus belli*, perhaps nowhere more so than in the Middle East. Before the rise of the nation state customary law generally provided for collective access to and even collective management of this precious resource. Where rainfall was sparse and water points rare, as in the Middle East, it was regarded as God-given and could be appropriated only at the risk of offending the Almighty. The nation state took that risk, at least *vis-à-vis* other nation states if not its own citizens. In most of the Third World the nation state is a recent phenomenon, at most thirty-odd years old. The political sovereignty for which Third World countries struggled so long will not, while it is so new, be easily surrendered for the sake of a more rational utilization of the world's scarce resources. In fairness it would be hard to find a developed nation that has taken effective steps toward a more enlightened attitude.

— We are already into a quarter century in which the nation state and the world's scarce, vital resources are tracked on a collision course. What will happen? Surely not a cataclysmic collision for sooner or later the perceived imminence of the collision and our instincts for survival will produce compromise. But one should not take much comfort in that, for it raises so many other menacing questions. How and when will the likely collisions be perceived and identified? How much damage must be done before steps are taken toward compromise? What will be the nature of the compromise, and can the damage done be remedied? A consideration of the likely fate of the Nile in the near future may provide clues (but no more than that) to the emerging global water crisis.

Our focus throughout this study is on the utilization of the River Nile, that is, the nexus of hydraulic technique and the fresh water resource itself. For when all the policies are devised, decisions taken, political susceptibilities indulged, domestic and foreign constituencies placated, it takes dams, irrigation canals, pumps, and buckets to put the water where it should go (and almost as frequently where it should not). No river remains passive in the face of technological manipulation, and how it reacts necessitates further hydraulic feats.

Herein lies the major question of this study: how do hydraulics and policy intersect and with what results for the use of the resource? In attempting to answer this question with respect to the Nile, it is hoped that some light may be shed, in terms of *process*, on what we may expect to encounter in other like situations in the Third World. It can be taken as a case study in resource management and policy elaboration that may help us understand why the world in general finds itself in such forbidding resource binds, but also why, in many instances, they are not worse than they are. Too much has been made of the bungling of the High Aswan Dam as well as other Third World ventures into sophisticated hydraulics. Too little has been made of how comparatively well this and other projects have been implemented or of what the consequences would have been had they never been undertaken. So while the message of what follows will be somber, it could have been more so.

It is here that the essential conundrum is posed: how can "sovereign" states, pursuing national self-interest and those policies that seemingly ensure a regime's survival, cope with the challenge of bi- or multinational coordination in the use of a common resource? The elements entering this equation in the Nile Valley are so structured as to thwart steps toward optimal usage. Why this is so, and what its implications are for the near future are the principal themes of this book; all others—such as choice of technology, elaboration of national growth targets, the search for external financing—are subordinate and explored only insofar as they illuminate the basic dilemma.

Along these same lines it should be emphasized that states are responsible in the Third World for policy planning regarding scarce resources. This facilitates our task for, although in some instances the state may derogate its authority in this domain to other actors (e.g., multinational corporations, foreign creditors, domestic pressure groups) we can still identify the locus of the decision whatever its repercussions. We are not thus confronted with a congeries of private actors whose individual acts and decisions defy coherent aggregation. For our purposes here, we are dealing with two autonomous decision-making bodies, the governments of Egypt and the Sudan, and one resource, the Nile.

These governments are the principal but not the only actors relevant to the disposition of the river. As we shall see other states, especially Ethiopia, are directly involved. Further, there are external interests, both governments and international aid agencies, that influence directly and indirectly this process of resource utilization. Nonetheless, an essential point is that the nation state with its national development goals and its national foreign policy and domestic concerns remains the framework for dealing with a transnational asset. The anomalies in resource utilization that derive from this situation are a theme that runs constantly through this study.

One of the gaps policy-makers have generally failed to bridge is also one that policy analysts have failed to bridge. It is the separation of the criteria for the adoption of specific technologies from the criteria guiding the political and economic decision-making process. National policy-making elites are generally preoccupied with the latter, and they expect the technocrats to adapt their needs to political decisions taken without regard to technological opportunity costs. Seldom do these two groups speak each other's language. Seldom do they clearly perceive the close interaction of their two spheres, that a political decision may determine the adoption of a certain technology but that once adopted that technology will then determine subsequent political decisions.

Similarly, academics compartmentalize the substance of policy-making. Political scientists (although this characterization is less and less true) have eschewed both the economic and the technological aspects of national decision-making. Non-Marxist economists have infrequently invaded the realm of political analysis and only somewhat less infrequently that of engineering and technology, while the engineers, except as regards project benefit-cost analysis, have kept clear of politics and macro-economics. The result, both in terms of the decision-making process itself and the analysis of that process, has been a fragmented and incomplete picture in which many interrelationships are left unexplored. In this situation one cannot properly assess cause and effect, and that after all is what the exercise is all about. It may well be the case, and indeed in the conclusion we so argue, that policy-making groups and external creditors *prefer* an incomplete picture for then unanticipated errors can be written off to incomplete information and poorly defined responsibilities. Academics presumably have no such motivation.

What then are the components that must be assembled for a complete picture? As concerns the Nile the components constitute the sequential ordering of this book. The first task is to understand the resource itself, its natural dynamics, and its evolution within the human ecosystem. Contemporary engineering has built upon techniques for manipulating the river that date back millennia. We may learn a great deal about today's hydraulic challenges by reference to the historical record. Moreover, we shall see that many of the problems and side effects attributed to the Aswan High Dam have plagued Egypt over the centuries. They may be more acute today, but they are not new.

Secondly, we must examine the relations and mutual susceptibilities among the riparian states. Our primary focus here will be upon Egypto-Sudanese relations in the modern era in order better to grasp the factors that have impeded effective steps toward political and economic integration — or, put another way, why there are still two decision-making centers rather than one determining the use of the river. The territory of the Nile basin is shared by nine states all of which could, to varying degrees, influence the flow and the quality of the water of the river. Egypt has always been acutely sensitive to the dangers of this broader regional context for, as the epitome of the downstream state, its economic life is at the mercy of upstream developments. In the last century this concern has become understandably obsessive. The current turbulence prevailing throughout Northeast Africa combined with increasing great power involvement has intensified all the visceral fears of Egypt and its regional allies as to the fate of the Nile. To underestimate or overlook this factor is to misread Egypt's and nearly to an equal extent the Sudan's deep concern with all that transpires politically in the vast Nile catchment. This concern has implicitly and on occasion explicitly led Egypt to reserve for itself the right to intervene in the affairs of other states to protect its vital water interests.

If one had to single out one factor that more than any other has determined the choice of hydraulic technology on the Nile in this century it would be exactly this downstream complex. Likewise no single project illustrates this better, nor is any more intrinsically important than the Aswan High Dam, a single, giant edifice totally within Egypt's borders that for a time seemed to be the country's ultimate insurance against seasonal or perennial water shortage. Yet the history of this project is testimony to the primacy of political considerations determining virtually all technological choices with the predictable result that a host of unanticipated technological and ecological crises have emerged that now entail more political decisions. It is not our intention to judge the dam or those who backed it, but rather to delineate as accurately as possible the process by which it came into being and by which its side effects are being confronted.

The next dimension of the overview is to assess the policy-making arena within the two states with which we are most concerned. It is unlikely that Presidents Sadat and Numeiry go to bed at night with visions of the Nile running dry or polluted beyond use torturing their sleep. Other visions probably *do* torture their sleep: war with Israel, domestic constituencies bent on their overthrow, immediate economic crises and pressures for unpalatable economic reforms emanating from international agencies and regional creditors, and so forth. The Nile, both these leaders may presume, is the one element in this scene upon which they can more or less rely. Beyond the day-to-day crises and challenges that each regime faces are the longer-term programs and strategies of national development that, if we are to believe the policy-makers of Egypt and the Sudan, will ensure prosperity for their peoples within this century. If we do not believe them, we can see these strategies as the proper public gloss on short-term survival tactics. In either case optimal use of the Nile is not at the forefront of their considerations. At the same time each nation harps on its capacity for autonomous growth, public bureaucracies indulge in project-mongering and international investors look for projects that will either pay off financially or have political propaganda value. The Nile may well be the victim of these short-sighted non-integrated policies.

Both Egypt and the Sudan are desperately short of the foreign exchange needed to cover their imports of basic consumer goods and investment requisites. They must struggle for access to international capital markets and important likely sources of "soft" funds. Both kinds of financing will be an important substantive sub-theme of this study. It is all the more pertinent in that Egypt and the Sudan figure prominently — but for very different reasons — in the movement of petrodollars within the Middle East. To understand why these as yet modest flows move where they do, we must look at the likely motives and apprehensions, within the regional framework, of the oil-rich, above all Saudi Arabia. These small states, powerful only through the financial resources (or so-called surplus earnings from petroleum exports) at their command, have great power patrons, primarily the United States, with whom they collaborate to make the most effective regional use of their financial leverage.

What these creditors seek to extract from Egypt and the Sudan may and probably does have little to do with optimizing the use of the Nile's waters. In exploring this subtheme we will thus be illustrating the permeability of the national decison-making process to exogenous forces that may, inadvertently, hasten the day of irreconcilable water demands. They may also hasten the day when they will be called upon to arbitrate the resultant disputes.

Thus the final question is to look to the future and estimate the impact of national development programs as currently enunciated upon existing water resources. This amounts to working out a budget and balance sheet for projected water utilization. Anticipating the result of this exercise (Chapter 8), it is found that the risk of a major water shortage by the mid-1980s is very high. Yet official pronouncements insist that there is no cause for alarm. One suspects that in fact some state officials may be aware of the coming crisis but that for a number of reasons we adduce in the conclusion, it is neither in their nor their government's interests to sound the alarm. Both as to the balance sheet and the final reaction to it, one also suspects that other major transnational rivers are now or will be in the near future in the same throes as the Nile.

So far we have emphasized the comparative lessons that might be drawn from this case study of the Nile but whatever they may be the fact remains that in and of itself the fate of the Nile is of immense importance. In Egypt and the Sudan alone it sustains a population of fifty to sixty millions. It is Egypt's unique source of water; Egypt can take from it but not add to it as there are no tributaries or rainfall within Egypt that could compensate for its demand upon the river. No one need be reminded of Egypt's long-standing geopolitical significance astride the east-west sea lanes and the north-south corridors linking the European land mass to Africa.

Egypt's pivotal role in the regional politics of the Middle East is recognized not only in Washington and Moscow but throughout the Arab world as well. With its forty millions, substantial industrial base, and large standing army, it is far and away the most powerful of all Arab states. According to the inclinations of its leaders and the state of its economy it can be a force for great good or ill depending on one's vantage point. Yet this nation that Winston Churchill once compared to a deep-sea diver whose air was provided by the long and vulnerable tube of the Nile has moved from the region's most prosperous and advanced society to a position of chronic economic distress and deteriorating living standards. The country has reached the outer limits of its agricultural growth and is enmeshed in a long-term holding action against further degradation of its agrarian base. Whether Egypt is able to hold its own, much less progress economically, is a question of momentous importance for the region as a whole. Habib Boulares, an Arab editor, summed up a general feeling.

> What will the Arabs do faced with the population increase in the Nile
> Valley from Khartoum to Alexandria, in an area they have outgrown and
> continue to outgrow? Forty million people or something close to it in
> Egypt alone and perhaps twice that number by the year 2000. It is
> obvious that we would be committing a cardinal error if we were to treat
> this as a purely Egyptian problem. It is not merely an Egyptian problem
> but that, at least, of its immediate neighbors: Libya, the Sudan, Saudi
> Arabia, and Palestine. For its vital living space is narrow. There can be
> only two outcomes. Either this living space is expanded through modern
> technology, or the human pressure will explode in the form of migration
> and colonization outside the Nile Valley.[2]

The Sudan enters the picture not only as Egypt's midstream
hinterland, erstwhile colony, and potential refuge for excess population, but as one of these rare corners of the world where great agricultural surpluses may yet be generated. It could come to meet an important part of the food deficits being forecast for the Third World in
general and the Middle East in particular. Egypt, if it can find an
appropriate means of payment, could become its largest customer.

INTRODUCTORY NOTE ON EGYPT AND THE SUDAN

There is little but the Nile and historical circumstances to join Egypt
and the Sudan. The claims of academicians and propagandists from
both countries notwithstanding, the socioeconomic differences between the two far outweigh their similarities.

Population and Population Density

In 1976 Egypt had a population of 38.3 million, of which 1.4
million lived abroad. This population was crammed into a habitable
area of about 30,000 km² or 11,200 square miles. With average densities
of 1,000 people per km², Egypt is on a par with Bangladesh. Seen from a
different perspective, Egypt's population survives in an area the size of
the Irish Republic or West Virginia. The Sudan, by contrast, is about
one-third the size of the continental United States, and 60 percent of its

surface is habitable. Average densities there are 6 to 7 persons per km², rising in the rural areas to a high of about 100 per km² in and around the Gezira Cotton Scheme. The contrast here is thus between extreme population concentration and crowding in Egypt and relatively pronounced dispersion in the Sudan.

Ethnoreligious Composition

Despite waves of exogenous invaders over the millennia, the Egyptian population is physically, linguistically, and culturally homogeneous. That is the result, as much as anything, of sharing limited land and water resources at very close quarters over long periods of time. According to the official census,[3] about 7 percent of the population is Coptic Christian although the Coptic Church claims 12 percent. Yet there is nothing physically (save an occasional tattooed cross) that would distinguish a Copt from an Egyptian Muslim. The Sudan, however, is markedly heterogeneous. The prevailing forms of rural social structure are still tribal units, unlike Egypt which is firmly village based. Sudanese tribes are of various ethnic groupings—such as Nilo-Hamitic, Arab, and Negroid*—and physical differences and life styles are pronounced. In this respect the Sudan is more like Morocco or Iran than Egypt. The fact that one-third of the population is non-Muslim and Negroid makes the Sudanese mosaic all the more striking. With the exception of the riverine populations of the Northern Province, which are closest to and most resemble Egyptian sedentary cultivators, one is most impressed by the mobility and wanderlust of the Sudanese.

Modes of Production

The differences between the extensive, shifting, low-yield, rain-

---

*The Sudanese mosaic comprises substantial exogenous elements. The term *fellata* refers to all non-Sudanese westerners (originally to northern Nigerians only), most of whom came to the Sudan on their pilgrimage route to Mecca, and who supplemented their meager finances by working odd jobs along the way. Over the years a large colony had assembled, now estimated at two million members, many of whom settled on the banks of the Blue Nile south of Sennar, and who have set up their own tribal hierarchy under a Sultan. Some of these *fellata* have been in the Sudan for more than three generations but are not considered to be strictly Sudanese by the natives. Peter Bechtold, *Politics in the Sudan* (New York: Praeger, 1976), p. 156.

fed agriculture practiced throughout most of the Sudan until a few decades ago and the intensive, fixed, high-yield irrigated agriculture practiced in Egypt extend into other domains of productive life. There is no question that in terms of agricultural techniques the Egyptians have been and remain far in advance of their Sudanese brethren. They have tens of centuries of experience in the generation of agricultural surplus, whereas the Sudanese are still for the most part rooted in subsistence patterns. In consequence, Egypt utilized its surplus to forge ahead in the development of urban centers, crafts and trades, industry, and the administrative-governmental forms necessary to attend to an integrated economy and culture. It was only in the twentieth century, however, that Sudanese public authorities began to aspire to the same degree of integration and centralization, and they are still a long way from achieving it.

Egypt is a much more urban society than the Sudan, with 44 percent of its population living in cities. Greater Cairo alone, housing more than 8 million people, accounts for more than 20 percent of the country's entire population. Only about 7 percent of the Sudanese population (ca. 17.5 million in 1975) can be considered urban, and the tri-city nexus of Khartoum/Khartoum North/Omdurman contained in the mid-1970s less than a million inhabitants. Urbanization and the spread of nonagricultural skills generally go hand in hand, and here again Egypt is relatively advantaged. Such skills in today's world may also be dependent upon literacy. In Egypt, 56 percent of the population 10 years old and older is illiterate (43 percent for males and 71 percent for females). This level is down from 70 percent in 1960. In the Sudan 80 percent of all those between 10 and 45 are illiterate.

National Consciousness and Civilization

The Egyptians are aware of themselves as a people, and they nurtured this awareness long before the imported Western label of "nation" was affixed to them. The geophysical characteristics of existence in the Egyptian Nile Valley produce an insularity and hence an intimacy that makes for feelings of common identity as strong as, say, those of the English. Moreover, the Egyptians take pride in their long history and their building and exportation of civilization and culture. They see themselves, not unjustifiably, as having been a beacon unto the Mediterranean world, purveyors of science, technology, and ordered life to the more backward societies surrounding their oasis. In that light, the Sudan was on all counts inferior, hardly more than a collection of barbarian bands. The Egyptian outlook on the Sudan has traditionally been colonialist, and backed by its heavy military preponderance, Egypt has periodically exerted direct control over parts of the Sudan. This historical experience has conditioned both peoples, and while all the talk today is of fraternity and equality, latent feelings of superiority and inferiority still underlie relations between the two states.

The Ties that Bind

Mitigating the long list of factors that set these societies apart are at least three that pull them together. Foremost among them is Islam, whose egalitarian doctrines have allowed the incorporation into the community of believers of most of the Sudan's population, leaving aside the three southern provinces. To be a Muslim automatically entails a status and degree of respect and acceptance on the part of all other Muslims, and while this mechanism may occasionally break down, it is an important factor for forging affinity. Concomitantly, both populations are bound together in the use of Arabic as the principal means of communication, although the elites of both countries may be proficient in English or secondarily some other European language. Even in the south of Sudan, with its myriad of tribal languages, a kind of pidgin-Arabic appears to be the *lingua franca*. Finally, Egypt and the Sudan were linked together through British control from 1898 on. The first steps toward economic and hydrological integration were taken after that date. At the same time, the nationalist elites of both countries achieved political maturity with the same adversary in their sights. They began to compare notes, share experiences, and articulate the commonality of their subservient status to British interests.

It is still at the elite level that communications and contacts are maintained. The overwhelming majority of Egyptians have little notion of who the Sudanese are or what their country is like, and in some ways they probably do not care. Conversely, despite the presence of half a million or more Sudanese living in Egypt, most Sudanese are equally unfamiliar with Egypt. If these two nations are to move closer together, it will require a willed effort on the part of their elites. Integration, if it is to take place, will come from the top down.

1

DEVELOPMENT OF THE RIVER SYSTEM

THE GREAT RIVER VALLEYS of the world witnessed humankind's first efforts to tamper with nature, to move beyond subsistence, and to engineer the environment. As we all know by now this manipulative urge has stimulated our greatest triumphs and yet laid the foundations for cataclysms of our own making. Of all river systems none beckoned so alluringly to be domesticated as the Nile. Its generally benign interaction with its valleys and inhabitants fairly dictated that they take the logical but fated step of attempting to improve on its natural attributes.

A river that for millennia was an object of worship, a beneficent and munificent symbol of fertility and renewal, is now no longer itself. The terrestrial force that so dominated the sacred and the profane of ancient Egypt is now trapped behind a manmade dam at Aswan, downstream from which is, for all intents and purposes, an enormous irrigation ditch. If the modern Egyptians are to have their way, every drop of the river's waters reaching the Mediterranean will have been utilized, and for months at a time no water will be allowed to escape at all.

For 7,000 years, or perhaps longer, the inhabitants of the Nile Valley have been mastering their river in order to master their land. But each technological advance has eventually entailed ecological setbacks. By the nineteenth century, as the population grew, the race between technological progress and ecological breakdown became particularly intense, so that by the twentieth century manmade imbalances had become so acute that the only solution was to try to correct one imbalance by planting the seeds of yet another. There was, by this time, no going back to the *status quo ante* short of plague, famine, or exodus.

In very broad terms one can outline a process of land and water degradation in nearly any river valley in which irrigation is extensively practiced, but particularly in those of arid regions. In essence, degrada-

12

tion takes place because water used to irrigate land upstream is generally drained back into the river, adding to the river's discharge the salts and chemical residues leached from the soil in the drainage process. Expressed more technically, with irrigation there is an increase in the surface-to-depth ratio of the water, thus increasing the evaporation potential. Further, by increasing vegetative cover, evapo-transpiration is increased which in turn augments the concentration of salts in the soil. In arid zones there is frequently a salt layer that is dissolved in the irrigation process and brought to the surface by capillary action. Thus the water brought to the fields further downstream is more saline and otherwise polluted, and after a point soil fertility is affected. The problem is compounded if natural or manmade drainage systems are faulty as salts will then be increasingly concentrated in the soil. Typically the lands lying furthest downstream, the river deltas with the richest deposits of alluvial soils, are the most severely afflicted by salinity, as salts in the irrigation water have attained maximum levels by the time it reaches the delta. Moreover, the low-lying delta lands tend to drain poorly and the water table is close to the surface. Poor drainage and the evaporation of excess water in the soil further concentrate salts, and whole areas risk being "salted out" or made unfit for cultivation. The irony is that in extending irrigation systems to increase production, the first victim of progress may well be the valley's most productive lands. The lower Tigris-Euphrates Valley has lost millions of acres to salt as have sections of the Indus. Over the centuries the same phenomenon has manifested itself in the Nile Delta and has reached crisis proportions in recent decades.

Nonetheless, for most of recorded history the inhabitants of the Nile Valley struck a fairly happy balance between their agricultural needs and the maintenance of soil and water quality. The balance was by no means entirely or even mostly of their doing; rather it was simply built into the natural functioning of the system, a fact which may explain the awe and reverence in which the river was held by its human beneficiaries. To understand the ecology of the valley and the strains under which the system now labors, we must first describe the basics, the topography and hydrology of the river.

TOPOGRAPHY AND HYDROLOGY

The most remote source of the Nile is the Luvironza River in Tanzania, 6,825 kilometers (4,200 miles) from the river's Mediterranean mouth.

The waterway length of the river, however, is 6,058 kilometers (3,728 miles), and its drainage basin is an area of nearly 3.1 million km² (1.2 million square miles), the equivalent of one-tenth of the African continent.[1] This drainage and catchment area today impinges upon the territory of nine African nations: the Sudan, the Central African Republic, Zaire, Uganda, Rwanda, Burundi, Tanzania, Kenya, and Ethiopia. Egypt, the river's primary beneficiary, is drained by the Nile but makes no contribution to its discharge.

TABLE 1

The Nile in Comparison to Other Major River Systems

River	Length in km	Drainage area km²	Annual discharge: billions of m³	Annual sediment load: millions of tons
1. Nile	6,825	3,100,000	84	110
2. Amazon	6,700	7,050,000	3,000	900
3. Congo	4,700	3,700,000	1,400	70
4. Hwang Ho	4,630	770,000	200	2,000
5. Mekong	4,200	795,000	400	800
6. Niger	4,100	1,890,000	180	40
7. Mississippi	3,970	3,220,000	600	600
8. Danube	2,900	1,165,000	200	80
9. Zambesi	2,700	1,300,000	500	100
10. Rhine	1,320	162,000	80	3

SOURCE: Democratic Republic of the Sudan, Ministry of Irrigation, *Control and Use of the Nile Waters in the Sudan*, Khartoum (June 1975), p. 7.

The Nile River has two major tributaries, the White and Blue Niles (Figures 1 and 2). The White Nile finds its principal source in Lake Victoria, a body of fresh water of 69,485 km² (27,000 square miles) in surface, second in size only to Lake Superior. Nearly a third of Victoria's entire inflow is derived from the 60,000 km² Kagera river catch-

FIGURE 1

Slope of the Nile from Lake Victoria to the Mediterranean

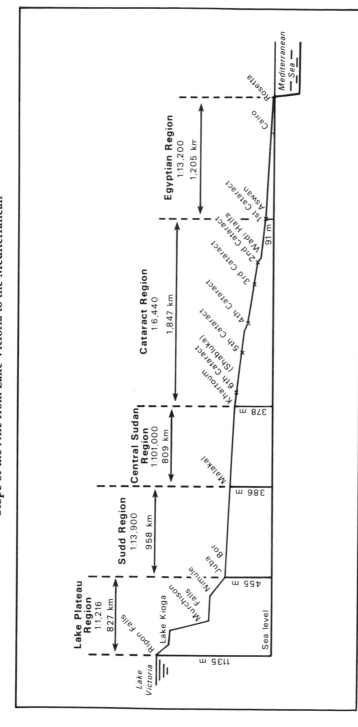

SOURCE: John Ball, *Contributions to the Geography of Egypt* (Cairo: Government Press, 1939).

ment to the southwest. Most of Rwanda and Burundi lie in this basin, while 33 and 10 percent of the catchment area fall within Tanzanian and Ugandan territory respectively. Straddling the equator, Victoria lies 1,133 meters (3,716 feet) above sea level and 5,611 kilometers (3,507 miles) from the mouth of the Nile. From this lake issues the Victoria Nile, dropping nearly 516 meters (1,700 feet) over 220 kilometers (138 miles), passing through Lake Kioga and then entering Lake Mobutu (formerly Lake Albert). This lake also receives the discharge of Lake Idi Amin (formerly Lake Edward) and the Semliki River, but in surface and volume it is only about one-tenth the size of Victoria. From Lake Mobutu to Nimule on the Uganda-Sudanese border, the river is known as the Albert Nile. After plunging through the Fola Rapids and into the Sudan, the Albert Nile becomes the Behr el-Jebel (literally Mountain Sea) and drops nearly 180 meters (600 feet) over a 168-kilometer distance to reach Juba, the capital of the southern Sudan. The river is now 452 meters (1,483 feet) above sea level but must still travel 4,787 kilometers (2,992 miles) before reaching the Mediterranean.

A great deal of the Behr el-Jebel's waters, however, never reaches the sea. A little north of Juba at Mongolla the river reaches the bottom of the bowl of its upstream drainage basin. Its slope flattens dramatically, and when in flood spills out over its banks and spreads in all directions forming a giant papyrus swamp known as the Sudd (the barrier). The permanent swamp here is about 6,000 km² (2,600 square miles) in surface, and in it the Behr el-Jebel loses about half of its total discharge (i.e., a loss of around 14 billion m³) through evaporation. Between Bor and the junction of the Behr el-Jebel and Behr el-Ghazal rivers, there rises a semi-independent, swamp-derived river, the Behr el-Zeraf, lying to the east of the Behr el-Jebel. Between the two rivers lies Zeraf Island. The probable origins of the swamps are worth noting. They are, in all likelihood, the remnants of a giant prehistoric lake, extending north of what is today Khartoum and with a surface of 230,000 km², four times the surface of Victoria. The lake emptied when the present-day Shabluka Gorge north of Khartoum was eroded and degraded.

Through the Sudd, the river maintains sufficient velocity to cut a sluggish, meandering 600-kilometer course until it reaches Lake No. There it is joined by another tributary, the Behr el-Ghazal, which receives its water from Zaire, the Central African Republic, and the Behr el-Arab and Lol Rivers of western Sudan. With this new surge of water the river is able to escape the swamps. Known now as the White Nile, the river jogs east, picks up the flow of the Sobat River that rises in the Ethiopian Highlands, and then turns north to Malakal (near the famous site of the Fashoda Incident). Malakal is 382 meters above sea level and 3,832 kilometers from the river's mouth. From this point to Khartoum, a distance of 807 kilometers, the White Nile receives no additional sources of water. Its slope from Malakal to Khartoum (see Figure 2) is even less than that between Bor and Malakal, but after evaporation in the swamps, so is its discharge.

FIGURE 2

Longitudinal profile of the Blue Nile

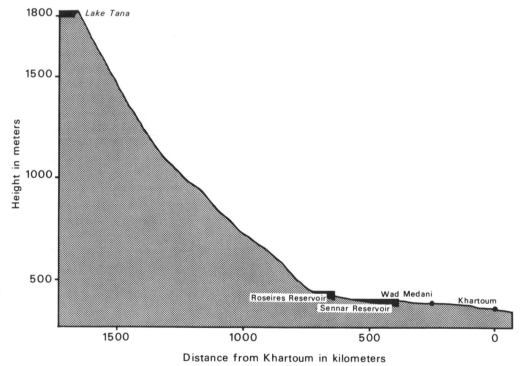

Distance from Khartoum in kilometers

Khartoum (literally the hose or the trunk) is located at the confluence of the White and Blue Niles at 370 meters above sea level. The principal source of the Blue Nile is Lake Tana (3,100 km²) lying nearly

1,800 meters above sea level and 1,500 river kilometers from Khartoum. Over that course the Blue Nile drops about 410 meters and picks up the flow of two seasonal tributaries, the Dinder and the Rahad.

From Khartoum downstream we are now dealing with the main Nile. Despite the seasonal discharge of the Atbara River that enters 320 kilometers north of Khartoum, the Nile receives no perennial sources of water over the rest of its 3,000-kilometer journey to the sea. This is probably the longest stretch of river in the world of which this can be said, and all the more notable for the fact that it cuts its way through the forbidding eastern reaches of the Sahara desert. The Nile is rightly described as an exotic river, nourishing a "linear oasis" nearly 1,000 kilometers long. En route the Nile once traversed five cataracts between Atbara and Aswan, until the Aswan High Dam and its reservoir submerged the next to last. (For some reason the most downstream cataract, that at Aswan, has been referred to as the first, and then one counts upstream to reach the fifth. It is the second cataract that has been drowned.) By the time the river reaches Aswan in Egypt it is only 87 meters above sea level but still 1,180 kilometers from its mouth. Its steepest slope thereafter is the stretch between Aswan and Cairo over which it drops 74 meters in 960 kilometers. Just to the north of Cairo the river forks into the Rosetta branch that empties into the Mediterranean on the western side of the Delta near Alexandria, and the Damietta branch which discharges on the eastern side. The slope of both branches is very gentle, dropping only 12 meters over roughly 240 kilometers.*

All of the waters of the Nile are derived from rainfall upon the Ethiopian plateau and upon the hinterlands of the Equatorial lakes. The contribution of rainfall further downstream, for instance in the Sudd swamp area, is negligible. The seasonal fluctuations of rainfall in the Lake Tana region (the headwaters of the Blue Nile), are much more marked than those prevailing at the source of the White Nile. This explains the important variation in the volume and timing of the peak discharges of the Blue and White Niles, a point to which we shall return. Maximum rainfall in both areas is about 800–1,200 millimeters per year. Over Victoria rainfall averages about 1,200 millimeters annually, slightly in excess of surface evaporation of 1,120 millimeters. Lake Mobutu generally receives 800 millimeters of rain but evaporation rates are well in excess of this. Throughout later sections of this study we

*One can express the slope of the Upper Egyptian (Sa'idi) Nile as 1:12,000 or a 1-meter drop for each 12,000 meters (12 kilometers) downstream flow. For the Delta or Bahrawi Nile the ratio is 1:20,000.

shall have occasion to come back to crucial questions pertaining to evaporation rates.

As one moves downstream from the Equatorial lakes and the Ethiopian plateau, annual precipitation declines in volume and increases in variability. In portions of the southernmost Sudan the climate is semitropical and rainfall averages 800–1,400 millimeters annually. Further north there is a broad belt (or in pluviometric terms, isohyet) on an east-west axis that comprises the extensive Sudanese savanna region and parts of the Sudd. Here, there is about 400 to 800 millimeters of rain each year concentrated in the late spring and summer months. Still further north, in the provinces of northern Darfur, northern Kordofan, and the Northern province, seasonal precipitation tapers to 75 to 400 millimeters annually. From there north to the Mediterranean rainfall is negligible or totally absent with the minor exception of the areas immediately adjacent to the Mediterranean along the northwest Egyptian coast.

While rainfall at the headwaters of both Niles is abundant, it is by no means consistent. The periodicity of precipitation in these regions is, as elsewhere in the world, only partially understood. Some years ago J. W. Beardsley speculated on the basis of 1,300 years of Nile floods, that the equatorial cycles of rainfall cluster into periods of 30 to 40 years or multiples thereof.[2] Such cycles have not been conclusively verified, but it is a fact that the Equatorial lakes, particularly Lake Victoria, are currently experiencing nearly a decade of overabundant rain. The lake levels have risen, flooding areas along their shores and increasing the volume of the discharge downstream. Victoria is releasing 150 million m^3 a day as compared with a more "normal" discharge of 100 million m^3. Downstream, extensive areas of the Sudd that would generally dry out and drain after the rainy season have remained perennially inundated for several years. This is the case in particular for the Zeraf Island between the Behr el-Jebel and the Behr el-Zeraf. In contrast, the recent decline in precipitation over the Ethiopian Highlands has been below average levels for this century. The conclusion to be drawn is that the two sources of the main Nile are subjected to differing climatic patterns. Indeed the Equatorial lakes, because of the enormous evaporation they generate, may sustain a kind of microclimatological environment relatively insulated from the fluctuations affecting the African continent as a whole.

Whether or not this argument is tenable, one must nonetheless call attention to some of the climatic changes that have occurred across all of West, Central, and East Africa. Both the Equatorial and Ethiopian

Highland regions are dependent upon the southerly flow of the Indian Ocean monsoon which sweeps across the horn of Africa in the summer months, and even reaches Yemen. The western tributaries of the White Nile and the rainfed areas of the western Sudan rely also upon the Guinea and Congo monsoons that water the Sahel zone of West Africa. It is of course well known that for nearly a decade, beginning in the mid-1960s, the Guinea monsoon "failed" and the Sahel zone underwent a catastrophic drought. The same phenomenon made itself felt over the Ethiopian Highlands, although the Equatorial lakes remained fairly impervious to the drought. In the opinion of Reid Bryson of the University of Wisconsin, what is at work is the "Sahelian effect." The southernmost edge of the prevailing dry, subtropical anticyclones is no longer retreating as far northward in the summer as has been the case in previous decades. This in turn blocks the southerly flow of moist air from the Atlantic and Indian Oceans during the monsoons. The shift in the latitude of the seasonal movement of the subtropical anticyclones has been small but nonetheless sufficient to lead to desertization* of vast areas, including parts of the western Sudan. It has seemingly contributed to the low discharge of the Blue Nile in the early 1970s and the resultant below-average floods on the main Nile. In recent years there has been some relief on all fronts, and the monsoon rains have returned. Still, if Bryson is correct, the globe is entering a secular trend in climate change that he refers to as the "little ice age." This general cooling is attributed to a number of factors that need not detain us here. The specific impact of this secular trend would be the recurrence if not prevalence of the Sahelian effect in the future.[3] One must at least entertain the possibility that the Indian Ocean monsoon will no longer regularly penetrate far enough north to provide the precipitation the Nile system requires for "normal" discharge. But having called attention to this possible and ominous eventuality, we shall ignore it from here on and assume that rainfall and river discharge will conform to averages established in the past century.

We come now to the heart of the matter: the total volume and seasonal availability of water in the Nile system. The average annual discharge of the main Nile as measured at Aswan is 84 billion m³. Substantial though this may be it is still dwarfed by the discharge of the Amazon (3,000 billion m³) or even that of the Congo (1,400 billion m³). Moreover, this average, which became the accepted figure by midcen-

---

*I conform here to one school that argues that "desertization" refers to the expansion of desert areas and aridity for whatever reasons, while "desertification" refers to aridity produced or caused by human activity.

tury, was founded on gauge readings taken over the most recent hundred-year period. It is known that the average volume of the Nile flood, like the rains at its source, has fluctuated over the millennia. Indeed some historians have attributed political and social decay in Egypt, most recently in late Ottoman times, to long-term declines in water discharge. Although it is by no means certain, the commonly accepted average may reflect a period of relatively abundant water, as Table 2 tends to indicate.

TABLE 2

Annual Discharge of the Nile

No. of years	Period	Mean in billion m³	Std. deviation in billion m³
30	1870–99	110.0	17.1
60	1900–59	84.5	13.5
90	1870–1959	92.6	19.8

SOURCE: H. Hurst, R. Black, Y. Samaika, *Nile Basin* (Cairo: Ministry of Irrigation, 1965), X: 81. The table as presented above was taken from Yusuf Shibl, *The Aswan High Dam* (Beirut: Arab Institute for Research and Publishing, 1971), p. 22. The entire historic record, approximate though it may be, reflects a marked secular decline in lake and river volume and river discharge over a period of 7,000 years. See Karl W. Butzer, *Early Hydraulic Civilisation in Egypt* (Chicago: University of Chicago Press, 1976), p. 31. See also Appendix.

For the most part, however, the cumulative readings of Nile discharge across history reveal a fairly familiar and steady pattern. Gauge readings supply annual measurements of the river's peak flood level and lowest dry season level. Since A.D. 622, shortly after the Arab conquest of Egypt, regular readings were taken at the Nilometer installed at the southern tip of Roda Island at Cairo. While allowance must be made for the drawing off of flood waters for irrigation purposes upstream of Roda, and for the tendency of Egypt's rulers, out of political expediency, to tamper with the readings in particularly low years, we may nonetheless treat the general orders of magnitude embodied in this cumulative evidence with some confidence.[4]

As the standard deviation figures in Table 2 reveal, the annual fluctuations in Nile discharge are substantial, and at their extremes entail agricultural collapse through drought or high floods. Anticipating a much more extensive discussion further on, it has been to cope with these fluctuations that various large-scale water storage schemes, including the Aswan High Dam, have been contemplated. It is also important to note that the *average* figure of 84 billion m³ has taken on a life of its own, and has been treated by several observers as an annual given upon which the Egyptians could depend. Obviously this is not the case. For instance, in 1878–79 (on the Nile, the "water year" runs from flood to flood or July to July) the total discharge was 150 billion m³ or nearly double the average. In 1913–14, it was 42 billion m³, or only a quarter the 1878–79 figure and just half the average (see Figure 3).

FIGURE 3

Nile discharge in the maximum and minimum hydrological years at Aswan

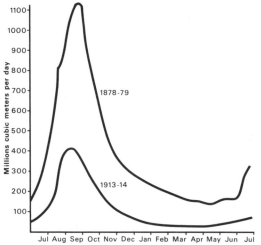

SOURCE: Michael Field, "Developing the Nile," *World Crops* (Jan.–Feb. 1973):13214.

More recently the discharge of the Nile, measured at Aswan, in 1971–72 was about 50 billion m³ while that of 1975–76 was on the order of 100 billion m³ (detailed recent flood readings are presented in Appendix I). Most of the world's rivers, great or small, are subject to the same unpredictability, but the phenomenon is especially important in the Nile Valley because of the almost total absence of rain and the exclusive reliance of its inhabitants upon the river's waters for their survival.

It also borders on the obvious to point out that the flow of the main Nile is not evenly distributed over the water year. More than 80 percent of the river's total discharge occurs from August to October while nearly 20 percent is spread over the remaining nine months. Moreover, the volume of discharge of the main Nile is dependent upon the Blue Nile flood. Over the entire year about 86 percent of the main Nile's waters derive from the Ethiopian Highlands while 14 percent are contributed by the Equatorial lakes (Table 3). During the flood, however, 95 percent of the water originates in Ethiopia and only 5 percent from the Behr el-Jebel (see Figure 4).

TABLE 3

Contribution of Main Nile Sources

	Tributary	12-month water year	Flood period
	Blue Nile	59%	68%
Ethiopian sources	Sobat	14%	5%
	Atbara	13%	22%
Equatorial lakes	Behr el-Jebel	14%	5%

SOURCE: Adapted from Michael Field, "Developing the Nile," *World Crops* (Jan.–Feb. 1973):13.

The reason for the disproportionate contribution of the Ethiopian tributaries is, as we have seen, the enormous evaporation losses of the Behr el-Jebel in the Sudd swamp. This same phenomenon tends to even out the flow of the White Nile downstream from the swamp, its discharge during flood generally being no more than three times that of the low season. By contrast the Blue Nile may discharge 60 times as much water during flood (beginning in the middle of May) as during the rest of the year. It is one of the peculiarities of this situation that if additional quantities of water are to be brought into the system, they will have to be found among the sources of the White Nile, heretofore the junior partner, as the Blue Nile's waters are already heavily committed for irrigation purposes.

The pre-eminence of the Blue Nile in the main Nile system is reaffirmed in its near monopoly of silt (suspended matter) supply. The Victoria Nile and the Behr el-Jebel neither pick up silt on the scale of the Blue Nile nor are they able to retain it as they move through Lake Mobutu and the Sudd swamp. The total volume of suspended matter reaching Aswan annually is variously estimated between 60 and 110 million tons. At the peak of its flood, the Blue Nile generally carries 4,000–7,000 parts per million (ppm) of suspended matter, but at Aswan, before the High Dam, the amount of suspended matter during

FIGURE 4

Nile discharge in the hydrological year at Aswan (mean 1900–52)

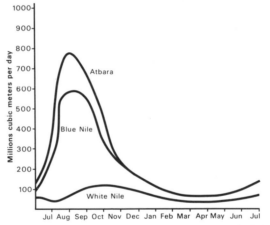

SOURCE: Michael Field, "Developing the Nile," *World Crops* (Jan.–Feb. 1973):13214.

the flood was 1,600 ppm, or a little less than one kilogram per m³ of water. The suspended matter consists of about 45 percent sand, 40 percent clay, and 15 percent silt. According to Gamal Hamdan, "It is this mud that, over the millennia, gradually constituted the Nile flood plain: the latter is thus in part an involuntary gift of the pastoral populations of Abyssinia whose overnumerous herds [have] favored the erosion of the soil."[5]

All the alluvial soil deposited along the banks of the main Nile, and above all, the soils of the Nile Delta, have been washed down several thousand miles from the Ethiopian plateau. On the average along the Egyptian section of the Nile, the deposit is 9 to 10 meters deep (30–33 feet). It increases in depth as one moves downstream, from about 6.7 meters between Aswan and Qena, 9 meters between Qena and Cairo, and 11.2 meters in the northern Delta. It is believed that the sediment has precipitated at a rate varying between .096 meters (3.8″) and .15 meters (5.9″) per century. This would mean that the rich cultivable flood plain of Egypt as it is known today was formed over a 7,000–10,000 year period. Even more impressive are the alluvial soils deposited by gravity flow between the Blue and White Niles in the Sudan. Not only are the soils extensive but in places well over 30 meters deep. The extent to which the annual deposits of suspended matter contributed to soil fertility is a matter of considerable debate. In terms of soil nutrients the answer is probably not much, but in terms of building a soil bank against river and coastal erosion and soil depletion the answer is probably a great deal.

Along with suspended matter, one should look at matter in solution carried by the Nile. The crucial element for our purposes is salt. On the whole the Nile is relatively salt free. Until recent decades the salt content of the waters passing Cairo was only 170 ppm, although with agricultural intensification and the storage of water back of the High Dam that figure is now about 220 ppm. The White is a saltier tributary than the Blue Nile. While Lake Victoria has only 80 ppm of salt, Lake Idi Amin has 670 ppm and Lake Mobutu 590. At Khartoum the White Nile has 140 ppm and the Blue Nile 130. With regard to this and all other aspects of water quality, the Nile has been classified as excellent by the U.S. Salinity Laboratory.[6]

PUTTING THE SYSTEM TO WORK

Up to this point we have described only the natural and unimpeded flow of the Nile, untouched, so to speak, by human hands. But it is of course the human symbiosis with the river and, eventually, willed interference with its natural patterns, that is of primary concern to us. Gamal Hamdan has distinguished four major historical epochs in the development of irrigated agriculture in Egypt which may have first made its appearance some 7,000 years ago. Prior to that time, by at least 10,000 years, paleolithic humans inhabited the valley but relied on hunting and gathering for their survival (the so-called eotechnic era).

During this preagricultural epoch the valley during flood was particularly marshy and inhospitable. Human settlement was consequently concentrated away from the river on higher ground rather than upon what is today the alluvial flood plain. It would seem, however, that 5,000–7,000 years ago some primitive village settlements were established on "tortoise-backs" on the flood plain, which are natural gravel or sand escarpments and outcroppings of subdeltaic deposits that remained permanently above the highest floods. It was from these villages that the first agricultural epoch, the geotechnic, was launched. It is interesting to note that settled agriculture was introduced into Egypt a good deal later than in the rainfed areas of southwest Asia. The probable reason, as Karl Butzer has argued, is that the Nile Valley was so ecologically hospitable to food collecting economies that there was little pressure at low levels of population to shift to more intensive modes of land use.[7]

Although it is conjectural, it appears likely that the valley's population initially took advantage of natural basins scooped out in the alluvial soils of the plain by the annual flood, and in which water would remain well after its retreat. It may have been in such basins that primitive cereal cultivation was initiated, and the only "engineering" that may have accompanied this phase would have been the construction of simple earthen dikes to trap water in basins and then, by breaching them, to allow the excess water to return to the river. Seed would be sown broadcast and harvested by hand. Cultivators owed their existence to this agriculture and to the flocks that they would move to higher ground during the flood. Although the terrain is very different and the animal herds consist of cattle, an agricultural system of roughly this level of technology has prevailed in large areas in and around the Sudd swamps until this day.

To move beyond this stage required the presence of a supra-village authority, and one may suppose that such an authority was present in 3400 B.C. The paleotechnic epoch of humanly engineered basin irrigation commenced at this point and endured until the nineteenth century. The last remnants of paleotechnic agriculture were not replaced in Egypt by more sophisticated methods until after 1964. Geotechnic cultivation may have been concentrated on the right or eastern bank of the Nile where the flood plain is narrow and the natural basins small. During the paleotechnic transformation, cultivation shifted to the broader plain on the left or west bank where much larger basins could be prepared for the flood and subdivided by manmade transverse barriers to spread and hold the water evenly over the entire basin. The scale and complexity of the new system necessitated the emergence of a central government to assure, above all, that upstream basins did not draw off more water than they needed, thus depriving downstream areas of their requirements.

Frequently, historians have concluded too much about the relationship between engineered irrigation systems and state authority. Karl Wittfogel has pinned the emergence of what he terms "oriental despotism" upon this interlinkage in several great river valleys. Butzer and others do not find convincing evidence in Pharaonic Egypt to support this view. To the contrary:

> It is significant that the plethora of Old Kingdom titles provides no evidence for a centralized, bureaucratic apparatus that might have served to administer irrigation at the national, regional, or local level.... It seems, therefore, that ecological problems were preeminently handled at the local level, at least until the opening up of the Faiyum in the Middle Kingdom. The development of a professional full-time bureaucracy must therefore be related to a different social impetus. In other words, there is no direct causal relationship between hydraulic agriculture and the development of the Pharaonic political structure and society.[8]

Supporting this hypothesis, but with reference to the Tigris-Euphrates system, are Robert Adams and McGuire Gibson.[9] According to Adams, ancient irrigation in this system was typically carried out by decentralized tribal units, and it was only in the Sassanian period (A.D. 226–640) that one can say that a centralized bureaucracy, the gathering of public revenues, and agricultural production were fully interdependent. Gibson goes further, claiming that state intervention typically led to deterioration of agriculture in Mesopotamia because it promoted intensification at the expense of fallows. In his view the Mongol invasions cannot be held responsible for the destruction of hydraulic agriculture in Muslim Mesopotamia; rather they applied the *coup de grace* to a system overdeveloped and in decline under the Abbassids.

Under the basin irrigation system humankind and the Nile river established a remarkable ecological balance *at moderate levels of population density*. The system's dynamics were simple. As the Nile's waters began to rise in flood in the late summer, teams of villagers would prepare off-take canals to channel the floodwaters into large basins. These varied in size from perhaps 2,000 feddans (one feddan = 1.038 acres) where the alluvial plain was narrow to 20,000 feddans in the broad deltaic zones. Basins of 40,000 and even 80,000 feddans were not unknown, but the average, at least in recent times, has been about 7,000 feddans. Each main off-take canal would feed about eight basins, and as these had a natural downstream slope, they had to be sub-divided by transverse barrages to hold the water evenly over the entire surface. The slope of the canals would be less than that of the river in order to slow the flow of the flood waters.

Each basin would be allowed to fill to a level dependent on the volume of the flood. In general in Upper Egypt each sub-basin would fill to about 1.5 meters and then the water would pass to the next downstream basin. In Lower or Deltaic Egypt the average depth was generally less, or about 1.25 meters. The water would then be allowed to stand for 40–60 days on what were to become cultivated fields, deeply penetrating and saturating soils that had dried and cracked during the dry months. Then any excess waters would be released to flow back into the Nile, now at a much lower stage because of the passing of the flood. If the flood had been high, the remaining waters would be evacuated directly from each basin into the Nile; if low, the waters in upstream basins would empty one after another into each downstream basin to maximize the amount of moisture in the soils.[10] While covering the fields the flood waters would precipitate and de-posit approximately one millimeter of suspended matter (silt), thus replenishing the alluvial soils. The manner in which sediment was annually precipitated — with the heaviest particles deposited close to the riverbed and lighter particles further away — led to the gradual elevation of the river bed itself above the flood plain with a gentle slope toward the furthest cultivable areas. In the Delta, where the two main branches of the Nile fed into a complex of canals and basins, the system could be likened to the back of a leaf with its raised veins carrying water to its lower-lying declivities. Water percolating downward through the topsoil would gradually drain by gravity into the low Nile through the subsoil water table, dissolving and leaching out in the process salts that may have been concentrated in the soil during the previous growing season.

Normally the basins would be submerged by the end of August and in turn be ready for cultivation by mid-October or the beginning of November. The growing season corresponded to the coolest part of the year and thus was best suited for the cultivation of cereals. The temp-erate winter months would be followed by a hot, dry period in which the grains matured. Barley was the backbone of Egyptian agriculture for centuries, although sometime before the Muslim era wheat dis-placed barley in importance. Broad beans, lupines, millet, sesame, lentils, clover *(berseem)*, and flax were also grown. Crops such as cotton, rice, sugar cane, and corn were much later innovations and depended to a considerable extent on more advanced hydraulic technology. In general the harvest would take place in May, and the land would then lie fallow until September. In contrasting this seasonal rhythm to that of the Tigris-Euphrates, we find yet another attribute sustaining the munificence of the Nile. In Iraq the rivers would flood in the spring after the snows melted upstream, the water arriving downstream when the crops had already been sown. Consequently the rivers had to be massively diked to protect the fields from erosion. In Egypt the flood, growing season, and fallow would succeed one another, minimizing the flood damage and the need for protective engineering while maximizing agricultural returns.

The regular generation of agricultural surplus under basin irriga-tion was problematic, and this type of technology did no more than lay the foundation for fairly advanced subsistence agriculture. The giant stride into a new era, the neotechnic, has consisted in the addition of a second growing season during the summer months. For it, the annual flood was of no direct use, and as often as not posed a direct threat inasmuch as summer crops (i.e., cotton, corn, and rice) would be well advanced when the peak of the flood moved downstream in late August. On the other hand, water had to be delivered to the newly cropped areas during the long hot spring and summer months, nec-essitating the development of year-round or perennial irrigation systems.

The conversion of most of Egypt's cultivable area to perennial irrigation has taken place within the past 150 years, but summer culti-vation in limited areas has been known in Egypt for centuries. Two kinds of fields were suitable for perennial irrigation: the elevated ridges and embankments of the Nile, the major basins, and the Deltaic canal banks; and fields accessible to subterranean water. Throughout the entire length of the valley, water is deposited in the water table, at a depth varying between 4 and 7 meters depending on the season. The water table is closer to the surface in the Delta than in Upper Egypt, and is replenished everywhere by the annual flood. Thus, using wells, it was possible to water certain fields during the dry season. Only in the northernmost areas of the Delta, where the ground water is brackish, were there major difficulties in supplementing the basin technology. These practices are very ancient, perhaps explaining the wealth of former capitals such as Memphis, Thebes, and Abydos where ground water was particularly abundant. Over the centuries as much as 15 to 25 percent of Egypt's cultivable area may have been susceptible to such practices, but whatever its extent there can be little doubt that wells drawing on ground water constituted the bridge from basin to perennial irrigation.

It is also the case, as in basin irrigation, that the state was called upon to play a direct role in regulating and supervising the utilization of irrigation water. One of the most remarkable undertakings along these lines was the development, beginning under the Twelfth Dynasty, of Lake Moeris and the Fayyum depression as a device for flood control and seasonal storage of flood waters. This lake and depression lies about 70 kilometers south of what is today Cairo, off the west bank of the Nile, or just upstream from where the Delta first begins to fan out. The depression is 42 meters below sea level and has a surface of about 2,400 km². It was used to siphon the peaks of excessively high floods in order to protect the Delta, and, in turn, could store water for redelivery to the system during the dry months. For Herodotus, who visited it, Lake Moeris was one of the engineering marvels of the world.

We can already discern in these technological innovations the elements of the transformation of the basic Nile ecosystem. Once one moves beyond basin irrigation, a new set of motivating factors comes into play: the production of agricultural surplus, state-building and the generation of revenues, the sacrifices of subsistence and symbiotic balance to the dictates of environmental engineering growth and expansion. The Aswan High Dam is but the most recent (and surely not the last) manifestation of Egypt's struggle to dominate rather than coexist with the Nile Valley.

It was not until about 4000 B.C. that the Delta could accommodate settled agriculture on a permanent basis. Even then the Delta, as described by Butzer and others, resembled the lower Brahmaputra and Ganges of Bangladesh of today, with much higher floods dictating shifting settlement and cultivation practices. Even then, subsidence and compaction of alluvial deposits rendered the northern third of the Delta inhospitable. Until the Christian era, the center of agriculture and population for the Egyptian Nile Valley lay in Upper Egypt. The major turning point in Egypt's hydraulic history lies in the Ptolemaic period, three centuries before Christ. The Delta had begun to take the shape we know today; river discharge and rainfall also stabilized at familiar lower levels. The population grew to the unprecedented level of about five million people, and a northward, Deltaic shift became apparent. This in turn was checked by a rise in the level of the Mediterranean during the first Christian millennium. Further, it was only under the Ptolemies, and based upon the intensive exploitation of the Fayyum oasis, that substantial agricultural surpluses were generated for state purposes. Again, Butzer has put the matter succinctly:

> The elaborate modern system of winter, summer, and flood crops characteristic of perennial irrigation could only begin to evolve after the introduction of the *saqiya* (buffalo-driven waterwheel) or after inauguration of a successful, high water head canal system. Both these prerequisites were first met in the Ptolemaic Faiyum, and it is therefore not surprising that complex cropping is first verified there in the third century B.C. . . . Egyptian agriculture under the Ptolemies was expanded and intensified to a degree unmatched until a century ago, after the introduction of perennial irrigation. Maximum development and population level appear to have been reached early in the first century A.D., in response to an exploitative, labor-intensive agriculture designed to supply Rome with food. . . . It is worth emphasizing that peak population coincided not with maximum prosperity but with the period of optimal colonial development and exploitation.[11]

The shift to perennial irrigation had a number of immediate and inescapable consequences. First, because of summer cultivation, the lands introduced to the new system were not fully exposed to the annual flood and were therefore deprived of the recurrent precipitation of silt sediment. This, in conjunction with the fact that fallows were much shorter, dictated three adaptive practices: (1) a complex crop rotation pattern, perhaps spread over two water years, to provide for periodic fallows and the cultivation of crops, such as clover, that fix nitrogen in the soil; (2) much greater reliance upon organic fertilizers ranging from manure and pigeon guano to potassium and phosphate-rich deposits (called *kufri*) at sites of ancient habitation; (3) the introduction of drainage networks to help draw off excess irrigation water. Thus we find at an early epoch of Egyptian history a trio of problems that are today at the heart of Egypt's agricultural crisis: cropping sequences, soil depletion, and waterlogging/salinity. Some observers, concerned only with the most recent developments, have tended to attribute all these problems to the construction of the Aswan High Dam, but the dam has been an additive rather than a causal element of imbalances with deep historical roots.

Under perennial irrigation, new types of crops were introduced into the Nile Valley, those indeed that were to become the source of surplus for domestic and foreign trade: rice, sugar cane, indigo, saffron, cotton, and to a lesser degree, onions and tobacco. By the Middle Ages of the Christian era all these crops were well known in Egypt. Sugar cane became the specialty of Middle and Upper Egypt at an early date, while Fayyum and areas around Rosetta and Damietta became famous for their rice. Corn, which became an essential element in rural diets, was introduced from Syria only 150 years ago and was grown primarily during the flood (nili) season.

It may be stating the obvious to note that perennial irrigation is much more labor-intensive than basin irrigation. The Egyptian peasant was obliged to work nearly the whole year round under the new system, and one of the most onerous tasks facing him was to lift or pump the water needed for his fields from irrigation ditches and wells.* In addition, the cultivator needed to maintain and clean irrigation and drainage networks and to engage in a constant process of mixing soil (often dredged from the canals) with manure and transporting it to the fields. All of these continuous and heavy labor demands still prevail today, and, as one observer suggested, Egyptian peasants have become a society of gardeners.

At the beginning of the nineteenth century, shortly after the Napoleonic invasion of Egypt, the Egyptian state — under Ottoman suzerainty and the rule of Muhammad Ali—undertook the engineering works whereby most of Egypt was converted to perennial irrigation based on seasonal water storage. This Ottoman governor, later to become Viceroy (khedive) of Egypt, had ambitious plans for Egypt's agricultural growth and industrialization, both of which hinged on the marked expansion of cotton cultivation. Cotton, as noted earlier, is a summer crop and requires so-called timely water when the discharge of the Nile is at its lowest point. To provide for improved delivery of timely water, new canals were dug (for example, the Mahmudia canal in 1817) in the Delta, and others were deepened so that they would be below the level of the river even during the dry season. Beginning in 1825, barrages were built on the main Delta canals to retain water and raise the level of the river on their upstream sides to facilitate the drawing off of water into secondary and tertiary irrigation networks. Both innovations necessitated the levying of labor brigades (the

---

*The three primary techniques for lifting water were the shaduf, a kind of fulcrum with a bucket at one end, counterbalanced by a heavy mass of dried mud at the other, by which water could be raised and swung to empty into field ditches; the tambur or Archimedes screw, cranked by hand; and the saiqa or waterwheel, generally driven by buffalo (gamusa) or donkeys. The last, introduced in Ptolmaic times, was a crucial technological innovation facilitating the spread of perennial irrigation.

notorious corvée) from the villages to dredge and clean the sediment from the canals and from behind the barrages, and to dig new delivery facilities. The work gangs frequently involved as many as 400,000 peasants (out of a total population of three to four million), and they owed the state 120 days of labor a year divided into two 60-day intervals during which they were presumably not overburdened with their own crops. [12]

Between 1843 and 1861, the Egyptian government initiated the construction of two main barrages, just north of Cairo, at the point where the Nile divides into the Rosetta (west) and Damietta (east) branches. These barrages functioned imperfectly until the British, who occupied Egypt in 1882, repaired and renovated them in 1890. They were then able to retain water during the summer season at 4 meters above the normal level of the river. Over these same years three major off-take canals were excavated to supply the Delta, and in 1873 the Ibrahimia canal in Middle Egypt was terminated, permitting the irrigation of the royal sugar cane plantations near Assiut and Bibeh as well as providing summer water for Fayyum (see Figure 5).

The process of seasonal water retention and the extension of summer cultivation accelerated after the British occupation and culminated in the construction of the first Aswan Dam in 1902. The height of the dam was raised twice, in 1912 and 1933, until the storage capacity of its reservoir grew from 1 billion m^3 to 5.7 billion m^3, but all this dam could do was to trap the tail end of the annual flood up to reservoir capacity. In fact, it was felt that striving for greater capacity would be self-defeating in that the impounded flood waters would precipitate their sediment upstream of the dam, and the reservoir would rapidly fill with silt. Thus, as in the past, the great bulk of the flood discharge was allowed to pass through the sluice gates and eventually to empty into the Mediterranean. Nonetheless, at various points downstream of Aswan, new barrages would entrap smaller increments of the flood waters for seasonal use in their immediate vicinities. In addition to the Delta barrages, new works were built at Assyut (1902), Zifta (1903), Isna (1909), Nag Hammadi (1930), and Edfina (1951).

In sum, at the peak of the neotechnic or perennial irrigation era, one finds a great intensification in land use through the lengthening of the cultivation period, the use of organic and, by the twentieth century, chemical fertilizers and the use of lift irrigation on perennially watered fields. The peasantry found itself continuously employed in farming and in maintenance of the water delivery system. Increasingly, the farmers were integrated into the production of cash crops, especially

FIGURE 5

**Schema of the Egyptian water delivery system before the
High Dam era**

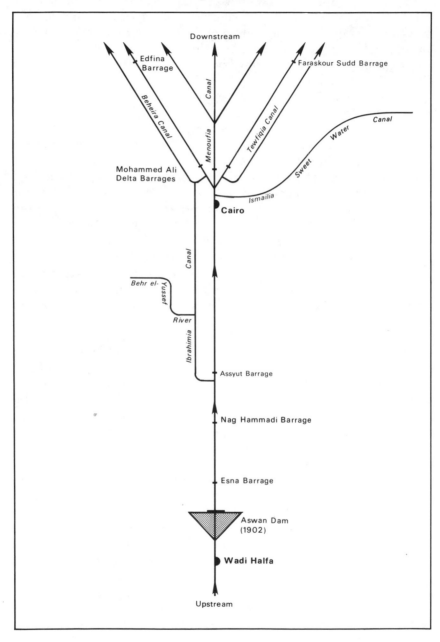

cotton. The new cultivation practices, in contrast to the basin system, also involved the ploughing of fields. For this, and for lifting water, animal traction became crucial to the countryside, and because Egypt has no natural pasturage, so, too, did the expansion of clover cultivation in the winter months. Finally, throughout all of these developments, there emerged the confirmation of the state's responsibility for and monopoly of the development of an irrigation infrastructure.

In terms of cultivated acreage, the conversion to perennial irrigation was somewhat as follows. By 1882, about one million of Egypt's 4.7 million feddans were perennially irrigated, mostly devoted to cotton. The completion of the Delta barrages in 1890 provided for the doubling of this surface, but the construction of the first Aswan Dam was the key to the conversion of most of the Delta to perennial irrigation. Even in Upper Egypt, where basin irrigation was still practiced, there was a continuous trend toward pump-irrigation in the summer months. Table 4 summarizes the remarkable transformation of Egyptian agriculture, and the equally remarkable growth of the Egyptian population, in the past century and a half.

At the same time, problems that are all too familiar to contemporary Egypt had appeared by the end of the nineteenth century. We shall dwell here upon only two: salinity and flood control. With regard to the first, its origins, like those of most other ecological side effects of irrigation, lay far back in Egyptian history. Sometime between the end of the Roman era and the beginning of the Muslim, as much as 1.5 million acres in the northern Delta (the *bararis* area) were lost to cultivation due to salt. It was commonly believed that there had been a sudden sea water infiltration, or, perhaps through the accumulation of alluvial sediment, a collapse of parts of the Delta. According to Hamdan, however, these low-lying lands had never been properly drained, and the evaporation of irrigation water in the upper layers of the soil led to the gradual accumulation of harmful levels of salt. Clearly such crises, albeit on a lesser scale, manifested themselves periodically throughout Egyptian history, but they became a permanent feature of Egyptian agriculture within the past century. Even before the British occupation of 1882, Mackenzie Wallace wrote of witnessing in areas of the Delta "white nitrous salts covering the soil and glistening in the sun like untrodden snow." He attributed the salt concentrations to faulty drainage, and noted as well that seepage from elevated canals such as the Ibrahimia in Middle Egypt and the Ismailia that delivered fresh water to the Suez Canal zone, had led to extensive waterlogging and salt buildup in the adjacent low-lying lands.[13]

TABLE 4

Growth of Egyptian Population and Cultivated and Cropped Land, 1821–1975

Year	Population*	Cultivated area (1000 feddans)	Per capita cultivated area	Cropped area (1000 feddans)	Per capita cropped area
1821	4,230,000	3,053	.73	3,053	.73
1846	5,290,000	3,764	.71	—	—
1882	7,930,000	4,758	.60	5,754	.72
1897	9,717,000	4,943	.53	6,725	.71
1907	11,190,000	5,374	.48	7,595	.67
1917	12,718,000	5,309	.41	7,729	.60
1927	14,178,000	5,544	.39	8,522	.61
1937	15,921,000	5,312	.33	8,302	.53
1947	18,967,000	5,761	.31	9,133	.48
1960	26,085,000	5,900	.23	10,200	.39
1966	30,075,000	6,000	.20	10,400	.34
1970	33,200,000	5,900	.18	10,900	.33
1975	37,000,000	5,700	.15	10,700	.29

*It is worth noting that as regards both land and population there is consensus on the figures presented for the period 1897–1966. Thereafter population estimates frequently follow growth rates established in the period 1960–66 rather than vital statistics registries, and the rate of loss of agricultural land due to expansion of built-up areas as well as the rate of effective land reclamation are subject to varying interpretations.

The cropped area of Egypt measures that surface that is cultivated more than once each year. As a rule of thumb, for every feddan (1.038 acres) of cultivated land under perennial irrigation there are 1.6–1.7 feddans of cropped land. The sources for this table are varied and not always in total accord. See Gabriel Baer, "The Beginnings of Urbanization," in his *Studies in the Social History of Modern Egypt* (Chicago: University of Chicago Press, 1969), pp. 133–48. The population estimates 1821–1882 are drawn from his table, p. 136. They do not correspond to a more prevalent estimate for 1821 (i.e., Helen Rivlin, *The Agricultural Policy of Mohammed Ali in Egypt* [Harvard: Harvard University Press, 1961], p. 256) of between 2,158,580 and 2,536,400, which Baer himself advances in order to refute it. He sets forth his reasons, which I will not reproduce here, for assuming that the 1821 population was grossly underestimated. The cultivated and cropped surface figures were taken from Patrick O'Brien, *The Revolution in Egypt's Economic System* (Oxford: At the University Press, 1966), p. 5 up to 1947. O'Brien, like Rivlin, uses a population figure of 2,514,000 for 1821. However, in another article, he rejects Rivlin's estimates of cultivated acreage for the same period. Rivlin uses tax records to suggest that the land under cultivation at the time of the French Occupation ca. 1800 may have been as much as 4,038,423 feddans in 1844 (pp. 265–70). O'Brien argues that Rivlin's sources are inadequate to sustain her argument. "The

Salinity and waterlogging became more severe after 1890, and especially after 1902. The twin causes of overwatering and inadequate drainage were a mystery to no one. For instance, cotton yields reached an all-time high in 1894 (5.2 cantars per feddan, one cantar = 157.5 kg. unginned), and then began to decline thereafter. One of the principal causes, along with the spread of the cotton leafworm, was salinity. During the first decade of this century, the effects of perennial irrigation on cotton yields became a topic of national concern. In 1908, Prince Hussein Kamil presided over a committee of the Khedieval Agricultural Society to study the problem. The committee recommended that cotton cultivation be limited to one-third of the summer surface. Later, in 1912, a British irrigation expert, Lawrence Balls, prepared a detailed study on the effects of excessive watering and poor drainage.[14] A partial solution was sought in obliging the peasants to lift their irrigation water to the greatest extent possible and thereby economize its use. At the same time the drainage system was extended, but never at a rate sufficient to match the more intensive irrigation that developed in the first half of the twentieth century, and which provoked a general rise in the water table, particularly in the Delta.

> On this day the Munadee [caller] goes about his district, accompanied by a number of little boys, each of whom bears a small coloured flag, called "rayeh"; and announces the "wefa en-Neel" [the completion or abundance of the Nile]; for thus is termed the state of the river when it has risen sufficiently high for the government to proclaim that it has attained the sixteenth cubit of the Nilometer. In this, however, the people are always deceived; for there is an old law, that the land tax cannot be exacted unless the Nile rises to the height of sixteen cubits of the Nilometer; and the government thinks it proper to make the people believe, as early as possible, that it has attained this height. The period when the wefa en-Neel is proclaimed is when the river has actually risen about twenty or twenty-one feet in the neighborhood of the metropolis; which is generally between the 6th and 16th of August. . . .

Long-Term Growth of Agricultural Production in Egypt: 1821–1962," in *Political and Social Change in Modern Egypt*, edited by P. M. Holt (Oxford: At the University Press, 1968), pp. 162–95, especially p. 173. More recent figures on land and population have been taken from the Central Agency for Public Mobilization and Statistics (CAPMAS), *Population and Development* (Cairo, 1973), p. 172, and CAPMAS, *Statistical Yearbook* (1952–71) (July 1972).

When the dam has been cut away to the degree above mentioned, and all the great officers whose presence is required have arrived, the Governor of the metropolis throws a purse of small gold coins to the labourers. A boat, on board of which is an officer of the late Walee (Muhammed Ali), is then propelled against the narrow ridge of earth, and breaking the slight barrier, passes through it, and descends with the cataract thus formed. ... The remains of the dam are quickly washed away by the influx of the water into the bed of the canal, and numerous other boats enter, pass along the canal throughout the whole length of the city, and, some of them, several miles further, and return.[15]

However predictable and benign in its fluctuations across the centuries, the Nile could be and frequently has been devastatingly fickle in its annual behavior. Regardless of the type of irrigation practiced, the extent of economic well-being or privation has always depended directly upon the volume of the flood. Too little or too much water would spell agricultural disaster. A low flood could reduce the potential cultivable area by half, producing the "tightening" or famine crisis known as the *shiddah*. By contrast, the high flood (*al-nabari*) destroyed the basins and left the flood plain pockmarked with pestilential swamps. Over a period of 500 years, from the fourteenth through the eighteenth centuries A.D., Hamdan estimates that Egypt was ravaged by epidemics and plague every eleven years on average. The years in which Egypt enjoyed a "Sultanic" flood that guaranteed abundance were relatively rare. And, with the gradual shift to perennial irrigation, the country's vulnerability to high floods was greatly exacerbated because of summer cultivation.

It is all too easy to forget this primordial fact when assessing the benefits, but particularly the costs, of recent hydraulic engineering schemes on the Nile. Not only could a high flood lay waste to summer crops already in the field, but because of their very commercial nature and their ability to generate revenues and foreign exchange for the state, the effects of below average yields of major crops would entail economic recession over a number of years. Protecting the perennially irrigated lands took on the character of national mobilization. One shares graphically in the annual crisis through the direct testimony of Sir William Willcocks:

> The terror reigning over the whole country during a very high flood is very striking. The Nile banks are covered with booths at intervals of 50 metres. Each booth has two watchmen, and lamps are kept burning

all night. Every dangerous spot has a gang of 50 or 100 special men. The Nile is covered with steamers and boats carrying sacks, stakes, and stone; while the banks along nearly their entire length are protected by stakes supporting cotton and Indian cornstalks, keeping the waves off the loose earth of the banks. In a settlement of a culvert in the Nile bank north of Mansourah in 1887 I witnessed a scene which must have once been more common than it is today. The news that the bank had breached spread fast through the village. The villagers rushed out on to the banks with their children, their cattle, and everything they possessed. The confusion was indescribable. A narrow bank covered with buffaloes, children, poultry, and house-hold furniture. The women assembled round the local saint's tomb, beating their breasts, kissing the tomb, and uttering loud cries, and every five minutes a gang of men running into the crowd and carrying off the first thing they could lay hands on wherewith to close the breach. The fellaheen, meanwhile, in a steady, businesslike manner, plunged into the breach, stood shoulder to shoulder across the escaping water, and with the aid of torn-off doors and windows and Indian cornstalks, closed the breach. They were only just in time. This is the way the fellaheen faced a breach. And this is how the old Governors of Egypt faced them. During the flood of 1887 I complimented an official on the Nile bank, whose activity was quite disproportionate to his apparent age. He told me that he was a comparatively young man, but he had had charge of the Nile bank at Mit Badr when the great breach occurred in 1878, and that Ismail Pasha had telegraphed orders to throw him and the engineer into the breach. He was given 12 hours' grace by the local chief, and during that interval his hair had become white; subsequently he was pardoned. These were the senseless orders which used to petrify officials into stupidity.[16]

In sum, as the economy moved beyond subsistence and into production for world markets, it lost its tolerance for poor agricultural performance and its capacity to absorb bad years. Sometime after World War I, the need for predictability in all elements of the Nile ecosystem became of paramount concern. Yet it was some of the architects of predictability who first voiced ominous premonitions of the costs. Once again it is Willcocks, writing in 1908, who senses something of the future: "It will be an evil day for Egypt if she forgets that, though basin irrigation with its harvest of corn has given way to perennial irrigation with its cotton fields, the lessons which basin irrigation has taught for 7,000 years cannot be unlearned with impunity. The rich muddy water of the Nile flood has been the mainstay of Egypt for many generations, and it can no more be dispensed with today than it could in the past."[17]

FROM SEASONAL TO OVER-YEAR STORAGE

The twentieth century transition from the neotechnic to what Hamdan calls the biotechnic era hinges on the fully predictable supply of summer or timely water for Egypt's, and, of late, the Sudan's cash crops. The principal milestone in this transition has been the construction of the Aswan High Dam which we shall consider in much greater detail further on, but the essential point is that the new era marks the total domestication of the Nile, transforming it downstream of the dam into nothing more nor less than an enormous irrigation ditch.

The dilemma the Egyptians faced in this century can be seen in the seasonal discharge of the river. Keeping in mind an average total annual discharge of 84 billion m³, less than 20 percent (or ca. 15 billion m³) was timely water. However, Egypt's summer needs rose, within a few decades of this century, to at least 22 billion m³. During the same period the Sudan's own entry into perennial irrigation raised total demand in the summer months to around 30 billion m³. By contrast at least 20 percent of the annual discharge was both untimely and unstorable, coming at the peak of the flood. About 60 percent of the discharge was untimely but theoretically storable. Before the construction of the Aswan High Dam, however, total storage capacity on the Nile was no more than 15 billion m³, and all of that capacity was seasonal.

The major problem, as noted earlier, was that seasonal facilities had to allow most of the flood waters to pass through their sluice gates in order to avoid rapid silting of their reservoirs. Yet seasonal storage, no matter how extensive, seemed unlikely to meet the growing needs of Egypt and the Sudan. Shortly after the turn of the century, serious studies of "over-year" storage were begun, and the rudiments of a two-pronged strategy were devised. A seminal figure in this process was Sir William Garstin of the Egyptian Public Works Department, the real father of the Century Storage Scheme. In 1902, Garstin undertook a pioneering hydrological survey of the Sudanese Nile system. Reflecting an Egyptocentric outlook that was to prevail for nearly half a century, Garstin proposed that the entire discharge of the White Nile should be reserved for Egypt and that of the Blue Nile, *when not in flood*, for the Sudan.[18] More important, Garstin delineated for the first time an integrated series of projects on the Upper Nile for seasonal and over-year storage which provided the stimulus for much more detailed studies in subsequent decades.

The essential elements of the strategy were to increase seasonal storage capacity at Aswan, to utilize the Wadi Rayyan depression of

Fayyum (formerly ancient Lake Moeris) to siphon and store excess flood waters downstream from Aswan, to build a discharge regulator at the outlet of Lake Mobutu in order to use it for over-year storage and release, and, most important, to cut down the water losses through evaporation in the Sudd swamps. For this, Garstin recommended dredging and improving the channel of the Zeraf branch of the Behr el-Jebel.

The Old Aswan Dam, as we have seen, was built and raised to its maximum height by the mid-1930s, but the other proposals were not advanced beyond the stage of technical appraisal and debate. Instead, the Sudan began to forge ahead with its own seasonal storage schemes. With the British in fairly effective control of both countries after 1898, conflicting water interests could be reconciled, although Egyptian needs were consistently given priority. As a result of a decade of studies and negotiations in the 1920s, a certain number of water storage projects were approved and some actually implemented.* First, the Sennar Dam on the Blue Nile was completed in 1926, thereby supplying irrigation water to the Gezira Cotton Scheme in the Sudan. Second, the barrage at Nag Hammadi in Egypt was approved and built, and approval in principle was given to a reservoir on Lake Albert, a channel through the Sudd swamp, a reservoir on the Upper Blue Nile, and the Jebel Auliya reservoir south of Khartoum. Only the last was implemented. In 1932 a formal accord was reached between Egypt and the Sudan to build this facility 45 kilometers upstream from Khartoum on the White Nile. Much more recently additional seasonal storage facilities have been constructed within the Sudanese system. The major completed projects are those of the dam at Roseires on the Blue Nile (1966) and the Khashm el-Girba Dam on the Atbara (1966). The Roseires' waters have been used to develop the Managil extension of the Gezira Scheme. The dam on the Atbara has formed a reservoir of 1.3 billion m³ and serves to irrigate 300,000 feddans at Khashm al-Girba, a cotton and peanut scheme where Nubians displaced by the filling of the reservoir behind the Aswan High Dam have been settled.

It is symptomatic of these seasonal storage facilities that Khashm al-Girba has been experiencing severe sedimentation problems. The technique developed to cope with it is to drop the level of the reservoir to almost nothing just before the peak of the flood and allow the flood itself to flush out accumulated silt through the sluices. Then the tail of

*Egyptocentrism was underscored by the fact that irrigation services in the Sudan were administered by an extension of the Egyptian Irrigation Service in Khartoum. It was not until 1925 that the Sudanese Irrigation Department became autonomous.

the flood is trapped for storage. Jebel Auliya on the relatively silt-free White Nile is not faced with these problems.

All these seasonal projects constitute the infrastructure of summer cultivation in the Nile Valley. Upon them depends the production of cotton, rice, and sugar cane, and, consequently, the fate of the two riverine neighbors' integration into world markets. But no matter how sophisticated and extensive, seasonal storage facilities could not remove all the unpredictables in the system's functioning. H. E. Hurst, the Nile's most authoritative twentieth-century student, pinpointed its fundamental weakness.

> Even with present day cultivation there will be years when it is not possible to fill both Aswan and Gebel Aulia reservoirs, thus increasing the shortage in the following summer. If further annual (i.e., seasonal) storage is provided, it will be possible to reclaim new land and extend cultivation in Egypt in many years, but it will be at the expense of increased losses in the very low years. It should be noted that there have been two years in the last fifty whose recurrence, even under present conditions, would cause serious loss to Egypt, and the disaster would be worse with an expanded area of cultivation. [19]

Hurst was not alone in his judgment, and after World War II the major hydraulic challenge became to devise an over-year storage capability that would eliminate the few low years each century that would spell disaster for the valley's economy. Two formulas were elaborated. The first, chronologically and by order of priority, was the Century Storage Scheme based on projects lying outside Egyptian territory but aimed at protecting Egypt's agricultural needs. The second, a relatively late arrival initially rejected as technologically unfeasible, was the proposal for a single great dam and reservoir within Egyptian territory. Whichever was chosen (and of course we now know that it was the latter project), a new era of predictable water supply and liter-by-liter water management was to be the result. And so indeed it has been. Over-year storage has ushered in Hamdan's final stage, the biotechnic, in which the Egyptian Nile is fully domesticated and made as manageable as a water faucet. The linchpin of the new era is the Aswan High Dam, and why it was chosen over all other alternatives will be the grist for further analysis. The basic point here is that by the middle of this century, Egypt's erstwhile divine gift was to be appropriated by central state authority.

2

POLITICAL AND ECONOMIC UNITY

"Long live Egyptian-Sudanese unity. This one nation is
building one destiny."
— ANWAR AL-SADAT *to a joint session of the Egyptian and
Sudanese Parliaments, October 23, 1977*

"Let unity not necessarily come at the hands of Gaafar or
Sadat today. Let it come tomorrow, or later, after building
it solidly."
— GAAFAR AL-NUMEIRY *to the same session*

A TRANSBOUNDARY RIVER or body of water is more difficult to manage than one that falls entirely or predominantly within the frontiers of a single state. If Egypt and the Sudan did constitute an integrated economic and political unit, then all of the midstream and downstream sections of the Nile would be subject to the domestic planning of a single political authority. Moreover, other concerned states, especially Ethiopia with its sovereignty over the headwaters of the Blue Nile, would have to tread with great caution in any matters that might affect the interests of what would be by far the largest state in Africa in geographic terms and nearly the largest in terms of population. But Egypt and the Sudan are not today unified politically or economically, and the reasons for this say much about the difficulties both states encounter in attempting to exploit the river rationally. Unity of sorts has been achieved in the past but always through the imposition of Egyptian, or at least Egypt-based, rule upon the Sudan.

In modern times an ideology arose, inspired by the Egyptians but eventually adopted by some Sudanese as their own, that all the peoples of the Nile Valley (but not the Christian populations of the Ethiopian highlands) are one, and only the nefarious designs of outside forces have kept them apart. The British were the most obvious of the spoilers, but a host of others—Russians, Cubans, Israelis, Americans, Libyans, according to the crisis of the day and the optic of the analyst—have taken their place. Egypt and the Sudan are still not one.

POLITICAL UNITY OF EGYPT AND THE SUDAN

"Unity of the Nile Valley" was one of the more potent slogans of the Egyptian nationalist movement. For a brief period of time, in the early 1950s, Sudanese nationalists added their voices to those of their northern brethren. The slogan reflected predominantly Egyptian interests and preoccupations. Throughout the history of the Nile Valley what was to become the Sudan was, for the Egyptians, no more than a backward hinterland. Some of its economic assets and its human resources perennially elicited Egyptian forays into its forbidding interior, but there was until recent times little that one could call cultural affinity or fraternal feeling between Egyptians and the patchwork of peoples inhabiting the southern reaches of the Nile.

Until the late nineteenth century, there was scant reason for the Egyptians to fear the Sudanese. No forces within the Sudan could have posed a credible military or economic threat to Egypt, and no European nations had yet been tempted to penetrate or seize the Upper Nile. Even the fact that Egypt drew virtually all its surface and groundwater from southern sources beyond its borders was a matter of little consequence, since there was more water available in the aggregate than anyone could conceivably use. The Sudanese had neither the technology nor the motivation to tamper with Egypt's lifeblood. Thus, while Egypt was, by objective measures, a vulnerable and hence classically "downstream" society, the reality of that situation had no practical political relevance until the past century. Indeed, to some extent the inverse was true. Egypt, throughout recorded history, had been the military, economic, and civilizational center of gravity for that part of the world. The Sudan's vulnerability to Egyptian military and economic incursions could in no way be offset by the purely potential leverage of sitting astride Egypt's principal source of water.

Some time after the American Civil War that *rapport de forces* was gradually and perceptibly transformed. The steady development of summer cultivation of cotton and its concomitant need for timely water — in seasonal terms, very much a limited resource — cast an entirely new light on Egypto-Sudanese relations. The great expansion in cotton acreage attendant upon the dramatic reduction of cotton exports from the Confederate States between 1860 and 1865 was one of those technological and cropping shifts whose ultimate implications were fundamentally geopolitical.* At once, the fate of Egypt's economic

*From a level of 147,000 cantars in 1830–34, Egyptian cotton production jumped to 515,000 cantars in 1855–59, to 944,000 in 1860–64, reaching 2.7 million cantars at the time of the British occupation in 1882. In that last year about one million feddans were put

well-being came to hinge upon the nexus of international market forces affecting the cotton trade, and "King Cotton" came to depend on an assured supply of summer water.

Initially the solution lay, as we have seen, in developing seasonal storage facilities within Egypt, but with the firm establishment of the Anglo-Egyptian Condominium over the Sudan in 1899, new constituencies claimed their due. Despite the nominal Egyptian connection, the Sudan had fallen under European domination. In-house lobbies soon took form among British administrators, military officials, and MPs, who were increasingly confronted with the issue of reconciling Egypt's extant needs with the Sudan's considerable agricultural potential. The Egypto-centric lobby generally dominated, but there were, nonetheless, countervailing lobbies. A relative shortage coupled with rising world-market prices for long-staple cotton led the British Cotton Growers' Association, after the turn of the century, to urge cultivation of cotton in the Gezira region of the Sudan. This would increase the supply to Lancashire, lower prices, and provide England with an alternative to Egyptian cotton under nearly monopolistic conditions.[1] It was nearly two decades before they got their wish, on the brink of a world depression when supply and price advantages were lost in the maelstrom. As for Egypt, its dependency had been multiplied by two: the supply of summer water could conceivably be altered by an upstream power; and the upstream power, however solicitous of Egyptian interests, was the leader of the European, industrialized world and no longer a disparate collection of Sudanese tribes and sects.

The first effective political unification of the Egypto-Sudanese Nile took place under British auspices in two phases. In 1876 the Khedive (an hereditary governorship granted to the family of Muhammad Ali by the Sublime Porte) of Egypt defaulted on the country's massive external debt. The finances of Egypt were placed in the hands of a debt commission dominated by the French and British. It applied stringent measures to skim the surpluses from all economic activities in Egypt in order to pay off foreign creditors. One such measure lead to the cashiering of nearly 2000 Egyptian army officers. These, plus many Egyptian civilians tired of Ottoman rule and European interference, rallied around Colonel Ahmad al-Arabi (a precursor of Egyptian nationalism) who compelled the Khedive to adopt an increasingly defiant stance *vis-à-vis* the debt commission. Matters came to a head when the British decided to intervene unilaterally to

---

under cotton. See E. R. J. Owen, *Cotton and the Egyptian Economy, 1820–1914* (Oxford: At the University Press, 1969), p. 186.

remove Colonel al-Arabi from the scene. The British military occupation of Egypt, begun in 1882, did not end until 72 years later.

That was the first step in consolidating the British grip on the Nile
Valley. Egypt was vital to the British not only for its cotton but also
because the Suez Canal, in which the U.K. was the largest shareholder
and along which the British fleet sailed to India and the eastern ex-
tremities of the empire, crossed Egyptian territory. It was a short step to
the conclusion that to protect Egypt and the canal, control of the Sudan
was inescapable.[2]

The problem was that the Sudan had broken away from Egyptian
tutelage. After 1820, Muhammad Ali had organized the slow penetration and conquest of much of what is today the Sudan — save, as
always, the southern reaches. This process, combining military action
with the mobilization of northern Sudanese populations friendly to the
Egyptians and ready to act as the Khedive's administrative agents, took
over fifty years to complete. In its course, slaving gradually came to an
end, but the image of the plundering Ottoman Egyptian, bent on gold,
ivory, ostrich plumes, and slaves, has been difficult to erase.

The period of Egypto-Ottoman rule, known as the al-Turkia,
came to an end in 1881. Muhammad Ahmad ibn Abdallah of Dongola in
northern Sudan, the man who would become the al-Mahdi or savior,
led a movement to break away from Ottoman control. In this he was no
doubt inspired by Col. al-Arabi in Egypt. The Mahdi's movement was
in marked contrast to the other great Sufi order of the northern Sudan,
the Mirghania or Khatmia founded by Muhammad Uthman al-
Mirghani. This order was, on the whole, favorable to Ottoman control
and had frequently cooperated in extending Egyptian suzerainty. In
these two movements we find the roots of a cleavage in Sudanese
politics that has persisted until today: A pro-Egyptian camp, whose
Khatmia core is built on distinctive ritual and tribal underpinnings,
countered by the Ansar, adherents of the Mahdi, who contested Egyptian control and rallied their own regional and tribal allies.

The Mahdi, in 1881, rallied his forces at Aba Island, just north of
Kosti on the main Nile, and launched an appeal throughout the Sudan
to drive out the Ottomans. One of those who answered his call was
Abdullahi ibn Muhammad of the Ta'isha tribe (part of the Beggara
group) of Southern Darfur. The Beggara of the western Sudan were to
supply the Mahdi with the bulk of his forces, and even today it is in the
west that Mahdism is most strong. In 1883 the Mahdists captured
al-Obeid. The Egyptians (now under British occupation) dispatched
General Charles "Chinese" Gordon to meet the threat. The Ansar

overwhelmed his forces and killed him at Khartoum on January 26, 1885.[3] The Mahdi himself died soon after, and was succeeded by Abdullahi, his deputy or *Khalifa*. The Khalifa could not master the loose and intricate tribal alliances assembled by his predecessor. Thus when Sir Herbert Kitchener undertook to reconquer the Sudan in 1896, the Mahdist forces had lost their cohesion. Omdurman fell to Kitchener in 1899, the Khalifa was killed, and the Anglo-Egyptian Condominium proclaimed. It was not, however, until 1928 that British forces overcame the Nuer and finally brought the southern provinces under the crown of Egypt. It was in that year that the geographic boundaries of the modern Sudan were set. After forty-six years, Great Britain had "unified" the Egypto-Sudanese Nile.

From this situation emerged a double fiction; first that Unity of the Nile Valley had become a reality in more than a geographic sense, and, second, that all the peoples of the valley and further afield were united under the crown of Egypt. The Egyptians, or at least those that thought about it, were more inclined to entertain either or both of these fictions than the Sudanese—who knew all too well the cultural differences setting them apart from the north, as well as the reality of British hegemony. The simple fact was that any effective Egyptian rule in the Sudan came to an end in 1881 with the advent of the Mahdia. It was reestablished in name only after 1898 through the Anglo-Egyptian Condominium. From that time on, the Sudan was in some ways more closely integrated with Britain's East African possessions than with Egypt. But however that may be, any influence Egypt retained in the Sudan was mediated through the British presence and was necessarily dependent upon their good will.

In the wake of the First World War, the British were confronted with an Egyptian nationalist movement that sought complete independence from Britain and unity with the Sudan. Violent mass uprisings in 1919 forced the colonial authorities to grant Egypt paper independence. On February 28, 1922, Egypt became an independent, constitutional monarchy. However, it was made clear to all concerned (but especially to Sa'ad Zaghloul, the leader of the Wafd Party, which was the backbone of the nationalist movement) that whatever constitutional arrangements were devised for Egypt would *not* extend to the Sudan. The basic document of the new monarchy had been worked out between the British and the first King, Fu'ad, a direct descendant of Muhammed Ali. Within its framework Britain carved out for itself four areas over which they would retain jurisdiction. The reserve clauses, as they became known, were (1) responsibility for security of communications (viz., Suez Canal); (2) defense of Egypt (hence continued garrisoning of British troops); (3) protection of foreign interests and minorities (so open-ended as to warrant, potentially, anything); (4) retention of the Sudan under British jurisdiction. The fourth clause was a red flag waved in the face of the Wafd. From 1922 on, Unity of the Nile Valley became the party's rallying cry.

Zaghloul's slogan found receptive ears farther downstream. In 1922, Lieutenant Ali Abdul-Latif of the Egyptian army in the Sudan, apparently of Dinka origins, wrote an article in the Egyptian newspaper al-Akhbar calling for the evacuation of British military from the Sudan. He was dismissed from the army and jailed. Upon his release in April 1923 he founded the White Flag League. The league contained civil servants, students of Gordon College, and military cadets. In August 1924, carrying pictures of King Fu'ad and Zaghloul, they demonstrated against the British.

These events were capped on November 19, 1924 by the assassination in Cairo of Sir Lee Stack, Sirdar or Commander of the Anglo-Egyptian armies. Lord Allenby, Egypt's High Commissioner, laid the blame squarely at the door of Sa'ad Zaghloul and the Wafd Party. On November 22, without London's go-ahead, Allenby issued a sweeping ultimatum to the Wafdist government, demanding, among other things, heavy compensation for Stack's death, and the evacuation of all Egyptian troops from the Sudan within 24 hours. The Egyptian parliament rejected the latter stipulation, but troop evacuation took place nonetheless. On November 24, a mutiny of all prisoners held in the Khartoum-North prison took place, but, deprived of Egyptian armed support, it collapsed.[4] Despite the spread of the mutiny to some Sudanese armed units, there was not to be another effective Egyptian effort to promote the collapse of British rule in the Sudan until 1953.

Egypt and the Sudan went their separate political ways for the next 30 years. The greater the political distance, the greater the clamor in the north for unity. The emotional thread between nationalist elites in both countries was never broken, although direct contacts were few and intermittent. The central Sudanese figure in this respect was Ismail al-Azhari, who brought about a fragile coalition of educated, urban Sudanese with the leaders of the Khatmia order, the two joined only by their hope that Egypt could aid their respective causes: Sudanese independence on the one hand, and the diminution of the Mahdist Ansar on the other.

In 1936, an Anglo-Egyptian Treaty was signed, which had the effect in the Sudan of allowing Egyptian troops back into the country and of liberalizing the entry of Egyptian nationals. As had been the case in the past, educated Sudanese felt they had been left out of a major decision affecting their country's future. In February 1938, the Graduates (of Gordon College, Khartoum) General Congress was held, a group consisting mainly of Sudanese civil servants. Its secretary was Ismail al-Azhari, at that time a math instructor at Gordon College. Within four years the Congress asserted itself as the major forum of Sudanese nationalism, at a time when Rommel was pushing toward Cairo and when the British had forced a nationalist and allegedly pro-Axis government from power in Egypt. Al-Azhari began to brandish the slogan of the Unity of the Nile Valley—free, of course, from British hegemony—and turned to the Egyptians as his allies. He then founded a genuine political party in 1943, the Ashiqqa (or Blood Brethren). The party was fundamentally urban and intellectual and made little effort to attract rural support.

Azhari's espousal of Unity of the Nile did not meet with universal approval even among Sudanese intellectuals. A rival faction, calling itself the Umma Party, proclaimed its goal as the independence of the Sudan *tout court*, without any mention of Unity of the Nile Valley. This party was linked to Sayyid Abderrahman al-Mahdi and the Ansar, and it was suspected of collusion with the British who obviously preferred that no coordination between the nationalist movements of the Sudan and Egypt take place. Al-Mahdi's open identification with the Umma forced Sayyid Ali al-Mirghani to associate himself, more discretely, with the Ashiqqa, and, after 1949, with its descendant, the National Unionist Party (NUP). Uneasy as these alliances may have been, what emerged after World War II was a major cleavage in the Sudanese political arena: the urban intellectuals, who coalesced with the Khatmia (whose rural roots were primarily in the northeast) to form the NUP, versus the Umma, which had broad rural support in the south, center, and west of the country, and was aligned closely with the Ansar, and hostile to Egypt. That cleavage, having gone through a number of permutations, has persisted up to the present time.

Although the Umma and the NUP held center stage in Sudanese politics in the postwar years, other political interests were also taking form. The workers and personnel of the Sudanese railroads, perhaps 25,000 strong, founded the Workers' Affairs Association at Atbara in June 1946. Three years later the railroad workers spearheaded a confederation of labor unions known as the Workers Congress, which had its headquarters in Khartoum. This was followed by the founding in 1950 of the Sudanese Workers Trade Union Federation (SWTUF), which had close contacts with the British Labor Party and the Sudanese Communist Party, the last founded in 1944 among Sudanese students who had studied in Cairo. The SCP called for Sudanese self-determination.

In the postwar period, Great Britain, weary and bled dry by the hostilities, began to reassess its colonial commitments, some of which would probably entail direct military involvement. In the Sudan, the British moved to head off growing nationalist sentiment by endowing the country in 1944 with its first representative institution, the Northern Sudan Advisory Council, which was replaced in 1948 by an Executive Council (six Sudanese and six British) and a legislative assembly with 65 elected members.[5]

The British were also under growing pressure in Egypt, before and after World War II. In 1936, King Fu'ad died and was succeeded by his young and then-popular son Faruq. As the implications of Hitler's rise in Europe became obvious, and as the Italians consolidated their hold on Ethiopia, Britain sought to ready its Egyptian fronts for hostilities. To appease the Wafd and other nationalist groups, the formal military occupation of Egypt was ended through the Anglo-Egyptian Treaty of 1936. However, this treaty allowed British troops to remain along the Suez Canal for 20 years, guaranteed the RAF training rights in Egypt, and gave Britain the right to reoccupy the country in the event of war. The Treaty also provided that the Sudan would remain under the 1899 Condominium, although Egyptian troops were to be readmitted to Sudanese units for the first time since the murder of Lee Stack.

During the war, Egypt served as a major staging area for the Allied campaign in the Middle East. In its aftermath, Egyptian nationalists (spearheaded by the Wafd, whose leader was now Mustapha Nahhas Pasha) were more adamant than ever in their demands for final evacuation of all British troops from Egypt and for the integral unity of the Nile Valley. No progress was made on either issue, so in October 1951, following a Wafdist victory in the parliamentary elections of January 1950, Prime Minister Nahhas unilaterally abrogated the 1936 Treaty and the 1899 Condominium. The British refused to accept the *fait accompli*, and Egypt was not strong enough to enforce it. As the British garrison in the Canal Zone was beefed up, the Egyptian government turned a blind eye to increasing guerrilla activity toward that presence. The situation deteriorated rapidly, and after one bloody encounter between British forces and local Egyptian police at Ismailia, riots broke out in Cairo on January 26, 1952, in which the center of the city was partially burned and sacked. "Black Friday" exposed the isolation of the Wafd and the incompetence of King Faruq. In addition, it was the catalyst to the activation of a conspiracy that had been simmering among a group within the Egyptian armed forces known as the Free Officers. On July 22, 1952, the Free Officers seized power in a near-bloodless coup. Four days later King Faruq was sent into exile, and shortly thereafter Egypt was proclaimed a republic. Its first (unelected) President was Muhammad Naguib, an officer of General rank whom the younger officers had selected as the figurehead of their movement.[6]

Before the *coup d'etat*, no Egyptian government was willing—or could afford—to dissociate the question of Egyptian sovereignty in the Sudan from that of troop evacuation. Nor could any civilian politicians agree to discuss the British suggestion that a referendum on self-determination be held among the Sudanese people. Such a referendum, declared Fu'ad Serrag al-Din, Secretary-General of the Wafd, would be like holding a referendum for the self-determination of Assiut (the capital of Upper Egypt). In January 1952, Muhammad Salah al-Din, the unfortunate Wafdist Foreign Minister, announced in an effort to corner the British, that Egypt would accept a referendum if all British civil servants left the Sudan. His suggestion was disowned by his government, and he was attacked in the Council of Ministers, especially by Taha Hussein, a cultured intellectual and Egypt's foremost man of letters, who accused Salah al-Din of high treason. The Foreign Minister was saved only by the Black Friday riots and the fall of the Wafdist government.[7]

Nasser and his Revolutionary Command Council (RCC) were in a position to be more flexible in negotiations with the British. While the eventual agreement (October 1954) on the evacuation of troops from the Canal Zone will not concern us here, the heart of the new approach was to treat evacuation and sovereignty over the Sudan as two separate issues. By November 1952, the RCC had come to accept the principle of self-determination with respect to the Sudan. Among the dozen members of the RCC, only three had any special relations with the Sudan. President Naguib was born in Khartoum, and his father served among Egyptian forces there; Anwar Sadat's mother was Sudanese; and Salah Salim was born in, but knew nothing about, the Sudan. Salah Salim was delegated by the RCC to supervise relations with the Sudan.

These were initiated with various Sudanese political parties in the fall of 1952. On the Sudanese side, such leaders as Ismail al-Azhari,

Mirghani Hamza, Muhammad Nur al-Din, and Dardiri Muhammad Usman met with Naguib, Salim, and Hussein Dhu al-Fiqar Sabry on the Egyptian side. An accord was quickly achieved by which all parties would accept the results of a referendum on self-determination, in preparation for which the Sudanese parties (minus the Umma) would join under Azhari's leadership within the National Union Party. The NUP's fundamental plank was evacuation of all British troops and unity with Egypt immediately following the referendum.[8]

The mercurial and exuberant Major Salim followed up this initial accord with a trip to the Sudan in January 1953 during which he met with representatives of the NUP, the Umma, and the Socialist Republicans, an ephemeral party of rural notables that did not outlive the 1953 elections. All agreed at that time on the necessity of home rule, Sudanization of the civil service, evacuation, and self-determination. As for the British, by accepting their suggestion for a referendum the new Egyptian regime had apparently outflanked them. On February 12, Egypt reached agreement with Britain on the setting-up of home rule for the Sudan pending a referendum at the end of a three-year transitional period. During that period the Governor-General would represent constitutional authority in conjunction with a five-member committee composed of two Sudanese, one Briton, one Egyptian, and one Pakistani. The General Governing Committee was to supervise elections to a constituent assembly that would deliberate the future status of the country.

The Egyptian reckoning was that if al-Azhari's NUP could dominate the assembly, union between the two countries would be a foregone conclusion. Because Naguib was fairly popular in the Sudan, the RCC banked on the isolation of the anti-Egyptian Umma forces in the elections. Salah Salim made a trip to the Sudan in August 1953 to show openly (and probably materially) with whom Egyptian favor lay. The southern provinces were actively wooed by all Sudanese parties, and, without authorization from the Governor-General, Salim visited the south, heard southern grievances, and drummed up support for union with Egypt. At one point in his tour, he sought to emphasize the ethnic unity of the Nile Valley by dancing naked with Dinka warriors, thereby earning himself the appellation in the British press of "the dancing Major." The Egyptian strategy seemed to pay off brilliantly: the NUP won heavily in the elections held late in 1953. Al-Azhari's supporters carried 51 of 97 seats in the new House and 22 of 30 in the Senate. On January 9, 1954, al-Azhari became Prime Minister. All that remained for Egypt was to await the end of the transitional period so that union could be plucked like a ripe fruit.

Ismail al-Azhari, however, had his own strategy, and although some Egyptians would like to believe otherwise, it did not include union with Egypt. Ahmad Hamrush, for instance, attributes the estrangement between the NUP and the RCC to the conflict emerging in the early winter of 1954 between Nasser and Naguib. The latter came to embody Egyptian opinion, civilian and military, that favored the army's return to the barracks, the issuance of a new constitution, and a return to parliamentary life. The Nasserists, by contrast, were seen as representing those mainly military forces that believed the "revolution," with all its authoritarian accoutrements, must be pursued until Egypt's political and economic affairs had been put right. As the conflict became known to the Sudanese, civilians all, they began to have apprehensions about a union in which the senior partner might be an entrenched military dictatorship. Such misgivings were legitimate, as Syrian civilian politicians later learned after 1958, when they cast their country into union with Egypt. In February 1954, when Naguib first resigned from his official positions, there were protest demonstrations in several Sudanese cities, and a delegation went to Cairo to find out what was going on. By the time it arrived, Naguib's resignation had been withdrawn following massive demonstrations of support in Cairo itself. But it was only a matter of time before Naguib and his few skilled allies were maneuvered by the Nasserists into isolation and eventually disgrace.[9]

Naguib flew to Khartoum on March 1, 1954 to attend the opening of the Sudanese parliament. He was accompanied by Salah Salim, and they were both greeted by a large crowd (40,000 or so) of hostile demonstrators organized by the Umma Party. The crowds chanted "no Egyptians, no British; Sudan for the Sudanese: la masri, la britani; as-Sudan lis-Sudani." In ensuing clashes with the police more than thirty people were killed, and Naguib had to retreat to Cairo the following day.

Prime Minister al-Azhari began to take his distance from Egypt. He refused a shipment of arms offered by the RCC; he did not send Sudanese troops for training in Egypt; and he blocked Egyptian disbursements for cultural programs in the Sudan. This policy of inaction corresponded to the gradual isolation of Naguib, culminating in his contrived implication in an attempt by a member of the Egyptian Muslim Brotherhood to assassinate Nasser. On November 14, 1954, Naguib was put under house arrest, and another Sudanese delegation was dispatched to Cairo. Its members were able to insure that Naguib would not be brought to trial, but there was no way that they could bring him back to a position of responsibility. For all intents and purposes, according to Hamrush, Sudanese union with Egypt became a dead letter. [10] By spring 1955, al-Azhari was announcing publicly that union was no longer the objective of any Sudanese groups, and at the Bandung (Indonesia) Conference of nonaligned states in May 1955, Nasser and al-Azhari, meeting for the first time, failed to patch over their differences.

Salah Salim still clung stubbornly to the hope of union, although he now considered al-Azhari an enemy and sought allies among the Sudanese left instead. As Minister of Culture and National Guidance, he saw to it that the Egyptian masses knew little of the real situation between the two countries, but by late August, as Abd al-Latif al-Baghdadi has written, all the RCC knew that the Sudan was on the road to independence. Salah Salim admitted as much but placed the blame on Nasser's *chefs de cabinet*, Ali Sabry, Anwar Sadat, Zakaria Muhy al-Din, and Abd al-Fattah Hassan. He accused them all of working for Anglo-American interests to prevent union between the two countries. His evidence ranged from circumstantial to nothing at all.

Ali Sabry's brother, Dhu al-Fiqar Sabry, was a member of the General Governing Committee in the Sudan and had reported consistently that Egypt's image was suffering there because of the extensive bribing of local politicians. So widespread had the bribing become that most Sudanese assumed that any pro-Egyptian politician was on the payroll. Likewise, a journalist friend of Sadat visited the Sudan and reported similar findings. Abd al-Fattah Hassan, Deputy Minister of State for Sudanese Affairs, was equally skeptical about the likelihood of union. The charge against Zakaria Muhy al-Din was not explicitly founded on anything. Salim claimed, however, that all opposed him because he had wanted a Soviet representative on the General Governing Committee. Despite Salim's maneuvers, the fact of the matter was that he had botched his job in the Sudan. Some members of the RCC recommended that Egypt try to salvage some of its image there by quickly "granting" the Sudan its independence before they simply took it. But Nasser noted that Egyptian public opinion had been so poorly informed about the real state of affairs concerning union that this would come as quite a shock. After several stormy sessions of the RCC, Salim resigned and officially went on "extended leave."[11]

Few months remained before the expiration of the transitional period, and by their end the very notion of a referendum had been scrapped. In December 1955, after Egyptian and British troops had left the Sudan, all Sudanese parties concurred that no referendum on self-determination was necessary. On December 19, al-Azhari proclaimed the Sudanese Republic, and on January 1, 1956, it officially came into existence. The Egyptians, sportsmanlike, were the first to recognize the new republic. Had they been duped? Conceivably, for P. M. Holt and P. K. Bechtold are both certain that even before the 1953 elections, al-Azhari did not sincerely espouse the cause of union but rather sought to mobilize Egyptian support to oust the British from the Sudan.[12] But al-Azhari fell victim to his own strategem, for once the goal of union with Egypt was shunted aside, the NUP lost its binding force. The Mirghani faction went its own way, forming the pro-Egyptian People's Democratic Party, and in July 1956, al-Azhari's parliamentary majority melted away. He was replaced as Prime Minister by Abdullah Khalil of the Umma Party.

Unity of the Nile Valley, if not dead, was in a deep coma from then on. Because the slogan never had much substantive relevance for either the Egyptian or the Sudanese masses, its de facto demise had few repercussions upon the man in the street. Vital interests revolving around the water supply and economic integration were safeguarded, but serious consideration of political union was not revived until 1969, when a beleagured Nasser, an upwardly mobile Qaddafi, and a tenuously seated Numeiry, sired the Federation of Arab Republics (see Chapter 3).

ECONOMIC INTEGRATION OF THE NILE VALLEY

Something of the skepticism with which some Sudanese regard economic cooperation with Egypt is summed up in the aphorism, "All the Egyptians want from the Sudan are water and doormen *(buwwab)*." Egypt's paternalist impulses and thinly veiled imperialist drive have occasionally been openly expressed. Prince Omar Toussoun, having been sent to the Sudan in 1935 to explore the possibilities of economic integration, allegedly reported, "If we fail to colonize the Sudan (idha lam nast'amir as-Sudan) then the Sudan (under the British) will colonize us."[13]

As contacts grew between the two countries after 1899, the Egyptian concept of integration hinged on two main objectives: first, attempting to relocate some of Egypt's burgeoning rural population to the virgin tracts of the Sudan, and, second, opening up Sudanese markets to Egyptian exports of raw produce and textiles. But however enticing these prospects, initially the Condominium was a net drain on the Egyptian treasury. In effect, Egypt subsidized the Sudanese budget, and in the period 1899–1908 total advances of £E 4,024,000 and subsidies of £E 3,950,000 were transferred to the Sudan. Through the intermediary of the Debt Commission it even financed the British expedition against the French at Fashoda (see Chapter 3). All this provoked considerable criticism among those who felt Egypt was helping to finance British imperialism. [14]

Skilled Egyptian labor in agriculture and construction had early on become familiar to the underskilled Sudanese. Already under the al-Turkia, Egyptian peasants in modest numbers had been imported into the Sudan to improve agricultural techniques in specific areas. It was, significantly, the Egyptian Governor of Suakin, Ahmad Mumtaz Pasha, who put 2,500 feddans under cotton at Tokar during the U.S. Civil War, thus launching the Sudan for the first time into cash-crop, export-oriented farming.

In the 1920s, Egyptian laborers helped the British to build the modern administrative city of Khartoum alongside Omdurman, and work gangs were used extensively in the construction of the Sennar and Jebel Aulia Dams. Although Egyptian immigration was restricted after the assassination of Stack in 1924, Egyptians began seriously to consider the desirability of population transfers to the Sudan. With the 1936 Treaty, restrictions on immigration were lifted but little occurred. To the contrary: the more dynamic Egyptian economy attracted considerable numbers of Sudanese to the north. While there has been a periodic hue and cry within and without the Sudan about hordes of Egyptian peasants seizing the good lands of the Upper Nile, the ironic fact is that most of the population flow has been in the opposite direction. In the early 1970s, Egypt's Sudanese population was probably on the order of 300,000 while the Sudan's Egyptian or Egyptian-descended population would not have numbered more than a few thousand.

Yet the hope of reversing the flow dies hard and may still be harbored by some Egyptians. More than thirty years ago, one of Egypt's most eminent geographers and sociologists, Dr. Abbas Ammar, drew up a scholarly brief for the benefits both Egypt and the Sudan stood to gain from population transfer and increased economic integration. First, he argued strongly for the hypothesis that all the peoples of the Nile Valley share common ethnic origins. He based his claim on the notion that a gradual Hamitic penetration of the Sudan, including the Equatorial provinces, invalidated the contention of colonialist anthropologists that the southern Sudan is Negroid.

He went on to describe the Sudan as, in essence, a *tabula rasa* upon whose vastness Egyptian skills, Egyptian industry, and Egyptian venture capital (there was some in 1947) could create new societies. Ammar envisaged private investors financing the transfer of peasants to the Sudan, thereby creating a class of dynamic yeoman small-holders. [15]

For Ammar, all that stood in the way of this natural harmony of interests was the obstinacy and enmity of the British. Nevertheless Egypt, beginning with Omar Toussoun's 1935 trip (under the auspices of the Royal Agricultural Society), began detailed investigations of the prospects for investment and development in the Sudan. In light of Toussoun's trip, the Society founded a special subcommittee to examine opportunities for land acquisition and development in the Sudan. There followed the establishment of a Permanent Popular Committee for the Sudan. It determined priorities for integration of the Sudan which have not fundamentally changed in forty years. The construction of transboundary transportation grids was emphasized, especially a rail link between Aswan and Wadi Halfa. Telephone connections to the Sudan were urged as well. Reciprocal tariff treatment to encourage each country's exports to the other were also on the agenda. In 1938, a special Directorate for Sudanese Markets was created in the Ministry of Commerce and Industry in Egypt. A long hiatus followed as the politicians on both sides played out the successive acts that led to Sudanese independence. It was not until 1961, when the military regime of General Abboud in the Sudan had arrived at a sort of *modus vivendi* with Nasser's Egypt, that joint ventures once again came up for discussion, including that of a commercial fleet on the lake that was to form upstream of the Aswan High Dam. The fleet was to move 100,000 passengers, 80,000 tons of goods, and 60,000 head of cattle a year between the two countries. Nothing substantive came of these talks.

There is an undeniable logic to greater interaction between these two economic systems, as there is for the Arab World in general, but actual performance has been disappointing. As a proportion of Egypt's total trade, that with the Sudan has seldom reached 5 percent and has frequently been less than one percent. For the Sudan, trade with Egypt has been only marginally more significant. In general, the balance of trade, however modest, has favored Egypt (see Table 5).

The content of trade between the two countries has predictably reflected the relative sophistication of their economies. Egypt has exported to the Sudan manufactured goods consisting mostly of yarns, textiles, building materials, and, until Egypt became a net importer, refined sugar. The only agricultural produce sent to the Sudan has

TABLE 5

Egypto-Sudanese Trade 1938–74 (selected years)

Year	Egyptian exports to the Sudan (in £E)	Egyptian imports from the Sudan (in £E)	Balance for Egypt (in £E)
1938	1,108,805	818,050	+ 290,755
1952	5,055,356	3,451,967	+1,603,389
1958	5,652,885	2,733,041	+2,919,844
1964	4,634,262	1,295,591	+3,338,671
1972	5,276,000	7,794,000	−2,518,000
1974	6,207,000	4,552,000	+1,655,000

SOURCES: For figures of 1938–64 see Tareq Ismael, "The UAR and the Sudan," *Middle East Journal* 27 (1) (Winter 1969): 14–28; for the period 1972–74, DRS, National Planning Commission, *Economic Survey 1974* (Khartoum: July 1975), p. 123.

been rice. By contrast, Sudanese exports to Egypt have been made up largely of livestock and livestock products (cattle, camels, skins, leather), and oil seeds. Because of rising domestic meat prices, a ban on all exports from the Sudan was applied in 1975, although there are signs that it was eased in 1977. A considerable trade in smuggled camels and cattle goes on nonetheless.* Still, whatever the volume and composition of this two-way movement of goods, it represents very little in terms of either country's total trade. In 1974, the Sudan's total trade stood at £S 381.7 million (153.4 million in exports and 228.3 million in imports) while for Egypt the total was £E 1,496 million (£E 587 million in exports and £E 909 million in imports). There was, in the same year, only £S 11 million of trade between the two countries. In the fraternal spirit established by Presidents Sadat and Numeiry in February 1974, trade increased substantially between the two nations, reaching about £E 22 million in 1975, a similar amount in 1976 and £E 27 million forecast in 1977. In addition, both countries adhere to the Arab Common Market, but, like the other members, neither has done much

*Michel Baumer probably exaggerates in arguing that 80,000 camels are smuggled by the Kababish tribe from the Sudan to Egypt annually: "Desertification Press Seminar," September 27, 1976; See "Cairo Consumes 100 Camels a Day," *Akhbar al-Yom*, December 16, 1972.

to comply with tariff reductions on imports from other Arab countries, especially those related to infant industries.*

Sometime in the early 1970s it began to dawn on the Egyptians that they might well need from the Sudan far more agricultural produce than they had ever contemplated, and that the Sudanese hinterland was coveted in some measure by other Arab states. Throughout the 1960s, Egypt plunged ever deeper into basic food imports, centered mainly on grain (wheat and wheat flour) but eventually including commodities that Egypt had always produced in abundance or even exported: corn, broad beans, edible oils, sugar, and so on. In the early 1970s, as international wheat and sugar prices soared, Egypt's chronic and growing food deficit bled the already anemic Egyptian treasury dry. All that agricultural potential lying to the south, about which various Egyptians had waxed eloquent since Omar Toussoun, became of vital concern to Egypt's economic well-being, if not survival. The Sudan's precarious military regime, in power since 1969, was in no position to shun the advances of its bulky downstream neighbor. Moreover, did not the Sudanese rightly count on the likelihood that between overture and performance the inertia of the Egyptian bureaucracy would intervene?

What had happened in the early 1970s was that the nations of Arabian peninsula, rich in petroleum and investment capital but agriculturally impoverished, began to regard the Sudan, just across the Red Sea, as their potential agricultural hinterland. With the proper investments, the Sudan could eventually generate a surplus of basic commodities destined for Arabian markets while providing a good return on capital invested. This state of affairs placed Egypt in an awkward position. Like the Sudan, it had experienced chronic foreign exchange deficits which dictated that the two countries try to conduct as much as possible of their mutual trade on a barter basis; manufactures against raw produce.

In the words of Egypt's most recent plan: "There is an advantage for Egypt in the event of Arab integration in that, in importing what is necessary to cover its food needs, it can obtain from neighboring Arab states secure supply with mimimal foreign exchange outlays and

*In this respect it should be noted that both countries are seeking foreign private investment which invariably lobbies for local protection. Moreover, in both countries proceeds from customs duties and trade tariffs may represent the single most important source of state revenues. See Ahmad Osman al-Hagg and Nagwa Ahmad al-Qadi, "The Experience of the Sudan in Planning with Regard to Arab Integration" (Cairo: Seminar of Long-Range Planning in the Arab World, Institute of National Planning, January 1976).

(avoidance) of world market fluctuations and other obstacles involving transportation, and storage if importation took place outside the Arab nation."[16] The foundation for expanded trade on that pattern would be rudely shaken if Arab investment led to a shift to world markets of most of the Sudan's future produce. Egypt could find that the beef, skins, edible oils, and sugar that it would like to import from the Sudan could not be had in exchange for low-quality manufactures, but only for foreign exchange.

Still, neither the Sudan nor the Arab oil-exporting countries (principally in this respect, Kuwait and Saudi Arabia) could afford to be too callous in their handling of Egyptian needs. For Egypt could be either a stabilizing or a disruptive political influence in the entire Red Sea/Arabian Peninsula region. With its relatively great military might, Egypt was and is in a position to underwrite the stability and survival of the moderate regimes of the area (a statement that cannot be made about any of the other states concerned), and it would serve no one's interests among the moderates to so ignore Egypt's economic needs as to undermine its present leadership.

Where the bargain will be struck has yet to be worked out. The first steps toward it, however, were taken in February 1974. After the relatively successful military encounter with Israel of the previous October, President Sadat of Egypt finally emerged from under the shadow of Nasser, having established his ability to strike out on his own. His initiatives included a move toward rapprochement with the United States, an opening of the economy to foreign investment, and a move to distance Egypt from the Soviet Union. It was precisely these steps that the Sudan had taken in 1971 and 1972, thereby earning Sadat's perhaps theatrical enmity. But as his own man, Sadat did not hesitate to follow his upstream neighbor. Once their basic foreign policy options came to resemble one another, concerted action on economic integration became possible. Thus it was that on February 11, 1974, Presidents Gaafar al-Numeiry of the Sudan and Anwar al-Sadat of Egypt signed the "Programs for Political Action and Economic Integration." The following April, both countries set up special ministries to follow up all policy recommendations, as well as a supreme ministerial council. In July of 1975 both presidents met in Khartoum to give their imprimatur to the execution of the projects that the two sides had drawn up in the interim. At that time, the protocols for the founding of three joint companies were signed: The Egypto-Sudanese Company for Agricultural Integration; the Egypto-Sudanese Company for Irrigation and Construction; and the Nile Valley Authority for

River Navigation. [17] In 1976 a joint mining company was added to the growing list of common ventures.

One of the facts of coexistence in the Nile Valley, to which we shall return in Chapter 8, was that both countries were on a collision course as far as available water supplies for planned projects was concerned. Consequently both sides agreed on the pressing necessity of construction of the Jonglei Canal along the eastern fringe of the Sudd Swamp in order to save 2 billion m³ for each country. Reaching back to the 1930s, it was also agreed that the two countries should be linked by rail and that, through the above-mentioned navigation company, river and lake transportation should be promoted. Over the long term, however, the most significant project was for the development of as much as one million feddans in the Damazin region, south of Roseires, for production of oil seeds, cattle, and fodder.

In November 1975 a joint company, capitalized at £S 2.5 million, was established to develop this region and to put one million feddans under cultivation by 1985. Three years later, some modest progress had been made, and a first harvest of sorghum had been brought in on 24,000 feddans. [18]

While these bilateral accords were being laboriously conceived and modestly capitalized, Arab interests, with less fanfare and more foreign exchange, began to implement their schemes.* It may have been in light of this state of affairs that Egypt finally realized that docile Sudanese compliance with Egypt's development priorities could no longer be taken for granted. In various ways, the Egyptians began to press the Sudanese to accelerate the pace of integration, accompanying the pressure with magnanimous gestures like the handing over of the Jebel Auliya Dam to full Sudanese control in February 1977. A large Egyptian ministerial delegation, led by Prime Minister Mamduh Salim, visited Khartoum on May 26–28, 1977, to activate various projects that had been approved in principle. The results were spotty, and those measures adopted were more of a procedural than of a substantive nature. They included the elimination of double taxation for citizens of one country residing in the other, the abolition of passports for citizens entering either country, reduction of air fares between the two, pledges

---

*For example, Prince Muhammad Faisal, through the Saudi-Sudanese Investment Company (49 percent Prince Faisal, 51 percent Sudanese), has taken out a ninety-nine year lease on one million feddans (900,000 rain-fed and 100,000 irrigated), all to be given over to fully mechanized farming and cattle-raising. *Ruz al-Yussef* 2579 (November 14, 1977).

gradually to reduce tariffs on bilateral trade, and the expansion of cultural exchanges.

More substantively, plans were outlined to establish a joint investment bank, initiate a shipping line between Suez and Port Sudan, and, in the all-important agricultural field, it was agreed in principle to develop a beef-fattening project, another for concentrated animal fodder, and a third to cultivate 100,000 feddans of coffee, tea, and tobacco. While the Damazin Scheme was not specifically mentioned, it was recommended that the Arab Organization for Agricultural Development be called upon to draw up a plan for agricultural integration between the two countries.

One may be permitted to conclude, tentatively, that Egypt has now cast itself in the role of suitor, but its own economic crisis is such that it has little with which to attract the Sudan. Procedural change requires little capital investment, but the numerous agreements in principle on development projects between the neighbors must be seen as acknowledgment that financing is not in hand. Until it is, Egypt may well be rebuffed in its advances.

3

WATER SUPPLY AND SECURITY

The definition of milieu includes the environed unit's own
ideas or images of the milieu, a concept designated herein as
"psychological environment." ... The data of physical geography have no intrinsic *political* significance whatever. Nor
have demographic, technological, economic, or other environmental data. Such factors acquire political significance
only when related to some frame of assumptions as to what
is to be attempted, by what means, when and where, and
vis-à-vis what adversaries, associates, and by-standers.[1]

THE PSYCHOLOGICAL ENVIRONMENT affecting water management in
the Nile Valley cannot be too strongly emphasized. The sense of vulnerability and the attendant fears of the downstream states—above all,
Egypt's — are at the center of all decisions affecting the choice of
projects and technology used to master the river. Not only is the river a
nearly unique life support system for the Sudan and Egypt, it is also
bounded by a congeries of nominally independent, poorly integrated,
politically unstable states whose policies, moods, objectives and big-
power alignments cannot be satisfactorily forecast from one year to the
next. To assure some sort of predictable use of its life support system,
Egypt has sought in this century to negotiate legal agreements
whereby the river's water is shared according to an explicit formula. To
hedge against the potential threat of their volatile neighbors, Egypt
and the Sudan have pursued various strategies for regional security.
Both avenues lead, it is hoped, away from the *casus belli* that lies
inherent in any tampering, or *threat* of tampering with the flow of the
Nile. No other major river valley is shared by so many autonomous
actors, and no other downstream state is so utterly dependent for its
livelihood as Egypt is upon its river. The acute awareness of the
juxtaposition of these geopolitical factors is at the heart of Egypt's
psychological response to all that goes on upstream.

NEGOTIATING WATER QUOTAS

The domino theory has empirical validity only to the extent that some power sets the pieces upright in the first place. So it was that Egypt came to be a giant domino in the entire structure of the British Empire in the late nineteenth century. Were it to have fallen, so too would have the southern flank of the Suez Canal. British-controlled sea lanes to the far eastern reaches of the Empire — the rationale for its East African possessions — and perhaps India itself could all have been placed in jeopardy by any change in the status of Egypt. In turn, Britain's rivals could threaten its grip on Egypt by seizing the sources of the Nile.

In the late nineteenth-century scramble for Africa, one of the determining events was Britain's decision in 1896 to advance militarily into the northern Sudan and toward Kassala in the east. The object was to head off a possible alliance between the Khalifa and Emperor Menelek of Ethiopia, the latter having subjected Italian forces in his territory to a series of military reversals. The French had it in their minds to stake a claim to the territories round the headwaters of the Nile and toward this end sought an alliance with Menelek and perhaps with the Khalifa. Ethiopian forces from the east were to link with a French expeditionary force, led by Major Marchand, coming from the Congo in 1898. They missed their rendezvous, and Marchand was left alone to face General Kitchener's much larger force at Fashoda, near present-day Malakal. Clearly outmanned, Marchand was ordered to withdraw, and from 1898 on the French sphere of influence was confined to those areas west of Darfur. With the Fashoda incident, Britain had secured the upper reaches of the White Nile in the name of Egypt.

Fashoda was the first, albeit indirect, attempt in modern times to tamper with the natural flow of the Nile to the detriment of Egypt. From then on Egypt has been acutely sensitive to any exogenous forces impinging upon its water supply. For half a century only one power, Great Britain, could exercise any kind of threat, and Egyptians always suspected its motives.

In 1920 Murdoch MacDonald put forth a variant of what was to become the Century Storage Scheme. Its major components would have provided for a flood-control barrage at Nag Hammadi (the only project in Egypt), a dam at Jebel Auliya to provide summer water for Egypt, a dam at Sennar to stimulate Sudanese cotton cultivation in the Gezira, and finally a storage dam at Lake Albert contingent upon a channel through the Sudd swamps. All of this is already familiar. What is important to note, however, is the Egyptian nationalist reaction to these suggestions. It saw in them a plot whereby the British could hold Egypt in thrall by direct control of vital waterworks outside Egypt proper, all the while stimulating a cotton producer that would reduce the value of Egypt's major export. If Egypt were somehow to break away from Britain (and this study was made public within one year of the 1919 revolt) Lancashire would still have unimpeded access to a major producing region of long-staple cotton. So intense was nationalist pressure that the Minister of Public Works, Ismail Sirri, tendered his resignation, and the British were compelled to make public assurances that no more than 300,000 feddans would be cultivated in the Gezira. Still, it was some years before further steps were taken toward construction of Jebel Auliya which would, in the new scheme of things, hold in its distant reservoir the fate of Egypt's summer crops.[2]

How empty British promises could be and how justified nationalist misgivings is nowhere better exemplified than in the capriciousness with which the imperial authorities handled the assassination of Lee Stack. One of the clauses of Lord Allenby's ultimatum to the Egyptian government following the assassination stated: "Notify the competent department that the Sudan Government will increase the area to be irrigated in the Gezira from 300,000 feddans *to an unlimited figure as need may arise*" (italics added).[3] The same authority only a few months later made something of a retreat once the matter had been thought over in London and Cairo, as High Commissioner Lord Allenby wrote to P. M. Ziwar Pasha of Egypt, on January 26, 1925: "I need not remind Your Excellency that for forty years the British Government watched over the development of the agricultural well-being of Egypt, and I would assure Your Excellency at once that the British Government, however solicitous for the prosperity of the Sudan, have no intention of trespassing upon the natural and historic rights of Egypt in the waters of the Nile, which they recognize today no less than in the past."[4]

However favorable, or at least unharmful, this particular outcome, the Egyptians could scarcely forget the extent of their vulnerability. Since the American Civil War, Egypt's agricultural economy had come to rely upon the summer cultivation of cotton and an assured seasonal discharge at Aswan that could then be variously stored. Already by World War I, however, the first timid steps toward perennial irrigation in the Sudan were being taken.

Curiously, it was William Garstin, the stolid Egypt-firster, who suggested in 1904 the feasibility of launching a major cotton scheme at the confluence of the Blue and White Niles south of Khartoum, using a seasonal storage facility on the Blue Nile to provide the water. Four years later, a formal proposal had been drafted to construct a dam at Sennar that would supply enough water to irrigate 500,000 feddans at what was to become the Gezira Cotton Scheme. Because of the disastrously low flood of 1913–14 (still the lowest on record for this century) and the outbreak of World War I, no effective steps were taken toward implementation of these projects. In their absence, the Egyptian Ministry of Public Works, in January 1904, authorized the Sudanese government to pump water during the timely season sufficient to irrigate 10,000 feddans. Five years later the authorization was raised to 20,000 feddans, although by 1919 only 16,416 were irrigated. [5]

With the end of the war it became clear that some sort of formal accord on the allocation of the Nile waters would have to be reached if both Egypt and the Sudan were to proceed with their respective development plans. An Egyptian government report of 1920 suggested that of the usable portion of the annual discharge, 50 billion m³ be reserved for Egypt and 6 billion m³ for the Sudan. Even at that ratio, strong criticism was voiced in Egypt that the country's real needs were being neglected. In the same year a special Nile Projects Commission was formed, with representatives from India, the United Kingdom, and the United States. The Commission estimated Egypt's needs at 58 billion m³ with the Sudan drawing enough from the Blue Nile to irrigate 300,000 feddans. The U. S. member, H. T. Crory, argued in a separate appendix to the main report that both countries should have fixed shares, should split any water gains or shortfalls 50–50, and that future water increments should be allocated according to prospective cultivable lands in each country. While neither Crory's particular view nor the recommendations of the Commission were acted upon, the principle enunciated was one, in the long term favorable to the Sudan, and consequently one that the Egyptians resisted each time it was subsequently raised.

The Lee Stack murder set back the process of negotiations, but in early 1925 a newly constituted commission made its report, which became the basis for a formal agreement four years later. The completion of the Sennar Dam in 1926 made such an accord all the more imperative. The formula finally settled upon in the Nile Waters Agreement of May 7, 1929, was to define Egypt's "acquired rights" as 48 billion m³ per year and the Sudan's as 4 billion m³. Equally important was that the entire flow of the main Nile was reserved to Egypt during the timely season, January 20–July 15. This meant, among other things, that cotton cultivation in the Sudan would have to be under-taken during the winter months. Underlying the paramount interests of the downstream state was the stipulation that Egypt be allowed to station on-site inspectors at Sennar and elsewhere. Egypt was also guaranteed that no works would be executed on the river or any of its tributaries which would prejudice Egyptian interests.* Within the context of this agreement, construction of the Jebel Auliya Dam, south of Khartoum on the White Nile, was begun in 1932, followed in 1952 by the raising of the reservoir levels at Sennar by one meter and at Jebel Auliya by 10 centimeters.

The reader will have noted the rather extraordinary message at the heart of this agreement: in effect the downstream state is saying that for every 10 or 11 million m³ it takes, it will cede the upstream state one million. The principle of the primacy of existing land usage and water needs versus potential use and needs had been resoundingly affirmed in this first attempt to legislate the international exploitation of the Nile. With hindsight we may say that such a lopsided and geopolitically unrealistic formula was not likely to endure. It did not. In time, as the Sudanese population grew, and especially once the country had achieved independence, domestic pressures for maximizing agricultural production at home would have become irrepressible. But the whole matter of a major follow-up to and modification of the 1929 Agreement came as a result of Egypt's decision in 1952 to seek funding for the construction of the Aswan High Dam, entirely within Egyptian territory.

This decision coincided with the brief honeymoon between the RCC in Egypt and al-Azhari's National Unionist Party (NUP) in the Sudan. It was imperative (as well as a condition of the IBRD, if it was to finance any aspect of the project), that Egypt and the Sudan reach agreement on the resettlement of population displaced at the High Dam reservoir, on compensation for any material damages caused the Sudanese, and, if need be, on the determination of a new formula for

*This is a crucial principle in the international law of river basins that cross or constitute international boundaries. The 1929 agreement represented an early codification of it, and one that has been recommended as a basic element of a code of conduct for river basin use by the so-called Helsinki Rules (1966) of the International Law Association. See C. Odidi Okidi, "Challenges to the Management of Water Resources," paper prepared for the UN Water Conference, Mar del Plata, Argentina, March 14–28, 1977. See also L. B. Sohn, "The Stockholm Declarations on the Human Environment," *Harvard International Law Journal* 14(1973):423; and UN Water Conference (UNWC)/ILC, *Work of the International Law Commission on the Law of the Non-Navigational Uses of International Water Courses*, E/Conf. 70/A.12, February 1977.

allocating the river's annual discharge between the two countries. Nasser and the RCC probably assumed that all steps could easily be taken once the British had left the Nile Valley and once an independent Sudan opted freely but inevitably for union with Egypt.

From its inception in fall 1952, the Aswan High Dam project was discussed by the new regime as a joint undertaking, but the RCC made no move to include the Sudanese in its preparation. It was only in September 1954, following the crisis between Naguib and Nasser that had so disturbed pro-union Sudanese politicians, that Egypt formally informed the Sudanese of their intentions with respect to the Aswan High Dam. The first bilateral negotiations over the dam were thus begun during the three-year transitional period, with British troops still in the Suez Canal Zone and British administrators still entrenched in the Sudan. The first round of talks lasted from September through December 1954, and the arguments employed by both sides reflect the factors that must be taken into consideration whenever allocation of international waters are at stake.[6]

In making their case, the Egyptians insisted on the priority of existing needs. Their country was totally dependent on irrigation water for agriculture and nothing could change that situation. For all intents and purposes, the only possible source of irrigation water was the Nile, and nothing much could change that either. By contrast, the Sudan, according to the Egyptians, had developed only the rudiments of irrigated agriculture and had vast opportunities for expanding rainfed agriculture. Moreover, water allocation should also reflect existing population levels which the Egyptians estimated at 22 million for Egypt and 8 million for the Sudan, with annual growth, respectively, of 2.5 and 1.6 percent.

On the basis of this summary, the Egyptians went on to recommend the following formula. First, they used an annual Nile discharge figure, as measured at Aswan, of 80 billion m^3 and claimed established rights of 51 billion m^3. Any water that might become available as a result of future hydraulic works should, they contended, be divided between the two countries according to the ratio of their populations, *after first deducting expected storage losses* (in the case of the Aswan High Dam, 10 billion m^3 in evaporation and seepage). The established rights of the Sudan and Egypt totaled 55 billion m^3, plus 10 billion m^3 in storage losses, thus accounting for 65 billion m^3. According to the Egyptian formula, 8/30 of the remaining 15 billion m^3, or 4 billion m^3, would be the Sudan's additional share, while 22/30, or 11 billion m^3, would be Egypt's. Total shares would thus be 62 billion m^3 for Egypt and 8 billion m^3 for the Sudan.

The final facet of the Egyptian case was to posit that the most efficient means of providing this additional water would be to construct one single large dam. The Century Storage Scheme, in their opinion, would cost more money, take longer, and entail greater storage losses than the Aswan High Dam, although, as one of the Egyptian negotiators, Samir Hilmy, conceded: "No doubt the Upper Nile projects combined with the High Aswan project will secure the maximum utilization of the water of the Nile."[7]

The Sudanese disputed the factual basis of the Egyptian argument and put forward different criteria for final allocation. They insisted first on the standard estimate of 84 billion m³ for annual Nile discharge and claimed that Egypt's acquired right was to 48 and not 51 billion m³. Secondly, they contended that their population was significantly greater than 8 and probably closer to 12 million. Assuming that it was at least half Egypt's,* then the Sudan would be entitled to one-third of any increments to the river's discharge over and above their acquired share of 4 billion m³. Finally, they rejected the notion that storage losses should be deducted before calculating the allocation. The Sudanese felt that if Egypt was determined to form a reservoir in an area with particularly high surface evaporation rates, then Egypt should absorb storage losses out of its share. Thus, in the Sudanese view, the total benefit to be derived from the Aswan High Dam was 32 billion m³ (84 billion m³ −48 for Egypt's share, −4 for Sudan's = 32) and that a third of this, or roughly 11 billion m³, would be their new share, yielding them a total of 15 billion m³ instead of 8.

This said, the Sudanese went on to question the very premise of the Egyptian approach. They argued for the lower cost and greater hydropower potential of the Century Storage Scheme as opposed to the Aswan High Dam. Further, they invoked the memory of H. T. Crory and advocated the relevance of potential growth to the determination of a formula of allocation. The Sudan would not, it was declared, accept total or even major reliance upon rainfed agriculture with its inferior techniques, low yields, and climatic vagaries. Instead, the Sudanese put forward a figure of 5.5 million feddans as suitable for irrigation. Assuming a water duty of 8,000 m³ per feddan, the country's annual need would become 44 billion m³. That was over five times what Egypt was prepared to offer, and to meet such demand Egypt would actually have to give up part of the share it acquired in 1929. This was clearly an unrealistic expectation, and one may suppose that the

---

*A sample census conducted in January 1956 estimated the population at 10.2 million, splitting the Egyptian and Sudanese figure nicely down the middle.

Sudanese were putting it forward for bargaining purposes. But the chance to find the *juste milieu* did not then present itself as relations at the political level between the two nations deteriorated rapidly.

The talks were broken off inconclusively, and briefly resumed in April 1955. These too were unsuccessful, and as Salah Salim waged a personal vendetta against al-Azhari, the Egyptian press and media, under Salim's supervision as Minister of Culture and National Guidance, heaped abuse upon the Sudanese negotiating team. With the talks suspended, Prime Minister al-Azhari warned "The Nile flows through the Sudan first, and we can no longer be content to receive our share last."[8] The eclipse of Salim in August 1955 was not enough to put matters right; of greater significance was the Sudan's inexorable progress toward complete independence in January 1956. Within six months of that date, as we shall see in greater detail further on, Egypt lost the possibility of Western financial support for constructing the Aswan High Dam. With that, the lack of progress in bilateral negotiations became for Egypt inconsequential. But the Sudan had projects of its own, including the construction of the Roseires Dam on the Blue Nile, to provide for a major expansion of the Gezira Cotton Scheme.

The Sudan's dilemma reflected the rather peculiar geopolitics of the Nile Valley. Despite its position as an upstream (or rather, midstream) state, it could not unilaterally press its geographic advantage against the much stronger military power of Egypt. Although the Sudanese had the tacit backing of the British in their dispute with Egypt, there was no way to move Nasser toward accommodation as long as the Aswan High Dam was on the back burner. Sudanese protests about the displacement of the Sudanese Nubian population around Wadi Halfa, which would occur if Egypt were to proceed unilaterally with construction of the Aswan High Dam, fell on deaf ears, in that Egypt had no prospects for unilateral action.

The domestic politics of the Sudan contributed to the paralysis that had come over the water management talks. Having dropped the goal of union with Egypt, al-Azhari lost a good deal of his Khatmia support, and, in July 1956, his position as Prime Minister as well. He was replaced by Abdullah Khalil, one of the leaders of the Umma Party, who inaugurated policies that were at once cold toward Egypt and warm toward the West. Khalil went so far as to endorse the 1957 Eisenhower Doctrine which provided for direct U.S. military support to Middle Eastern states threatened by "Communist aggression." By contrast, Egypt, having weathered the tripartite assault of France, Israel, and Great Britain upon the Canal Zone in November 1956, headed in the other direction, developing its economic and military links with the Soviet Union and insisting that all Arab states remain free from entangling Western alliances.

Within this general context of distance and mistrust, relations became particularly poisoned in February 1958. The electoral maps drawn up by the Sudanese authorities in preparation for parliamentary elections included territory along the common border that Egypt claimed as its own. On the eve of the elections Egypt dispatched a military force into the disputed territory of Halaib, north of the 22nd parallel. The net result was to consolidate a solid victory of the anti-Egyptian Umma Party in the elections, and to rally Sudanese support for a military counterforce that successfully withstood the Egyptian penetration.[9] The following summer, the Sudanese proceeded unilaterally with the raising of the Sennar Dam to increase storage capacity and to deliver more water to the Gezira Cotton Scheme. With that act, the 1929 Agreement was openly repudiated, and, in the absence of any other, the Nile was without international governance.

A break in the mounting crisis came with surprising speed. The Sudan's parliamentary experiment was working poorly, with various coalitions coming unstuck as a result of opportunistic "floor-crossings" by several Members of Parliament. Simultaneously, economic conditions worsened because of a poor cotton crop and falling foreign exchange reserves. Prime Minister Abdullah Khalil turned to his old schoolmate, Major General Ibrahim Abboud, and invited him and the army to take over the mess. The transfer took place on November 17, 1958, and there were few parliamentarians sufficiently motivated to oppose the establishment of military rule.[10] Egypt was the first foreign country to recognize the new regime.

It was only three weeks prior to the advent of Abboud in the Sudan, that the Soviet Union made Egypt a formal offer to help fund construction of the first stage of the Aswan High Dam. Thus within a month the High Dam project came to life; and the Sudan was firmly controlled by a military regime with which Cairo was confident it could do business. Both countries now had ample incentives to reach an accord.*

---

*An accord had been the precondition for IBRD funding, but it was apparently not for Soviet funding. Still, the Sudanese needed an agreement to insure IBRD funding for the Roseires Dam, and Egypt presumably never had any intention of establishing the dangerous precedent of unilateral action. In another instance the USSR assisted Syria in its construction of the Tabaqa Dam on the Upper Euphrates in the late 1960s, without any prior agreement with downstream Iraq. Once the dam was completed in the early 1970s and its reservoir began to fill, Iraq lodged international protests that its water needs were not being met.

Talks were renewed in early 1959, and both delegations were headed by military figures: Zakaria Muhy al-Din for Egypt and General Muhammad Tala't Farid for the Sudan. As if to stimulate the fears of both parties as to the machinations of neoimperialist forces, the British attempted to insert themselves into the picture. At that time Kenya, Uganda, and Tanganyika were all represented by the United Kingdom. Therefore, in August 1959, Britain sent notes to the United Arab Republic (the UAR was formed by the merger of Egypt and Syria in February 1958), the Sudan, Belgium (responsible for the Congo), and Ethiopia, reserving the rights of three co-riparians with respect to any accord concluded between Egypt and the Sudan. Beyond that, Britain called for an international conference to assure the rights of all riparian states, and to found an International Nile Waters Authority, of which the United Kingdom would be a member. Coming in the wake of suspect proposals like the Suez Canal Users Association of 1956, and the British attack upon the Canal Zone in the same year, the British suggestion had an ominous ring to it. D. C. Watt has nicely summarized the spirit in which the British initiative was taken:

> There can be little doubt that among the motives which lead the British Government to plead for the establishment of an international authority ... there was included the notion that Egyptian nationalism could be domesticated and instructed in the complexities of contemporary international politics; that its nativist, expansionist, national-centric aspects could be diverted into that kind of "constructive" administration, which the paternalist-colonialist philosophy of latter-day British imperial sentiment used to contrast with the "destructive" nationalism of nationalist politicians.[11]

Egypt and the Sudan, however, moved toward agreement undeterred. On November 8, 1959, the Agreement for the Full Utilization of the Nile Waters was signed. The heart of the agreement lay in the following calculation: the mean annual discharge of the Nile at Aswan was taken to be 84 billion m^3. Of this Egypt would receive 55.5 billion m^3, or 7.5 billion m^3 more than its 1929 share. This 7.5 billion m^3 is Egypt's net water gain from the Aswan High Dam. The Sudan was to receive 18.5 billion m^3, 14.5 billion m^3 over its 1929 share and over twice as much as Egypt offered when the talks first started in 1954. The Sudan was not then capable of absorbing that much water, and a special section of the Agreement provided for an annual "water loan" of 1.5 billion m^3 from the Sudan to Egypt, through the water year ending in the fall of 1977. Egypt's effective share thus became 57 million m^3. The remaining 10 billion m^3 were written off to evaporation and seepage at the reservoir.

Further, the Sudan won another major concession. Any increase in the natural yield of the river would be split 50–50 between the two countries rather than in proportion to their respective shares. The same principle would obtain with respect to increased yield resulting from implementation of the Upper Nile projects. The costs of these projects were also to be borne equally, and, recognizing Egypt's more pressing need for additional water, provision was made for Egypt to begin execution of the Upper Nile works, at its own expense, and in the absence of Sudanese participation. The 50–50 principle likewise would apply to the sharing of water losses resulting from water withdrawals by upstream riparians.

Implementation and supervision of the agreement was to be placed in the hands of a Permanent Joint Technical Commission (PJTC), that would station inspectors in each country's territories, gather hydrologic data, and supervise studies and implementation of the Upper Nile (or any other) hydraulic works. If low floods ever caused a shortage of the water stored upstream, the PJTC would also determine the water allocations to both countries.* In addition, it would study and prepare common negotiating positions *vis-à-vis* any other riparian states.

Finally, Egypt agreed to pay the Sudan £E 15 million in compensation for the displacement and relocation of some 50,000 Nubians of the Wadi Halfa district and for the flooding of about 20,000 feddans of their land. Predictably, the agreement was not welcomed with universal enthusiasm. In Egypt, it was pointed out that, under its terms, the Aswan High Dam undertaking would yield only 7.5 billion m^3, or a good deal less than the anticipated storage losses at the reservoir. Similarly, in the Sudan there were still those who felt that Sudanese potential warranted a larger water share and that, in any case, the best approach to over-year storage was to begin first with the Equatorial

---

*For many international waterway accords, the Final Act of the Congress of Vienna served as a source of precedent. Article 108 of the Act is particularly relevant here. "The Powers whose States are separated or crossed by the same navigable river engage to regulate, by common consent, all that regards its navigation. For this purpose they will name Commissioners, who shall assemble, at latest, six months after the termination of the Congress and who shall adopt, as the bases of their proceedings, the principles established by the following articles." From G. F. Martens, *Nouveau Receuil de Traités* 2:427, cited in UNWC/ILC, *International Water Courses*, p. 7.

projects. Despite this niggling, the agreement has been faithfully applied, the PJTC has regularly met whatever the political climate between the two countries, and both have without exception received their designated shares. One of the few omissions one may discern in the agreement is that it made no provision for maintaining minimal levels of water quality. This could become a problem for Egypt as the Sudan expands its irrigated acreage with greater run-offs of leeched salts and chemical residues. But that deficiency must be put in its proper context. About half the world's international rivers (of which there are ca. 170) have no accord at all among riparians governing their use. Among those that do, few undertake to specify quality standards. Certainly among African* and Middle Eastern nations, the 1959 agreement should serve as an example of a successful instrument for water management.

Other riparian states were concerned to varying degrees in the 1959 agreement. As indicated, Uganda, Kenya, and Tanganyika reserved their rights as to the future and hypothetical disposition of the waters of the Equatorial lakes and sources of the White Nile. Since 1967, however, all three states have participated in the hydro-meteorological survey of the Equatorial catchment launched under the auspices of the World Meteorological Organization.† But if and when Egypt and the Sudan are ready to propose the use of Lake Victoria as a major overyear storage facility, with the concomitant effect of raising the lake's level and flooding habitable areas along its shores, then some sort of understanding will have to be reached with the three above-mentioned nations.

Of greater importance is the position of Ethiopia from whose territory issue the sources of the Blue Nile and the Atbara. Soon after its occupation of Egypt, Britain set about to assure these crucial flows. In April 1891 the United Kingdom and Italy signed a protocol in Rome, in which Italy, then in control of Ethiopia, undertook to avoid any works on the Atbara that, as Garretson noted, might sensibly alter its flow into the Nile. As Italy's fortunes waned in Ethiopia, Britain was compelled to seek an accommodation with Emperor Menelek II. This was consummated in the 1902 Addis Ababa Agreement which obliged

---

*Of the fifty-five river basins in Africa shared by two or more states, only fourteen are governed by international treaties, the most important of which are the Nile, the Niger, and the Senegal.

†Initially Egypt, the Sudan, Uganda, Kenya, and Tanzania participated in the project, and were joined in 1972 by Burundi and Rawanda. Ethiopia joined at that time as an observer, and Zaire remained aloof.

Ethiopia to seek prior accord with the United Kingdom before initiating any works that might affect the discharge of the Blue Nile, Lake Tana, or the Sobat. Once again Ethiopia fell under Italian domination, and in an exchange in December 1925, the United Kingdom extracted Italian recognition of the prior hydraulic rights of Egypt and the Sudan, accompanied by pledges not to construct any works likely to modify the flow of Ethiopian tributaries to the Nile.

After World War II, Ethiopia once more became independent under Emperor Hailie Selassie. Despite inconclusive talks with Egypt and the Sudan over the utilization of Lake Tana as an over-year storage facility, no new agreements were reached among the three riparians. Once Egypt had set its sights after 1952 on the High Dam, Ethiopia took a reserved position. In a note of September 1957 to Egypt and the Sudan, Ethiopia referred to its projected water needs and natural rights to Nile waters originating in its territories. Implicit in the note was the rejection of the 1902 pledge, inasmuch as it was totally non-reciprocal, as well as a repudiation of the validity of any agreements signed by Italy in Ethiopia's name.[12] In short, Ethiopia is at present bound by no agreement and may exercise its sovereignty over the headwaters of the Blue Nile and Atbara with as much latitude as the ire of its downstream neighbors will permit. So far, Ethiopia has done nothing provocative, but (as will be set forth in Chapter 8), fairly ambitious water development plans are under consideration.

Despite the attention paid by the 1969 Agreement to the Upper Nile and Equatorial projects to reduce water losses in the Sudd swamps, no steps were taken in that direction until 1974, There were three major reasons for this. First, and most important, was the fact that construction of the High Aswan, Roseires, and Khashm al-Girba Dams monopolized both countries' time and financial resources, and their water benefits would have to be fully employed before moving on to new projects. Full utilization was achieved in the early 1970's.

Second, the southern provinces of the Sudan had been rendered insecure since 1955 as a civil war sputtered on between local Negroid populations and northern, Arab troops and administrators under the orders of Khartoum.

Third, Egyptian and Sudanese politics were out of phase. Nasser's Egypt took a radical turn in 1961–62, manifested in widespread nationalizations of private, nonagricultural assets; closer economic and military ties with the USSR; and involvement in such regional arenas as the Congo and the Yemen. Abboud's Sudan could not bring itself to follow either the economic or diplomatic innovations of Egypt. The brief restoration of civilian parliamentary rule in the Sudan between 1964 and 1969 did little to bridge the political distance between the two countries. Ministerial musical chairs led to wide and unpredictable oscillations in foreign policy positions. The June War of 1967 inexorably drew the Sudan into more intimate relations with its Arab brethren. Sudanese troops were dispatched to Egypt's aid, and diplomatic relations with the United States were broken. By default, greater reliance upon Soviet military and economic support became inescapable. This state of affairs was significantly altered by the advent of Major-General Gaafar al-Numeiry who overthrew the civilian government in May 1969.

The new Sudanese regime pushed the country toward membership in the Federation of Arab Republics (FAR) along with Egypt and Libya. (We shall look more closely at the FAR in the next section.) The situation in the three southern provinces of the Sudan, where the civil war dragged on, aborted the Sudan's membership in the FAR. Southern non-Arab leadership could not contemplate accommodation with the north if Khartoum were bent on integrating the Sudan into some larger Arab entity. Numeiry needed a settlement in the south more than union with Libya and Egypt and held the Sudan out of the FAR. Libya has never forgiven Numeiry, and Egypt, under the leadership of Sadat after the death of Nasser in September 1970, was momentarily miffed.

By 1974, however, matters had begun to fall into place. Egypt, too, abandoned the FAR. Its successes in the October 1973 war with Israel gave Sadat the pretext to turn Egypt's attention toward development rather than war, and by this time it was clear that further agricultural expansion would hinge to some degree on moving ahead with the Upper Nile projects. Correspondingly, Numeiry reached an accord with the southern guerrillas in 1972, granting them regional autonomy, and the situation began to return to normal in the provinces which would be involved in the proposed hydraulic works. The Sadat-Numeiry talks of February 1974 led directly to joint endorsement of a revised plan to excavate the Jonglei Canal around the Sudd swamps.

This important and controversial project will receive detailed treatment further on. Suffice it for the moment to point out its immediate political repercussions. In October 1974, only three months after the Egyptian and Sudanese Ministers of Irrigation had initialed an accord to proceed with the Jonglei Canal, riots broke out in Juba, the capital of the autonomous southern region, in which three people were killed. The rumor had spread that once the canal was completed and portions of the swamp drained, Egyptian peasants would pour into the area to cultivate the new lands. It may have been that local politicians and ex-guerrilla fighters who were not beneficiaries of the patronage system in the south exploited this issue in an effort to discredit the incumbent southern leadership. The Southern Regional President, Abel Alier, went before the regional assembly to debunk the notion of Egyptian colonization and to make the case for Jonglei, including endorsement of Arab funding for construction if such could be obtained. Because of the great increase in earnings from petroleum exports following the October War,

> it was thought that the present financial climate in the Arab World was conducive to obtaining financing easily and at advantageous terms. It was therefore imperative to implement the project immediately while this climate existed. ... Need I also assure the honourable members that no Egyptian nationals will come to settle in the area? The Egyptians are presently engaged in developing their own country and in recovering their lost lands. They have the sense to know the bitterness generated against those who occupy other people's land. ... The people (in the South) cannot even have one full meal a day, and children of school age cannot go to school because of our underdevelopment, backwardness, and poverty. Yet we are asked to accept all this ... and remain in a sort of human zoo for anthropologists, tourists, environmentalists, and adventurers from developed countries of Europe to study us, our origin, our plights, the sizes of our skulls and the shape and length of our customary scars. ... I wish to say that although this is a Central Government [i.e., Khartoum] project, the Regional Government supports it and stands for it. If we have to drive our people to paradise with sticks, we will do so for their good and the good of those who come after us.[13]

Whatever their technical and engineering difficulties, Jonglei and other Upper Nile works must be handled with the greatest political discretion so that Southern susceptibilities are not provoked nor their economic well-being ignored while downstream, Arab, interests are served. A renewal of southern dissidence could force everyone back to the drawing board and postpone that increase in the White Nile's yield upon which both Egypt and the Sudan are banking.

REGIONAL SECURITY: THE FASHODA COMPLEX

In Chapters 2 and 3 we have so far examined the difficulties encountered by Egypt and the Sudan in promoting political and economic integration, the need for which is more keenly felt by Egypt than the Sudan. The two countries have elaborated legal and supervisory mechanisms to assure an equitable sharing of the Nile waters—at least within the current configuration of water utilization—and this is no mean achievement. But no formula is immutable and surely adjustments in the 1959 Agreement will be required. Moreover, it is unlikely that in the next decades sufficient progress will be made toward political and economic integration to assure a stable and harmonious environment for the working-out of new formulae. If this assumption is correct, then the "Great Geopolitical Game" of the Nile Valley and the Horn of Africa, in which Egypt and the Sudan are only two of several actors, assumes potentially dramatic proportions.

As indicated above, the weak link in the chain of regional security as seen from Cairo and Khartoum is primarily the southern Sudan and, secondarily, Ethiopia. It is sincerely feared that if hostile forces were somehow able to exploit regional dissidence in the Sudan, the downstream water supply could be jeopardized and the Sudanese and Egyptian regimes threatened. It is not so much a question of whether or not it is plausible—or even conceivable—that any power would engage in such a crude geopolitical game, for that could only be considered an act of war; rather it is a question of Egyptian and Sudanese decision-makers, reacting instinctively in accord with what might be called the Fashoda Complex, finding such threats credible and shaping policy accordingly. Although a certain amount of hyperbole is surely involved, the fears aroused in Egypt by the presence of Cuban troops in Ethiopia, coupled with two abortive uprisings in the Shaba Province of neighboring Zaire in 1977 and 1978, are real and not easily dismissed. Thus President Sadat, in May 1978, warned, "we depend upon the Nile 100 percent in our life, so if anyone, at any moment thinks to deprive us of our life we shall never hesitate [to go to war] because it is a matter of life or death." Who is the unnamed enemy? Sadat's ally, King Hassan of Morocco, has repeatedly voiced the opinion that the USSR has a long-range plan to destabilize African regimes, bring strategic resources (copper, uranium, cobalt, and even agricultural produce) under the control of "friendly" regimes, and then disrupt Western economies by manipulating supply. That strategy, he feels, provided the logic of the Shaba Province insurrections, but Hassan II fears that "the Sudan could well be the next field of battle for it is potentially the richest country of Africa. Soon 70 million hectares [sic] will be cultivated there. They have just discovered oil. Strategically, it controls the sources of the Nile; finally it is within artillery range of Saudi Arabia."[14] Sadat, Mobutu, King Khalid, Numeiry, Giscard d'Estaing, and Zbigniew Brzezinski all share to some degree this perception of Soviet objectives.

To the extent that they are accurate, these perceptions indicate a geopolitical game in the classic sense of the term: fairly crude physical control of strategic real estate and vital resources that can be used to further national and super-national power advantages. In the Horn of Africa the implications of the game are especially far-reaching, for the real estate is very important. The struggle for the Nile, real or imagined, is literally paralleled by the struggle for the Red Sea, or at least the entrance thereof. The movement of a significant portion of the world petroleum trade (and of other goods), through the Bab al-Mandab straits depends in part upon which power controls them. This control of the straits would also bear directly upon the viability of the Saudi monarchy.

These are very high stakes, and Egypt has always sought arrangements for regional security that would cushion it against unforeseen and uncontrolable developments in and around its hinterland. This has meant, since the British re-occupation in 1898, a constant effort to maintain Egypt's pre-eminence in the Sudan so as to neutralize whatever unfriendly regimes might emerge in Ethiopia, Kenya, Uganda, and Zaire. Saudi Arabia, with its vast oil wealth and conservative regime, now has the same interest in a solid Egyptian-Sudanese tandem, provided they are both well disposed toward Saudi interests.

This was not the case in the late 1960s, when Egypt actively pursued formal collective security arrangements with the Sudan and Libya. In May of 1969 Ga'afar Numeiry came to power in the Sudan, and the following September Mu'ammar Qaddafi overthrew King Idris and proclaimed Libya a republic. These two young, untried, and insecure officers were both great admirers of President Nasser of Egypt and sought his support as they attempted to consolidate their authority. Nasser at that time was in a peculiarly difficult situation. His image and authority throughout the Arab World had been greatly impaired as a result of the defeat in June 1967 at the hands of the Israelis. He had been obliged to accept the largess of his old regional adversaries (especially that of King Faisal of Saudi Arabia), who were avowed spokesmen for United States interests in the area, except as regards the Arab-Israeli issue. Simultaneously, Nasser was driven even deeper into reliance upon the USSR for military aid and economic support for Egypt's public industries. Diplomatic relations with the United States had been severed for two years, and aside from the Saudi financial influence the West had little leverage over Egypt.

As Nasser returned from the Rabat Arab Heads of State meeting of December 1969, at which the conservative oil-producing states would not meet his request for increased military aid, the opportunity that Numeiry and Qaddafi could offer must have been plain to him. Oil-rich Libya, land-rich Sudan, and people-rich Egypt could become allies under the authority of Nasser and build a unit that would be the center of gravity of the Arab World. Saudi Arabia and the other conservative oil-rich states would be put in their proper place. The federation must have seemed to Nasser a way out of the morass. He and Numeiry stopped in Tripoli to meet with Qaddafi. On December 27, 1969, the three leaders issued a document known as the Tripoli Charter, proposing a federal union among their countries. In November 1970, Hafiz al-Assad of Syria, himself freshly arrived to power, announced his interest in joining the Federation. [15]

By the time Assad expressed his interest, Nasser had been dead for two months, an event that was the turning point for the Federation of Arab Republics. Nasser's political weight and prestige made him the linchpin of the Federation. Qaddafi, fiercely anticommunist, anti-United States, anti-Faisal, and ebulliently pro-Nasser, could be swallowed by the Egyptian left, the Sudanese communists associated with Numeiry, and the USSR, which aided both Egypt and the Sudan only so long as Nasser dominated the scene. His presence was insurance against the abandonment of Egypt's socialist experiment and the severing or diminution of ties with the Soviet Union and the socialist countries of Eastern Europe. Even with Nasser at its head, both the Sudanese and Egyptian left ranged from skeptical to hostile toward the proposed federation. Let us note at this point the states of Northeast Africa and the adjacent areas that were considered radical. Egypt seemed solidly aligned with Moscow; the Sudan potentially so, as Numeiry was initially compelled to rely upon domestic Marxist support; and Libya, through confrontation with Western oil companies and the closure of the U.S. airbase (Wheelus), appeared even-handed in its animosity to the great powers. Syria, also fundamentally dependent upon Soviet military and economic aid, was frosting on the radical cake. On the Western side were a disparate assortment of friends with few or no contacts among them: Israel, Jordan, Saudi Arabia, and Ethiopia (see Map 1).

With the accession of Anwar al-Sadat to power in Egypt in fall 1970, regional alignments began slowly to come apart. Sadat paid perhaps more than lip service to the FAR, for, after all, foreign-exchange–starved Egypt could scarcely forego a pliable benefactor like Libya. Qaddafi, it may have been thought for a time, with his tiny population and only oil for leverage, could not present any real challenge to Egypt or Sadat. But the real issue was not there but in Egypto-Saudi relations. Having overthrown a monarchy to come to power, Qaddafi was hostile to those that remained: King Faisal of Saudi Arabia, King Hussein of Jordan, and Hassan II of Morocco. For the Saudis, the Qaddafi menace was considerable. Conceivably one of the prices that Qaddafi might have exacted for his financial participation in the FAR would have been

MAP 1

Nations of the Middle East

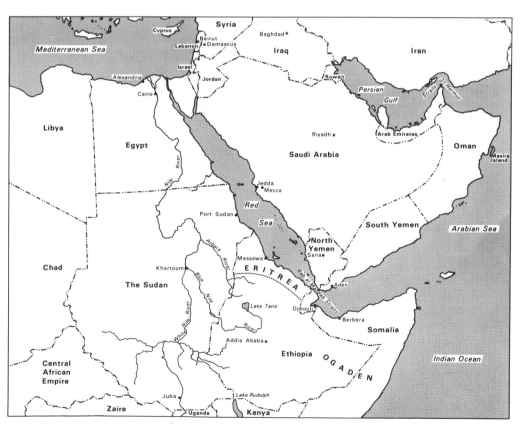

to force Sadat to adopt the same confrontationist stance toward the Saudi monarchy as had Nasser until 1967. Indeed, if the FAR, with Syria included, were to have pursued such policies, Saudi Arabia, Jordan, and all the lesser entities of the Arabian Peninsula would have found themselves isolated and exposed.

Fortunately for Saudi Arabia, President Sadat was not personally inclined toward this course. On the contrary: he became convinced that relations with the United States must be improved if progress toward a settlement with Israel was to be achieved. He was confident that he could coax from the oil-rich Arab states the kind of investment and financial support that Nasser had tried to extort. In brief, the market that was gradually developed in the early 1970s was to trade Egypt's political docility *vis-à-vis* the pro-Western regimes for their financial support. But Sadat could not have both Saudi Arabia and Libya as benefactors, and a choice between the two was inevitable.

Similarly, Numeiry in the Sudan was facing some difficult alternatives. The civil war in the south had sapped the country economically, and in its intractability, denied to successive regimes in Khartoum the chance to consolidate their legitimacy and demonstrate their effectiveness. If only for his own survival, Numeiry needed to normalize the southern situation, and it became abundantly clear that normalization would be impossible so long as the Sudan intended to adhere to the FAR. Southern leaders who signaled their willingness (through the good offices of Haile Selassie of Ethiopia) to accept a compromise on the basis of regional autonomy, insisted that such autonomy would be rendered meaningless if the Sudan simultaneously immersed itself in some larger Arab unit. Such a move would deprive the southern region of much of its bargaining power and weight (one-third of the territory, one-third of the population) within the Sudan. Numeiry came to accept this perspective, and when the FAR was officially proclaimed in September 1971, the Sudan was "temporarily" out of it. Numeiry later stated that the Sudan would reconsider membership only after the restoration of complete normalcy in the south and once the Sudan as a whole had overcome its basic economic problems.[16] From that point on, Sudanese-Libyan relations reached a nadir from which they have yet to rise. That left within the FAR Libya, Egypt, and a rather aloof Syria. Integral union between Egypt and Libya was to be proclaimed on September 1, 1973. It never was; for Sadat had become fully convinced of his Saudi Arabian option and had also taken the decision to launch his limited war to "explode," as he put it, the military and diplomatic stalemate prevailing in the Arab-Israeli dispute. The October War set the stage for an astonishing realignment of regional forces.

The FAR was dead and its three original founders all mutually hostile. It was Saudi Arabia, representing Western (especially U.S.) interests, that began to pick up the pieces. Here it is important to note that Saudi initiatives were part of a much broader reassertion of U.S. influence in the Middle East. Saudi Arabia became the swing state in an interest group—some would say axis, others "Holy Alliance"—that also included Iran, Egypt, and the Sudan.

With the collapse of the FAR, the quest for regional security within a framework of formal political unity was abandoned for the time being, replaced by a kind of pro-western entente among the four powers mentioned above. For all its looseness, its tasks were nonetheless challenging in view of the perceived threat from the Soviet Union and the entente among its disparate supporters: Ethiopia, after the overthrow of Hailie Salassie in 1974, Libya after 1973, Uganda, and South Yemen. There is little purpose in trying to seek ideologic consistency in the alignments that have emerged in this regional cockpit, and whatever they are, they will surely have changed by the time these lines are read.

The focal point in most respects is Ethiopia. The radical military regime that has installed itself there since 1974 has failed to find any accommodation with two secessionist movements that would not only cut off Addis Ababa and the Amharic Christian heartland from the sea, but lead to the dismemberment of the state as well. Firstly, the radical armed struggle for Eritrean independence that has been under way since 1962 found Ethiopia's new masters to be as intransigent as the Emperor.[17] The revolutionary fronts have been able to deny Addis Ababa access to the Red Sea through Masawa (see Map 1). Secondly, radical, pro-Soviet Somalia simultaneously aided the cause of Somali irredentism in the eastern buttress of Ethiopia, the Ogaden region. In the course of the armed struggle there, the rail link between Addis Ababa and Djibouti was severed so that Ethiopia became effectively landlocked. If that were not enough, it seemed possible that once the French gave up control of Djibouti in the spring of 1977 the majority of the population, being ethnically Somali, might drag it into union with Somalia. How these struggles played themselves out would determine who controlled the Bab al-Mandab straits.

This situation as it stood in 1977 must have seemed frustratingly absurd to the Soviet Union. Nearly all the local actors, save Egypt and the Sudan, were avowedly revolutionary with close links to Moscow, yet they seemed bent upon destroying one another. Territory and national sentiment obviously weighed more heavily than ideology. The USSR tried to salvage the situation by proposing a loose confederation of South Yemen (including the port of Aden), Ethiopia, Djibouti, Eritrea, and Somalia. Former President Podgorny raised the question on his trip to Africa in the spring of 1977, but it was Fidel Castro who made the case for it in Aden on March 16, with the leaders of South Yemen, Somalia, and Ethiopia present. President Sayyid al-Barre of Somalia vetoed the suggested confederation.[18]

A pro-Western counter-alliance, already in the making, turned out to be no more effective. In February 1977 in Khartoum, Presidents Sadat, Numeiry, and Assad met and indirectly denounced combined Libyan-Ethiopian machinations against the Sudanese regime as well as Soviet designs on the area as a whole. Saudi Arabia meanwhile utilized monetary blandishments to try to lure South Yemen and Somalia away from the Soviet camp. Three developments threw the counter-alliance into disarray: Numeiry's need to come to terms with internal opposition elements; Sadat's peace initiative in the fall of 1977; and the direct involvement of Soviet and Cuban military personnel in Ethiopia's fight against the insurgents in the Ogaden.

The latter move represents the Soviet assessment that a pro-Soviet Ethiopia, with its large population and territorial expanse, must be kept intact. In other words, neither a friendly Somalia nor Eritrea could offer the same strategic advantage in the Horn and the Nile Valley as could Ethiopia. Thus the USSR, having failed to promote the idea of a confederation, decided to give Ethiopia the armaments and logistic support to hold in check, if not suppress, the insurgents in Eritrea and Ogaden. In early 1978 the entire region of the Ogaden was once again restored to the control of Addis Ababa while Sayyid al-Barre, having burned his bridges with Moscow, waited forlornly for arms from the West that never came. However, as regards Eritrea, whose absorption into Ethiopia in 1962 was at best arbitrary, the Cubans and Soviets have been more circumspect, urging a negotiated settlement that would probably lead to some form of Eritrean autonomy.

That, indeed, is the solution long recommended by Gaafar al-Numeiry. With Hailie Selassie's good offices, such an arrangement had been worked out for Southern Sudan, and Numeiry hoped that either the Emperor or his military successors would espouse the same formula for Eritrea. These two regions and their ethnic problems are closely interrelated. For instance, if the Sudan overtly supports the Eritreans, then the Ethiopians will seek to revive the dissidents in the

Southern Sudan, or actively abet the subversive activities of the Mahdi's Ansar, who sought refuge in Ethiopia by the thousands following the Aba Island massacre in 1970. The ruling Dergue in Addis Ababa after 1974 revealed itself insensitive to this tradeoff, engaging in hot pursuit of Eritrean rebels on Sudanese territory* (and allegedly assisting an attempt to overthrow Numeiry in 1976). The Sudan countered by giving greater support to the Eritreans, particularly to the more conservative front most favorable to Saudi Arabia.

This gambit was shortlived, as Numeiry found himself compelled to come to terms with several forces of internal opposition so as to overcome his isolation. This led to his reconciliation with the exiled Sadiq al-Mahdi, leader of the Ansar and the Umma Party. One of the al-Mahdi's recommendations, if not a pre-condition for his return from exile, was that the Sudan not be provoked into alienating so great and powerful a neighbor as Ethiopia, nor, by the same token, should it sever all links with Libya. Consequently, after the Ethiopian reconquest of the Ogaden, the Sudan made conciliatory gestures both toward the Dergue and toward Colonel Qaddafi. At the meeting of the OAU in Khartoum in July 1978, Numeiry was elected President of the Organization.

The third episode that stimulated the disaggregation of the regional security arrangements encouraged by Egypt and Saudi Arabia was President Sadat's decision, in the fall of 1977, to go to Jerusalem in order to make a breakthrough towards a peace settlement with Israel. This was accomplished without any prior consultation with Egypt's friends and tactical allies. The result was that Syria considered Sadat thenceforth a traitor to the Arab cause while Saudi Arabia remained studiously silent about the advisability of the move. Only the Sudan (and Morocco) gave tepid endorsement to Sadat's initiative. The Libyans, having recently emerged in June 1977 from a brief border war with Egypt, took comfort in the new isolation of Sadat's regime.

Looking at the local actors in and around the Nile Valley, as well as at their extra-regional benefactors, one finds almost total disarray. The tentative alignments along great power lines of 1976–77 have been dissolved. In their place have appeared at least a dozen states, many of which are undergoing agonizing reappraisals of their foreign policies, or are confronting severe domestic challenges, or both. It is this proliferation of actors that has characterized the Nile basin in modern times.

---

*The Sudan has provided sanctuary, sometimes reluctantly, to Eritrean freedom fighters as well as a home for some 200,000 refugees.

The British dealt with it for a time by imposing imperial control from Cairo to Capetown. But the local actors most directly menaced by the unknowns of the present confusion—Egypt and the Sudan—are not capable of reimposing the same kind of order. Their visceral fear that the disorder might well be exploited by hostile powers to their disadvantage is similar to British apprehensions of the French presence at the headwaters of the Nile at the turn of the century. One particularly important conclusion for the purposes of this study can be drawn from this assessment. Until the reasonable fears of the downstream states regarding their water supply can be allayed, none of the technical arguments for optimum use and management of the Nile, however compelling, will sway these states sufficiently for them to run the risk of implementing such projects. It is precisely in the context of alleviating downstream fears that the Aswan High Dam scheme must be placed. A material need—adequate summer water—and the engineering key to satisfying that need *within Egyptian borders*, led to a revolution that transformed the river below Aswan into something else altogether.

4

INTERNATIONAL HYDROPOLITICS

The High Dam has simply eliminated the flood: there will be no more flood from now on. It has converted the destructive river into a giant irrigation canal. — GAMAL HAMDAN[1]

Mean years are of no value since the surplus of one year is not available for the next. — SIR WILLIAM WILLCOCKS[2]

DURING THE FIRST sixty years of this century, the average annual discharge of the Nile as measured at Aswan was 84 billion m³. The standard deviation from that mean, however, was about 20 billion m³ annually. At the same time, toward midcentury, Egypt's estimated water needs stabilized between 55 and 63 billion m³, the bulk of it for agriculture. Thus, while discharge fluctuated widely from year to year, real needs were constant and high. Years of low floods spelled economic disaster, but high floods, as in 1946–47, could be equally menacing. After World War II, Egypt's economy and growing population could no longer tolerate the uncertainties inherent in the Nile's natural discharge.

Since the turn of the century, pioneers in the hydraulic engineering of the Nile, such as William Willcocks, William Garstin, and H. E. Hurst, all of the Egyptian Irrigation Department, saw the need for overyear storage throughout the Nile Valley and began tinkering with various aspects of a multifaceted solution that came to be known as the Century Storage Scheme. Many others, it should be noted, made major contributions to the elaboration of the project. The basic notion is simple: to remove the unpredictable element from the Nile discharge would require storing several successive annual floods; that is, storing the annual difference between real needs and total discharge. In this manner a series of reservoirs could be used to bank water against low years or to hold excess water if the flood promised to be especially high.

There are numerous reasons why some variant on this notion was not pursued in the first half of this century, but the two principal obstacles were technical and diplomatic. On the technical side was the problem of impounding silt and other sediment along with the flood-waters. Until 1960 and the beginning of the construction of the Aswan High Dam, all water storage facilities on the Nile were seasonal in capacity. They could entrap a portion of the tailend of each flood (that portion varying with the volume of the flood), allowing the bulk of the flood and most of the silt to sluice through unimpeded. If reservoir capacity had been enlarged, more silt would have been impounded upstream of the dams, and the reservoirs themselves would have silted up fairly rapidly.* In light of this constraint we find the seasonal storage facilities on the Nile described in Table 6. The final entry is for the only over-year storage facility, the Aswan High Dam.

TABLE 6

Water Storage Facilities on the Nile

Facility	Completed	Area km²	Capacity billion m³	Location
Old Aswan				
3rd raising	1933	—	5.3	Aswan, Egypt, Main Nile
Sennar	1925	160	.9	The Sudan, Blue Nile
Jebel Auliya	1937	600	3.5	The Sudan, White Nile
Khashm al-Girba	1966	150	1.2	The Sudan, Atbara
Roseires	1966	290	3.0	The Sudan, Blue Nile
Aswan High Dam	1971	4000	164.0	Aswan, Egypt, Main Nile

The largest of the seasonal facilities, Old Aswan, could impound only about 6 percent of the average annual discharge. The other dams could together hold less than 12 percent so that reliance upon seasonal storage meant that at least 80 percent (except in very low years) of each

*What silting can mean is demonstrated by the Roseires Dam on the Blue Nile. Between 1966 and 1975, the maximum depth of the reservoir was reduced from 50 meters to 17. See Christaan Gischler, *Present and Future Trends in Water Resource Development in the Arab States* (UNESCO/ROSTAS, August 1976), p. 40.

flood had to be released downstream. In low years these facilities could not make up the shortfall, and in high years both the Sudan and Egypt risked flooding. The Aswan High Dam, from a purely theoretical point of view, could impound two average annual floods without letting a drop through its sluice gates.

Aside from silting, the Century Storage Scheme had to coordinate a series of complicated engineering projects over a period of twenty years among some nine African states.* This aspect can best be understood by getting at the heart of the project itself. The linchpin of the proposed system would have been Lake Victoria (today Kenya, Tanzania, and Uganda are all riparian states), which was to be used as the major over-year storage reservoir. Victoria is the second largest lake in the world (after Superior) with a surface area of 67,000 km². Raising its level by just one meter would represent an increment in stored water of 67 billion m³ or the equivalent of nearly 80 percent of the Nile system's entire annual discharge. However, only about 5 billion m³ of the additional stored water could be delivered into the Behr el-Jebel River at the lake's outlet each year. Supplementing the over-year storage function of Victoria would be Lake Idi Amin and Lake Tana, at the headwaters of the Blue Nile. Lakes Kioga and Albert would operate in tandem with Victoria and Idi Amin to regulate the discharge into the Victoria Nile and the Behr el-Jebel River. It may be appropriate at this juncture to note that in 1948 the Owen Falls Dam at the exit of Victoria (Jinga, Uganda) was begun, and construction was completed in 1954. Egypt paid £1 million to raise the dam one meter higher than planned in order to increase storage, but the main objective was to regulate the discharge from the lake and to generate 150 megawatts of hydroelectric power annually for Ugandan industry.

The real challenge to the proposed system lay further downstream where the Behr el-Jebel River enters the great Sudd swamp north of Juba in the Sudan. Here the Behr el-Jebel reaches the flat bottom of its drainage basin and spills over its banks to form a swamp some 5,000–6,000 km² in surface. Half the total discharge of the Behr el-Jebel, or some 14 billion m³, are herein lost through evaporation each year. Over-year storage at Victoria would go for naught if the additional stored water could not be delivered through the swamps. Total losses due to evaporation in the swamps, and comprising the spill-over of all

---

*They are today Egypt, the Sudan, Ethiopia, Kenya, Uganda, Zaire, Tanzania, Rawanda, and Burundi. All are now independent states, but at the time the project was being considered, all were under direct or indirect colonial control, mainly British but also Belgian and Italian.

the main White Nile tributaries (Behr el-Ghazal and the Sobat) is on the average 40 billion m³ per year.

The problem, therefore, was to cut a channel through or a diversionary canal around the swamp. Early suggestions centered on embanking and deepening the channel of the Behr el-Jebel to prevent spillage into the swamps during the flood. In the interwar years, a new objective was added, that of excavating a canal, known as the Jonglei, to take off north of Juba at Bor and to skirt the swamp to the east for some 280 kilometers, delivering its discharge to the Nile at Malakal. The Egyptians sought approval for this scheme as early as 1938.

What was proposed was a canal with a capacity of 55 million m³ per day that would make an additional 7 billion m³ available for Egypt during the so-called timely season from December through July. This period corresponds to the months of the low Nile in Egypt, after the discharge of the flood, and to the season in which foreign exchange earning crops are grown: principally cotton and rice. Even with Jonglei, it was still proposed that the Behr el-Jebel be embanked from an upstream point at Tombe north to the barrage that was to be built at the canal's off-take on the River Atem (see Map 2).

The proposal's major drawback for the Sudanese was that the canal itself, and the seasonal pattern of its discharge, would invert the Sudd's natural regime. It was known from the start that this inversion would adversely affect the populations living in the area. These consisted mostly of pastoral tribes subsisting on rainy season agriculture and year-round cattle raising. The principal tribal groupings of the Sudd region are the Mandari, Dinka, Nuer, and Shilluk. In 1954, when a survey of the area was finally undertaken, it was found that there were about 700,000 people with nearly one million cattle exploiting the area that would be disturbed by Jonglei.

Most of these peoples established their permanent settlements on high ground, generally to the east of the swamp. The area around their settlements would be cultivated during the rainy season (mainly with millet and sorghum) from May to October. Then, as upland pasture dried out, the herdsmen would move westward and down toward the swamp, until they reached flood plain areas from which the swamp recedes during the dry season. The islands of pasturage that thus emerged constituted the "toich" lands and were sufficient to provide adequate grazing throughout the dry season. In that capacity the toiches were, and still are, vital to the survival of the pastoral tribes.

The inversion in the delivery of water to the Sudd, upon which the original Jonglei Canal project was based, would have threatened sub-

MAP 2

Jonglei Canal

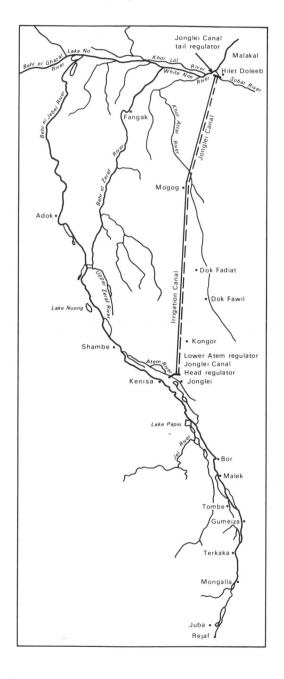

stantial areas of toich lands with desiccation. First, some of the water of the Behr el-Jebel, whose discharge reaches its peak in August-September, would be retained in Lake Victoria, because at that time of year Egypt receives all the water it can utilize—and more—from the Blue Nile flood. The water stored at Victoria would be released during the timely months (December through May), through the now-embanked upstream portions of the Behr el-Jebel, and from there into the Jonglei Canal, which would carry 55 million m³ a day to the White Nile at Malakal. Spillage and flooding in the Sudd would thus be minimized and large areas of toich land deprived of water at precisely the time of year that the pastoralists moved to lower ground in search of pasturage. The areas so affected would have included 700 of 1,100 km² along the stretch between Mongolla and the Atem River; 2,100 of 2,500 km² in the central Sudd; and 1,100 of 1,500 km² in the northern sectors. Most of the permanently flooded areas would also have been drained, reducing the fish stock: the livelihood for significant numbers of the swamp's fishing population. (One source estimates that the permanent swamp would have been reduced from 6,500 km² to 360 km².)³

The extensive socioeconomic disruption inherent in the Jonglei project, plus the fact that only the Egyptians stood to gain substantially from it, made the Sudanese reluctant to acquiesce to the plan. After the interlude of World War II, the Sudanese, in 1946, instituted a special Jonglei Investigation Team to devise counterproposals, which were presented in 1954. The general aims were (1) to regulate discharge so that it conformed more closely to the natural pattern; (2) abandon embanking the Behr el-Jebel; and (3) reduce the total discharge of the Jonglei Canal. The goal was to minimize the loss of toich pasturage to about 19 percent of the total available and to protect swamp fisheries.⁴ At this juncture the Jonglei project, as well as all other facets of the Century Storage Scheme, fell into abeyance as the Sudan moved toward independence and Egypt became enamored of the Aswan High Dam project.

The Jebel Auliya Dam, 40 kilometers upstream from Khartoum on the White Nile, cannot be considered a functional part of the Century Storage Scheme. Rather it owes its existence to the fact that over-year storage projects remained for so long planners' dreams. Its construction, as noted earlier, was at the behest of the Egyptians and was agreed upon in 1932. The dam itself was completed in 1937. At the time it reflected the imperative needs of Egypt for more summer water when the Sudan, after construction of the Sennar Dam, was drawing more heavily on the discharge of the Blue Nile. The Jebel Auliya Dam was designed to store the Sobat flood (which joins the Behr el-Jebel and Behr el-Ghazal at Malakal) in a reservoir of 3.5 billion m³ capacity. Although the dam provided some additional seasonal storage, it did so at the cost of high evaporation rates amounting annually to about half the water stored. Egypt shared in the expenses of the dam's construction, supplied most of the labor, and compensated the Sudanese for riverine areas flooded by the reservoir. Had the Century Storage Scheme become reality, Jebel Auliya would surely have become superfluous if not an outright liability. Indeed, as it now stands, with the construction of the High Dam at Aswan, the destruction of the Jebel Auliya Dam could add 1.5 billion m³ to the annual discharge of the Nile by doing away with the heavy evaporation losses at the reservoir. This the Egyptians would most like to do, but the Sudanese are reluctant to go along because, since 1937, considerable pump irrigation schemes have been installed along the reservoir's banks.* The dam also serves as a barrier to the spread of the water hyacinth downstream.

Within the framework of the Century Storage Scheme the Blue Nile did not present the same challenge as the White Nile. The major project was to develop over-year storage at Lake Tana (3,100 km²) in Ethiopia. It has been estimated that raising the maximum lake level from 81.5 meters to 83 meters would provide a water reserve of 5 billion m³. Raising it to 85 meters would give an additional storage of 7 billion m³, of which 2 billion m³ could be set aside annually for Sudan's use, and the remainder stored against low years or as an element in flood control.[5] The only benefit to Ethiopia from the project would be the generation of hydroelectric power, but even then the power station would be far from the major consumers of electricity.

An initial agreement between Egypt and the Sudan concerning Lake Tana was reached in 1935, but the Italian invasion of Ethiopia precluded an accord with the party most directly involved. Although the 1935 agreement was modified in 1946 to allow for increased storage at, and greater discharge from, Lake Tana, the now-independent Ethiopians could not be coaxed into acquiescence. There, as with Victoria, the matter lies as the Aswan High Dam project pre-empted center stage.

Until the mid-1960s, the only dam constructed on the Blue Nile was

---

*Dr. Abd al-Aziz Ahmad argued that with a backwater extending 600 kilometers upstream, Jebel Auliya could be a direct hindrance to increased discharge during the timely season if the Century Storage Scheme were pursued. He called for the dam's "discontinuance." See his "Recent Developments in Nile Control," paper 6012, *Proceedings of the Institute of Civil Engineers* (U.K.) 17 (October 1960):174. See also Michael Field, "Developing the Nile," *World Crops* 25 (1) (January–February 1973):14–15.

at Sennar (1925), about 350 kilometers upstream from Khartoum. The reservoir's capacity (900 million m³) was designed to impound a portion of the Blue Nile flood to irrigate the Gezira Cotton Scheme, without depriving Egypt of any water that it could effectively utilize. (It was precisely the bulk of the Blue Nile flood that Egypt had to release through the sluice gates at the Old Aswan Dam. Much of the released water simply flowed into the Mediterranean unused.) Sennar Dam could have played a role in the Century Storage Scheme, for it would have provided additional storage for expanding Sudanese agriculture. Instead, once construction of the Aswan High Dam began, plans were laid for a second Blue Nile Dam at Roseires, 620 kilometers upstream from Khartoum. The dam was completed in 1966, and has a reservoir capacity of 3 billion m³. Paid for in its entirety by the Sudanese, the project's benefits accrue exclusively to the Managil extension of the Gezira Cotton Scheme. However, the Sudan's increased use of Blue Nile water is fully consonant with the terms of the 1959 agreement allocating water between Egypt and the Sudan.

Moving downstream on the main Nile, we come to the site of another crucial element in the proposed Century Storage Scheme: a major dam and storage facility at the fourth cataract just upstream from Merowe. Despite high evaporation rates, as at Jebel Auliya, such a dam would be vital for flood control below the confluence of the White and Blue Niles, and would rapidly supply additional summer water to Egypt (the fourth cataract is 800 kilometers close to Aswan than Jebel Auliya). The proposed capacity of this seasonal storage facility was about 3 billion m³. Like the other components of the Century Storage Scheme, interest in the fourth cataract dam faded in the early 1950s, and because neither flood control nor *seasonal* storage are of any further concern to Egypt, interest in the project has not been revived.*

The Old Aswan Dam, built in 1902 and raised to its present height in 1933, would have continued its role as the major seasonal storage facility on the Nile within the framework of the Century Storage Scheme. No additions to or modifications of that structure were contemplated (except for the indirectly related question of whether or not to install a power station at the dam site). Thus, within the Century Storage Scheme, there remains to be considered only Egypt's Wadi Rayyan depression, which lies just to the south of Fayyum province, and was used for flood control and storage of excess flood waters. (In

*The Permanent Joint Technical Commission (PJTC) in July 1977 recommended the construction of a fourth cataract dam to expand summer cropping in the Dongola-Merowe area of Northern Province and to provide some hydroelectric power.

ancient times, Lake Moeris, lying in the same depression, was used for similar purposes by the pharaohs.) The depression is about 50 meters below sea level, has a surface of 700 km² and is situated 60 kilometers west of the Nile. Both seasonal and over-year storage have been suggested for Wadi Rayyan. In either case a barrage would have to be built across the Nile just downstream of an off-take canal, to deliver flood waters to the depression. The depression could contain over 20 billion m³. Once full, the reservoir could store unused flood water, and then, once the river level had dropped during the timely season, redeliver water to the Nile by gravity flow—some 2 billion m³ could be returned to the system during the dry months in this manner. After this water had been drawn off by free flow, it would then be necessary to pump additional quantities up from the depression to the river. In the view of Abd al-Aziz Ahmad, one of the most compelling reasons for electrifying the Old Aswan Dam was to provide seasonal power (February–July) to run these pumps. An over-year variant on this suggestion was to allow only the free-flow portion of the stored waters to return to the Nile, holding the rest against particularly low years. Over-year or annual storage would require both major pumping stations and an assured energy supply. A problem related to this project was its probable effect on the water table in the Fayyum province. Dr. Ahmad stated his opinion that silt deposits in the depression would effectively seal its bottom so that seepage into the adjacent area would be negligible. At the same time, he noted that the capacity of the reservoir was such that it could be used for 650 years before silting up. H. E. Hurst echoed that view, adding that the main effect of gradual siltation would be the addition of new land to Egypt's cultivable surface.[6] Table 7 gives an estimate of the total benefits in timely water that could have been derived from the Century Storage Scheme.

Hurst judged that the cultivation of 7 million feddans in Egypt and 2 million in the Sudan during the same months would require about 30 billion m³ of water, so that there would be some margin for extending cultivation into new areas (see Figure 6). Summarizing his position as of 1946, Hurst wrote:

> We again emphasize: a) that only by over-year storage in the lakes can the cultivation of Egypt and the Sudan be protected against the menace of low years which increases with the proportion of storage water to that of natural supply. b) That the projects are interdependent and the efficient control of the Nile in the future requires that they be considered as essential parts of one scheme. c) That if the population of

Egypt continues to increase at its present rate the full development will be needed in 1980. As the projects for "Century Storage" and the Sudd will take twenty-five years before they are in full operation, it is obvious that preparation for what is sometimes called the "far future" must be begun now. Decisions on these combined projects must be made within the next year or at most within the next two. In fact we may say that the "far future" is already upon us.[7]

TABLE 7

Timely Water (February–July) as Measured at Aswan
(excluding High Dam, Roseires, and Khashm al-Girba)

Natural Flow of the River	15.4 billion m³
Stored at Lakes Victoria and Albert	5.3 billion m³
Stored at Lake Tana	2.1 billion m³
Stored at Sennar	1.0 billion m³
Stored at Jebel Auliya (net of evaporation)	2.5 billion m³
Stored at Aswan	5.2 billion m³
Stored at Fourth Cataract	3.0 billion m³
Subtotal	34.5 billion m³
Downstream Aswan; Wadi Rayyan	2–5 billion m³
Grand Total	36.5–39.5 billion m³

That was in 1946. No action was taken on any facet of the Century Storage Scheme, with the exception of the Owen Falls Dam, during the waning years of the Egyptian monarchy. When Gamal Abd el-Nasser came to power in July 1952, the "far future" was even more upon Egypt than when Hurst issued his warning. It is to the credit of Nasser and his colleagues that they immediately came to grips with the problem. It was not their decisiveness but the nature of their decision that roused the ongoing controversy. They decided to drop the Century Storage Scheme, at least temporarily, and to opt for a visionary project known as the Aswan High Dam. A series of relatively small projects was thus scrapped in favor of one giant project, but the fundamental goals were the same: over-year storage and adequate summer water for Egypt's commercial agriculture.

FIGURE 6

Diagram of the Century Water Storage Scheme as conceived around 1950

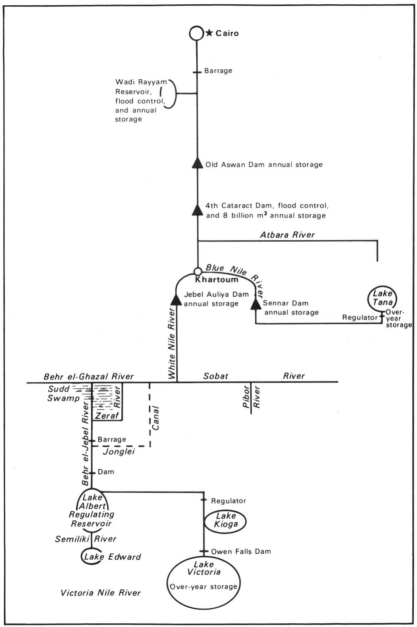

SOURCE: Adapted from H. E. Hurst, *The Nile* (London: Constable, 1957), p. 282.

THE DAM AS SYMBOL: FUNDING

Egypt's very survival depends on the $1.3 billion Aswan High Dam project. ... President Nasser [stated] that if the Western proposal were properly revised, he would give categorical assurances against Soviet bloc participation in the High Dam project.

The Egyptian Premier was driving a hard bargain, but Western diplomats were confident that they and he could come to terms. Agreement would consolidate a resounding victory for the free world in the oil-rich Middle East. — *Newsweek*, January 16, 1956, p. 25.

Here are joined the political, social, national, and military battles of the Egyptian people, welded together like the gigantic mass of rock that has blocked the course of the ancient Nile. Its waters now spill into the largest lake ever shaped by human kind and which will be an everlasting source of prosperity. — GAMAL ABD AL-NASSER, May 14, 1964: Speech at first closure of the Nile at the High Dam Site.

The decision to build the High Dam was taken by the small band of middle-ranking Egyptian army officers who had overthrown a patently corrupt monarchical regime. However popular their action, the Free Officers enjoyed no constituency of their own. The specific decision regarding the High Dam must thus be set in the general context of a new and unknown regime seeking to establish its credibility and to signal its citizens, and make known to the nations abroad, that it was prepared to do what no previous regime had dared contemplate or advocate to promote the country's well-being.

Gamal Abd el-Nasser and his eleven principal co-conspirators had no blueprint in mind for Egypt's economic strategy when they came to power on July 23, 1952, but they did have some goals and principles to which they tenaciously adhered. Foremost among them was to encourage prosperity for the many by engineering an equitable distribution of economic goods within Egyptian society. With one or two exceptions there were no ideologues and no doctrinaire revolutionaries among the young officers. What bound them together was an overriding concern with Egypt's independence, in all its political, military, and economic aspects; an independence they rightly viewed to be contingent on the emergence of a materially secure and educated citizenry. They justifiably accused the *ancien regime* of having grossly— even criminally — neglected these goals, tolerating sham independence, continued British military occupation, growing class cleavages, and the absolute pauperization of the largely illiterate peasantry. Nor on this unhappy landscape could one discern any determined effort to move the society on to an industrial footing. Such a transformation, in the eyes of the officers (and in those of many other Egyptians as well) was the prerequisite of balanced growth and eventual economic self-sufficiency. Continued reliance on the agricultural sector, and upon Egypt's major commercial crop, cotton, was seen as not only economically unfeasible over the long term, but also as tantamount to an acceptance of indefinite economic backwardness and international dependency.

The new regime sought a spectacular gesture to signal its visions and intentions to the Egyptian people and to the world. Within two months of the July Revolution, the Aswan High Dam project was under active and favorable consideration by the Revolutionary Command Council (RCC). There is no evidence that the conspirators had given any consideration to the High Dam Scheme before coming to power. Indeed, it is unlikely that they had even heard of it before it fell, somewhat fortuitously, into their laps. But once before them, the project's political advantages, as well as its economic strengths, became immediately apparent. Politically it had the advantage of being gigantic and daring, thrusting Egypt into the vanguard of modern hydraulic engineering. Moreover, during its construction and after its completion, it would be highly visible and fittingly monumental. In addition, it would meet the well-known problems of over-year storage through an edifice lying entirely within Egypt's borders. Thus Egypt, the classic downstream state, would not be hostage for its economic survival to upstream riparians. The fact that some of the most important of these — the Sudan, Uganda, and Kenya — were under the control of Egypt's chief great power adversary, Britain, made it all the more imperative for the RCC to treat the Century Storage Scheme cautiously. Economically, the project held out the prospect of improving Egyptian agriculture while (through the generation of massive amounts of hydroelectric power), simultaneously furnishing a cheap source of energy to fuel the transformation of Egyptian society to an industrial mode. Finally, it was believed that the High Dam could be completed in a decade — whereas all the projects comprising the Century Storage Scheme would have required at least twice as long— and that the High Dam would cost no more than any of its alternatives. In light of these considerations, the decision of whether or not to adopt the project devolved upon the Egyptian and international technical consultants whose task it became to pronounce upon the dam's feasibility.

The High Dam's most fervent advocate, and the man who brought it to the attention of the new regime, was Adrien Daninos, a Greco-Egyptian engineer and visionary. He had been the promoter of apparently lost causes ever since 1912, when he first argued for the electrification of the Old Aswan Dam in order to stimulate Egyptian industry, especially for the production of fertilizers. While others shared his concern, it was not until the mid-1950s that anyone in authority acted upon his suggestions. Shortly after World War II, as other technocrats crowded him from the scene, Daninos (in conjunction with Luigi Gallioli, an Italian engineer at the head of Studio Tecnice Ingegnore Gallioli) came to the conclusion that a single dam upstream of Aswan could impound an entire flood of the Nile and, through over-year storage, generate as much as 16 billion kWh of power per year. While these estimates were over 20 percent in excess of the reservoir capacity of the High Dam that has become reality, and over 60 percent in excess of the actual power station, it is indisputable that in 1948 Daninos fathered the High Dam project.[8]

Daninos had tirelessly peddled his notion to anyone willing to listen, both inside Egypt and abroad. Experts, such as H. E. Hurst of the Ministry of Irrigation, treated his suggestions with equal measures of respect and skepticism. Hurst had argued as early as 1944 that over-year storage in places such as Aswan, subjected to scorching heat and high winds, would cancel its benefits by excessive rates of surface evaporation.[9] Daninos himself was primarily worried by the possibility that the reservoir he proposed would rapidly silt up, while others, such as Ali Fathi, Dean of the Faculty of Engineering at Alexandria University, anticipated severe downstream "scouring," or erosion of the riverbed, if the Nile's waters no longer bore their customary load of suspended matter.*

While others carefully deliberated on his scheme, Daninos seized the opportunity of the advent of a new regime in Egypt to go straight to the top with the Aswan High Dam proposal. Within a month of coming to power, two army engineers, Samir Hilmy and the late Mahmud Yunis, both members of the Free Officers conspiracy, were approached by Daninos in their capacity as heads of the RCC's technical office. They were favorably impressed by the project and referred it for an initial critical review to Dr. Muhammad Ahmad Selim, professor of hydraulic engineering at Cairo University. By September 1952 he had reported positively on the dam, at which point Hilmy and

*Fathy was enough impressed by Daninos' plan that he allowed him to lecture on it at the Faculty of Engineering at Alexandria in the early 1950s.

Yunis put the project before the RCC. Samir Hilmy explained the scheme and urged its adoption. The RCC approved it in principle, pending further technical studies, and it was only then that the project was presented to the Ministry of Public Works (later to become the Ministry of Irrigation) for comment.

Samir Hilmy accompanied one of the members of the RCC, Anwar al-Sadat, to discuss the matter with the Minister of Public Works, Murad Fahmy. They were invading a bureaucracy that was reputedly hostile to any over-year storage project other than the Century Storage Scheme, which the government had formally endorsed in 1948. Yet eventually, and probably not surprisingly, the ministry came out in favor of the High Dam. The project was scrutinized there by the Water Resource Committee, consisting of H. E. Hurst, R. P. Black, and Yussef Samaika. They seemingly reversed earlier stances on the project, and several colleagues came to feel that they had opportunistically sold out. One of their peers summed up his view of their change of heart by citing a phrase from the *Rubayyat of Omar Khayyam*: "When the King says it is midnight at noon, the wise man says behold the moon." The experts themselves simply argued that with careful design, evaporation losses — the core of their previous objections — could be kept within tolerable limits, and that silt precipitation in the reservoir would eventually seal its bottom and thereby minimize seepage.[10] In opting for the dam, the Water Resources Committee stressed that the project was not a substitute for the Century Storage Scheme but rather a politically manageable and technically sound antecedent. They maintained that optimal utilization of the Nile would ultimately require implementation of the Equatorial projects. The young officers concurred in this view, hoping that with the elimination of the colonial presence from Africa, the multinational complications of managing the Nile could be pursued without the threat of upstream blackmail.[11]

In April 1953, a special committee was constituted and attached to the National Production Council to oversee the project. Its members were Colonel Samir Hilmy, Dr. Muhammad Ahmad Selim, and Dr. Hassan Zaky (chief adviser to Murad Fahmy). At nearly the same time (January 1953), Egypt's Minister of Finance, Abd al-Galil al-Amary, approached the International Bank for Reconstruction and Development (IBRD) with regard to funding the project. At that point the project was still loosely conceived, and the IBRD agreed to finance only $200,000 worth of engineering feasibility studies.*

_____

*Al-Amary wrote directly to Eugene Black, the President of the IBRD, and Daninos paid him a personal visit in Washington, D.C. In February 1953 Black toured the

This modest support was unnecessary, as Egypt had already reached an accord with the Federal Republic of Germany (FRG) to finance and undertake the engineering study. German financial participation was readily forthcoming as a counterweight to its announced intention to pay Israel DM 3 billion as compensation for Jewish suffering under Hitler. When Germany made its intentions public in September 1952, the Arab states denounced the policy as direct aid to a hostile state. Agreeing to help Egypt with the High Dam allowed West Germany to save some face in the Arab World. The FRG government awarded the study contract to an association of two German firms, the Hochtief and Dortmund Union, and by November 1952 Egypt invited technical experts from the Union to visit Aswan and begin drafting designs. The preparatory work took two years, during which Hochtief and Dortmund drew up two alternative plans. They were reviewed by an international advisory panel constituted in February 1953 upon the invitation of the Ministry of Public Works.* In December 1954, this panel endorsed the plan calling for a clay-core, rock-fill dam 6.5 kilometers upstream from the Old Aswan Dam. In October 1955 the British engineering firm of Sir Alexander Gibb was enlisted to review the implementation of all aspects of design and specifications with the panel of experts.

In sum, we find that the new regime placed the High Dam project at the top of its priority list and pursued its design and implementation with what some came to regard as indecent haste. At the time, however, none of their Western consultants or potential donors cautioned against the speed with which the project was being developed. Moreover, a subsequent IBRD review of its own involvement in the scheme revealed that the ecological ramifications of the dam, which have provoked so much recent criticism, did not figure prominently in its own positive evaluation of the project. By 1955, all that stood in the way of beginning construction were the problems of hard currency funding and the need to reach agreement with the Sudan on allocating the Nile waters after the dam became operational.

From the very beginning, Egypt focused its attention on the IBRD in the not unreasonable hope that the bank would become the catalyst to the formation of a Western aid package to finance the dam. The

proposed site of the dam. See Edward S. Mason and Robert Asher, *The World Bank Since Bretton Woods* (Washington, D.C.: Brookings Institution, 1970), pp. 627–42.

*Initially the panel consisted of I. F. Harza and A. S. Steele (United States), Andre Cogne (France), and Max Pruss (Federal Republic of Germany). They were later joined by C. Terzaki and Lorenz Straub.

IBRD, as already indicated, proceeded cautiously. On the one hand, its president, Eugene Black, was favorably disposed toward large hydraulic projects and was already involved in arduous negotiations with India and Pakistan for the development of the Indus Valley. At the same time, the World Bank was not then (nor is it now) fully autonomous in setting its aid policies; it had to take into consideration the foreign policy goals and economic philosophies of its major depositors, foremost among them being the United States. It was understandable that Black, an American himself and a Wall Street banker, would consult closely with the administration in Washington, D.C., concerning any IBRD programs with far-reaching international implications. As far as the High Dam project was concerned, these considerations inevitably drew the scheme into the context of the Arab-Israeli conflict and superpower rivalries.

A first indication of this state of affairs was Black's reluctance to accelerate the IBRD's examination of the project while Egypt and Great Britain were still at loggerheads over the question of the repatriation of the 70,000 British troops stationed in the Suez Canal Zone. Western aid for the dam would be appropriate *after* the two parties had reached an accord but not before. Almost a year and a half after the bank was first contacted, Black indicated in an *aide memoire* (June 1954) that the IBRD would not necessarily accept the recommendations of the German consultants and that the bank would undertake its own independent study. In October 1954, two bank-appointed engineers were dispatched to Cairo, along with an economist who was to assess Egypt's ability to meet loan obligations and to mobilize domestic savings towards construction. Simultaneously, the Egyptians and British came to terms over the evacuation of British troops from the Suez Canal Zone, a process to be completed by June 18, 1956.* With that stumbling block removed, the bank could move on towards negotiations with Egypt with greater alacrity.

The engineering report, prepared by the IBRD engineer, Gail Hathaway, was ready in April 1955. It was generally favorable, stating the project to be technically sound, economically beneficial (with minor reservations about some proposed land reclamation sites), but of such size that it would require strict fiscal discipline and "a rigid limitation on the Egyptian government's commitments to other pro-

---

*On the Anglo-Egyptian Treaty of October 19, 1954, see Anthony Nutting, *Nasser* (London: Constable, 1972), pp. 70–72. The treaty provided for reoccupation of the Suez Canal bases by British troops if Egypt, Turkey, or any Arab state were to be attacked by an outside power (excluding Israel but implicitly including above all others, the USSR).

jects."[12] With this green light, such as it was, the IBRD and Egypt were then able to talk directly of a capital package and contracting for construction. Therein lay an important obstacle in that the IBRD required open bidding on all contracts, while the Egyptians, in order to begin construction as quickly as possible, were inclined to award a management contract for implementation to Hochtief and Dortmund Union.

At the very time the IBRD was preparing its assessment of the Aswan High Dam, a new and dangerous phase in Egypto-Israeli hostilities began. On February 28, 1955, Israeli Minister of Defense, David Ben-Gurion, ordered a surprise attack on an Egyptian army outpost in the Gaza Strip, which, he suspected, was aiding and abetting Palestinian guerrillas. The so-called Gaza Raid was successful from the Israeli point of view, with the outpost overrun and forty Egyptians killed. For Nasser and the RCC, however, it was a stinging humiliation, and one that persuaded the regime to pursue the rearmament of the Egyptian armed forces, whatever the source of arms. Inasmuch as the United States, Great Britain, and France had jointly applied a partial embargo on arms sales to the belligerents in the first Arab-Israeli war of 1948, Nasser had to give serious consideration to a source of arms he would otherwise have preferred to ignore: the USSR. The result was protracted negotiations throughout the spring and summer of 1955, and the announcement in September of an $80 million purchase of Soviet equipment, with Czechoslovakia acting as the supplier.* For the first time, Soviet arms had entered an Arab country, and it remained for the leader of the Free World to decide how best to respond to the challenge.

The initial reaction to the arms deal in Washington, D.C., was to seek a highly visible means to shore up U.S./Western influence in the Nile Valley. For John Foster Dulles, the U.S. Secretary of State (1953–59), American participation in the High Dam scheme was particularly appealing in that it would symbolize the constructive policies of the Free World in contrast to the destructive arms-mongering of the Soviet bloc. Great Britain's Prime Minister, Anthony Eden (1955–57), shared Dulles' support for the project: all the more so in that, during the fall of 1955, there were persistent rumors that Daniel Solod, the Soviet Ambassador in Cairo, had expressed Moscow's interest in helping fund the project. With this kind of high-level backing, there was a positive

*Most analysts present the *denouement* much as I have, although at least one is convinced that the Gaza Raid was a pretext rather than the cause of the Soviet arms deal. See Uri Raanan, *The USSR Arms the Third World* (Cambridge, Mass.: MIT Press, 1969).

incentive for Eugene Black to proceed as rapidly as possible towards concluding an agreement with the Egyptians.

Accordingly, in November 1955, Dr. Abd al-Moneim al-Qaissuny, Egypt's Minister of Economy (accompanied by Dr. Muhammed Ahmad Selim and Colonel Samir Hilmy), was invited to Washington to confer with the bank's executives. In final negotiations, concluded on December 2, Black, representing the IBRD, was joined by Herbert Hoover, Jr., of the State Department and Sir Robert Makins from the Foreign Office. The tentative accord that emerged from their talks was that the United States, Great Britain, and the IBRD would jointly provide the foreign exchange component for the construction of the dam. The total cost of the project, including the power station, was estimated at $1.3 billion, with $400 million in foreign exchange. The IBRD agreed to lend Egypt $200 million at 5.5 percent interest, while the United States and the United Kingdom promised grants of $70 million, ($56 million from the U.S. and $14 million from the U.K.) toward the first stage (diversion tunnels and coffer dams), with the understanding that the two countries would loan Egypt a further $130 million at a later date.

There were, understandably, a number of fairly stringent conditions attached to the disbursement of the aid. First, it was an all-or-nothing deal: the IBRD would not go ahead with its loan unless the two Western powers also went ahead. This in turn meant that the whole project hinged on Egypt coming to terms with the United States and the United Kingdom. The suggested terms were severe: (1) that Egypt concentrate its development effort on the dam, diverting one-third of internal revenues to the project over ten years; (2) that relevant aspects of the country's economy be subject to periodic IBRD review; (3) that contracts be awarded through open bidding with a prohibition on any being awarded to a communist country; (4) that Egypt would have to avoid incurring new foreign obligations (such as acquiring more arms), and any new loans or credits would require prior approval by the IBRD; (5) that no disbursement would take place before Egypt reached a new agreement with the Sudan over the allocation of the Nile's waters.

This was the offer that Dr. al-Qaissuny brought back to Cairo in mid-December, and it was received with heavy criticism in the local press and with indignation by President Nasser. The terms were not only patronizing but ominously reminiscent of the Anglo-French Caisse de la Dette which had allowed the two Western governments to take over Egypt's economy in 1879. Moreover, Nasser suspected that the U.S.–U.K. two-stage funding offer was a gimmick to keep him on a short leash; once the project was under way, Egypt would have to be subservient to Western financial and political desiderata in order to obtain a second round of funding. It was logically assumed that the U.S. and the U.K. would try to use the dam to pressure Egypt toward a settlement with Israel, and toward closer cooperation with the emerging system of Western military alliances (NATO, CENTO, SEATO, etc.). In short, Nasser saw the terms as a trap whereby the fate of Egypt's economy would lie in American hands for at least a decade.

Dulles requested that Black go to Cairo to allay Nasser's fears, and, on February 9, 1956, after ten days of deliberations, an accord in principle was reached. Black succeeded in convincing Nasser that the financial conditions for the $200 million loan reflected standard IBRD procedure, and Nasser acquiesced to periodic review of Egypt's finances by bank officials. In the same month the IBRD issued a report on the High Dam in which it was estimated that after completion the dam would generate annually an internal rate of return of 28.5 percent. Yet, despite this progress, Egypt had not reached agreement with the United States and the United Kingdom, nor had they formally approved and appropriated their shares of the $70 million grant.

It is reasonably clear that Western enthusiasm for the project of fall 1955 had been seriously eroded by midwinter 1956. A number of incidents contributed to the reassessment: Nasser's implacable hostility to the Bagdad Pact (CENTO) sponsored by the United States; his attacks on Jordan when Britain tried to coax that kingdom into the pact; and the conclusion of a second Soviet arms deal worth $200 million. Eden became convinced that Nasser was a megalomaniac criminal who should be brought down rather than bolstered up, and Dulles, with less personal venom, came to share that view. By spring 1956, it became apparent that Dulles hoped that Nasser would find the Western terms unacceptable and reject the offer. At the same time he was convinced that the USSR was merely bluffing in expressing interest in funding the project itself. The mood of the two leaders was reflected in Parliament and in Congress. Members of Parliament seized upon the question of excessive evaporation at the dam site, and the lack of an agreement with the Sudan, as grounds for refusing aid to Egypt. Some argued for the establishment of an International Nile Waters Authority to force Egypt into collective arrangements for managing the river. Similarly, in the U.S. Congress, southern cotton interests (allegedly alarmed that the High Dam would increase Egypt's competitive advantage in world cotton markets) and the Zionist lobby opposed the $56 million grant to Egypt, and Dulles was no longer prepared to do any counterlobbying.

According to Nasser's confidant, Muhammad Hassanein Heikal, Nasser soon got wind of Dulles' ploy. At first he tried to haggle over the terms of the U.S. grant, although his ambassador in Washington, Ahmad Hussein, and Eugene Black, who paid another visit to Cairo in June, assured him that Congress would accept no watering down of the grant conditions. Both men urged Nasser to accept the offer as it stood, but, at least to Ahmad Hussein, Nasser reportedly warned that if need be he would nationalize the Suez Canal and use its revenues to build the dam. Finally, Nasser was so convinced that the United States would not approve the grant under any circumstances that he instructed Ahmad Hussein to inform Dulles that Egypt accepted *all* the U.S. terms. On July 19, Hussein met with Dulles, George Allen, and Herbert Hoover, Jr., and announced Egypt's readiness to accept the offer. It is said that he also added that if the United States did not respond positively then Egypt had assurances that the Soviet Union would. Dulles' mind was already made up, and he wished to chastise Nasser for having imprudently made the Nile Valley a focal point of the Cold War. Dulles told Hussein that the United States was now convinced that the Egyptian economy could not bear the strain of building the dam (presumably because of the arms purchases) and that the United States was withdrawing its offer. The United Kingdom followed suit a day later. There was no small irony in this turn of events, for, just a few days before, Eugene Black had written Dr. al-Qaissuny expressing the bank's confidence in the soundness of the Egyptian economy. Some months later, after a third arms deal, the U.S. Embassy in Cairo estimated Egypt's annual obligations as a result of these acquisitions at $25 million, a substantial but hardly crippling burden.[13]

When Nasser received the news of the renege he was on his way to Cairo with India's Jawaharlal Nehru, after having met with President Tito at Brioni in Yugoslavia. In his message to Nasser, Ambassador Hussein claimed that Dulles had at one point interrupted him, declaring, "We believe that anybody who builds the High Dam will earn the hatred of the Egyptian people, because the burden will be crushing." Upon hearing this, Nasser told his Foreign Minister, Mahmud Fawzy, "This is not simply the withdrawal of an offer; it is an attack on the regime and an invitation to the people of Egypt to bring it down."[14] Just one week later, on the fourth anniversary of King Faruq's departure into exile, President Nasser proclaimed the nationalization of the Suez Canal Company and placed engineer Mahmud Yunis in charge. Before a wildly enthusiastic audience in Alexandria, he pledged that the foreign exchange revenues from the Suez Canal would be utilized to defray the construction costs of the High Dam. His action led the following November to a direct military assault on Egypt by Great Britain, France, and Israel. That story is beyond the scope of this essay, but it warrants brief mention as yet another example of the highly charged atmosphere that had by then, and would in the future, envelop the High Dam project.

The series of crises in Egypt in 1955 and 1956 effectively paralyzed progress toward the dam's construction. The Suez Canal was blocked during the November hostilities, and when revenues from it did begin to flow, they were used to replace military losses or to compensate for Egyptian assets frozen in Western accounts abroad—including those in the United States. Even had adequate foreign exchange been available, it is unlikely that any Western firms would have bid for contracts at Aswan. In addition, Western credits for completing the electrification of the Old Aswan Dam, a prerequisite for the construction of the new dam, were halted, and Western technicians working on the project were withdrawn. Little wonder then that Nasser and his associates could no longer regard the dam as simply a big engineering project, but rather came to hold it up as the symbol of Egypt's will to resist imperialist endeavors to destroy the revolution.

In the face of Egypt's financial dilemma, the Soviet Union was unwilling to advance credits beyond those already committed to various industrial projects in Egypt. It was believed that if the USSR were to come to Egypt's rescue, it would demand that the High Dam become a showcase for Soviet technology and engineering. Egyptian hesitation and Soviet aloofness forced the project into the background. The dam's economic benefits, that Egyptian officials had so broadly touted, were seen to be attainable through other projects. Targets in land reclamation, for example, were whittled down, and with the "discovery" of large amounts of fossil ground water in the western desert, it was suggested that this area could be the site of Egypt's agricultural boom. In May 1958, Dr. al-Qaissuny noted that Egypt's recent union with Syria reduced the acuity of Egypt's land problem. (The United Arab Republic was founded in February 1958 and dissolved in September 1961.) The discovery of modest amounts of oil, he felt, held open the possibility of meeting Egypt's industrial energy needs through thermal power generation. [15]

Yet Nasser had not abandoned the project; and indeed his increasing desperation in attracting financing led him to acquiesce to the Soviet showcase approach. On October 23, 1958, Khrushchev informed Abd el-Hakim Amer (Egypt's Chief of Staff and Nasser's close friend) that the USSR was prepared to offer a credit of 400 million rubles (ca. $100 million) toward the first stage of construction. A formal agreement was signed December 27, providing for repayment after completion of the first stage over 12 years at 2.5 percent interest.

The sudden entry of the USSR into the project foiled Western bluff-calling and rekindled Western interest in the dam. It was believed, or perhaps hoped, that the Soviet Union would be unable to advance second-stage financing and that this would allow Western powers to participate in the scheme.* West Germany went so far as to offer Egypt credits of DM 200 million toward the second stage. But these timid signals were overlooked by Egypt, and on August 27, 1960 an agreement was signed with the USSR for $120 million in credits toward the second stage.

In the meantime, Soviet experts had gone over all the accumulated feasibility studies and recommendations. They modified the Hochtief and Dortmund design principally by situating the power station in the tunnels of the diversion channel rather than in tunnels specially dug for the purpose; by shortening the north-south length of the dam; and by proposing a well-tested Soviet technique for sluicing and compacting sand in the dam's core. The Soviet plans were ready in May 1959, and Egypt referred them to a board of international consultants that made counterproposals on the power station and methods of sandfill. The Soviet experts chose to disregard the counterproposals, and Egypt did not see fit to make an issue of it. Project execution was put under the supervision of the Soviet Hydroproject Institute with complete authority for all subcontracting operations. Agreement having been reached with the Sudan in December 1959, work at the dam site began on January 9, 1960, almost eight years after the Free Officers had endorsed the project.

CONSTRUCTION

The rock-fill coffer dam, which would allow work on the main dam itself, was completed in May 1964 with Nikita Khrushchev and Nasser witnessing the closure of the Nile. Within a few months the coffer dam was to withstand one of the highest floods of the century (see Figure 7).[16]

*See Dougherty, "The Aswan Decision," who was so confident that the USSR would fail to meet its obligations that Nasser would have had to beg the West to bail him out on the second stage.

FIGURE 7

Cross section of the High Dam

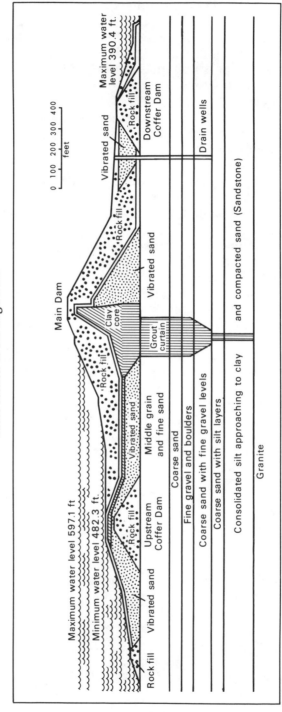

SOURCE: From Tom Little, *High Dam at Aswan* (London: Methuen, 1965), p. 80.

From then until the official completion of the dam on January 15, 1971, work proceeded on construction of the main body, an edifice nearly a kilometer wide at its base, made up of a clay core, capped by rock fill, buttressed by walls of impacted sand, and flanked by the up- and downstream coffer dams. The crest of the dam stands 111 meters above the riverbed, and the whole structure is anchored into the sediment upon which it rests by a grout curtain thrust over 200 meters down to granite substrata (see Table 8). On the west side of the dam is

TABLE 8

The High Dam in Figures

Measurement of the Dam

Length at Crest	3,600 meters
Length of Part in River	520 meters
Length of Right Wing	2,325 meters
Length of Left Wing	755 meters
Max. Height above Bed Level	111 meters
Width at Crest	40 meters
Width at Base	980 meters
Vol. of Construction Materials	42.7 million m³
River Bed Level above Sea Level	85 meters
Crest Level above Sea Level	196 meters

Measurements of the Reservoir

Max. Water Level of Reservoir	182 meters (above sea level)
Total Capacity	162 billion m³
Dead Storage Capacity	30 billion m³
Live Storage Capacity	90 billion m³
Excess Flood Storage Capacity	37 billion m³
Length of Reservoir	500 kilometers

Power Station Capacities

Turbines: Type	Francis
No. of Turbines	12
Capacity of Each Turbine at Design Head	180,000 kw
Discharge at Design Head (57.5 m)	346 m³/sec.
Diameter of Turbine Runner	6.3 meters
Rated Speed	100 rpm
Head	77–35 meters
Generators: capacity	175,000 kw
Voltage	15.75 kv
Rated Speed	100 rpm
Total Installed Capacity	2,100,000 kw
Max. Available Annual Energy	10 billion kWh

the powerhouse transecting the diversion channel. Six tunnels feed water through 12 turbines with the capacity to generate 10 billion kWh per year. The first of the turbines was installed on January 9, 1968, and the last on July 23, 1970.

After completion of the upstream coffer dam, the High Dam reservoir slowly began to fill, and with the 1975 flood reached its maximum level for safe storage of 90 meters above bed level, or 175 meters above sea level. The body of water thus formed is known as Lake Nasser, while its southern, Sudanese tail is called Lake Nubia. The entire lake is 500 kilometers long and averages 10 kilometers wide, with numerous side arms or bays (khour). Its surface area, depending on the level of stored water, varies around 5,000 km². The volumetric capacity of the lake is 162 billion m³, of which 30 billion m³ are set aside for "dead storage" and to receive precipitated sediment; 90 billion m³ for live storage of usable flood water and 37 billion m³ for excess flood waters. Dead storage, strictly speaking, refers to reservoir capacity of a fixed volume or head, while live storage designates the variable volume or head of the reservoir. While the dam and its reservoir are among the largest in the world, neither is *the* largest. Its grout curtain is, however, the largest of its kind.

Final cost estimates of any reliability are hard to come by, and, in some ways, they are never really final. Payments on the first Soviet loan began in 1964 and should have terminated in 1976; payments on the second began in 1970. In early 1978 Minister of Irrigation Aba al-Atta informed Parliament that all loans for the Aswan High Dam had been paid off. Land is still being reclaimed and the power grid extended. Moreover, as we shall see, more engineering will surely be required to cope with some of the direct or indirect effects of the dam. With that caveat in mind, we may look at 1973 estimates that the main body of the dam and the power station cost £E 320 million. At the official rate of exchange, this would be the equivalent of $820 million.[17] Far more difficult to estimate is the cost of the land reclamation, for it is still under way. Initially, it was believed that reclamation would cost at the most £E 250 per feddan, with all socioeconomic infrastructure included. Subsequently, these costs have been revised upward to £E 1000 per feddan and more (see Chapter 5). Thus, if reclamation of 1.2 million feddans is completed, total outlays may substantially exceed £E one billion or between $1.5 and $2 billion at non-official exchange rates. We may contrast these figures to those of IBRD projections of 1955. The bank believed that construction costs at Aswan (not including interest or loans) would be about £E 167 million, and that downstream irrigation and reclamation projects would require another £E 283 million. In other words, due to long construction delays and rising costs, the final price tag may be upwards of three times the initial forecasts.

CONCLUSION

Gamal Abd al-Nasser, who died in September 1970, did not live to see the completion of the High Dam. His successor, Anwar al-Sadat, presided over the official ceremonies on January 15, 1971, in the company of Nikolai Podgorny, President of the USSR. Egypt's new head of state obliged his guest by a speech castigating the United States for its perfidy and eulogizing Egypto-Soviet solidarity:

> America's broken promise [of 1956] is neither the first nor will it be the last. And Soviet support in building the High Dam is neither the first nor will it be the last, for it is an expression of aspirations for freedom and peace for peoples eager for them and who resist colonialist exploitation and imperial subjugation.
>
> America's broken promise is but one link in an unending chain that leaves us no alternative but to believe it represents a political plan designed to thwart the aspirations of the Arab people. . . .
>
> For each of America's broken promises — O my brethren — there is a Soviet promise fulfilled or on its way to fulfillment; in every sphere of hope and work; in industry, in land reclamation, in electrification, in armaments, in training, in unconditional and unlimited diplomatic support. For the Soviet Union is confident that its stance is one of defense of liberty and defense of peace.[18]

It was the Nasserist rhetoric of socialist Egypt of the 1960s, and it seemingly consecrated the massive monument the Soviets had built in the preceding decade. Near the dam's eastern end, a somewhat more elegant monument of Soviet-Egyptian friendship was built in the form of a five-pronged lotus flower, 70 meters high.

Yet, within months of the official inauguration of the dam, Sadat had purged his regime of those closest to Moscow, and in July 1972 he expelled all the Soviet military advisers. Relations deteriorated steadily until, in March 1976, Sadat unilaterally abrogated the Soviet-Egyptian Friendship Treaty that had been signed in 1971. It was an irony that

MAP 3

Lake Nasser and Lake Nubia

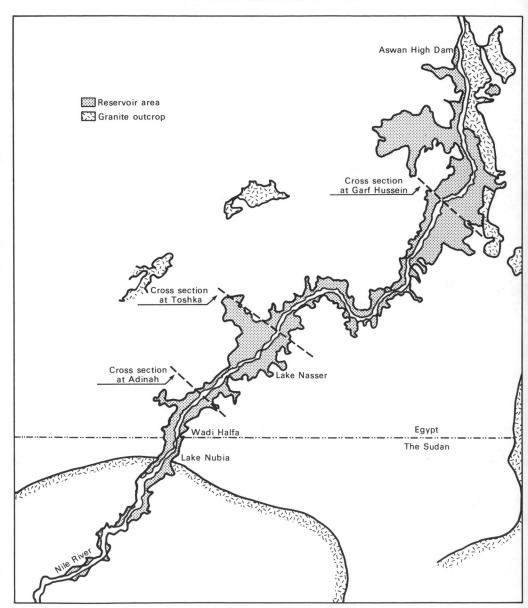

John Foster Dulles might have appreciated but, like the rest of us, would probably never have fathomed, that, in October 1975, when Aswan swarmed with officials to celebrate the filling of Lake Nasser (see Map 3), there was not a Soviet among them. In an Orwellian way, their contribution to the dam had (temporarily at least) become nonhistory, as had America's broken promises.

Whether a triumph of Soviet-Egyptian solidarity or a triumph of the Egyptian people, the diplomatic history of the dam dictated that it be a triumph of some sort. On the other hand, the dam is real and not merely a symbol. It performs functions, some well and some badly, and its real contributions to Egypt must be given as much weight as its symbolic impact in international politics. Nonetheless, the domestic and international assessment of the technical performance of the High Dam has never remotely approached the dispassionate and scientific neutrality that alone would provide the basis for a balanced accounting. Once the great powers got into the High Dam act, objectivity from any quarter was either ignored or doomed.

5

THE NILE STOPS AT ASWAN

We must play the hand nature dealt us — we must learn to use wisely the water we have, and not think we can go to some other country or some other region and bring in new supplies when we already waste enormous amounts of water. — STEWART UDALL[1]

It became clear that competent technicians in government circles were collectively determined to overlook any signs of the deterioration of soil fertility as a side effect of the High Dam, even as a hypothesis. This was the result of what might be called "the High Dam Covenant," a psychological state born of political and other circumstances which has cloaked the project from its very inception. — ALI FATHY[2]

IN JANUARY 1965, Gamal Abd el-Nasser was going through the formalities of standing as Egypt's sole candidate in elections to the presidency. At that time construction of the High Dam was about half completed, and it is reported that crowds outside Egypt's parliament chanted the following ditty:[3]

Nasser, Nasser, we come to salute you; after the Dam our land will be paradise

Nasser, Nasser, our beloved; next time (lead us) to Tel Aviv.

Small wonder, then, that in the face of the High Dam's carefully nurtured image—a symbol of prosperity and resistance to imperialism —Egypt's technicians would be party to the "Covenant" alluded to by Ali Fathy. But that was years ago. One day in the spring of 1975, I was in a taxi crossing the Nile on Cairo's Qasr al-Nil bridge. The water flowing

116

below was a startling yellow color and full of tree branches and other debris. More by way of conversation than anything else, I asked the driver what accounted for the strange color. "It must be the dam," he replied. In fact what had happened was that freak torrential rains had caused flash flooding around al-Minia in central Egypt, and what we saw in Cairo was the runoff of desert soil. But no matter, for popular opinion had seized upon the High Dam as the root cause for everything that was inexplicable or just plain wrong in Egypt. How had this symbolic transformation come to pass?

The answer to that question is complex. First, as we have already seen in Chapter 4, the dam from its inception was the focal point of superpower rivalries in the Arab World. It came to symbolize a national patriotism, and therefore any criticism of it was thought of as subversive or even treasonous. In the middle 1950s, there were Egyptian experts who considered the dam to be technically unsound (and only incidentally some of them harbored a dislike for Nasserist politics). Their critiques were seized upon by Western enemies of the Egyptian regime, and thus technical criticism — at least in public — became tantamount to aiding and abetting the enemy. Early technical criticism was pretty thoroughly stifled, and international bodies eager for the political gains to be reaped from participating in the High Dam project were none too meticulous in their own analyses.

This conspiracy of silence lasted until about 1970, the year of Nasser's death. At that time, events and circumstances combined to usher in a new era of hydropolitics, this time largely centered in the Egyptian domestic arena. Two processes were at work. First, it had become increasingly evident that a number of negative side effects, directly or indirectly related to the High Dam, were making themselves felt. The problem of how to deal with them could no longer be avoided. Second, a muted debate now began about the alleged abuses of Nasserist rule. The new evidence that Nasser's "pyramid" might be the cause of some of Egypt's economic problems added fuel to these fires. The 1950s critics became quasi-cult heroes, and it was not long before the anti-Nasserist forces were in full cry against the dam and its patron. The real side effects of the dam became thoroughly entangled with the magnified ones of political polemics. We shall not try to disentangle them here, but shall rather advance the best evidence available concerning the technical issues and, where relevant, show how they relate to the domestic debate. Our purpose is not to provide definitive judgments on those questions but rather to outline them as clearly as possible, given the general dearth of specific or accurate data.

ACCENT ON THE POSITIVE

In 1958, once Soviet funding was in hand for the construction of the first stage of the High Dam, a litany of its expected benefits was drawn up and passed on to various choirs of enthusiasts. The refrains are still intoned today, and some reflect terrestrial reality. The expected benefits were essentially ninefold:

1. to expand Egypt's cultivated area, through land reclamation, by 1.2 million feddans;
2. to convert about 800,000 feddans of basin irrigated land in Upper Egypt to perennial irrigation;
3. to expand the area under summer rice cultivation to one million feddans;
4. to improve cultivation in the Delta by lowering the river level and hence improving drainage;
5. to protect the country against the danger of high floods;
6. to improve year-round navigation conditions;
7. to generate hydroelectric power of 10 billion kWh per annum (with all its implications for industrialization);
8. to improve the economic efficiency of the Old Aswan Dam power station by year-round operations;
9. to provide the Sudan with enough additional water to increase its cultivated area threefold.

It was estimated that the High Dam would add £E 235 million annually to the national income. Preliminary cost estimates of the entire project in 1964 were put at £E 416 million, so that in two years of full operation the dam would have more than paid for itself.[4]

Some of these objectives were mostly or partly achieved, but somehow, for enthusiast and critic alike, admitting to anything less than 100 percent success seemed like abject failure. A brief review of these achievements, however, is necessary to an understanding of the contemporary situation discussed below. Land reclamation has begun on nearly one million feddans, although this can hardly be termed a success, as it has yet to contribute to national income. All the Upper Egyptian land under basin irrigation has been converted to perennial irrigation, with commensurate increases in the number of crops harvested annually — but with deleterious effects on soil fertility. Rice acreage has been expanded beyond the target, and yields have been good. Whether for home consumption or export, this derived benefit has been, so far, an unmitigated success. The only blemish on the picture, and one unrelated to the High Dam, is that rising domestic consumption of rice has forced cutbacks in the exports of this lucrative,

foreign-exchange earning crop. The expected improvement of drainage in the Delta has not been achieved; indeed, the inverse is the case.
On the other hand, it can be said that Egypt no longer faces any
dangers from high floods and, indeed, could be threatened only by an
uninterrupted series of low floods. Moreover, navigation conditions
have been improved by eliminating the annual flood. The power
station at Aswan has not yet generated—probably never will—its full
capacity of 10 billion kWh per annum, although this figure continues to
be touted. Undeniably, utilization of the old Aswan Dam power station
has been made more efficient. Penultimately, the Sudan can dispose of
more water for its own purposes—and in 1975–76 was doing so—up to
its allotment under the 1959 Nile Waters Agreement. We might add to
the above an achievement that is seldom given any attention: with the
construction of the High Dam, Egypt's obsession with timely or summer water came to an end. No longer would it have to twist and bend
the Sudan's pattern of water use to fit its seasonal needs, a source of
vast relief for the Sudanese, as well as a factor making for greater
understanding between the two countries.

   Today it is neither fashionable nor tenable to deny that anything
has gone wrong with the dam and its downstream goals. Yet in several
official quarters, the tendency has been to dismiss any shortcomings as
the inevitable consequences of any daring engineering scheme. The
claims made for the dam have become apologia; their empiric justifica-
tions unclear, their judgments Olympian and declamatory. In May
1973, Engineer Ahmad Daud, Deputy Director of the High Dam Authority, claimed that the return on the project had already covered all
its costs. From the official point of view, that was that.[5]

ACCENT ON THE CRITICAL

Evaporation and Seepage

   It is likely that members of the RCC, especially those with technical
expertise, were well aware that the High Dam could not and would not
be perfect. But they could not afford months and years of wrangling
over possibly erroneous estimates, ecological side effects, and technical shortcomings.

   Instead, early critiques were discussed privately, generally in the
absence of the formulators, and these critiques and the rebuttals to
them were never made public. This convention was broken early on by

Dr. Abd al-Aziz Ahmad who not only went public but did it in a non-Egyptian forum. He became, and has remained, a *cause célèbre*.

Dr. Ahmad was an old hand, technical consultant to the Ministry of Public Works and Chairman of the State Hydroelectric Power Commission. He was familiar with Adrien Daninos' High Dam scheme even before it was adopted by the RCC. He felt that the project should have been treated with the greatest caution, because a reservoir in an area as arid and windswept as Aswan risked surface evaporation rates of such magnitude that all projected gains in timely water could be wiped out. H. E. Hurst, the British expert on Nile hydrology attached to the Egyptian Ministry of Public Works, shared this view, but reversed his position after the RCC came out in favor of the High Dam.

Dr. Ahmad wrote up his views in two papers in 1955 and submitted them for discussion at the annual meetings of the British Institute of Civil Engineers. That decision was fatal on several counts; airing dirty linen abroad was bad enough, but to pick a forum in the ex-colonial master's home turf was particularly ill-conceived. Moreover, submission of the papers coincided with the renege on Western funding of the High Dam and the subsequent Suez crisis. It is conceivable that British MPs, hostile to the Nasserist regime and to British aid to the High Dam project, adopted Abd al-Aziz Ahmad's technical arguments as weapons in their own crusade. The upshot was that Dr. Ahmad was seen by the Egyptian regime as being in league with its enemies, and his technical arguments received scant attention thereafter.

Yussef Simaika, one of the authors (along with Hurst and Black) of a multivolume study of the Nile, later recounted that Dr. Ahmad had submitted his critical report simultaneously to Musa Arafa, the Minister of Irrigation. Arafa, Simaika, and Ahmad Kemal (who became Minister of Irrigation in the early 1970s) reviewed the report. Allegedly they convinced Ahmad that his findings were in error. He assured them that because of the Suez crisis he had no further intention of presenting the findings in Britain. Arafa urged Ahmad, under these circumstances, to turn in all copies of the reports for "safe-keeping"; and this Ahmad did. Some time later, Simaika received an invitation from the Institute of Civil Engineers to come to London as a discussant at a public presentation of Ahmad's papers. It became apparent that Ahmad, whatever his contrition, had sent off to London, in October 1959, a revised version of his paper in which he defended his initial criticisms. He repeated these criticisms in the public discussions in London in mid-November 1960.[6]

Abd al-Aziz Ahmad was disgraced. In 1964, a state election committee voted him the State Prize for Outstanding Achievement only to have the decision reversed from on high. Ahmad wrote the Deputy Prime Minister protesting that arbitrary action and stating that his criticisms in the past had been directed mainly at H. E. Hurst and not the Egyptians who had come to believe in Hurst's technical gloss on the dam. His protests were to no avail, and in March 1967, Dr. Ahmad died unvindicated.[7] The controversy surrounding him remained unabated as the High Dam debate moved into its post-Nasserist phase. Among foreign critics of the High Dam, Claire Sterling and others have called attention to his arguments and to his mistreatment; and he has been hailed by Egyptian anti-Nasserists as one of the few who dared challenge the accepted wisdom of the President. An indication of the gradual shift in the official assessment of the dam came in the form of a decision by the Academy of Scientific Research, in April 1976, to award the State Achievement Prize posthumously to Dr. Ahmad.

Abd al-Aziz Ahmad's entanglement in the politics of the dam should not obscure the importance of his critique. First, it should be stated that for all the furor raised by his report, the specific arguments he advanced have never been aired in the Eyptian media. Second, anyone who reads them will find them clincial, dispassionate, and impressively documented; they are valuable as a general reference on Nile hydrology.[8]

There were three main components to Dr. Ahmad's argument concerning possible water losses through evaporation, seepage, and reversal of the hydrostatic pressure of the underground water table. He looked logically to the Old Aswan Dam reservoir for clues about storage losses. On the average, during the nine months of each year when the dam performed storage functions, the mean loss over the period 1921–34 was 640 million m³, which he calculated to be 25 percent of average reservoir capacity.[9]

At its maximum storage capacity of 5.6 billion m³, it was found that annual surface evaporation at the Old Aswan Dam reservoir averaged about 7.5 percent of gross volume stored. Extrapolating from this, Dr. Ahmad projected that the High Dam reservoir with a mean surface area of 3,180 km² (probably an underestimate) and a mean gross storage volume of 130 billion m³, would lose about 10 billion m³ per year in evaporation. Here he was merely following the arguments of Hurst and others. But Dr. Ahmad went on to hypothesize that experimental testing of evaporation rates had neglected the wind velocity factor at the reservoir site. His own calculations led him to believe that high winds there could increase the evaporation rate by as much as 40 percent, or 4 billion m³. Inasmuch as Egypt stood to gain an additional 7.5 billion m³ annually from the High Dam, as agreed upon with the Sudan, underestimating the wind factor could substantially reduce the projected benefits.

Dr. Ahmad did not stop there, however. He considered seepage of stored water into the rock and sediment underlying the reservoir more important than evaporation. Since its filling after 1902, the Old Aswan Dam reservoir had probably lost 120 percent of its capacity annually, declining over 30 years to about 9 percent of capacity. The decline is attributable to saturation of the underlying strata and to the deposit of silt in many of the faults and fissures running through the reservoir's bottom. There is good reason to believe, Dr. Ahmad contended, that the High Dam reservoir would behave similarly, with immense water losses in the initial years. Assuming the reservoir's live storage capacity to be 100 billion m³, Abd al-Aziz Ahmad estimated that for the first 20 years, total losses due especially to seepage and the long period of rock saturation, and to evaporation, would be 124 percent of reservoir capacity . . . and that after thirty years losses would reach a stable state of 17 percent per year. At that level, losses would cancel out all the High Dam's expected gains.

Finally, Dr. Ahmad was convinced that the filling of such a large reservoir would reverse the hydrostatic pressure of the underground water table, and where this table had once added water to the river, it would now take water away from it. He calculated the mean annual gain of water seeping into the river prior to 1902 (when the old dam was built) at 3.4 billion m³.

Dr. Ahmad drew the following conclusions from these observations:

1. "The above results seem to set a limit to the size of reservoirs to be created on rivers which are known to traverse permeable beds, so that their storage levels should not be much higher than the water-table prevailing in the district" (p. 195).

2. That if the basic objective is a regular supply of summer water of ca. 34.6 billion m³, and if the natural flow averages 15 billion m³ and one billion m³ is stored at Sennar, then a storage facility at Aswan of only 18 billion m³ (allowing for seepage and evaporation) would be adequate to meet these needs in *most* years. The Jebel Auliya Dam, because of the enormous evaporation losses, should be destroyed.

3. There is no sense in building storage capacity against the one or two low floods that might occur each century. To guard against floods as low as that of 1913–14 could be done with over-year storage of only 9

billion m³. Dr. Ahmad believed that the Wadi Rayyan depression near Fayyum would be the appropriate site for such storage. "To take a larger capacity than actually needed in order to play for safety would involve not only the expenditure of capital outlay proportionately in excess of the yield, but also would entail larger losses. On the other hand no damage is done by taking too small a reservoir. It could always be raised in future should experience prove this to be necessary" (p. 152).

What can actual experience at Aswan since 1964 tell us about Dr. Ahmad's prognostications? In several respects they have been unconfirmed, but not sufficiently to deprive them of all validity. Evaporation and seepage are still sensitive issues. Little explicit attention has been paid to the wind velocity factor, but there is general agreement that surface evaporation in the Aswan area is about 2.7 meters per year. In 1959, when the Sudan and Egypt reached agreement on the allocation of the Nile waters, 9 billion m³ of the annual discharge was written off to evaporation. This is an anticipated average and in some years will be more or less. While figures are hard to come by, it would appear that the 9 billion m³ figure is much too conservative. The determining variable is reservoir level. At 160 meters above sea level, the reservoir surface is 3,084 km², and at 180 meters it is 6,200 km²; that is, the exposed surface is almost doubled.[10] Surface evaporation is exacerbated in the *khors* or side arms of the reservoir. There are more than one hundred important *khors* with a surface area of 4,900 km² (79 percent of total lake surface), but because they are so shallow they contain no more than 55 percent of the water stored. Lake level will vary with flood size against Egypt's annual and fairly steady draw-down. A series of low floods will entail a low lake level and thereby minimize surface evaporation, but such an eventuality can hardly be considered desirable. Rather, the dam and the reservoir will function best at maximum storage levels between 172 and 175 meters (see Table 9). At that level, evaporation losses would be between 12 and 13 billion m³ per year. Above that level, evaporation would rise commensurately, but that would not be too serious, as storage above 175 meters is designed largely to contain excess floodwaters. In short, if the reservoir is kept at optimal levels of 170–175 meters, evaporation will be well in excess of initial estimates. Direct, although not Egyptian, support is given to this surmise by a publication of the Economic Commission for Africa prepared for the UN Water Conference at Mar del Plata, Argentina. The report states that "the evaporation from Lake Nasser in Egypt represents about a quarter of the flow of the Nile River at Aswan."[11] If

TABLE 9

Rate of Reservoir Fill and Estimated Evaporation Losses

Year level was reached	Reservoir height meters	Reservoir surface km²	Reservoir volume billion m³	Estimated evaporation losses billion m³
1964–65	127.6	550	9.8	1.4
1967–68	151.2	2,200	41.1	5.9
1970–71	164.8	3,500	78.5	9.4
Oct. 1975	175	5,168	115.0	13.9
never attained	182	6,200	157.4	15.3–16.7

this refers to one quarter of the mean annual discharge (84 billion m³) then total evaporation would be 21 billion m³. More likely, it refers to that mean minus the Sudanese share, which would correspond to a loss of 15 billion m³. As Egypt had a hand in drafting this report, one must assume that it concurred in the wording of the reference to Lake Nasser evaporation. The official Egyptian claim is, however, that an average 10 billion m³ in evaporation losses annually was anticipated from the outset, but the wording of the 1959 Nile Waters Agreement refers to total "storage losses" of the same magnitude and presumably includes seepage.

The questions of seepage and hydrostatic pressure are not equally moot. Experimental studies were not begun at Aswan until 1962, two years after the dam's construction had actually begun. On this question, Claire Sterling, operating as we all have in an informational void, assumed the worst and intimated that because of seepage and evaporation, the reservoir might not fill for 200 years. She suggested that seepage is infinite. "Lake Nasser is losing more than a third of the water flowing into it, 30 billion m³ yearly. Downstream, the Egyptians are getting nearly 10 billion m³ less than they used to, 53.7 billion instead of 63 billion."[12] Neither Sterling's nor Ahmad's gloomy forecasts have been borne out; otherwise Egypt would have been subjected to drought. On the other hand official statistics do not sound plausible. In their study published in 1966, Hurst, et al., dismissed the threat of large-scale seepage as negligible. In their view the sediment precipitated in the reservoir would soon seal its floor so that little water would escape. It is now known that due to the shape of that floor and the reservoir's length (400–500 kms) the sediment is not being deposited uniformly but is concentrated at its southern end.

The most serious study of seepage at Aswan has been carried out by Taher Abu Wafa and Aziz Hanna Labib. Their findings can be briefly summarized. Should the reservoir rise to 180 meters, saturation of the Nubian sandstone underlying most of it would require 48 billion m^3. This "vertical" seepage might take up to 8 years, with annual losses of up to 6 billion m^3 per year. Beyond that, one may anticipate annual losses due to "horizontal" seepage of one billion m^3 per year.[13] This results from the natural seasonal rise and fall of the lake level, causing periodic saturation, desiccation, and resaturation of the exposed sandstone. Thus, in recent years, one would have expected seepage losses of at least 5 billion m^3 over and above evaporation losses. Yet official figures do not reflect this. The figure for 1971 is 11.4 billion m^3, of which 9.4 can be attributed to evaporation. The remaining two billion m^3 for seepage is too low to fit into Abu Wafa's and Labib's calculations. Either they are wrong (and both gentlemen were top officials in the High Dam Authority) or the figures released for public consumption are being doctored.

Finally, it should be noted that little attention has been paid to Dr. Ahmad's contention that the old reservoir at Aswan, and probably the new, has reversed the flow of groundwater into the river. Nonetheless, the Ministry of Irrigation estimates the "return flow" to the Nile in Upper Egypt, consisting mainly in drainage water, at 2.5–4 billion m^3.[14]

All in all, when one is dealing with a net benefit to Egypt of only 7.5 billion m^3 per year, any miscalculation in evaporation or seepage rates could change credits to debits. It may be surmised that for at least a decade of operation at optimal levels, Egypt's benefit may be nearly canceled by storage losses. Once vertical seepage has been arrested, one may anticipate evaporation losses of 2–3 billion m^3 in excess of predicted rates plus about one billion m^3 in horizontal seepage. In sum, under the best of circumstances, more than half Egypt's incremental gain from construction of the High Dam will be lost in storage.

Silt Deprivation, Scouring, and Drainage

While Abd al-Aziz Ahmad achieved unwonted notoriety in making his criticisms public, another eminent Egyptian expert, Ali Fathy, worked from inside. Fathy, now retired, was formerly the Supervisor of the Old Aswan reservoir as well as Professor of Irrigation at Alexandria University. While there are several problems connected with silt precipitation upstream of the dam, Fathy consistently concerned himself with one of them: riverbed scouring.

Each year the Nile waters have carried about 100–110 million tons of silt, clay, and sand either to Egypt's fields or to the Mediterranean. Now nearly all that sediment is being entrapped by the High Dam reservoir, where the "dead storage" capacity available for this purpose is 30 billion m³. On the assumption that the average silt load year is 60 million m³ (or 110 million tons) annually, dead storage would be used up after 500 years. In the past, most of the sediment washed down from the Ethiopian Highlands by the Blue Nile, reached Egypt during the flood at an average of 1,600 parts per million (ppm), or a little less than one kilogram per m³.

Before the High Dam was built, the annual flood would inevitably erode sections of the river's bed and banks (the phenomenon known as degradation or scouring) occasionally jeopardizing bridges, embankments, and barrages. This was especially true in the Upper Egyptian stretch between Aswan and Assyut where the slope of the bed is steepest (i.e., 1:12,000 or a one meter drop for each 12,000 meters downstream). In the past, erosion was localized and temporary, with silt deposits either from the same flood or subsequent ones filling in the damage. Of particular importance was the compensatory mechanism of the return flow of silt-laden water just downstream of each of the main barrages (Isna, Nag Hammadi, Assyut). Floodwaters sluicing through these barrages would scoop out "scour holes" at the bases of the barrages but, by a backlash effect, the surging water would turn on itself and deposit silt on the hole's upstream side, thereby stabilizing its depth. When silt is removed from the water, the backlash effect is lost, the scour hole is deepened without any compensatory silt-fill, and the riverbed downstream is scoured along its entire length.[15] Instead of temporary riverbed erosion, silt-free scouring sets in motion a secular trend of degradation that can be halted only when some new and indeterminate equilibrium is achieved. The implications of this are far-reaching. First, the downstream sides of the major barrages could be so deeply scooped out that they would risk toppling over on themselves. Second, all bridges and embankments would be subject to permanent undermining, that could be corrected only by costly engineering works.

As early as 1957, Ali Fathy called attention to this danger in a technical memorandum sent directly to President Nasser. Nasser never replied to it directly but did appoint a committee of experts (of which Fathy was not a member) to consider its merits. The committee evidently concluded that Fathy's fears were exaggerated, but while ignored, he never suffered Abd al-Aziz Ahmad's virtual ostracism. Indeed, some others shared his apprehensions. One of them, Abd al-Khaleq Shinnawi, was Minister of Irrigation, and in December 1967 he prompted the formation of a special committee under Ahmad Ali Kemal to investigate the extent of scouring. When he left the ministry, however, the committee's investigations were terminated. Shinnawi himself, who has of late become a critic of some aspects of the dam, has concentrated his attacks on silt deprivation as it affects soil fertility, but not on riverbed scouring.[16] For his part, Ali Fathy claims to have peppered the authorities over the years with more than 50 memoranda and studies on silt deprivation and scouring. He maintains that the 1954 panel of international experts urged that further studies of scouring be undertaken, but that their advice was ignored by Hurst and others.[17]

Fathy's arguments have recently been spelled out in more detail.[18] The extent of scouring will hinge ultimately, in Fathy's view, on the rate of discharge at the High Dam. Agricultural needs have dictated a peak daily rate of 250 million m³ and an annual average of 153 million m³ per day. At that rate, since 1964, the riverbed has been lowered by one meter downstream of the Isna barrage, by 55 cm downstream of Nag Hammadi, and by 70 cm downstream of the Assyut barrage. Ali Fathy concedes that, as the Ministry of Irrigation contends, the river appears to have reached a new equilibrium at this rate of discharge. But, he asks, what would happen if the rate went up to 350 million m³ daily as the result of one or more outsized floods?

To answer this question Fathy turns to a report prepared by Soviet experts in the early 1970s.

> They say . . . that degradation of the riverbed will reach a stable state at an average (slope) of one centimeter per kilometer [whereas at present the slope is 6–9 centimeters per kilometer], and that the water velocity would be .5 meters per second. If we recognize that discharge of 350 million m³ per day is the equivalent of 4,000 m³ per second and that the average width of the river is 500 meters, then we can easily calculate that the [new] depth of the water in the riverbed will be 16 meters, and that this exceeds by 6 meters the greatest depth reached by any floods in the past.[19]

At the new depth, the head of water upstream of each barrage would be far in excess of the barrage's structural capacity to withstand it.

Fathy's argument is premised on the supposition that once the High Dam reservoir fills (as it did for the first time in October 1975), one or two high floods would result in water releases from the reservoir far above the peak 250 million m^3 per day. After the High Dam was completed, Fathy says, an experiment was carried out in which for one day the rate of water release from the reservoir was increased from a normal level to 500 million m^3. The silt content downstream rose from insignificant amounts to 890 grams per m^3 at Cairo. This is roughly the same concentration common during the epoch of annual flooding, but its source, during this experiment, could only be sediment scoured from the riverbed itself. Were this experiment to replicate itself naturally, then all Fathy's fears might be confirmed.

So far, such massive releases have not been necessary. Moreover, a project is being carried out to use the Tushka depression, 250 km south of the High Dam, as a spillway for excess floodwaters. To bring this about requires a 50 km canal and considerable investments which are not yet in hand, but this approach could obviate the scouring disasters foreseen by Fathy.[20] Until the Tushka scheme or an alternative is realized, however, Fathy's critique cannot be dismissed lightly, nor is it. The Specialized National Committee, in one of the more candid admissions in 1975, stated:

> Studies are now being made to estimate the overall erosion, with the object of determining the protective structures to be erected all along the Nile from Aswan to the Delta barrages.
>
> The importance of protecting the barrages against erosion can hardly be exaggerated. It should be given priority. The Council draws attention to the need to conclude all protective measures satisfactorily in good time, and to support these measures at every stage with a proper plan of researches and studies.[21]

A number of ideas have already surfaced. In the early 1960s, Swedish consultants recommended constructing additional barrages in Upper Egypt to transform that stretch of the river into a series of cascades with relatively still water between each. Ali Fathy rightly debunked this proposal, and he was not alone. It was demonstrated, in addition to the enormous cost of constructing seven or eight new barrages, and regardless of the amount of hydroelectric power each could generate, that their principal effect would be to raise the river level, increase surface evaporation, inhibit natural drainage, and raise the water table of the surrounding lands. While momentarily in vogue, the cascade model has been quietly shelved.*

A more plausible solution, although its implementation is still in the distant future, is a series of weirs downstream of each existing barrage. These would be mini-barrages whose effect would be to slow the river's velocity immediately downstream of the three main barrages. In 1970, discussions were begun with the USSR to construct the weirs, possibly along with a fourth main barrage between Aswan and Isna, by 1978. Indeed, the former Minister of Irrigation, Ahmad Ali Kemal, stated flatly that work on the project had begun in 1975, although there is no evidence to substantiate this claim. With the marked deterioration in Egypto-Soviet relations since the expulsion of the Russian military advisers in July 1972, followed by the abrogation of the Egypto-Soviet Friendship Treaty in March 1976, it would seem unlikely that any progress on weir construction will be made, and no other sources of expertise or funding are apparent.[22]

Riverbed degradation thus remains a major problem, although within manageable proportions. Ali Fathy's apprehensions were given sustenance when in 1975 the reservoir filled to its optimal level. If another above-average flood were to follow, potentially devastating water releases would have to be accepted. His misgivings are shared privately by irrigation officials, who note the inadequate maintenance of embankments and barrages against scouring. The Tushka depression appears to be the key to security against this particular calamity.

Scouring is not the only problem arising from silt deprivation. Equally serious, in the view of Fathy and others, is the question of soil fertility in the absence of the annual flood. No lesser figure than Sayyid Marei, perennial Minister of Agriculture since 1952 and Chairman of the World Food Conference in 1974, launched a parliamentary investigation into the dam's side effects because of his fears about soil fertility. "I say in all candor, as loudly as possible, I am worried, extremely worried, because of the threat to the fertility of our soils."[23]

What is in this sediment that built the Delta and Egypt over the millennia? Of the average 110 million tons moved by the river annually, 40 percent is silt, 30 percent fine sand, and 30 percent clay. The suspended matter in the Nile is volcanic in origin and, before the dam's

---

*The notion dies hard. *The Egyptian Gazette*, April 25, 1974, said a chain of dams across the Nile would be constructed with Soviet help over a ten-year period. Earlier it was estimated that six new barrages would cost £E 138 million.

construction, contained the chemical nutrients and minerals listed in Table 10.[24]

TABLE 10

Estimated Amounts of Nile Sediments and Total Nutrients Annually Deposited over the Cultivated Land of Egypt prior to the High Dam
(in 1,000 tons)

Region	Sediments	K_2O	P_2O_5	N	Organic matter
Upper Egypt					
Basin	8,800	94	20	11	218
Perennial	2,900	31	7	4	72
Lower Egypt					
Perennial	1,500	16	4	2	37
Total	13,200	141	31	17	327

SOURCE: H. A. El-Tobgy. *Contemporary Egyptian Agriculture*, 2nd ed. (Cairo: Ford Foundation, 1976), p. 34.

The impact of its loss downstream has been variously estimated, but it is clearly far greater than had been anticipated. The official view from the beginning has been that the silt was of minor nutritive value and could easily be replaced by chemical fertilizers. Moreover, because of the silt's low nitrogen content, Egypt had relied heavily on chemical fertilizers even before the High Dam was built.* It was also noted that about 80 percent of the annual silt load was flushed out to sea (a fact to which we shall return when we consider coastal erosion) while only 13 million tons actually reached Egypt's fields, the major beneficiary being the 800,000 feddans under basin irrigation in Upper Egypt, which received about 7 million tons of sediment annually. Abdel Rakeeb calculated that Egypt's fields would be deprived of only 1950 tons of azote yearly, an amount that could be compensated for by

*Consumption of nitrogenous fertilizers rose from 648,000 tons in 1952–53 to 1.2 million tons in 1964–65; phosphate fertilizer consumption rose from 92,000 to 322,000 tons over the same period.

applications of 13,000 tons of calcium nitrate fertilizer. While this argument may be valid, it fails to take into account other trace elements—especially iron, zinc, and magnesium—whose absence is now increasingly being felt.[25]

Similarly, initial assessments attached insufficient importance to the replenishment function of the silt deposits. This has made itself felt in two respects: soil depletion due to more intensive cropping, and soil removal to supply a basic ingredient to the local brick industry. Silt has been essential to Egyptian brickmaking over the centuries. Until recently, the 7,000 or so brick kilns scattered along the Nile were able to obtain silt gratis from canal cleanings. Total production was over one billion bricks a year in 1964 but, by 1967, fell off by more than a third. The major cause, one may surmise, is that silt had become a scarce commodity. Yet Egypt's construction sector remains dependent upon the silt bricks, sand brick production having reached a level of only 50 million a year by 1973. The predictable result was the brickmakers began to buy topsoil from peasants, and in certain areas the price for one feddan of topsoil up to a meter in depth reached £E 800 (ca. $1,600). For a peasant who stands to make only £E 100 net from his crops, the economic incentives for running down his plot are irresistible.[26] Government policy aims to phase out the burnt-brick establishments as soon as possible and to phase in sand brick factories. The time frame would appear to be ten years, but neither compensation for local interests nor foreign exchange for imported plants have been much discussed. Moreover, none of this touches the equally important village manufacture of unfired, sun-dried mud bricks for local construction.

More urgent than any of the negative side effects so far discussed are the twin problems of inadequate drainage and soil salinity. In brief, what has occurred since the High Dam's construction is the intensification of a process that began with the introduction of perennial irrigation over a century ago. Basin irrigation, even when supplemented by pump irrigation during the summer months, relied primarily upon the annual flood, whose excess waters would drain through the aquifer into the river, carrying with it salts leeched from the soil. With perennial irrigation, fallows were eliminated, and water applications were increased, leading to a rise in the water table. Drainage was impeded, waterlogging occurred and, through evaporation, the salts concentrated in the soil's upper layers.

The hope had been that with the construction of the High Dam, the average level of the river and canals would be lowered, and that this would actually improve the natural flow of drainage water through the aquifer back to the riverbed. In light of this assumption, a 20-year project, announced in 1958, to introduce main and field drains to all of Egypt's cultivated lands was abandoned for 12 years. By 1969–70 the new reality had begun to sink in.[27]

The phenomenon has several manifestations. One, to which we shall turn later, results from the extension of cultivation to new areas that generally lie higher than the river's flood plain and delta, and hence drain into the lower-lying land, raising the levels both of the water table and of the dissolved salts. This is the case not only all along the Delta's western edge, but also at Kom Ombo and other areas in Upper Egypt. Second, the High Dam has made water so readily available, especially in the summer, that over-use by the peasants is a major problem. In quantitative terms, it is believed that 10 billion m^3, or nearly 20 percent of Egypt's agricultural water needs, represent overirrigation and a further stimulus to a rising water table (see Chapter 8).

Waterlogging and salinity are particularly acute in the low-lying Delta, but, as in all other areas of Egypt, the nature of the problem varies from zone to zone (see Map 4). The Delta is built of alluvial deposits with a clay cap 9 to 10 meters thick overlying coarser sand and gravel deposits that constitute the aquifer for groundwater. The cap, in general, has low permeability and contains its own groundwater. The coarser substrata are fully saturated with water. In the southern Delta, the piezometric head of the aquifer groundwater is lower than that of the clay cap. Hence irrigation and groundwater drain naturally into the aquifer. In the northern Delta, by contrast, the situation is reversed. The piezometric head of the aquifer is higher than that of the clay cap, thereby producing upward seepage. While the addition of massive amounts of irrigation water has hindered drainage in both zones, clearly the northern Delta is the most afflicted. Artificial pump drainage could benefit both zones, but there is some possibility, because of the low head in the northern aquifer, that improved surface drainage will lead to seawater invasion of the aquifer with eventual seepage upward to the clay cap.[28]

While reducing on-field waste would be a step in the right direction, the most feasible way to cope with waterlogging and salinity is by the widespread installation of main drains, pumping stations, and covered field drains. In 1975, only about 2.7 million feddans (2 million in the Delta and 700,000 in Upper Egypt) had drainage of any kind. It was reckoned that adequate drainage could raise crop yields by 20–30 percent at far less expense than by land reclamation. Not only was

MAP 4

Lakes of the Nile Delta

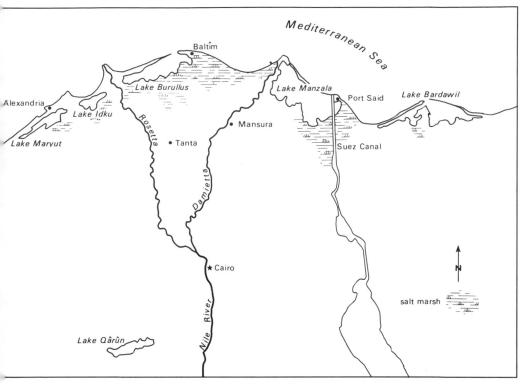

drainage not seen as a problem in the High Dam era, but Egyptian planners failed to provide for its installation on Upper Egyptian acreage converted from basin to perennial irrigation. Again, in 1975, of the 800,000 feddans so converted, only 393,000 had any drainage at all while a scant 61,000 had covered field drains.

The situation is grave. A few years ago an FAO study contended that 35 percent of Egypt's cultivated surface is afflicted by salinity and 90 percent by waterlogging. A USAID mission reported in 1976 that 4.2 million feddans were undergoing slight to severe effects from inadequate drainage, and unless something were done, all would be severely affected.[29] The question of why so little had been done became the subject of polemics and direct assaults upon the judgment and integrity of Egypt's masters during the 1960s. Sayyid Marei, although one of them, intimated that he had warned his colleagues of the follies of horizontal expansion (land reclamation) at the expense of vertical expansion (drainage, improved seeds, fertilizers, etc.). Others were nearly apoplectic in their denunciations of "Marxists" who had ushered Egypt into the High Dam era. Ibrahim al-Ba'athi fumed: "Even the soil of Egypt lost its fertility as a result of their stupidity and their faith in people who were incompetent and irresponsible."[30]

What can be done now to rectify the situation? First, there is a general recognition that an extension of the drainage network is of the utmost importance. Nonetheless, progress will be slow. By the year 2000 open drains may be extended to 1.3 million feddans in Upper Egypt and to 1.9 million in the Delta. This would cover just about all Egypt's cultivated area, but, in its excavation, such a network would take land out of cultivation. In addition, Egypt has entered into a long-term project with the IBRD to introduce tile (covered) drains to Egypt's fields. This project was begun in 1969 when only 200,000 feddans were serviced by such drains. Installation is currently progressing on 300,000 feddans in Upper Egypt and 950,000 feddans in the Delta. By the year 2000, 1.4 and 2.5 million feddans in Upper Egypt and the Delta may benefit from tile drainage. The Minister of Irrigation in 1978 estimated that total outlays for both field and main drains through 1985 would reach £E 700 million or nearly twice the cost of the High Dam itself. While awaiting the system's gradual installation, the best Egypt can hope for is (1) to promote more economical water use among farmers, and (2) to protect existing crop yields through more intensive fertilizer and pesticide applications, regardless of chemical runoffs into the water table, the river, and the northern lakes.

Ali Fathy has presented another, albeit draconian, solution to the problem. He advocates the return of the flood. The High Dam would be maintained but two diversion canals capable of discharging 860 million m³ per day would be used during the flood to protect Egypt against high floods. Over-year storage as a hedge against low floods would have to be transferred to the Equatorial lakes. If crop rotation allowed for a significant fallow, Fathy's scheme would restore silt to the land, maintain soil fertility and improve drainage, and obviate the danger of scouring. He concedes one major drawback; his proposal would necessitate the elimination of the hydroelectric power station which, for the promoters of Egyptian industrialization, would be a near-mortal blow. He seems unaware of a second drawback: under his scheme Egypt would once again become obsessed with the flow of timely water and thus would be forced to pressure the Sudan to adapt its own irrigation needs and regional development plans (viz., the

Jonglei canal and its impact on the Sudd populations) to Egyptian priorities.[31]

Coastal Erosion

Directly related to silt deprivation, and largely unanticipated, has been the steady erosion of the Mediterranean coast along the northern Nile Delta. Here again the High Dam's construction has been additive rather than causative. Muhammad Kassas has put the matter simply: "The Delta shoreline that had obviously been advancing throughout the history of the Delta formation is now retreating."[32] The phenomenon is not new. Measurements at both outlets of the Nile show that their promontories advanced 5–8 kilometers between 1800 and 1900 but then evidenced a yearly retreat of 29 meters at Rosetta and 31 meters at Damietta.

With or without the High Dam, the northern Delta would be under attack. Since Roman times, the level of the Mediterranean has risen some two meters, accompanied by some indication of a tilting of the eastern end of the basin from north to south. Second, under the sheer weight of its sediment, the Delta may be settling or sinking. During the nineteenth century, the Delta held its own against the sea, but, probably with the heightening of the Old Aswan Dam in 1934, the diminution in silt discharge began to shift the balance. Over the past decade, something like 600 million tons of sediment have never reached the sea. The Delta is clearly no longer holding its own.

There are two lines of defense along the northern coast: (1) the narrow sand spits that protect the northern brackish lakes (Idku, Burullus, Manzalla; .8–1 percent saline as opposed to 3.5–3.9 percent in the Mediterranean) from seawater invasion, and (2) the southern shores of the lakes themselves, which border on cultivated land (mainly salt-tolerant rice). It would not take much to breach either line of defense, and much of the Delta, lying only one or two meters above sea level, would go under.

Experts rightly point out that the actual process is poorly understood, but the long-term trend is unmistakable. Generally, surface currents in the eastern Mediterranean move counterclockwise, so that in the past, discharged Nile sediment moved west to east, building the tapered sand spits between the lakes and the sea. The process has been going on for millennia; for instance, the now-extinct Pelusiac branch of the Nile provided the silt by which Lake Bardawil in the Sinai peninsula was built. If these spits are breached, the lakes will simply become coastal bays. This process accounts for Abukir bay just to the east of Alexandria. But while the general trend is known, conditions may vary at specific locations. The movement of subsurface currents is poorly understood, and defensive engineering works have backfired in the past and could easily do so again.

The danger is clear. The ecology of the northern lakes may be transformed by seawater invasion. This would jeopardize existing and planned reclamation projects, and would also lead to increased seawater seepage into the northern Delta aquifer.[33] Minimalists stress that the most threatened areas are confined primarily to the two main Nile exits at Damietta and Rosetta. The fragile sand peninsulas that shelter these outlets are being eaten away rapidly. However, the inlet to Lake Burullus at Baltim and the coastal road from Damietta to Port Said are also threatened. With appropriate jetties and rock groins, the minimalists argue, the coast can be saved at a cost of no more than £E 200 million, "a very modest figure if compared to the benefits accrued to the High Dam."[34]

Other experts point out that the general problem has been recognized for years, and that the dam cannot be blamed for it, but that despite the clear and present danger nothing was done in sufficient time to study the phenomenon or to take protective measures against it. The first display of official concern may have resulted in the visit of the Soviet expert, Dr. Zukovich, in 1969, who recommended the kind of intense monitoring that UNESCO is now carrying out. It is also noted that if protective seaworks had been constructed in the early 1960s, they could have trapped and held the silt the Nile was still discharging. What might have occurred is evidenced by the original rock groin put in to protect the entrance of the Suez Canal at Port Said. Much of that city's physical expansion has taken place on the sediment trapped by the groin. By contrast, any works undertaken now will have to be massive, for there is no silt left to trap. Around 1973, costs were put at roughly £E 200 million, but if work is delayed until 1980 or later, the probable cost will be closer to £E one billion. There are no indications that any plans are now afoot to cope with the situation.

Land Reclamation

Our density is our destiny. — Gamal Hamdan[35]

In no other domain connected with the High Dam were so many

hopes deceived as in land reclamation. With around 1,000 people per km² of inhabited area, it was only natural that Egypt's government should want to break loose from the confines of the Nile Valley. It is said that in 1959, when Nasser reviewed land reclamation efforts since 1952, he was dismayed to find that there were only 50,000 feddans in the initial stages of reclamation. Nasser demanded that reclamation be begun on 100,000 feddans per year so that they would be ready to receive the additional 7.5 billion m³ of water alloted to Egypt once the High Dam reached completion.[36]

Horizontal expansion became Egypt's top agricultural priority. In the first five-year plan, 1960–1965, of total investment outlays in the agricultural sector of £E 208 million, £E 154 million were set aside for reclamation and related projects. Concern with vertical expansion, particularly the installation of adequate drainage on the old lands, fell by the wayside and a number of new myths arose to replace it:

1. Because the average annual water application per feddan in the old lands was about 7,500 m³, then Egypt's additional water would cover reclamation of about 1.5 million feddans. This facile transposition overlooked the heavy water requirements of the reclamation process itself, as well as the other goals of increasing sugar cane and rice acreage (thirsty crops) and converting 800,000 feddans from basin to perennial irrigation with concomitant increases in water used;

2. Real costs were minimized and the time to bring new acreage up to marginal levels of productivity was consistently underestimated;

3. It was assumed that the new lands would prove sufficiently fertile to permit the transfer of significant numbers of peasants from the old lands to them.

The new orthodoxy became unassailable. One of Nasser's closest confidants, Muhammad Hassanein Heikal, prophesied that by 1970 Egypt's cultivated surface would be nine million feddans: the six million already cultivated, plus two million from reclamation projects using the Nile waters, and one million using artesian water in the western desert and elsewhere.[37] By 1970, cultivated acreage was in fact more like 5.9 million feddans, and in March 1972, Mustapha al-Gabali, the Minister of Agriculture and Land Reclamation, put a halt to any further reclamation.

One element in the dilemma, perhaps a surrogate for all the others, was real cost. Here the reader may permit some amplification on a problem common to virtually all reporting on the Egyptian economy: on any day, for any project, according to any source, there is a different authoritative figure on level of production, cost, rate of return, etc. Consider the experience with reclamation.

First, just what has been reclaimed? For some years it was alleged that 1.2 million feddans had been reclaimed. By the time the reclamation effort was halted, the figure had shrunk to 912,000 feddans *gross area*, of which 770,000 feddans represented the net *cultivable* surface. But even this figure contains several ambiguities. The implication was that all this land was being fed by Egypt's post-1959 additional increment of water where, in fact, the figure includes pre-1959 projects and sites relying on ground water — such as 80,000 feddans in the New Valley. In addition, the impression was given that reclamation referred to cultivated acreage. When it came time to settle accounts, it was found that in 1972 less than 600,000 feddans were being cultivated, of which a maximum of 345,000 feddans had reached marginal levels of productivity. The rest was still under preparation.[38]

What has this rather marked underachievement of declared goals actually cost? We should note immediately that real costs cannot yet be known because so little acreage has become self-sufficient, but nevertheless, costs from the outset were grossly underestimated. In 1964, the Ministry of Land Reclamation insisted that gross outlays per feddan would not exceed £E 165. Real costs during the first five-year plan turned out to be more like £E 310 per feddan, but projected outlays per feddan during the second five-year Plan (which was never launched) were held to £E 263.[39] By the end of the 1960s, when this sacred cow had been partially desanctified, diverse cost estimates abounded in press reports. In 1974, Abd al-Azim Abu al-Atta, former Director of the General Authority for Cultivation and Agricultural Projects and now Minister of Irrigation, stated that total investment in reclamation had reached £E 300 million at an average of £E 328 per feddan (*al-Ahram*, July 2, 1974). Ahmad Yunis, head of Parliament's Agricultural Committee, claimed gross outlays of £E 382 million, plus an annual £E 10 million loss in operating expenses. Yet none of these figures tallies with those of Osman Badran, who stated that in the period 1960–71 £E 429 million were invested in reclamation for an average of £E 470 per feddan (*al-Ahram*, June 10, 1972). An equally authoritative source, Sayyid Marei, who, like Badran, had been Minister of Agriculture, told a group of students that land reclamation had cost the state £E 625 million at £E 525 per feddan (*al-Ahram*, May 10, 1975). One of Marei's close associates, Saad Hagras, Director of the General Authority for Agrarian Reform, indicated that all future efforts in land reclamation should be calculated on the basis of £E 1,000 per feddan (*al-Ahram*, May 13, 1974), while Abd al-Azim Abu al-Atta reverted to a figure of £E 480 per feddan (*al-Ahram*, June 10, 1976).

Hagras may be the more credible. The 1978–82 Five Year Plan declared total outlays on the reclamation of 912,000 feddans over the period 1954–75 at £E 865 million (£E 383 million for preparation; £E 340 million for initial cultivation; £E 141 million for canals, drains, and pumping stations) for a per feddan average of £E 950. The same feddans contributed only 3 percent of the total value of agricultural output, and their return does not begin to cover annual operating expenses.

The remaining question is why is this so? An important element that will not be dealt with here is that of state management versus private ownership of the new lands. Sayyid Marei and others have insisted that part of the plight of reclaimed areas can be attributed to the bungling of incompetent state bureaucracies and misguided socialist models. But whatever the form of ownership, technical problems must be the determinant factor. Consider the question of soil quality, for example. Typically, no serious soil surveys of prospective reclamation areas were carried out before the construction of the High Dam. Not until 1964, in conjunction with the FAO, were such surveys undertaken, covering 14 million feddans. By that time Egypt had already begun reclamation on nearly 600,000 feddans. Of the area surveyed, a little over two million feddans were designated as suitable for reclamation. The soils were classed within six categories ranging from excellent (I) to poor (IV) to uncultivable (VI). Most of Egypt's old lands are in classes II and III (4.6 million feddans), but the new lands surveyed were distributed as follows:

Class	No. of Feddans
I	8,328
II	217,000
III	604,542
IV	1,391,682

A recent USAID mission noted: "Of the 500,000 [reclaimed] feddans now producing crops, about 70 percent are Class IV, 25 percent Class III, and the remaining 5 percent are Class II. Soil Classes III and IV have severe limitations for crop production, particularly Class IV which requires special soil treatment to obtain moderate yields at relatively high cost."[40] So indeed was the case. The poor quality of the soils has lengthened the time to eight to ten years from the start of reclamation to the attainment of marginal levels of productivity. Yields are generally low, and, for the most part, the traditional valley crops—cotton, wheat, corn, rice, and sugar cane—cannot be grown on the new lands. Instead, melons, grapes, citrus, alfalfa, potatoes—and perhaps one day sugar beets—have so far proved the most suitable for these soils. The combination of state ownership, low yields, and the nature of the crops have militated against significant population transfer to the new lands. Most labor is provided by field hands who frequently commute to work. By 1975 only 35,000 families were living in reclaimed areas.[41]

The crisis of the new lands does not end there, however. Their productivity has been further diminished by inadequate drainage and increasing salinity. While old lands are going out of cultivation at the rate of at least 20,000 feddans a year, owing to urban and village sprawl, large chunks of the new lands have returned to a state of nature — 160,000 feddans by one observer's estimate.[42] The highest hopes were pinned to the reclamation of 500,000 feddans along the western edge of the Delta. By 1973–4 some 117,000 feddans were being cultivated and the rest prepared. Water applications amounted to 10,000 m³ per feddan per year.

By focusing on one major sector of this area (south of Alexandria on Map 5) we may gain some insights into the unanticipated crisis that is plaguing reclamation as a whole. A number of main canals—the most important being the Nubaria, Tahrir, and Nasir canals—were built to bring water to these lands. Water from these canals is pumped uphill to land lying as much as 40 meters above sea level and as far as 40 km from the main canal. When irrigation first started at the reclamation sites, the water table in the westernmost sectors was 40–50 meters below the surface. Because the soils are sandy and calcareous with high permeability, it was felt that they would drain naturally and no drainage system was installed. At the same time, lateral delivery canals were excavated stepwise uphill, with each section being quite deep in order to minimize the number of steps and overall costs.

The field delivery system was designed according to a ten-day watering cycle that has proved to be at the heart of the problem. The cycle is inappropriate for the soils under reclamation. Because of their high permeability, they retain water only at the beginning of the cycle, and the rest percolates down to the water table. The plants' root systems suffer from lack of water toward the end of the cycle, while the unused water stimulates a general rise in the water table. Over the period 1969–72 the water table rose at a rate of four meters per year.

As the volume of water in the aquifer increased, other processes were set in motion. First, it is believed that the natural drainage flow of

MAP 5

Areas of Reclaimed Land

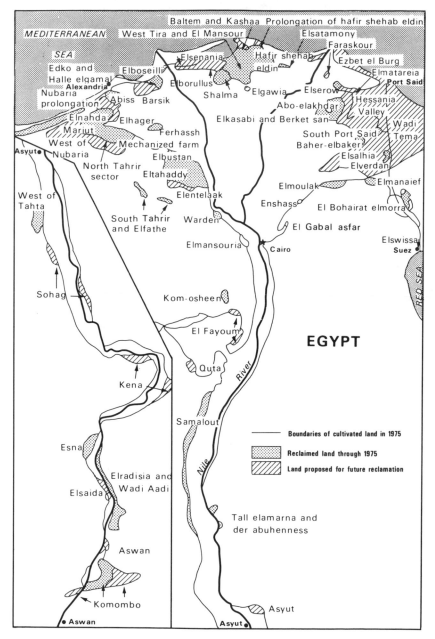

this area had been east-west (i.e., away from the Nile and toward the western depressions of Natroun and Qattara). With the massive water applications on the reclaimed land, this flow has been reversed, and the new lands now drain into the Nile after traversing lower-lying old lands.[43] Second, the water table has risen in many areas to the root level of the plants. Waterlogging has been compounded in that the westerly flow of the irrigation water has dissolved salts in the soil and carried them to low-lying lands. Third, because the main canals are not lined, this highly saline groundwater (in places 3,000 ppm as opposed to 300 ppm for the Nile at Cairo) seeps into them and is pumped back onto the fields. Likewise, the feeder canals are cut so deeply that there is heavy seepage into them (see Figure 8). The problem became so

FIGURE 8

Western reclaimed areas. Cross section showing water table and soil strata

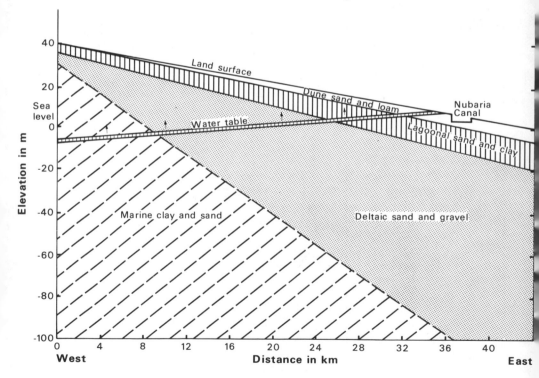

acute in the early 1970s that some main canals fell into disuse (Tahrir, Nubaria), and many pumping stations, relying on electrical power through uninsulated copper wiring, had to be closed down because of the seepage.[44]

There will be no inexpensive way to meet this situation. Irrigation networks can be redesigned to provide water at different intervals; existing irrigation canals can be transformed into main drains and new feeder canals dug and lined; sprinkler or trickle irrigation can be introduced to reduce water loss. However, any or all of these will cost substantial sums, and Egypt's general economic crisis has not permitted allocation of funds toward such ends. It is not at all clear what state policy is toward the new lands. The tendency seems to be to transfer these lands to private individuals through auctions, to joint ventures with foreign companies interested in agroindustries, or to public sector companies that will promote processing and exports.

Despite the reclamation's unhappy record, the mood since 1976 has been bullish. Perhaps Egypt's policy makers could not be otherwise as the population expanded to 40 million people and cultivated acreage continued to shrink. Abd al-Azim Abu al-Atta, Minister of Irrigation (and also of Agriculture until February 1977), has talked of bringing in another 2.5–3 million feddans by the year 2000, over and above those lands upon which reclamation has already been begun (al-Ahram, March 14 and June 10, 1976). Some of the proposed new sites, such as those in Sinai and the Port Said-Ismailia region of the Canal Zone have not been adequately surveyed, and foreign experts doubt whether many of these areas are worth reclaiming. The previously cited USAID study was of the opinion that, "Based on present information, it seems unlikely that additional new land worth developing over the next ten years or so would exceed one million feddans and the actual amount may be considerably smaller than this."[45]

Some Lesser Agricultural and Social Side Effects

There is growing evidence that water quality in all its forms is a factor that Egypt can no longer afford to neglect. One aspect, already alluded to, is that of increasing water salinity. The high evaporation rates at the High Dam reservoir have led to 10 percent increases in salinity; that is, water entering the reservoir has about 200 ppm, and when it leaves, 220 ppm. Because Upper and Middle Egyptian lands drain back into the main Nile, salinity around Cairo and in the Delta is in excess of 300 ppm. In itself, this is no cause for alarm, but agricultural intensification in Egypt and the Sudan cannot fail to aggravate the problem. Moreover, in developing new water resources from the Equatorial lakes and the Jonglei scheme, the White Nile, with a higher salt content than the Blue Nile, will figure more prominently in downstream discharge.

The High Dam reservoir has affected the water quality in other ways as well. This large body of water has become highly eutrophic,* producing a variety of phytoplanktons and algae. These are released downstream, and in the fall of 1974 caused a considerable flap in Cairo as that city's drinking water turned murky and unpleasantly odoriferous. The algae had clogged Cairo's decrepit water filtering system. Ali Fathy seized upon this to suggest that if the algae could do this to sand filters, one could imagine their effect upon the permeability of the soil and the functioning of the tile drains in Egypt's fields.[46]

Accompanying increased salinity and algae are chemical runoffs due to the heavy use of pesticides, herbicides, chemical fertilizers, and copper sulphates (to kill snails that host bilharzia). Added to these regular runoffs are periodic crash programs; in 1975, for example, herbicides were applied to 50,000 km of canals and drains to kill heavy concentrations of Nile hyacinth (al-Ahram, May 15, 1975). For the most part, these residues would be an inescapable facet of agricultural intensification and unrelated to the High Dam per se. Nonetheless, they are part of the ecological disequilibrium that now characterizes the Egyptian Nile.

The most ecologically disturbed areas are the northern lakes into which most of the Delta farmlands currently drain. Several billion m³ of drainage water pour into these lakes annually: 6 billion m³ in Manzala alone. One consequence of this is that lake levels have risen and salt content actually diminished in the past decade (1,400 ppm in south Manzala to 2,800 ppm in the north). But chemical and sewage discharge have led to a marked deterioriation in the water environment. "If Lake Manzala (and by extension the other northern lakes) is to survive as anything more than a relatively stagnant inland lake or a

---

*If nutrient inputs exceed the response capacities of the aquatic organisms, a process termed eutrophication can ensue. Basically, a state is reached where insufficient dissolved oxygen (DO) is present to maintain an aerobic stabilization of organic nutrients, so anaerobic decomposition becomes dominant. At certain levels of eutrophication, fish and plants cannot survive. The precipitation of sediment in the reservoir allows for greater penetration of sunlight there and downstream which in turn stimulates algae growth.

eutrophied swamp, then a detailed comprehensive study will have to be undertaken of the lakeland ecosystems and of their existing and proposed uses."[47]

The northern lakes have traditionally provided Egypt with the bulk of its annual fish take. Deterioration of the ecosystem has already led to a sharp drop in fish production. From Lake Burullus, for instance, 60,000 tons were taken in 1966, while in 1975 production fell to 14,000 tons, according to *al-Ahram*, July 22, 1975. Water quality is by no means the sole factor governing levels of fish breeding; periodic closure of sea inlets, fishing techniques, and lake bottom drainage have all played a role. A crucial question today concerns the opportunity costs of draining and reclaiming as much as 25 percent of the lakes, as opposed to developing and managing them as fish farms (see Table 11). Reclamation costs might run as high as £E 600 per feddan while fisheries development could be done at £E 200 per feddan. Fishery returns per feddan are estimated by some at £E 480 annually per feddan against £E 150 for agricultural use.[48]

TABLE 11

Characteristics of the Northern Lakes

Lake	Area/ feddans	Fish production/ tons	Areas reclaimed/ feddans
Manzalla	314,000	21,000	26,000
Burullus	136,000	15,000	3,000
Idku	45,000	4,000	2,000
Maryut	33,000	7,000	10,000
Total	528,000	47,000	41,000

The overall question of Egypt's fisheries has stimulated considerable debate. The lack of sediment in the Nile discharge, and the drop in the amount of fresh water discharged annually, has adversely affected Egypt's Mediterranean fisheries, especially the sardine take. In the early 1960s, Egypt's *total* fish production was about 100,000 tons annually, of which some 25,000 tons were taken from the sea. Half of that 25,000 consisted of the sardine take, while the remaining 75,000 tons were taken from the Red Sea, the lakes, and the river. Between 1962 and 1971 the sardine catch fell from 12,500 tons to 1,500.

Defenders of the High Dam argued that the sardine loss would be easily replaced by the fish catch from the High Dam reservoir. They are essentially correct as the take has grown from 781 tons in 1967 to around 15,000 tons in 1975. But now production is lagging behind projections, some of which were clearly fanciful.[49] A primitive fishing fleet, lack of refrigeration and transportation facilities, and the fact that freshwater fish do not move in schools have held down overall fish yields. Still, takes of 25,000 tons a year would appear attainable, although the needed investment is not in hand.

The final question to be considered under this rubric is bilharziasis (schistosomiasis), a tiny blood fluke that infests humans, lodging in the urinary tract or the intestines. The fluke's eggs are released by the human host in the urine or feces, and in the Egyptian countryside this generally means that the eggs enter the river and irrigation canals. In stagnant water, as in the canals, small snails act as intermediate hosts for the hatching of the eggs. New larvae are released into the water, where they penetrate the skin of humans working or playing in the water, thereby reentering the bloodstream. The disease is mainly debilitating, causing internal bleeding and general fatigue. In 1965–66 it was estimated that about 40 percent of the entire population was affected by bilharziasis, and that it was costing the economy £E 80–100 million annually in lost production.[50]

Bilharziasis has spread with the gradual conversion of all Egypt's acreage to perennial irrigation. In the 1930s, the process was measured in four districts into which perennial irrigation was introduced. Infestation rates rose in three years from an average of 7 percent of the population to 58 percent. The impact of perennial irrigation is in this respect threefold: it eliminates fallows during which the snail host would be killed off as canals dried out; it increases the amount of still or stagnant water and the amount of aquatic weeds to which the snails cling; and it increases the amount of time the *fellahin* (peasants) spend in the water. Little wonder, then, that the conversion of 800,000 feddans in Upper Egypt to perennial irrigation after the construction of the High Dam has caused a sharp rise in infestation rates in these areas (Sohag, Qena, Assyut).

In theory it would be relatively easy to eliminate bilharziasis. All that is required is that people neither urinate nor defecate in the irrigation canals, thus breaking the cycle between hosts. But theory could become reality only if the entire context of rural living in Egypt was completely transformed. When most villages do not yet have electricity, it is ludicrous to talk of modern plumbing. After all, modernization of the countryside was one of the goals Egypt's policy makers set for the High Dam, and until that day comes (if ever) the quiet plague of bilharziasis will have to be tolerated.

Hydroelectric Power

Surely the Nasserist regime would not have gone ahead with the High Dam had its anticipated benefits been limited solely to agriculture. The dam's catalytic effect in providing a cheap source of power for Egypt's ambitious industrial growth plans was probably a major determinant. But here, too, the regime's hopes were not fully realized.

The question of power generation and industrialization had for some time been politically loaded. It was widely believed that Great Britain and its local allies (the Palace, local landlords, cotton merchants, etc.) were opposed to Egypt's industrialization, and that their primary concern was to assure steady supplies of cheap raw materials (chiefly cotton) to British industries. As soon as the first Aswan Dam had been built, various foreign and Egyptian experts advocated installation of a power plant at the dam site so that Egypt, oil-poor and reliant on thermal generators, could at least have the energy to found a fertilizer industry. Yet, as we have already noted, it took a *coup d'état* in 1952 and the determination of the young officers to bring the project to fruition in the late 1950s.[51] The Old Aswan power station's maximum generating capacity is two billion kWh annually, and nearly all of it is consumed by the Kima Fertilizer Company at Aswan.

The Soviet design for the High Dam provided for a power station with *installed capacity* (12 turbines) of 10 billion kWh annually. This power station was completed in January 1971. In the preceding years, the 10 billion kWh figure had taken on a magical quality; it was blithely assumed that because the capacity was there it would be fully used. Industrial planners began to look to the future on that assumption, and even today the figure is used as if it described reality (for example, cf. Ministry of Electricity release, *al-Ahram*, May 15, 1975).

Not surprisingly, it does not and it never will. The least important element in the explanation is that, at any one time, only 10 of the 12 turbines are in use. Of crucial importance, however, is the head of water available at the dam to drive the turbines, and the rate of water release. Both in turn are governed by several other factors. The main dilemma lies in meshing the wide variations in seasonal water requirements for agriculture with the fairly constant power needs for industry and other purposes. Although this problem was recognized early on, the question of optimality has still not been fully aired. An early examination of optimal patterns was presented by Revelle, et al. Their table (see Table 12) summarizes the basic conundrum.[52] Rate of

TABLE 12

Seasonal Distribution of Inflows into Lake Nasser and Water Demands for Agriculture and Power Generation
(% of annual supply and demand)

Season	Inflow to Lake Nasser	Hydropower Demand %	Proportion of Power Demand met by meeting irri. demand %	Irrigation requirement %
January–March	9	28	53	15
April–June	3	25	136	34
July–September	53	22	159	35
October–December	35	25	64	16

All figures are estimates and represent neither real discharge nor real power production.

release and available head are not synonymous, and the tradeoff is complex. For instance, in late January and early February, it has been the custom to minimize water release in order to drop the river level at a time when agricultural needs are low, so that irrigation and drainage canals can be dredged and all waterworks repaired. This winter closure would last up to 40 days, with daily releases as low as 85–90 million m³. Agriculture still calls the tune on the pattern of water release, but industry's pressing need for energy has led to a shortening of the winter closure to 21 days, during which 3 billion m³ are released in order to satisfy nonagricultural demands. The point is that during this period, the head may be held constant, but releases are insufficient to meet power needs. With the flood, or just after it, releases are more than is needed for power, although the head is dropping (see Figure 9).

FIGURE 9

Water heads for hydroelectric power generation, Old Aswan and High Dams

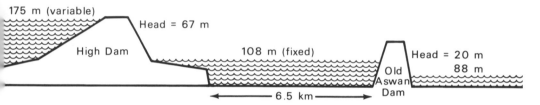

Thus the most power the High Dam and the Old Aswan Dam could generate *together* is nine billion kWh, of which the old dam's share is two billion. A study made in March 1966 claimed that simulation studies using data for the period 1870–1965 indicate that *on the average* the High Dam power station would generate about 5.7 billion kWh a year, although if a monster flood like that of 1879 were to arrive, installed capacity might be put to full use. As it is, the power generated at the High Dam reached 4.4 billion kWh in 1974, less than half of installed capacity, but slightly more than half of all power generated in Egypt. By 1976, the High Dam power station generated 6.6 billion kWh with another 2 billion kWh coming from Old Aswan and nearly 5 billion kWh from thermal generators.[53]

Some suggestions have been made as to how to reconcile, at least partially, agricultural and industrial needs in water release. One suggestion is to release more water during the slack agricultural season and then store it further downstream, at Wadi Rayyan perhaps, or use it to recharge the Delta groundwater table, which could be more heavily pumped during the peak season. Whatever the merits of such suggestions, little has been done about them, mainly, one supposes, because Egypt's energy needs in the near future are liable to be much greater than any incremental gains provided by optimal release projects at the High Dam.

In 1973, the Ministry of Industry stated that Egyptian industries consumed 5.1 billion kWh of the 7.6 billion kWh that represented the country's entire energy supply. Kima Fertilizer Company alone uses 2 billion, the Helwan Iron and Steel plant one billion, the Nag Hammadi Aluminum Complex eventually 2 billion, and the Suez-Mediterranean Pipeline 600 million. By 1982 the same Ministry estimates that industrial energy consumption will rise to 15.6 billion kWh. The Ministry of Electricity, which one must suspect will not underestimate future needs, is talking of generating 29.2 billion kWh by 1985 and 85 billion kWh in the year 2000. Clearly, were such levels to be attained, the Aswan High Dam could contribute only about 10 percent of the load.

These figures are surely inflated and probably reflect normal ministerial empire-building and project-mongering. Yet even if reduced by 20 percent, future needs still dwarf High Dam capacity. To meet these demands, Ahmad Sultan, former Minister of Electricity, pinned his hopes on two projects, either or both of which contain the seeds of glory and disaster more than equal to those of the High Dam. The first is the acquisition of nuclear reactors to generate electricity, but this technology is tied to the question of the accumulation of fissionable materials that could be used to construct explosive devices. The United States has been reluctant to provide this technology to other countries, including Egypt, although France may not be so circumspect if financing can be found.

The second avenue is the Qattara Depression project which in scale makes the High Dam look insignificant. For three-quarters of a century, some Egyptians have envisioned a canal running from the Mediterranean near al-Alamein some 76 kilometers inland to the northern head of the depression, whose lowest areas lie 50–60 meters below sea level. The surface of the depression is 19,500 km². One major question to be answered is whether excavation of the canal can be carried out by controlled nuclear explosions (estimated costs for the entire project equal £E 500 million) or whether it must be dug by conventional means through the *massif* that separates the depression from the sea, thereby quadrupling the price. The project would transform the depression into a large salt lake with as yet uncalculated effects upon the water table of the western Delta. Water entering from the sea would be dropped through turbines to generate five times the High Dam's installed capacity, or 50 billion kWh. Water inflow would be regulated to balance with the rate of surface evaporation from the lake. The Federal Republic of Germany is financing the feasibility studies connected with the project. If begun within two years, its full power benefits would come on-stream gradually until full capacity was reached in the year 2000. The official view of this project, whose side effects, not to mention feasibility, are very poorly understood, is eerily reminiscent of the High Dam at its inception. Sanctification seems but a step away.

Nonetheless, we may suppose that the High Dam's role as cheap power provider to Egyptian industry will become obsolete within a decade or so. If it has not, that would simply mean that Egypt's industrial base had failed to expand. New energy sources will have to be found; in addition to Qattara and nuclear reactors, investigations are being carried out as to the feasibility of developing solar and wind power generators. As—or if—these alternatives are implemented, an intriguing possibility opens up: would Ali Fathy's radical solution of bringing back the flood by eliminating the power station at the Aswan High Dam, and allowing the silt-laden waters to skirt the dam through diversion canals appear more sensible and practical?

CONCLUSION

Despite the hue and cry, domestic and international, that has been raging about the High Dam since 1955, it is now apparent that it is simply unequal to the problems it was designed to solve. Egypt and the Sudan need more water than the Nile can now provide and must pursue the old Equatorial lakes projects and the partial draining of the Sudd swamps as rapidly as possible. The costs have not been calculated, but both countries should consider themselves fortunate if they are able to increase their share of Nile water by 9 billion m³ each within 20 years. For Egypt, especially, future expansion of its cultivated area to meet population growth will be entirely dependent on new hydro-projects. Similarly, the crucial domain of industrial expansion will rest squarely on the development of new energy sources, and not upon the hydropower of the High Dam.

The High Dam has performed several notable services. Above all else, it has guaranteed Egyptian agriculture a steady and predictable water supply, year-in, year-out. The importance of this gain cannot be minimized, for wide fluctuations in agricultural production would effectively cripple an economy already in a parlous state. It is perfectly justifiable, therefore, to cite, along with Egyptian apologists, the low flood of 1972. Without the High Dam's over-year storage there would have been inadequate summer water and about a third of the cotton and rice crops would have been lost. They were not, however, and in that one summer the High Dam went a long way toward paying for itself.

Still, there is no denying that the High Dam has caused new problems or exacerbated old ones. The distinction is vital and too many observers have ignored it. The questions that must be asked are (1) what side effects are *directly* attributable to the High Dam? (2) what side effects are attributable to poor downstream planning? and (3) what side effects has the High Dam produced that no other over-year storage scheme would have? *The assumption here is that Egypt could not possibly have foregone some form of over-year storage or complete conversion to perennial irrigation.*

Directly attributable to the High Dam are the high rates of evaporation and perhaps seepage at the reservoir. Alternative projects would suffer from the same phenomena but perhaps not on the same scale. Likewise, silt deprivation may be attributed to the dam, but again with the caveat that the Century Storage Scheme would have led to silt entrapment on a lesser scale (viz., at Wadi Rayyan). Consequently, riverbed degradation *on its present scale* can be chalked up to the High Dam, but degradation would have occurred under any alternative scheme. So, too, coastal erosion, although surely poor planning of seaworks along the coast is the real culprit. Soil salinity and waterlogging are the results of failure to install a good drainage network in the 1960s and of neglecting to train the peasantry in economic water use. Any system of over-year storage and perennial irrigation would have posed the same challenge. The fiasco of land reclamation is entirely independent of the dam, being the direct result of sloppy soil analysis and downstream planning. Any over-year storage project would have contributed to the deterioration of the northern lakes, the drop in the maritime fish take (without the compensatory development of new fish resources as at Lake Nasser), and the spread of bilharziasis. Finally, the High Dam provided more hydropower than any conceivable alternative, although less than what its planners predicted.

The policy errors that have studded the High Dam's history are rooted in the highly political atmosphere in which the project has been appraised. Quiet and serious technical debate and analysis became impossible because the analysts' motives were suspect. Frequently, such suspicions of technical criticisms were well founded; just as frequently, they were not. Once the decision had been made to go ahead with the dam—in the teeth of Egypt's enemies, as it were—there was no going back. That is understandable. The real tragedy lay in the subsequent difficulty in presenting anything but the most positive and most exaggerated benefits to be derived from it. Anything less than superlatives became potentially treasonous, and, one suspects, policy makers who knew they would not be around to pay the price of their Polyannaism, severely rebuked the sowers of doubt. Now that Nasser is dead, and it has become fashionable in some quarters to castigate his style of politics and governance, it is possible to place responsibility for the unforeseen consequences of the High Dam on such things as the exaggerations of socialist ideologues, the perfidy of the Soviet Union, lack of democracy, and police rule. For the many who were closely associated with the project and are still around, the stock defense is "I tried to warn them/him, but no one would listen." So everyone may be off the hook, but the problems are real and must still be confronted. No regime ever built a monument to itself with tile drains, but it is at that level that Egyptian planners must focus their attention.

6

EGYPT: THE WAGES OF DEPENDENCY

As BEFITS any Third World state, Egypt has ambitious plans for economic development. Yet, in marked contrast to the Sudan, where all plans are directed toward future growth, Egyptian growth strategies are preponderantly designed to cope with the cumulative problems and errors of the past. These derive primarily from the fact that for nearly a century, Egypt came to rely more and more for its economic well-being on agricultural intensification and the export of cotton. Over this same century Egypt's population grew dramatically, taxing the agricultural sector's capacity to provide adequate land, employment, and revenues for the new millions. Nonagricultural alternatives in the sphere of industrialization had not, until the Second World War, been given the priority they deserved. In a sense, Egypt was trapped by an outsized population and agricultural specialization. Nasser sought to free his country from that trap, but in pursuing state-guided industrialization created a host of new problems without resolving the old.

Like the Sudan, however, Egypt has confronted these problems within a national framework. It has always believed that the capacity for autonomous economic growth lies within its borders and that with the proper mix of good planning and luck it can achieve some sort of prosperity. In this light, the various attempts at political union or economic integration with other Arab countries have been undertaken primarily to generate advantages along the margins of national development and the process of undergirding the regime. The attempts have never been seen as crucial to Egypt's survival, nor as entailing the surrender of any major proportion of the country's sovereign rights. A prevalent view is that Egypt will always somehow manage to pull its chestnuts from the fire and that it is far too important a country to be

The core of this chapter, as well as its title, has been taken from my "Egypt: the Wages of Dependency," in A. L. Udovitch, ed., *The Middle East: Oil, Conflict and Hope*, (Lexington, Mass.: Lexington Books, 1976), pp. 291–351.

allowed to go under. Consequently, Egyptian elites have evinced little sense of urgency in seeking regional solutions to national problems. Nowhere is this more striking than in Egypt's approach to the Sudan (Chapters 2 and 3), and it has a direct bearing upon the use of the Nile. Egypt and the Sudan have long exploited the Nile from the standpoint of their own national objectives; and the point at which their demands on the river become irreconcilable with the quantity and quality of the available water depends on the extent to which they continue to do this. Thus, the task in this and the following chapter is to look more closely at the domestic context of policy-making in the two countries, and at the political constraints that have kept the attention of the national leaders in both so firmly fixed on maximization of national advantage at the expense of the rational mobilization of resources on a regional basis.

In these two chapters we must also examine the increasingly important role of Arab and western capital in financing the development of Egypt and the Sudan. For if there is one thing both countries share, it is their weak foreign exchange position, large external debt, and unfavorable balance of trade. These add up to a kind of international vulnerability and dependency upon external sources of credit—generally provided with implicit political strings—that make pretensions to autonomous growth and political sovereignty all but hollow. Where has the capital come from, and where will it come from now and in the future? What are the political and economic expectations of the creditors? To anticipate a fuller response to these questions, suffice it for the moment to note that, external credit to date has flowed into the Sudan with the expectation of a good *commercial* return, while it has entered Egypt to stave off an economic crisis that might undermine the moderate regime of Anwar Sadat. Capital has been going to both from the same sources. With such widely divergent motives behind the transfers, how would the creditors react to a situation in which pursuit of the development goals of the two debtors brought them into conflict over available water supply? We will postpone a discussion of that question until Chapter 8.

ECONOMIC CHANGE AND SOCIAL STRATIFICATION

Since the inception of the revolution, Egypt's leaders have had no perceptible commitment to any particular economic ideology. What seems to have informed Nasser's economic preferences was a concern to bring Egyptian resources under Egyptian control, to strengthen the Egyptian economy so that it bolstered independence, to institute a certain degree of distributive justice, and to protect the revolution (a term that came to be synonymous with the regime) from regional and great power machinations. Nasser did, it is true, maintain an abiding suspicion of the Egyptian bourgeoisie of the *ancien regime*; in a general sense, he was apprehensive of any groups that appeared able to accumulate wealth and, derivatively, political leverage. Many of the nationalizations that accompanied the overtly socialist phase of the revolution can be seen as simple pre-emptive maneuvers to destroy potentially dangerous sources of material wealth.

The Free Officers who came to power in 1952 were sprung from the urban and rural *petite bourgeoisie*. Their image of the Egypt of the future was one of a powerful and prosperous state, without class antagonisms, and internally cohesive and disciplined. They rejected liberalism without rejecting capitalism, and what models they had came from the political experiments of the 1930s: Attaturk and Mussolini, with favorable historical references to Muhammad Ali.[1]

Prosperity consistently eluded the new regime. A liberal foreign investment code in the early 1950s failed to attract any capital except in oil exploration and in tourism. The regime inched its way towards bolstering the public sector of the economy as it planned for the Aswan High Dam, the Helwan Iron and Steel plant, Kima Fertilizers, and so forth. The nationalization of British and French assets following the Suez War of 1956 committed Egypt to a path that it had already hesitantly begun to follow. Before 1956, government holdings in mixed enterprises amounted to £E 17 million. By 1957, paid-up public capital in mixed and entirely public enterprises rose to £E 59 million.[2] From then on, the state moved inexorably toward the consolidation of its grip on all major establishments in manufacturing, banking, insurance, cotton, foreign trade, and transportation. Two processes were at work: the state was creating new industrial and manufacturing units under public ownership, and, at the same time, nationalizing or taking controlling interests in existing private enterprises. The takeover of Abboud Pasha's companies and the effective nationalization of Bank Misr and thus of the companies in the Misr Group (principally spinning and weaving at Mehalla al-Kubra) were the first steps toward the massive nationalizations of July 1961.

These measures can be seen as the counterpart of the land reforms of 1952, 1961, and 1969. The first of these was aimed primarily at

destroying a landed class of a few thousand families, which had dominated Egyptian politics in the twentieth century and which the new
regime regarded as the natural allies of the British and of foreign
interests. Redistribution of agricultural resources was an important,
but secondary, consideration.[3] All three land reforms resulted, by 1971,
in the distribution of about 800,000 feddans to no more than 400,000
rural families: i.e., about 14 percent of the cultivated surface was
parcelled out to about 10 percent of all rural families.[4] Similarly, in the
nonagricultural sectors, once British, French, and Belgian interests had
been eliminated after 1956, came the turn of the Levantine and Egyptian bourgeoisie. The Socialist Decrees of 1961 were probably inspired
by three basic motives: first, to cut the grass from under the feet of any
"counterrevolutionary" force that might oppose the growing importance of the state sector of the economy; second, to acquire new assets
that would help finance the Five Year Plan; and third, to put at the
disposal of the regime the industrial capacity and financial institutions
of the country, in order to underwrite Egypt's increasingly dynamic
role in the Arab World. The fact that the private sector, in the first year
of the Five Year Plan, failed to live up to the investment levels expected
of it by the government, and the fact that it had been distributing about
two-thirds of all profits as dividends to shareholders, were the ostensible but perhaps not the dominant causes of the nationalizations. The
process of politico-economic consolidation was continued after the
secession of Syria from the United Arab Republic in September 1961, as
several hundred families suspected of complicity in the secession had
their assets sequestered. Other sequestrations followed in 1964 and
again in 1966. The upshot was that by the early 1970s, the state dominated the nonagricultural sectors of the economy. By 1974, capital
invested in the public sector totaled £E 4 billion, exclusive of agriculture, and that invested in the private sector £E 400 million.

The right of private ownership was never attacked; rather, systems
of exploitation and "feudalism" were to be destroyed. Either evil could
of course be defined in many ways. The inverse of the exploitationists
and feudalists were the "national capitalists" who invested their earnings, treated their workers well, and served national interests. The line
between exploiter and national capitalist was politically determined
and varied over time.

Despite these momentous changes, the private sector continued to
thrive and flourish. Most of Egypt's cultivable land is still privately
owned. Seventy percent of all commercial operations are still in private
hands. Over 25 percent of all industrial production still comes from the

private sector, which employs about 40 percent of the work force.

Somewhere around 1969 the efforts to redistribute national wealth more equitably came to a perhaps unintended halt. In that year, individual land holdings were limited to 50 feddans, but Nasser announced that there would be no further reductions. The so-called kulak class of Egypt was still intact: 5.2 percent of all landowners (168,000), owning between 5 and 50 feddans, possessed 32 percent of all cultivated land (i.e., 1.9 million feddans).[5] The economic options open to Egypt had begun to polarize markedly by 1969 if not before. The choices were to intensify the revolution through more land reform, nationalization of commercial activities, and rigorous efforts to collect taxes and force savings, or to open the Egyptian economy to a combination of private Egyptian and foreign capital investment, combined with a diminution of economic links with the socialist countries. Nasser never fully committed himself one way or another, although there are signs after 1965 that he was leaning away from further intensification.

In the shadow of socialism as it were, a new bourgeoisie came into existence that thrived on its access to the public sector. Contacts were made along three main avenues: influence peddling, subcontracting, and black market operations. Ironically, its members began to accumulate wealth at the same time the state began to concentrate more and more economic activities in its own hands. The elimination of the Levantine and a part of the Egyptian business community left the way open for them, and the administration of investments during the first plan played directly into their hands. It has been estimated that about 40 percent of all investments in that plan, (about £E 660 million), was channeled through private contractors, who in turn recycled some part of those funds through subcontracts.[6] Much the same phenomenon has occurred even in the absence of formal development plans: reconstruction of the cities of the Canal Zone after 1973 has maintained the basic symbiosis.

As a result of the Socialist Decrees of 1961, it was difficult for this stratum to find outlets for productive investment. It constituted the only discernible group that could lay claim to the title "national capitalists" (i.e., the nonexploitative bourgeoisie), but nationalized banks, low interest rates, and long-term government bonds could not attract its savings. A heavy profits tax proved a disincentive to investment in manufacturing, although not an insuperable one: investment has taken place, and also presumably, widespread tax evasion. Accumulated savings went instead into housing in urban areas, while in recent years, private investment in housing has been outstripping public outlays five to one.

Another sphere that has attracted the new bourgeoisie is the distribution networks of goods administered by the public sector, sold at subsidized prices, and always in short supply. A few examples will give some idea of the scope of the problem: cement, window frames, steel reinforcing bars, copper, copper cable, scrap iron, fertilizers, pesticides, seed, spare parts, Kastor cloth, cooking oil, sugar, flour, rice, tea, newsprint, school books, bottled gas, and kerosene. All these items are either imported by the state or manufactured by state enterprises, and in either case the state is supposed to control retail prices. Some of these goods are simply allowed to slip into private hands and are sold at market value. Public servants and private entrepreneurs make a killing, and the poor, whom the public subsidization policies are designed to serve, are the victims. So well-known is this state of affairs, that public officials who privately advocate the abolition of subsidies in the name of capitalist efficiency, have done so publicly with the disingenuous argument that they only serve to line the pockets of profiteers.

Throughout all phases of Egypt's recent economic history, highly placed public officials and their allies in the private sector, have been able to promote contracts and deals with foreign governments and investors, in return for legal and illegal rewards. Commissions, brokerage fees, and kickbacks were not uncommon when Egypt traded mostly with socialist countries, but now that it is trying to woo Western capital and aid, there is greater scope for freelance brokers and other intermediaries. In sum, the growth of the bourgeoisie accentuates certain forms of consumption which are dependent on imports from the West at the expense of imports of a directly productive nature. Egypt's drive toward socialism in the 1960s (Attaturk's phrase of "etatism" is perhaps more appropriate), with all its attendant laws and decrees aiming at a massive redistribution of income, failed, on the one hand, to raise real per capita income for the mass of Egyptians, and, on the other, to prevent the accumulation of wealth in the hands of the middle strata.

It has been frequently argued that the Nasserist regime represented the *petite* (especially rural) *bourgeoisie*, but this is too facile a judgment. There has been no coherent set of objectives to represent. There have been loose strands of an ideology, which is socialist to the extent that social harmony and the narrowing of class differences have been espoused, but it is fiercely anti-Marxist, occasionally pious Islamic, and also advocates a greater role for Egyptian private capital while seeking to contain, without destroying, the public sector. The ideal of the middle strata or the upwardly mobile *petite bourgeoisie* would be the maintenance of the public sector as the major channel for disbursing investment, while allowing the private sector to develop its symbiotic relationship with the public sector. In many respects, Nasser stood in the path of this sentiment, but Sadat has given it full rein.

FINANCING DEVELOPMENT

In the late 1950s, Nasser apparently became convinced that Egypt's economic development could be brought about without social pain. Except for the politically suspect, the better-off would not have to pay excessively nor, on the other hand, would the workers and peasants be sweated. The late president somehow hoped to combine welfare socialism and forced-draft development. At the outset of the first five year plan, this reckoning did not appear absurd.

Total gross investments in the plan were £E 1.5 million. Prior to 1960, rates of domestic investment had been low: 12–13 percent of GNP for most years. The objective of the regime was to raise this to 20 percent during the plan period mainly by *transferring* to public ownership agricultural and business assets whose earnings would accrue directly to the state and thus be available for reinvestment. This is what happened through the land reform and Socialist Decrees of 1961. The total capital of the companies nationalized at that time was £E 258 million or two-thirds of all registered capital.[7] The second approach to financing was to enlist foreign support on a massive scale. The USSR had already shown its willingness to advance credit on easy terms for large-scale infrastructural projects, such as the High Dam and the Helwan Iron and Steel Complex, while the United States began to sell large amounts of wheat to Egypt under the Food for Peace Program, paid for in local currency. Table 13 shows the proportions of domestic and foreign sources in gross investment for the decade 1960–70.

The first five-year plan was in large measure dependent upon foreign sources of financing, particularly for the importation of requisite capital goods and raw materials. Moreover, Egypt's chronic food deficit was being met through surplus U.S. wheat deliveries under PL 480, "Food for Peace," which amounted to £E 286.5 million throughout the period. At the time, this was judged as a temporary and acceptable level of dependency. This judgment evidently grew out of the belief that the plan would be both import-substituting and export-generating. At the outset, it was predicted that by the last year of the

TABLE 13

Aggregate National Investment and Sources of Financing, 1960–70

Year	Total Investment		Local Savings		Foreign Financing	
	Mill. of £E	% of NI	Mill. of £E	% of Investment	Mill. of £E	% of Investment
1960–61	225.6	15.5	210.1	93.1	15.5	6.9
1961–62	251.1	16.6	164.7	65.6	86.4	34.4
1962–63	299.6	17.8	195.6	65.3	104.3	34.7
1963–64	372.4	19.7	236.8	63.6	135.6	36.4
1964–65	381.7	17.4	307.2	80.5	74.5	19.5
1965–66	446.2	18.7	309.6	69.4	136.6	30.6
1966–67	385.6	15.7	370.7	96.1	14.9	3.9
1967–68	342.2	13.6	288.2	84.2	54.0	15.8
1968–69	318.2	12.0	341.0	107.2	−22.8	7.2
1969–70	416.1	14.2	395.0	94.9	21.1	5.1

SOURCE: Muhammad Sultan Abu Ali, "A Test of the Domar Model as a Model for Economic Growth with Reference to Egypt," l'Egypte Contemporaine 64 (352) (April 1973):104. The first five entries do not reflect the indirect aid of the Food for Peace Program nor do the entries for 1968–70 reflect the £E 110 million in annual subsidies paid Egypt by Saudi Arabia, Kuwait, and Libya following the June War.

plan, the value of imports at 1959 prices would have dropped from £E 299.2 million to £E 214.9, and that the economy would register a balance of payments surplus of £E 40 million.[8] Both predictions proved illusory. Imports in 1966 were valued in current prices at £E 405.8 million, and there was a balance of payments deficit of £E 142.2 million (see Table 14).

It is an irony of this plan that it was able to generate an admirable rate of growth in GNP (6.5 percent per year) and an unprecedented rate of capital investment (16–19 percent of NI a year), and yet it failed in the crucial respect of generating exports and hard currency earnings. (Much the same failing befell the Sudanese Five Year Plan of 1971–75.) Exports rose substantially at the beginning of the plan, but a good part of the increase was not real, having resulted from the devaluation of the Egyptian pound from $2.87 to $2.30 in June 1962.

In the final analysis, what this meant for the Nasserist regime was that it approached a major watershed in 1965–66, in which it was

TABLE 14

Commercial Balance of the ARE, 1951–76

(in £E million)

Year	Imports		Exports		Commercial Balance	
1951	283.2		205.0		−78.2	
1952	227.7		150.2		−77.5	
1957	182.6		171.6		−110.0	
1958	240.2		166.3		−73.9	
1959	222.2		170.4		−61.8	
1960	232.5		197.8		−34.7	
1961	243.8		168.9		−74.9	
1962	300.9		158.3		−142.6	
1963	398.4		226.8		−171.6	
1964	414.4		234.4		−180.0	
1965	405.8		263.1		−142.2	
1966	465.4		263.1		−202.3	
1967	344.3		246.1		−98.2	
1968	289.6		270.3		−19.3	
1969	277.3		324.0		+46.7	
1970	342.1		331.2		−10.8	
1971	540.8	(399.9)	369.7	(343.2)	−171.1	(−56.7)
1972	559.2	(390.7)	353.7	(358.7)	−205.5	(−32.0)
1973	657.6	(361.1)	396.3	(444.2)	−261.3	(+83.1)
1974	1,357.5	(920.1)	653.9	(593.3)	−703.6	(−326.8)
1975	1,691.1	(1,539.3)	653.9	(548.5)	−1,078.3	(−990.8)
1976	1,480.1	(1,489.9)	628.5	(595.4)	−851.6	(−894.5)

SOURCE: Adapted from Federation of Egyptian Industries, *Yearbook 1973* (Cairo: 1973), p. 42 up to 1971. Thereafter the entries are from "Egypt," *The Financial Times*, August 1, 1977, table p. 13, the sources of which are Central Bank of Egypt, and the IMF Balance of Payments Yearbook. The entries for the past six years may be in current prices. In parentheses one finds a rival series of entries from the Central Agency for Public Mobilization and Statistics, published in *al-Ahram al-Iqtisadi* (527) (August 1, 1977): 15. The discrepancies, all too common in Egyptian data, are not readily explained, except to note that the Central Agency figures on imports may *not* include imports that did not officially clear customs.

obliged to work out a strategy to cope with Egypt's growing external debt and to ascertain how the second five-year plan could be financed. Foreign borrowing stemmed from poor export performance (aggravated by the loss of a third of the cotton harvest to leaf-worm infestation in 1961) and was abetted by Nasser's costly commitment of Egyptian troops to the republican side in the Yemeni civil war, and by the U.S. decision in 1966 to suspend Food for Peace shipments to Egypt because of its "trouble-making" in the Yemen, the Arabian Peninsula, and the Congo.

Nasser was caught on the horns of a dilemma; he did not want, in financing the second five-year plan, to further deepen his dependence upon Soviet aid and technology. Yet he had to some extent alienated the West, and could not accept Western counsel as to the proper economic course to follow without losing face. Nonetheless, he did take some steps that indicated his desire to patch things up with the West. Ali Sabry, who was considered to be "Moscow's man" was dismissed as Prime Minister in 1965 and was replaced by the efficiency-minded, pro-American Zakaria Muhy al-Din. The government acceded to the advice of the IMF and introduced a program of stabilization and austerity in which public outlays and imports were sharply curtailed. With that, the second five-year plan was stillborn. No further attempts were made to bleed the middle classes or force savings, yet no major steps toward liberalization, i.e., a return to a fairly open market economy, were taken at that time. Indeed, the agonizing choices that Nasser then faced were put aside as the crushing defeat of the June War seemingly reduced these questions to insignificance.

The most obvious consequence of the June War was that retrenchment was no longer a matter of choice but of absolute necessity. Imports fell off precipitously (see Table 13), and the Egyptian public sector was plagued by idle capacity due to the lack of raw materials and capital goods. Overshadowing the stagnant level of production and unfavorable balance of trade were the costs of rebuilding Egypt's armed forces. These rose steadily after 1967, averaging £E 700 million per year between 1968 and 1973 and substantially exceeding £E one billion annually thereafter.

A second consequence of the June War was that Egypt had to accept the aid of its erstwhile regional enemies: Kuwait, Saudi Arabia, and Libya. At the Khartoum Conference of August 1967, it was agreed that these countries would pay Egypt an annual subsidy of £E 110 million to compensate for the country's loss of oil, tourist, and Suez

Canal revenues. In accepting the contributions of his rivals, Nasser had to curtail his regional ambitions and mask his hostility to the conservative, pro-Western, oil-rich regimes.

The problem in 1960 had been to find a way to pay for development while minimizing and diffusing the level of sacrifice Egyptian society was called upon to sustain. After 1967, the problem was to find a way to mask the sacrifices inherent in a state of "no war, no peace," massive arms expenditures, increasing inflation, and economic stagnation. What one finds is an unpatterned ebb and flow of belt-tightening and political largess. Bent Hansen felicitously characterized this as the policy of seeking "the line of least popular dissatisfaction."[9] On one side of the ledger, we find various forms of forced or obligatory savings that apply to most salaried personnel in the public and private sectors, accounting in 1973 for about 85 percent of all national savings. The peasantry was called upon throughout the 1960s to pay, in some measure, the price of industrialization. The government's means of leverage consisted of setting the prices of the main crops below world market levels, while selling inputs (fertilizers, seed, pesticides, etc.) above world market prices. The middle and upper classes were hedged in by a series of laws that limited their incomes, profits, the rents they could charge, the goods they could import, and their ability to travel abroad. No matter how poorly applied these measures may have been, they had some impact in restraining middle class consumption.

All of these measures were of the belt-tightening variety, but when the breeze seemed to carry the feeling that the tolerable limits of sacrifice were being approached, the authorities would habitually try to placate whatever constituency appeared most vocal or most dangerous. Thus, on the other side of the ledger we find the politically-motivated give-aways.

The work force has been given periodic wage increases without any discernible relation to production increases. President Sadat has sponsored a number of like measures: tax relief for various artisans and craft groups, a raise in the minimum wage from 9 to 12 pounds per month in 1974, a doubling of social security payments, the abolition of the forced savings of one day's pay per month in the public sector, and the exemption of all peasant landowners of less than 3 feddans of all taxes.

The administration of price subsidies itself is part and parcel of treading the line of least popular dissatisfaction. For foodstuffs, cloth and clothing, fertilizers, pesticides, agricultural production subsidies, public transport, medicine, petroleum products, etc., total subsidies by 1976 were well in excess of £E 600 million, whereas in 1965–66 they had cost the state no more than £E 52 million. At the levels of the mid-1970s, subsidies represented about a seventh of national income. Not only has their absolute cost grown dramatically since 1973 (despite some downturn in world wheat prices in 1976), they have also introduced a nearly impenetrable series of distortions into internal pricing and distribution of basic goods. As Sadat moved Egypt westward in quest of Western investment, his would-be benefactors stressed repeatedly the necessity to do away with the subsidies. His first major attempt to do so came in January 1977, in compliance with IMF requirements, and the result was the most severe rioting that Egypt had experienced since the Black Saturday conflagration of 1952. The government rescinded all proposed price increases.

At the risk of overdrawing our conclusion, it can be argued that the policies of least popular dissatisfaction have encouraged immediate consumption at the expense of investment, reduced the efficiency and competitiveness of the public sector, stimulated inflation and increased demand for foodstuffs, and hence intensified Egypt's need for nonproductive imports and its dependence upon external credits and import financing. The major benefit drawn from these policies has been to stifle or contain latent social conflict and thus to enhance the political stability of the regime.

THE OPENING

These policies could not be applied indefinitely so long as the country remained on a war footing with a stagnant economy and without the capital to pay for its imports and debt servicing. Sadat had to make hard decisions on the issues of war, peace, and economic strategy: issues about which Nasser had long temporized. Limited war and economic liberalization were selected by Sadat as the keys to a new era. With startling candor, Sadat emphasized the primacy of economics in all fields of policy. Speaking to Egyptian student leaders in August 1974, he said:

> I will not hide from you, my sons, that before the decision to go to war (on October 6, 1973) we had reached a very difficult economic situation, for without economic resistance there could be no military resistance. Our economic situation, six days before the battle, was so critical that I

called a meeting of the National Security Council and told them that we had reached zero. My calculation was simple. The army cost us £E 100 million a month, and all our tax receipts were worth (in one year) £E 200 million; just two months' expenses for the armed forces. There was nothing left for us but to enter the battle whatever happened. We were in a situation such that if nothing had changed before 1974 we would have been hard-put to provide a supply of bread (raghif al-aish) ... after the 6th of October War we received $500 million (from Saudi Arabia and other Arab states) which saved our economy and gave us new life.[10]

The war cleared the air, re-established Egypt's military honor, and allowed Sadat to talk volubly of the quest for peace. The atmosphere, it was hoped, would be conducive to bringing in that foreign investment that war conditions had probably scared away. To pursue this policy required a major overhaul of the rhetoric, programs, and even structure of the state-capitalist-cum-socialist system that had been erected during the 1960s. The new economic look was dubbed al-infitah al-iqtisadi or the economic open-door policy.

Internal pressures towards liberalization had been building since the balance-of-payments crisis of 1965 and the initiation of the retrenchment policies. External prodding came from bodies such as the IMF while domestically, the new bourgeoisie searched profitable investment outlets for the capital it had acquired through its dealings with the state during the first five-year plan. Public-private interest groups began to lobby for a relaxation of state controls on profits levels, sectorial investment restrictions, and the entry of foreign capital into the country.[11] Nasser resisted these pressures, but Sadat openly identified himself with them after 1973.

The first step was to enact a liberal foreign investment code (Law 43 of June 1974, later modified by Law 32 of 1977) providing for tax holidays, duty-free importation of raw materials and equipment, guarantees against nationalization, liberal rules for profits repatriation and, in 1977, the ruling that all capital transactions would take place at the incentive rate for the pound ($1 = 70 piastres, as opposed to the official rate of $1 = 39 piastres). The supposed attraction of Egypt to foreign investors is its large domestic market, relatively skilled yet low-cost work force, relatively developed infrastructure in power, ports, and communications, strategic location, and ready access to growing African, Middle Eastern, Asian, and southern European markets. Egypt's policy makers envisaged a happy alliance of Western know-how and management, Arab capital from the super-rich such as

Saudi Arabia, and Egyptian human and natural resources. Supplementing the open-door policy were the expected earnings from increased tourism, revenues from the reopened Suez Canal, the exportation of crude petroleum, and earnings repatriated by the Egyptian community abroad (in 1977 several hundred thousand Egyptians abroad remitted about $400 million in hard currency and an equivalent sum in gifts).

In the first three years of the law's application, the results were meager. By the end of 1976, only 66 projects worth a total of £E 36 million (most of it Egyptian capital) and employing 3,450 Egyptians were operating, although a much greater number of projects had been approved by the Investment Authority. Arab capital was most attracted by the rapid payoff of real estate and touristic investment, while Western firms plumped for projects that would sell to the Egyptian market (Seven-Up for instance), earn Egyptian currency, but draw on treasury reserves to repatriate earnings in hard currency. The Egyptians have resisted such investments, thereby leading to stalemated projects.

In terms of political constraints, President Sadat found himself trapped among unpalatable alternatives. Of all Egypt's economic problems, none was more pressing by 1976 than servicing the enormous external debt and thus decreasing the country's reliance upon short-term banking facilities and suppliers' credits to finance the annual import bill. The external debt stood at £E 600 million in 1965 (exclusive of military debt) and servicing amounted to only £E 15 million or only about 5 percent of revenues from exports. By 1977, the debt had grown to £E 4.8 billion (or $12.2 billion at the official rate of exchange). It has four major components: $2.1 billion in short-term obligations bearing interest rates up to 18 percent; Arab bank deposits of $2.5 billion; long-term loans of $3.4 billion; and debts to the socialist countries, mainly military, totalling $4.2 billion. Frequently, Egypt has been in arrears in servicing its commercial debt, and had Egypt faithfully met all its obligations, it would have paid out in 1976 the equivalent of 90 percent of export earnings.[12]

To break loose from this increasingly intolerable situation, Egypt had to seek massive balance of payments support and long-term credits with which to pay off its costly short-term debt. Such funding became available through the Gulf Organization for the Development of Egypt, set up in April 1976, and with capital of $2 billion subscribed by Saudi Arabia (40 percent), Kuwait (35 percent), United Arab Emirates (15 percent), and Qatar (10 percent). In winter 1976–77, it guaranteed a loan of $250 million managed by Chase Manhattan Bank, and directly loaned Egypt $1.47 billion at 5 percent interest, repayable over five years after a five year grace period. But Arab creditors share the view of the IMF that balance-of-payments support should be contingent upon major economic reforms, which will be politically distasteful. These reforms include raising internal interest rates, shifting a substantial part of foreign trade to the incentive rate for the pound (thereby raising the domestic price of imported goods by over 40 percent), eliminating unprofitable public enterprises, reducing public outlays in the recurrent budget, and, most important, whittling away at the price subsidies. We have already noted that the first attempt in this direction resulted in riots that shook the regime, and because Egypt's Arab creditors have every interest to keep Sadat in power, they had to rethink how much pressure they were willing to exert in pushing Egypt towards economic overhaul. Nonetheless, Egypt needs over $13 billion to finance its long-awaited second five-year plan (1978–82), and it is an open question as to what conditions will be imposed if and when some part of this financing is forthcoming. If the economy has not taken a major turn for the better by 1980, Egypt will be faced with a debt burden thereafter that will dwarf that which it presently bears. He is not at all clear that Egypt's tenuous peace with Israel will provide any relief for its economy.

It is understandable that Egypt's leaders do not dwell upon these negative aspects of the economy. In their view the next five years are crucial, which is indeed the case. But caution seems to have been cast to the winds in approaching this critical period. A draft of the new plan was ready in spring 1977, and it was conceived in ambitious terms. Gross Domestic Product over the plan period is to grow by 9.8 percent per year, investment outlays by 16 percent a year, and domestic savings by 23 percent a year. The proportion of local financing of the investment is to rise from 60 to 80 percent by the last year of the plan, but even then, external financing worth $13.1 billion will be required over the five years. By 1980, the debt servicing ratio to the value of exports should fall to 29 percent, which is by most standards an alarmingly high level of repayment (see Table 15). It still represents stunning progress.

In some of the preplan working papers, it was made clear that Egypt's long-term economic salvation would lie in an extraordinary growth in nonagricultural exports, especially industrial manufactures. These would have to rise from their level of £E 275 million in 1974 to £E 561 million in 1980 and to £E 6.1 billion by the year 2000; that is, a

TABLE 15

Egyptian Five-Year Plan, 1976–80, Sectoral Output Targets
(at constant 1975 prices, millions of Egyptian pounds)

Sector	Value of Product						Average Annual Growth Percentage
	Actual 1975	Actual 1976	1977	Planned 1978	1979	1980	
Agriculture	2,052	2,116	2,182	2,247	2,315	2,384	3
Industry, Mining	3,332	3,449	3,665	4,103	4,595	5,145	12
Oil and products	385	581	598	747	859	989	15
Power	90	100	123	145	171	200	17
Construction	465	416	513	589	678	780	15
Suez	42	146	200	230	264	304	15
Transport, Communic.	300	371	456	501	551	606	10
Trade, Services	2,612	2,830	3,100	3,410	3,751	4,126	10
*Total Gross Output	9,278	10,009	10,889	11,975	13,186	14,538	9
Annual Growth Rate Percentage		7.9	8.8	9.9	10.1	10.2	

SOURCE: Ministry of Planning, published by *The Financial Times* (August 1, 1977), "Survey, Egypt," p. 16.

*Due to rounding, totals may not add up.

thirtyfold expansion. Total exports, including invisibles, should grow over the same period from ca. £E 600 million in 1974 to £E 2.2 billion in 1980 and £E 12 billion in 2000. [13] This may well be the only way out, but the problem of how to achieve it has scarcely been studied. What will Egypt produce, upon whose technology will it rely, where will it find financing and where will it find markets? These questions are without ready answers, for Egypt finds itself in the company of India and other Third World "giants" who are already pursuing this strategy. Further, the most rapidly expanding markets in the Middle East region are those that can afford to buy the best quality the West has to offer.

The industrial future cannot obscure the agricultural present. In this respect, Egypt's dependency has become chronic and is likely to worsen in the coming decade.

Reliance upon outside sources of food grains has become an over-whelming fact of life in contemporary Egypt, and the hopes of self-sufficiency, still stubbornly harbored in some official circles, appear unfounded. Per capita grain production has increased almost imper-ceptibly in the past 25 years. In 1950–54 Egyptians produced, on the average, 202 kilograms per capita per year. In 1971, the figure was 221 and may have declined subsequently.[14] Per capita consumption, how-ever, is considerably higher. For instance, in 1975, it was estimated that four million tons of wheat and wheat flour (108 kgs. per capita) would be consumed in Egypt. Only about a third is produced locally while the rest is imported. Of the other grains consumed, only rice is grown in sufficient quantities to meet local needs. The result has been that the value of food imports, which stood at £E 160 million in 1967–68, ballooned to £E 700 million in 1975. Some relief has come in the form of declining world market prices for wheat coupled with U.S. wheat shipments to Egypt under PL 480 that were resumed in 1975, but that merely changes the terms—not the degree—of Egypt's vulnerability.

It is illuminating, although hazardous, to project present trends to the end of the century, but the exercise is necessary to at least establish some order of magnitude of future food needs. It has been assumed that current levels of *consumption* include, on a per capita basis, 190 kgs. of locally produced grains and 60 kgs. of imported grains for a total of 250 kgs. per annum. Without any change in that level, and assuming a population in the year 2000 of 60 million, total grain requirements would be 15 million tons. Barring any increase in acreage under cultiva-tion (although that may be unduly pessimistic) and assuming a 30 percent increase in wheat production, and a 20 percent increase in maize production, current levels of rice production, and slight in-creases in barley and millet, local grain production might reach 8.5 million tons. Egypt would be faced with a gargantuan deficit of 6.5 million tons. This would not include imports of food oils, meat, poul-try, and sugar which are growing each year. It would also omit the importation of agricultural production inputs, whose costs have risen substantially: e.g. fertilizers, pesticides, herbicides, and farm machin-ery.

It is conceivable that Egyptian agricultural exports of rice, cotton, onions, potatoes, fresh vegetables and fruits may some day be suffi-cient to pay for grain imports. This does not seem likely, however, and even if it were to occur, Egypt would nonetheless have to choose the sources of annual grain imports. At present there is little room for maneuver: the United States, Canada, Australia, Argentina, and, to a lesser extent, the EEC are the only likely providers. It is also the case that in the years to come these countries may not regularly produce large exportable surpluses. Other importers, such as India, Indonesia, the People's Republic of China, and Bangladesh, may generate aggregate demands well beyond the capacity of world markets.

To survive economically, Egypt must become a pioneer in advanced techniques of resource planning and management. In order to intensify agricultural production, Egypt will have to be at the forefront of perennial irrigation technology: an innovator in the use of chemical fertilizers, pesticides, and high-yield seeds. Unfortunately, it must explore the problems of the degradation of the Nile ecosystem, as the cumulative impact of intensive agriculture and heavy industry make themselves felt in the waters of the Nile and the northern lakes. Coping with this degradation will entail integrated planning on a level so sophisticated that it must result in a kind of cybernetic model of the functioning of the entire Nile system. Rationalized crop rotation, appropriate fertilizer imports, mechanization, agricultural supplies to existing and projected agro-industries, shipping and marketing abroad, and the planning of water and power needs so that all sectors can be serviced in an expanding economy, are but a few of the closely interrelated elements that must be built into a dynamic model. These in turn must be closely meshed with available foreign exchange, export maximization, and the satisfaction of local demand. The official credo of Egypt endorses centralized planning and decentralized execution. To date, there has been little planning at all, and what has been executed has been centrally determined. The fact that, by some estimates, 60,000 feddans of good land are annually lost to nonagricultural sprawl is but one indicator of the present system's failure to cope with the basic challenges facing the Egyptian economy.*

In the face of all this President Sadat in 1976 launched the campaign for "food security" and this has become the *leit motif* of the agricultural section of the five-year plan. What this slogan means is not that Egypt will become agriculturally self-sufficient, but rather that it will reduce its external dependency enough to free itself from being at the mercy of any one exporter or the vagaries of supply in world markets. Part of the

---

*According to former Minister of Agriculture, Mustapha al-Gabali, the *net* land loss over the period 1963–73 was 200,000 feddans. Dr. Kemal Ramzi Stino, Director of the Arab Organization for Agricultural Development, warned that Egypt's cultivated surface in the year 2000 might be no more than 4 million feddans, i.e., only about 25 percent more than in 1820 but with 20 times the population dependent upon it. His remarks are in *al-Ahram,* September 4, 1975.

strategy would entail even more ambitious reclamation schemes — despite the high cost and poor performance of those already tried — and the moving of millions of Egyptians out of the valley and into new areas of habitation (the NW coast, the southern New Valley, the Canal Zone, the Red Sea Coast) at costs no one has attempted to estimate. We come up once more against the view that with a little peace, a little capital, and a little ingenuity all will be well for Egypt's future 70 or 80 millions. Still, Egypt's planners cannot escape some hard statistical realities. In Vol. 4 of the 1978–82 Plan, a document evidently re-written numerous times since 1976, the authors argue at the beginning for the feasibility of achieving food security but essentially discard it toward the end. By 1985, they estimate that Egypt will need to import 175,000 tons of meat, 1.2 million tons of milk, nearly 3 million tons of fodder and about 4 million tons of wheat. There is no agro-technological solution on the horizon that could provide a way out. Food security appears thus a rather empty slogan, but because, politically, it must be espoused, attention is focused away from the practical steps that would be necessary to move toward *regional* food security. In either case, and for the foreseeable future, Egypt must borrow more than it earns in order to feed itself.

It is likely that a good part of the investments, aid, and credits that Egypt will receive will continue to be politically motivated; Saudi Arabia, Iran, the United States, and the USSR are all willing to invest in Egypt's subordination to their interests. For the time being, however, there is little doubt that Egypt will consolidate its reliance upon Saudi Arabia, with the consequence that its foreign policy will in most respects be aligned with that of the United States. This kind of alignment, one that Nasser found so repugnant, may be the price of development for a poor, welfare state wary of radical social change.

The most disturbing question is whether or not Egypt's Arab creditors really want to see such development take place. Leaving aside the leverage of their oil revenues and foreign exchange holdings, Saudi Arabia, Kuwait, and the lesser sheikdoms are economic and military dwarfs alongside Egypt. In fact, their regional power is in no small way derived from the fact that they have Egypt as a client. Would Saudi Arabia be willing to trade away this kind of leverage by financing real growth in the Nile Valley? If Egypt does overcome its basic economic problems in the next decade, it would be a country with over 50 million inhabitants and a large industrial base; the most powerful military establishment among the Arab states. It would, presumably, have no further need for Arab largess and could cooperate with the

Saudi monarchy or not as it saw fit. Dreams of regional hegemony, shelved since the early 1960s, might once again come to haunt Egypt's leaders, and the small states of the Arabian peninsula would be hard put to thwart them. From the point of view of their survival, the wiser policy might well be to string Egypt along, making available emergency credits to meet specific crises and to void the collapse of a moderate regime, but not enough to break the links of dependency.

7

THE SUDAN: IN QUEST OF A SURPLUS

The southern half of the Sudan is potentially one of the
richest farming regions in the world, with the soil, sunlight,
and water resources to produce enormous quantities of food
—as much, perhaps, as the entire world now produces! The
water is useless today; the headwaters of the White Nile,
blocked in their northward flow by high plateaus, spill out
over the land to form great swamps. To unlock the promise
of the southern Sudan those swamps would have to be
drained, a rural infrastructure put in place, and the nomadic
cattle raisers of the region somehow turned into sedentary
farmers. The capital costs of such an undertaking would be
as large as the promise ... Yet the potential is real and untapped, and as world food shortages persist such a reserve
cannot long be neglected. — W. DAVID HOPPER[1]

Agricultural development, both in terms of plant and animal
production, is considered the foundation of the national
economy in its entirety, and the development of all other
sectors is closely linked to agricultural expansion. — From
"Highlights of the Sudanese Six-Year Plan, 1977–83"[2]

I T IS A FACT that the only remaining virgin land tracts with great
agricultural potential are to be found in the developing countries, and
the Sudan is one of them. Hopper's statement above is merely an
indication of the unfortunate extremes to which qualified observers
occasionally go, thereby nurturing great expectations that are unlikely
to be met. Nonetheless, there is no doubt that the Sudan *could* produce
major agricultural surpluses that in turn *could* meet some part of the
region's, if not the world's, future needs.

The Sudanese population on the whole is poor, but that portion
still living at or near subsistence levels — perhaps the majority —
includes cattle herdsmen, dirt farmers, migrant laborers, and fishermen, who survive and, to some degree, thrive in traditional subsistence modes. Must they be driven from these modes, and, if so, in

174

whose or what interests? The leaders of the independent Sudanese republic have taken the view that to build a modern nation state, founded on a cohesive national identity, requires that all Sudanese reduce parochial loyalties which are sustained by subsistence patterns, and participate economically and politically in the emerging state system.

But it is not only the bureaucratic elites of Khartoum, the merchant trading groups, and the intelligentsia that wish to see the emergence of an all-embracing national market system but the Sudan's Arab neighbors as well. Poor states such as Egypt in search of reliable food supplies to meet their growing deficits, and the rich but agriculturally deprived states of the Gulf that would like to meet the soaring domestic demands for imported foodstuffs have all turned their attention to the Sudan. In 1977 alone food imports by states of the Arabian Peninsula and Gulf totalled nearly $2 billion while those of all the members of the Organization of Arab Petroleum Exporting Countries (OAPEC) exceed $5 billion.

Estimates of the Arab Fund for Social and Economic Development (AFSED) are that the Arab region will be importing one million tons of edible oils, over two million tons of sugar, 900,000 tons of meat, and 9 million tons of wheat by 1985. The same organization believes that the Sudan should be able to meet 42 percent of edible oil imports, 20 percent of sugar, and perhaps 20 percent of meat requirements by the same year. Despite periodic talk to the contrary, the Sudan is not likely to be the region's "breadbasket" as average temperatures are too high to assure maximum wheat yields. Iraq, Syria, and Morocco are more suited for extensive grain cultivation.

The regional and international mood about the Sudan is fairly bullish. The question is not so much its potential, but rather how to generate and move its surplus. Massive capital investments that the Sudan cannot muster alone will have to be solicited. In April 1974, before the UN General Assembly, the Sudanese Minister of Foreign Affairs, Mansur Khalid, set the tone for the Sudan's image of the future.

> What we are trying to do in the Sudan is to proffer this wealth of land to our friends: those who have the money, and those who have the technological know-how, with a view to financing its utilization and cultivating it with the latest possible tools man has yet discovered. In other words, a tripartite venture between us who have the land and the water; the moneyed who are willing to invest in agriculture, and our friends whose technological abilities we lack.[3]

A vast area and a scattered population are major factors in the perpetuation of subsistence patterns of rural life in the Sudan. Intensification of agricultural practices generally requires either major concentrations of population (e.g., Egypt) or capital-intensive machinery (e.g., U.S. Midwest), or both. Not only does the Sudan lack a peasantry with peasant skills, but it lacks the sheer numbers necessary for a labor-intensive strategy (see Table 16). Occasional labor shortages and chronic labor instability have been and remain major problems in the Sudan.

The sharp skew of income distribution in the Sudan, coupled with the very low average per capita income ($120 per annum in the early 1970s), also indicate a great deal about subsistence patterns and the marginal or nonparticipation of most Sudanese in the national economy. One survey, based upon 1971–72 tax receipts, states that only

TABLE 16

Population of the Sudan

Province	Population of capital	Total population	Density per km^2
Khartoum	300,000	945,000	45
Northern	10,000	1,220,000	2.6
Red Sea	123,000	407,000	5.1
Kassala	106,000	1,347,000	n.a.
Blue Nile	82,000	3,398,000	23.9
Kordofan	73,000	3,027,000	7.9
Darfur	59,000	1,825,000	3.7
Upper Nile	38,000	1,380,000	5.8
Behr el Ghazal	55,000	1,537,000	7.2
Equatoria	57,000	1,403,000	7.1
Total	903,000	16,489,000	Average: 6.6

SOURCE: Ministry of Culture and Information, *Sudan Facts and Figures* (Khartoum: November 1974), p. 12. All figures are estimates and tend to adjust the census figures returned a year earlier and which reportedly underestimated the real population. The Sudan's principal urban centers were populated as follows: Khartoum, 200,000; Omdurman, 289,000; Khartoum North, 149,000; Port Sudan, 123,000; Kassala, 106,000.

346,000 individuals were subjected to income tax in that year—that is, about 2 percent of the population—and that their assessable income totaled £S 151 million or *nearly 20 percent* of GDP.* The same survey postulated that the top 13 percent income earners controlled 63 percent of all income, while the bottom 40 percent disposed of only 14.5 percent. Thus there is a small stratum of very rich that occupy a major place in the modern economy, and this stratum tends to be overwhelmingly urban.[4] In terms of income distribution, the Sudan does not differ substantially from other Arab countries and developing states, but that observation does not detract from the fact that concentration of wealth in the hands of a few has great significance for the development of local industry, as well as for the makeup of the import package, which will tend to be overburdened with nonessential consumer items.

WATER AND LAND

Between rain and river water, the Sudan has the basic ingredients for agricultural expansion and intensification. It also has abundant agricultural land, probably more than can be serviced by existing water supplies. There has been a tendency both within and without the Sudan to exaggerate available cultivable acreage. The public relations figure is around 200 million acres, of which only about 15 million are actually farmed (see Table 17). However, while in a technical sense much of the remaining 185 million acres *could* be farmed, this is not practically feasible because of the destruction of forests, groundcover, and pasturage; poor soils; an inadequate water supply; the absence of roads; and the existence in some areas of the tsetse fly. A 1973 FAO survey of Sudanese agriculture provides a suitably cautious, but nonetheless impressive, view of Sudanese land resources.[5]

From this table we see that arable land in 1970 amounted to 25 million feddans, and that, at the expense of forest and pasturage, it could be increased to 39 million feddans by 1985. Irrigated and nonirrigated acreage could be increased by 40 and 70 percent over the same period. The low cropping intensity rates of 1970 are worth noting. They reflect the current need for annual fallow periods in the irrigated schemes, and the multiyear fallows and short growing seasons of the

*In 1976 one Sudanese pound was worth $2.87 at the official rate, but $2.50 for a considerable number of foreign commercial transactions. In 1978 the pound was devalued 20 percent.

rainfed areas. Presumably, it was the opinion of the FAO that cropping intensity can only be increased marginally for both types of agriculture by 1985.

Indeed, since this survey was completed, expansion in irrigated and nonirrigated acreage has taken place. Harvested rainfed acreage grew to 11.6 million feddans in 1974–75 and harvested irrigated land to 2.5 million feddans. Table 18 shows clearly that on five times the

TABLE 17

Present and Proposed Land Use in the Sudan
(in 1,000 feddans)

Distribution of surface	1970		1985	
	1,000 Feddans	% of total	1,000 Feddans	% of total
Total Surface Area of the Sudan	596,383	100		
Not suited for agriculture; total:	304,595	51		
of which water courses	(30,895)			
swamp, desert	(273,700)			
Suitable for agriculture total:	291,788	49		
of which: forests	(212,335)	(35.7)	(202,594)	(34.1)
permanent pasture	(54,400)	(9.1)	(49,520)	(8.3)
arable land	(25,053)	(4.2)	(39,674)	(6.6)
Arable land breakdown				
Irrigated	3,218	.54	4,438	.7
Nonirrigated	21,835	3.66	35,236	5.9
Area harvested				
Irrigated	2,348	.39	3,548	.6
Nonirrigated	8,734	1.47	15,856	2.65
Cropping intensity				
Total		44%		49%
Irrigated		73		80
Nonirrigated		40		44

SOURCE: FAO, *Perspective Study of Agricultural Development in the Sudan.*

TABLE 18

**Trends in Area and Production of Main Crops by
Type of Water Supply**

Type of Water Supply	1965–66 1969–70 (Five year average)	1972–73	1973–74	1974–75 (est.)
Total area				
1,000 feddans				
Rainfed	6,729	10,498	11,064	11,563
Irrigated	1,685	1,994	2,210	2,480
Flooded	123	149	144	181
Total	8,537	12,641	13,418	14,224
Production				
1,000 metric tons				
Rainfed	1,731	1,948	2,135	2,856
Irrigated	1,657	2,385	2,565	3,165
Flooded	46	54	45	55
Total	3,434	4,387	4,745	6,076

SOURCE: DRS, National Planning Commission, *Economic Survey 1974* (Khartoum, July 1975).

acreage, rainfed lands achieve only about two-thirds the level of production of irrigated lands. Moreover, despite increases in total production, due mainly to expanded acreage, per-feddan yields for several crops have stagnated over the past fifteen years.[6]

LAND TENURE

Land utilization and agricultural production are to some extent a function of land tenure patterns. Here, as elsewhere, the evolution of the Sudan has been in marked contrast to that of Egypt. Egypt has traditionally had a dominant rural class that monopolized the usufruct of the land nominally belonging to the state. Privatization of land in the late nineteenth century merely made hereditary the basic inequalities of the countryside. When a revolutionary regime came to power in 1952, its first act, as we have noted, was to place a ceiling on land ownership in order to destroy the land-owning class. No such land reform has been needed in the Sudan because there is no dominant land-owning or usufruct-monopolizing class. Its absence is yet another token of the general absence of agricultural surplus.

A pre-Islamic, feudalist land tenure system did exist in the Sudan based on matrilineal succession. The system was prevalent in the riverain areas of Nubia, but it was gradually transformed, as Muslims married into local matrilineages. Once property was transferred to their heirs, it was thenceforth bequeathed according to Muslim shari'a law: property is divided among male heirs according to their relation to the deceased, with half-shares for female descendants. Over the centuries, this led to excessive fragmentation of riverain holdings to the extent that today in Northern Province, where Muslims first settled, there is an average of 300 co-owners for each ten-feddan plot.[7]

Outside the riverain areas, in the rainfed zones where seasonal agriculture and animal husbandry prevail, land was utilized collectively. Each tribe controlled a large tract (or dar) which was regarded as the property of the whole tribe. Each tribesman was allotted land for his own use, and because of the vastness of the dar and the practice of shifting cultivation, untilled land was never in short supply. Attempts to subjugate the transhumant tribes and Bedouin did not greatly alter intratribal relations. Ottoman control in the nineteenth century perpetuated the system of de jure state ownership and de facto tribal-communal control. The short Mahdist period (1885–98) saw considerable upheaval in this system, in that tribes that failed to rally to the Mahdi were dispossessed, while loyalist tribes were granted new lands. But the principle of tribal management of the dar was not challenged.

Nonetheless, a titled rural class had begun to emerge in embryo under the Funj Sultanate and the Ottomans (neither of which penetrated into the far western or southern Sudan), especially in what is now the Blue Nile Province. Certain tribal chiefs were able to obtain title (wathiqa) to large tracts of land whose tribal inhabitants then became tenants tied to the land and burdened with debts. Had this new class been allowed to develop, the Sudan might have come to look more like Mamluk Egypt or early twentieth century British Iraq.

Somewhat uncharacteristically, the British in the Sudan resisted the expansion of this class. The Gezira Cotton Scheme was developed after 1920 on lands held by some of the nobility, and they were offered a small fixed rent for their holdings. On other estates, the government introduced strict control of rents and tenancy terms to protect the cultivator. Moreover, the government resisted the incursions of foreign investors, real estate speculators, and land companies, and all land transfers became subject after 1905 to the oversight and veto of provincial governors.

Traditional forms of land tenure thus survived up to and beyond Sudanese independence in 1956. The Gezira Cotton Scheme is a major exception; started by a private company and then transferred to the state, its cultivators are all tenants. This model has been replicated on the Managil extension, Guneid, and Khashm al-Girba. Since 1956, the only measure approximating a land reform came about for political reasons. After 1969, Gaafar Numeiry entered into direct conflict with the Ansar, and, borrowing a leaf from the Mahdi's book, confiscated most of the 40,000 feddans that the Mahdi family had accumulated around Kosti. The Mirghanis began preemptive sales of their own land, not knowing where Numeiry might strike next.[8]

In sum, with the exception of six million privately owned feddans, the rest of the Sudan is nominally owned by the state. This principle was confirmed in the Unregistered Land Act of 1970. Tribes have formal rights only to the usufruct of the land they cultivate. These communal lands, including pasture and forest, cover about 40 percent of the Sudan's surface, and are found in the western sand (qoz) plains, the central clay plains, and the ironstone plateau of the south.

If the Sudan is to generate a major agricultural surplus before the turn of the century, the existing patterns of land use and tenure will be rudely shaken and frequently shattered. The fact that the state can dispose of the bulk of the Sudan's land as it sees fit will facilitate various land-development schemes under Sudanese and foreign auspices. At the same time, the Sudan faces not only the challenge of capital mobilization and investment, but also that of social engineering. In a country the size of the Sudan (see Map 6), with its strong tribal, regional, and ethnic identities, centrally planned social transformation can be a very risky proposition.

TRANSPORT

Along with the shortages of capital and reliable labor, transportation constitutes a major impediment to growth in the Sudan. This is the

MAP 6

Provincial Boundaries of the Sudan, 1976

Arab Republic of Libya

Arab Republic of Egypt

Red Sea

Northern Nile

Chad

Nile

Red Sea

Nile

Northern Darfur

Khartoum

Khartoum ✱

El Gezira

Kassala

Northern Kordofan

White Nile

White Nile

Blue Nile

Southern Darfur

Southern Kordofan

Blue Nile

Ethiopia

Upper Nile

Central Africa

Behr el-Ghazal

Jonglei

El Buheyrat

Western Equatoria

Eastern Equatoria

International Boundary

Provincial Boundary

0   50   100
Miles

Zaire

Uganda

Kenya

"getting it out" side of the surplus equation. Sudan's needs in this respect are enormous and costly, yet infrastructure development seldom attracts foreign investment. As it exists today, the transport system of the largest country in Africa consists of 4,800 kilometers of railroad track, 400 kilometers of asphalted road (mostly in and around greater Khartoum and Wad Medani), 2,000 kilometers of gravel roads, and 18,000 kilometers of dry weather earthen roads. In addition, there is significant Nile steamer traffic on the 1,400 kilometer stretch between Juba and the rail crossing at Kosti. The southern capital, Juba, relies on river transport from Kosti and Malakal, subject to long delays. It may well be that Mombassa in Kenya will become the south's major port, as a few hundred kilometers of all-weather road are all that is needed to link Juba to the existing Ugandan and Kenyan grids.[9]

ECONOMIC PERFORMANCE

It is a tribute to the country's untapped bounty that there has been such bullish talk—and some bullish investment—while the Sudan remains in nearly all respects a deficit country. Cotton, groundnuts, sesame, and gum Arabic have been steady export items, although their quantity has varied considerably from year to year. Of those items which the Sudan may eventually supply to the region, it is today a net importer of two: rice and sugar. The Sudan's export potential must thus be placed firmly with a context of an overall deficit in foodstuffs. Unlike the heady prognostications of David Hopper, the IBRD has projected growing shortfalls of food grains for the Sudan through 1985. Local production of such items as wheat, maize, millet, sorghum, and rice may rise from 2.324 million tons in 1974 to 3.052 million tons in 1985. Domestic consumption, however, is likely to grow from 2.424 million tons in 1974 to 3.510 million tons in 1985. The cost of importing the 458,000 tons that constitute the deficit may be on the order of $43 million.[10]

While the bulk of the Sudanese population draws its livelihood from agriculture, its low levels of production give rise to the fact that agriculture contributes only 38 percent of GDP. Fifteen years ago, it contributed 58 percent of GDP, but other sectors, especially services and trade (with 34 percent of GDP in 1974–75), have expanded much more rapidly.[11] However, over the same period, agriculture has continued to account in value for 83 to 90 percent of all Sudanese exports.

Cotton alone generally represents 60 percent of all export earnings. Export markets for cotton have been uncertain (see Table 19). The Sudan markets about 8 percent of all cotton traded internationally, but in 1973–74, for instance, it was able to market only a third of its exportable production. In short, even in those areas where surpluses can be expected with fair regularity, they fail, in and of themselves, to assure economic success. As important as generating a surplus is the ability to maintain and market it.

Throughout the 1960s and early 1970s the gross domestic savings rate seldom exceeded 10 percent of GNP. In 1975, for instance, the rate was 9.7 percent of GNP (i.e., domestic savings were £S 130 million and GNP £S 1,325 billion), a rate which, even with heavy foreign borrowing, has failed to stimulate much real economic growth. Over the plan period, 1970–75, the average annual growth rate in GNP was 4.6

TABLE 19

Exports of Some Crops of the Sudan

(quantity in 1,000 tons, value in £S millions)

Crop Year	Cotton Q	Cotton V	Dura* Q	Dura* V	Millet Q	Millet V	Groundnuts Q	Groundnuts V	Sesame Q	Sesame V	Gum Arabic Q	Gum Arabic V
1965	117	31	112	2	5	.164	159	9	71	5	58	7.5
1966	143	35	79	1.8	6	.180	108	7	167	6	56	7
1967	172	41	.5	.02	.7	.03	109	6	75	6	52	8
1968	184	48	55	1.1	2	.056	88	5	85	6	51	8
1969	172	49	2	.4	1.2	.037	82	6	112	8	49	9
1970	232	65	2	.6	2.6	.116	69	5	82	9	47	9
1971	241	69	37	1.1	1.7	.077	121	9	86	8	43	8
1972	248	74	55	1.7	5.6	.214	114	9	86	9	44	9
1973	226	81	102	3.1	6	.214	138	13	104	11	36	8
1974	103	58	98	4.8	4	.174	130	18	108	21	31	14
1975	144	66	48	2.4	3	.133	206	34	57	12	15	7

SOURCES: DRS, *Foreign Trade Statistics*, Dept. of Statistics, for period 1965–73. For 1974–75, DRS, Statistics Section, Ministry of Agriculture, *Current Agricultural Statistics* 1 (2) (June 1976):21–3.

*Dura = sorghum.

percent. Like many other developing nations, the recurrent outlays of the central government of the Sudan have consistently outstripped the growth in public revenues and in development expenditures.

Taking the patterns of real investment and recurrent administrative expenditures in combination, one comes up with a picture of administrative parasitism in which the civil service is growing in some measure at the expense of directly productive investment. This fact, added to sluggish economic growth, poor export performance, and growing capital needs, has led to a serious balance of payments crisis and growing foreign indebtedness. In 1971, the trade deficit stood at £S 26.5 million, but after the general rise in world prices following the oil crisis of 1973, the deficit increased to £S 119 million in that year and then to £S 254 million in 1974. To cover the deficit and meet foreign exchange needs, the Sudan has resorted to heavy external borrowing. By 1976, the country's external debt reached the equivalent of $1.25 billion, with servicing requirements representing 30 percent of all export earnings.[12] Sudanese planners anticipated disbursing £S 370 million in debt servicing over the period 1977–84 which itself is 30 percent of all planned public investment for the same years. By 1978, for all its growth prospects, the Sudanese debt had mounted to £S 2 billion by official estimates. The IMF, long active in guiding the Sudan's external finances, proposed a stringent stabilization program in exchange for a $170 million standby credit and ca. $700 million in soft loans to be provided by Saudi Arabia. The program sought a substantial devaluation of the Sudanese pound, higher taxes on income, higher lending rates, curtailed investment outlays and subsidies, *and*, significantly, an end to the country's annually-negotiated trade agreement with Egypt. Initially, the Sudan complied only with the devaluation.

GROWTH STRATEGIES

From its inception, the modern economic sector of the Sudan — and here we mean that sector utilizing relatively advanced technology to produce regularly a marketable surplus — has been under the direct guidance of the state. For the entire period between the world wars, this sector consisted almost exclusively of the Gezira Scheme for cotton production. In the initial stages of this project, the British authorities of the Anglo-Egyptian Condominium allowed a prominent but minority role for private capital. The main project was inaugurated in 1925 on

300,000 feddans, upon completion of the Sennar Dam on the Blue Nile. Under the British, extentions were made in 1931 and 1937, raising the surface to 840,000 feddans. In 1950, the gross area of the project was nearly one million feddans. At that point, the private companies' concessions came to an end, and the entire scheme was handed over to a public authority known as the Sudan Gezira Board. Thus the denoument was a modern agricultural project in the public domain, based on tenant agriculture rather than private ownership. [13]

The Gezira was a small, dynamic enclave in a vast expanse of subsistence agriculture and animal husbandry that the British left largely untouched. As a colonial administration, the condominium was not interested in balanced growth nor the edification of a largely self-sufficient national economy. However, after the Second World War, as the entire British Empire came unstuck, a belated effort was made to move beyond a dualistic, enclave economy. Development programs, the forerunners of formal economic plans, were drawn up for the periods 1946–50 and 1951–5. Their impact was minimal, and when the Sudan became an independent state in 1956, its primary assets remained the Gezira Cotton Scheme and the Sudanese Railways.

It was not until the seizure of power by Lieutenant General Ibrahim Abboud in 1958 that a concerted effort was made to conceptualize a growth strategy and embody it in a national plan. Given the economic backwardness of the country and the constraints to growth, the basic objectives were inescapable and self-evident. The only path to follow was to maximize agricultural production and gradually feed surpluses either into exports or agro-industries of relatively simple technology. Inevitably, the government would have to provide the bulk of investment funds for heavy infrastructural, agricultural and industrial projects.

The Sudan's first ten-year development plan was launched in 1961–62. At that time, the country had a fairly manageable foreign debt of £S 26 million, with annual servicing amounting to about 4 percent of export earnings. Foreign exchange reserves stood at £S 61 million. The goals of the plan were to (1) increase real per capita income by 25 percent, preliminary to doubling it over 25 years; (2) diversify agricultural production and the industrial base; (3) spread the benefits of growth regionally; (4) move toward import substitution and where possible, exports; (5) improve social conditions and both general and technical education; (6) maintain a relatively stable price level; and (7) achieve an overall growth rate of 5 percent per annum (6.7 percent for the modern sector and 3.3 percent for the traditional).

Import substitution was to be served by increased production of sugar and wheat in irrigated areas, and of tea and coffee in the south. A greater proportion of the cotton crop was to be processed locally in order to reduce finished textile imports. At the same time, cotton and oil-seed exports were to increase substantially. It was expected that some 800,000 Sudanese would transfer from the traditional to the modern sector over the decade, but the plan did not seem to take into account that this transfer, which involved the traditional sector's most dynamic elements, would make it very difficult for that sector to attain its targeted growth rate. In turn, the modern sector growth rate was dependent on a high level of private investment.[14] Of a total investment of £S 565 million (i.e., £S 56 million a year) the private sector was to provide £S 228 million and the public sector, £S 327 million.

Public investment was concentrated in large hydraulic schemes and land reclamation. The Roseires Dam on the Blue Nile, for instance, was completed in 1966 at a cost of about £S 25 million. The Khashm al-Girba Dam on the Atbara and the Nubian resettlement scheme there required outlays of £S 30 million. Another £S 14 million was allocated for the 290,000-feddan Managil Extension to the Gezira Cotton Scheme.

In terms of actual performance, the first ten-year plan only partially fulfilled its objectives. Both public and private investment outlays exceeded plan forecasts, but the government was forced to deplete its own cash reserve of £S 44 million and resort to heavy bank borrowing to meet its investments. The major public investments took place before 1965 and tapered off thereafter. Then the heating up of the insurrectionary war in the south, with attendant military outlays of £S 15 million a year, began to have a negative impact upon the economy. In brief, the slower than predicted rate of growth, and the financial disequilibria that manifested themselves, led to the scrapping of the ten-year plan in 1967 and the drafting of a new plan for 1969–73. The first plan had survived the fall from power of Abboud in 1964, but the second became a dead letter after the *coup d'état* of Gaafar Numeiry in 1969.

The new regime soon came up with its own five-year plan for the period 1971–75. It differed from the previous plan in that it sought a much higher level of investments, rising from £S 38 million in the first year to £S 114 million in the last. Moreover, it held agricultural and hydraulic investments steady while increasing the investment shares of industry (sugar refineries, fiber sacking, textiles, fertilizers, cement) and transportation. But actual disbursements during the plan averaged only 50 percent of planned investments. This serious shortcoming was attributed to continued liquidity problems, slow preparation of projects, shortfalls in foreign currency in-flows, and soaring project costs due to world market inflation after 1973.[15]

In 1967, the civilian government had decided to try to attract private foreign investment and toward that end, issued the Organization and Promotion of Industrial Investment Act. Not long thereafter, the same government nationalized all trade in tea, coffee, and salt. Not only was the government incapable of handling this new responsibility, but the takeover was symbolically inappropriate for a country trying to stimulate foreign investment. Throughout the early 1970s, the problem of mixed economic signals continued.

General Numeiry's first government included prominent Marxist members and there was constant talk of various kinds of nationalizations. Nevertheless, one of the first economic measures of the new regime, in August 1963, was to de-nationalize the coffee, tea, and salt trade and to turn them over to autonomous companies with public and private shareholders. The same formula was extended to gum arabic and building materials. The Prime Minister, Babiker Awadalla, stated that it was official policy to encourage the Sudanese private sector and foreign capital to play an important role in the country's development. Then, in May 1970, the government undertook a series of nationalizations of private Sudanese businesses and foreign concerns, including six banks. This move was widely attributed to the communists in the government, but during their short-lived coup of July 1971, the communists condemned Numeiry for carrying out the nationalizations without consultation and for placing corrupt, bourgeois elements in charge of the nationalized enterprises. It became clear that these concerns were poorly run, and, in yet another flip-flop, most of the Sudanese assets were returned to their owners and the owners of foreign assets were compensated for the takeover.[16] At the same time, Soviet Gosplan advisers were removed from the Planning Commission, although it is not clear if any major changes were made in the plan itself. Since 1971, the Sudan has moved fairly resolutely toward a more liberal economic system.

After the inconclusive experience of the 1970–75 plan, the Sudan has launched itself into the first of three six-year plans destined to carry the country to the turn of the century. The plan for 1977–83 puts agricultural growth at the heart of the investment program. Concomitant with this priority are the goals of rectifying the balance of payments picture and promoting import substitution. By the end of the plan, total investments are to rise to 23 percent of GNP. The private sector is expected to nearly match public sector outlays of £S 1.1 billion; 55 percent of public and half of private investments are to come from external financing for a total of £S 1.5 billion (see Table 20).

TABLE 20

Sudanese Six-Year Plan Investment Outlays
(£S millions)

Sector	Outlays for on-going projects	% of total	Outlays for new projects	% of total
Agriculture/Irrigation	80	19	540	33
Industry/Mines	155	37	390	24
Transp./Communic.	123	30	468	28
Soc. Serv./Admin.	60	14	246	15
Total	418	100	1,644	100

SOURCE: Democratic Republic of the Sudan, Ministry of Finance, Planning, and National Economy, *Initial Highlights of the Six-Year Plan* (Khartoum: July 1976). In each sector save social services and administration, private investment is forecast to exceed public.

TRADE, AID, AND INVESTMENT

The evolution in the Sudan's growth strategy has been similar to several of its Arab and African neighbors. After a brief and partially unsuccessful application of heavily *étatiste* policies, tinged with socialism, the country found itself with improved infrastructure, but also with an insufficient growth rate, a sprawling public bureaucracy, and a sizable foreign debt. Future growth would continue to be dependent upon massive injections of foreign exchange to cover imports, but the export sector had clearly demonstrated that it could not meet these needs. The Sudan's foreign exchange conundrum has meshed with the need of the Arab states of the Arabian peninsula to find high-return investments for their surplus oil earnings, and a source of agricultural produce for their own burgeoning home consumption.

This has been translated into a considerable influx of Arab capital into the Sudan since 1970; thus the oft-sought but seldom-applied formula of "triangulation," bringing together Arab capital, Western know-how, and Middle Eastern human and natural resources, may have its first real test in the Sudan.

Although state-to-state aid grew rapidly between the Arab oil-rich and the Sudan in the last decade, the *fer de lance* of the investment effort has been constituted by a handful of Arab (and one Western) entrepreneurs. Unquestionably, the key element in this thrust has been one man, Dr. Khalil Osman, and only secondarily a company, Gulf International. Osman, who is Sudanese, made his fortune in Kuwait. Osman was able to get financing to start a shrimping and freezing business in the Gulf that eventually became Gulf Fisheries, which now owns the world's largest shrimping fleet. From there, Osman spread far and wide — into textiles, paint manufacturing, hotels, drugs, matches — putting together 45 companies scattered from New Guinea and Nigeria to the Bahamas and California. The conglomerate is called Gulf International (GI), and is a private partnership, owned 75 percent by the family of Kuwait's Foreign Minister, Sheikh Sabah al-Ahmad al-Jabir, and 25 percent by Osman.

As a Sudanese, Osman was willing to begin forging ahead in his native country even when there was considerable opposition to foreign investment. He established a good relationship with President Numeiry and, by 1975, had ten companies worth about £S 25 million in full swing. With the Johns Manville Corporation, the GI will undertake a $100 million asbestos mining and production project. However, the Sudan Textile Company at Khartoum alone accounts for 80 percent of GI's investments in the Sudan. This is one of the largest composite textile mills in the Middle East and Africa.

The major Saudi Arabian actor in the Sudan is Tri-Ad Natural Resources, Incorporated. This is an affiliate of Tri-Ad, Incorporated, the conglomerate run by one of the Arab World's most flamboyant moguls, Adnan Khoshoggi. Khoshoggi put together a 200 million Eurodollar loan to the Sudan, the largest ever made to a developing country, and he managed to obtain a Saudi Monetary Authority guarantee for it, after having arranged a meeting between the late King Faisal and President Numeiry. More recently, Tri-Ad Natural Resources won approval for a one-million feddan (1 feddan equals 1.038 acres) cattle breeding and finishing project in the Damazin area, worth nearly $100 million. The project will be managed by the Arizona Land and Cattle Company in which Tri-Ad is the single largest shareholder.

Without doubt, the most ambitious and crucial of all foreign investment ventures in the Sudan is the Kenana Sugar Scheme, put together primarily by Lonrho Ltd. of London. As this project will test the Sudan's potential for large-scale cane cultivation, sugar refining, and export, much of the country's future growth strategy may come to rest on its success or failure. The impetus behind the project has been largely dependent upon the personal commitment of Lonrho's managing director, R. W. "Tiny" Rowland. He may be one of the last great Western entrepreneurs, and his individual style has made him attractive to the new Arab money men. His career, however, has been marked by considerable controversy. Some of it has stemmed from the fact that Kuwaitis, in fact Gulf Fisheries, own 22 percent of all Lonrho's stock, and there are three Arabs on the board of directors: Sheikh Nasser Sabah al-Ahmad of Kuwait, Khalil Osman, and Muhammad al-Fayed of the United Arab Emirates. This Arab connection was considered unsavory, and Rowland's determination to move into the Sudan on a large scale, unwise. A major row in the board of directors in 1973 caused the departure of several of its members. It also put the company in the public view. Prime Minister Edward Heath referred to it as the "unacceptable face of capitalism" and official investigations into its operations were initiated by the Department of Trade and Industry.

Rowland's move into the Sudan was typically daring and grandiose. It began in the summer of 1970, shortly after the Sudan had carried out a sweeping series of nationalizations. Rowland visited the Sudan to look over the possibilities of sugar cane cultivation and sugar refining, in which Lonrho has great expertise. He liked what he saw and, in a private meeting with President Numeiry (arranged one must assume by Khalil Osman), Rowland made some sweeping proposals. "You know," said Rowland, "that Cuba is the foremost exporter of sugar in the world. But your country does not produce enough for its own local consumption. What would you think if I told you that the Sudan has the potential, if it is developed, to take over first place from Cuba?" President Numeiry agreed to allow Rowland to put together a project.[17] It took six years to do, and 72 personal trips to the Sudan by Rowland, but, by the end of 1975, the Kenana Sugar Scheme was breaking ground.

The project consists of the initial development of 80,000 feddans of cane 19 kilometers east of Rabak on the White Nile, and the construction of one of the largest sugar refineries in the world to produce 300,000 tons by 1980. After 1980, the project may be expanded to cover

300,000 feddans and to refine one million tons of sugar. The initial phase alone is worth over $350 million, and the main canal, at $40 million, is nearly as much as the project's initial subscribed capital.

The subscribers are a significant group. The Sudanese public share in the project was at first 51 percent, although a good bit of that was loaned by Saudi Arabia. Lonrho itself held 12 percent plus the management contract, the Arab Investment Corporation (headquartered in Riyadh) has 17 percent, Gulf International 5, Nisso-Iwai 5, and the Sudan Development Corporation 10. Between the SDC and the Sudanese government, the local share amounted to 61 percent. The initial subscription was hardly adequate to cover the real needs of the project. More Kuwaiti capital was sought, apparently from the KFTCIC. As this became available, it was learned that cost over-runs on the project had grown to the point that estimates for outlays on the first phase had soared to $500 million. The new Kuwaiti investors demanded that Lonrho be stripped of its management contract, and, pending final litigation, were successful in doing so. Many interests, Sudanese and other, were damaged in what may have been a Kuwaiti in-house fight.

It is hardly likely that the Sudan will move into the same league with Cuba in terms of exports (over 4 million tons a year) or even production. Nor can the Sudan be assured of steady world market prices for its sugar. The euphoria of January–November 1974, in which these prices rose from US $.16 to $.65 per pound were shortlived, as they subsequently tumbled down to their former levels. Moreover, beet sugar and high-fructose corn syrup could become serious rivals to cane sugar. The fact is, however, that today, nearly all the 20 million tons of sugar traded annually is cane sugar, and world demand has been growing between 2 and 4 percent per year. A. D. Little and others therefore expect world prices of $.18–.22 per pound by the early 1980s.[18]

Kenana will be the first Sudanese project to get into the export market and may well dominate it if production grows to one million tons in the 1980s. Guneid, Khashm al-Girba, and newer state projects at Hajar Assalaya (35,000 feddans) and Sennar (32,000 feddans) will supply the domestic market, whose needs are expected to grow to 600,000 tons per year by 1985. Farther down the road are projects at Melut (45,000 feddans near Malakal), Mangalla (28,000 feddans near Juba), Renk-Gelhak (400,000 feddans in Upper Nile Province), and Seteit (60,000 feddans near Khashm al-Girba).[19]

THE AFSED PLAN

The operations of Gulf International and Lonrho are large-scale by almost any measure. But potentially the biggest growth project is that being worked out by the Arab Fund for Social and Economic Development (AFSED). This Fund is subscribed to through public commitments of most members of the Arab League of States, but in fact the biggest subscribers are Kuwait and Saudi Arabia.

In September 1974, AFSED dispatched a team of agricultural experts to the Sudan to carry out a thorough survey of the country's potential. After four months in the field, the AFSED team drafted a comprehensive ten-year development program with specific suggestions on the levels, sources, and administration of funding (see Table 21). The initial proposals have undergone a number of permutations,

TABLE 21

AFSED Projections on Production Increases in
Selected Crops and Commodities

	1970		1980	
	Exports 1000 tons	Value £S mill	Exports 1000 tons	Value £S mill
Commodity				
Oil seeds	266	15	772*	60
Vegetable oil	9	1	185	19
Oil cake	237	5	530	11
Cotton fiber	232	65	260	79
Meat & fish	20	5	173†	52
Sugar	—	—	405	24
Gum arabic	48	9	100	20
Grains	—	—	630‡	15
Fruits & vegetables	—	—	205	14
Others	—	—	—	7

SOURCE: AFSED *Basic Program for Agricultural Development in the Sudan.*
    *500,000 tons groundnuts, 200,000 tons sesame, 72,000 tons sunflower seeds
    †12,000 tons poultry, 10,000 tons fish, 151,000 tons beef and mutton
    ‡130,000 tons wheat and 500,000 tons white sorghum

but AFSED officials insist that the original targets have not been altered. These were, in brief, to invest over the period 1976–85 the equivalent of £S 2.2 billion (ca. $5.5 billion). In essence, however, AFSED's initial efforts will center on the funding of the current six-year plan, the agricultural component of which is largely inspired by the Fund's recommendations. In this respect, AFSED is expected to mobilize about £S 510 million in foreign exchange, or nearly half of all the foreign exchange funding now under negotiation for the plan period. Out of the hundred projects examined, AFSED has singled out 17 in the six-year period for which it will be directly responsible.* In these and others, the Sudanese government will have the option of taking at least a 50 percent interest.

The Fund's expectations are appropriately optimistic. They forecast crop production increases over the next decade of 1,100 percent for rice, 350 percent for sugar, and 105 percent for wheat. Such increases may be possible, but are not likely. Over the next 20 years, the Fund envisions expansion of irrigated acreage to 9 million feddans and rainfed acreage to 22 million. Again, this may be possible, but in terms of water alone (a question to which Chapter 8 is entirely devoted), supplies may not be adequate to meet this expansion.

Of equal significance is the administrative instrument that AFSED will use to disburse its investments. In January 1977, the Sudanese parliament approved the establishment in Khartoum of the Arab Authority for Agricultural Investment and Development (AAAID) which had been proposed by the meeting of Arab finance ministers at Rabat in April 1976. The formula is similar to, and indeed, preceded, the Gulf Organization for the Development of Egypt, with the difference that the AAAID is aimed at all Arab states. In either case, the invasion of national economic sovereignty is only lightly veiled. The AAAID will have a non-Sudanese director and a Sudanese deputy. It would take a direct financial interest in the projects it promotes while enjoying quasi-extraterritorial status, guarantees against nationalization, and would be allowed to repatriate earnings free of taxes. The Authority will be in the form of a corporation, a relative majority of whose shares will be held by the Gulf states and Saudi Arabia. A 10 percent participa-

*Six projects are in crop production: two for mechanized cultivation of sorghum, sesame, and groundnuts; another two for sugar in the south and the east (presumably Melut and Seteit); another for southern coffee, tea, and rice cultivation; and the last for irrigated truck farming. There are five animal production schemes concentrated in the Damazin area: a poultry scheme, concentrated fodder, and agro-industries in textiles, glucose, and cement.

tion has been sold to the Sudanese goverment in Sudanese currency, and the rest offered to other Arab governments. Like the GODE, the Authority is a privileged multi-national agency that, through its ability to mobilize desperately needed foreign exchange, is in a position to determine basic economic options. In Egypt, GODE's objective may be to assure political stability, while in the Sudan, the AAAID will seek to make a sound financial return on actual investments. Neither Egypt nor the Sudan, despite considerable misgivings, could afford to reject this kind of succor.[20]

THE NORTHEAST GROWTH AREA

In their original proposal, AFSED indicated that 60 percent of all program investment would go to the north and east of the country, 24 percent to the west, and 16 percent to the south. If these priorities are followed it will serve to reinforce existing regional imbalances, but in orthodox economic terms, these regional priorities make sense.

The northeast has the greatest potential for growth of any region of the Sudan (see Map 7). This is so for two principal reasons. The first consists of the fine heavy clay soils deposited by the Blue Nile, the Atbara, and their tributaries (the Dinder, Rahad, Seteit, and Gash), all originating in the Ethiopian Highlands. These soils are highly suitable for irrigation, especially in the triangle south of Khartoum formed by the junction of the White and Blue Niles, both of which are tapped for irrigation water. No other region of the Sudan can boast this combination of good soils and available water. The second factor is the relative proximity of this region to the political/administrative hub of the country at Khartoum and its only seaport at Port Sudan on the Red Sea. While still grossly inadequate, the road and railroad links in this area are the best in all the Sudan, and a new road under construction between Khartoum and Port Sudan will loop southward to serve the entire region. Taken together, these two factors endow the northeast with a marked advantage in producing a surplus and in getting it out. In all probability, this comparative edge will be accentuated over the next decade.

In terms of existing projects, the lead is already considerable. The Gezira-Managil Cotton Scheme, with over one million feddans, produces 75 percent of the Sudan's long-staple cotton, 12 percent of its sorghum, and 15 percent of its groundnuts. Average yields for all these

MAP 7

Northeast Growth Area

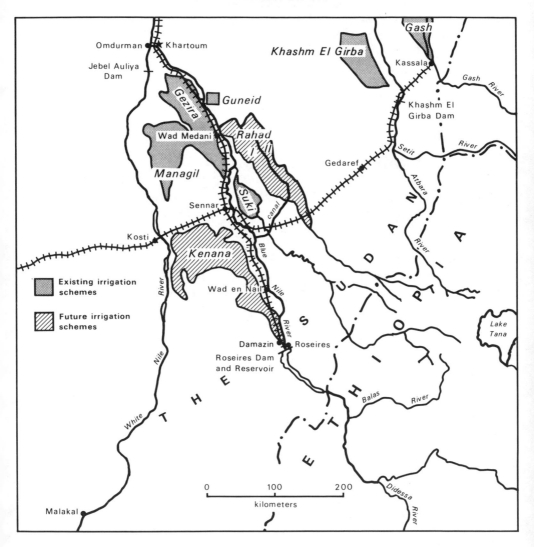

crops are four and five times those of the rainfed areas. All the Sudan's
wheat is grown on irrigated land with 75 percent of total production
coming from Gezira-Managil. Fifty percent of the Sudan's rice acreage
is at Gezira.

The next biggest project after Gezira-Managil is that of Khashm al-Girba on the Atbara River. This project originated in the need to resettle 25,000 Nubians who were to be displaced by the rising waters of the lake forming behind the High Aswan Dam. The Khashm al-Girba Dam was built in the mid-60s to irrigate 360,000 feddans downstream of the barrage.

In the future, more irrigation schemes will be concentrated in the northeast. We have already given sufficient consideration to Kenana, Assalaya, and Sennar. These could add another 400,000 feddans to the Sudan's irrigated acreage. Then, if a barrage is built on the Seteit River near its junction with the Atbara, a vast project of some 600,000 feddans near Khashm al-Girba could become reality. In addition, work is already well under way on Phase I of the Rahad Scheme which will bring 300,000 feddans under irrigated cultivation. The project will be based on cotton and groundnut cultivation and will accommodate 14,000 tenants and 90,000 seasonal laborers. Raising the height of the Roseires Dam by ten meters would double the capacity of its reservoir and thereby permit Phase II of the Rahad scheme, i.e., an extension of 800,000 feddans. It would also provide water for a southern extension of Kenana. When all these projects are completed, there will be a nearly solid block of large irrigation schemes running in an arc from Kenana in the southwest through Gezira, the old Suki pump irrigation scheme, and Rahad in the center to Khashm al-Girba, Seteit, and the flood irrigation areas at Gash and Tokar in the northeast.

The northeast will be favored in rainfed agriculture as much as in irrigated agriculture, and for the same reason—soils, and proximity to Port Sudan. The rainfall zone of 400–800 millimeters cuts a swath across central Sudan. At its northeastern end, it covers most of Kenana, the Damazin area to the south of Roseires, and the Gedaref area between the Rahad and Atbara Rivers. Thus there is a broad belt of deep cracking, self-mulching clay soils running along the southern and eastern fringes of the irrigated heartland, in which mechanized rainfed agriculture and modern animal husbandry will be developed. Both kinds of projects will be extended into the western Sudan in southern Darfur and southern Kordofan, but while these areas have equivalent rainfall, they do not have the same quality soils as the lands to the east.

Mechanized rainfed agriculture in the Sudan is particularly risk-laden. Rains can and will fail. Private entrepreneurs may continue to mine the soil. A combination of successive years of low rainfall and millions of plowed acres could create a Sudanese dust bowl or a variant of the Soviet Union's central Asian steppes debacle of the 1960s. The west, where the soils are poorer and lighter and the rains less predictable, could be particularly victimized. Even short of such calamities, the risks of soil depletion are great. The excellent soils of the northeast savannah could be depleted in a decade and lost to cultivation for an incalculable period of time. With careful soil management, this need not occur, but whether a failure or a success, the focal point of mechanized farming will remain the northeast.

THE FAR WEST

The far west of the Sudan, Darfur, and Kordofan provinces, consists of 850,000 km² of savannah grazing lands. The northern reaches fall in the 75–400 mm rain isoyet and the southern areas in the 400–800 mm isoyet. There are pockets of higher rainfall in the Nuba mountains of Kordofan and at Jebel Marra between al-Fasher and Nyala. Predictably, these latter zones are also the only places in the far west where purely sedentary agriculture is practiced—mainly by the Negroid Nuba and Fur peoples. In the rest of this area, transhumant tribes of the Beggara group, who provided the Mahdi with the bulk of his troops, move their cattle herds on long north-south treks, following the rains. Further north are camel herdsmen who ply the caravan routes to Libya, Chad, and Egypt.

The challenge of this region is not so much to generate prosperity as to make the habitation of it viable for existing and future populations. This is a challenge of considerable magnitude, and the steady eastward stream of western migrants would indicate that it has not yet been met. Survival and subsistence in the west depends on maintaining rather fine ecological balances. Under the best of circumstances, any surplus would be difficult to obtain, and to date it has been of two kinds: cattle and groundnuts. Food grains, mainly millet, were seldom in excess of local demand. But the best of circumstances no longer prevail, for rapid population growth and the Sahelian drought have upset the ecological balance. Rainfall in the period 1965–72 was 10 percent less than the average for the preceding 30 years, and the 400–800 mm isoyet shifted 75 kilometers southward. This put severe pressure on the central rainy season grazing lands, which are also where the tribes maintain permanent quarters and their area of cultivation. At the same time, the population had grown from 3.1 million in

1956 to over 5 million by 1975. In lockstep with population growth has been the growth of the region's herds. The net result of inadequate rainfall and the growth of human and animal populations has been a marked deterioration in soil quality through overcultivation, and in pasturage through overgrazing. Even if the rains come back, as now seems the case, they can do little to restore the pasturage and soil balance.

"What this can do to agriculture is dramatically illustrated in Kordofan province, one of the worst affected areas. There, in 1973, the crop area needed for a given quantity of groundnuts was almost five times more than in 1961. In that year, the sesame crop area was 47,040 hectares; in 1973, it was 326,760 hectares. Rainfall in both years was approximately the same, but the total crop went down from 38,000 metric tons in 1961 to 14,722 tons in 1973. In terms of average yield per hectare, this went from .8 tons down to .04 tons."[21]

There are two facets to the strategies currently being considered to deal with these problems. The first is to improve traditional subsistence agriculture, animal husbandry, and patterns of transhumancy. Some experts feel that if this could be done, it would in itself constitute quite an achievement. The second facet is to skim a surplus from the cattle herds and to modernize the pockets of traditional agriculture with the greatest promise.

For this approach to work, there would have to be (1) a major reduction — perhaps as much as 50 percent — in current herd sizes, which would necessitate (2) a major and continual shift of migratory herdsmen to sedentary agriculture, so that they may survive with fewer animals, and (3) careful supervision of soil use and farming practices to minimize soil depletion. At present there is little incentive for herdsmen to shift to sedentary agriculture. The only possible one would be the promise of a cash income, but many of the tribesmen remain stubbornly indifferent to such appeals. In this respect, as well as in that of private property, their capitalist instincts would have to be cultivated. Moreover, those who do enter the cash economy must be guided in the use of earnings.

Western underdevelopment may reinforce the regional dualism already prevailing. As one body of foreign experts put it:

> Steadily decreasing returns to land and labor in the traditional sector will stimulate an increase in the supply of seasonal migrants which will serve to keep wages down. On the other hand, enterprises in the modern sector employing the seasonal migrants become increasingly adjusted to

cheap labor. As time passes this trend towards dualism becomes almost impossible to reverse because all the parties concerned become attached to its maintenance. The pattern will be all the more difficult to break if the modern sector produces largely for export, rather than for domestic markets, since the expansion of the modern sector would then not depend on the expansion of domestic markets.[22]

In this situation, already very nearly a reality, the far west would be an auxiliary prop of northeastern modernization.

THE DEEP SOUTH

The three southernmost provinces of the Sudan have been only tenuously—and most often forcibly—attached to the rest of the country. Reciprocal resentment and antipathy toward Muslim, putatively Arab northerners, and non-Muslim Negroid southerners, erupted into a civil war that lasted 17 years (1955–72) and devastated the already primitive southern economy. Since the 1972 Addis Ababa accord, and the granting of regional autonomy to the south, the challenge to that region has not been to generate a surplus, but to achieve subsistence— the literal survival of hundreds of thousands of southerners being at stake.

The population of the south cannot yet be accurately known, as over 300,000 of its people sought refuge across its borders between 1965 and 1972. Most have returned, perhaps with additional dependents. Hundreds of thousands more took to the bush during the "troubles," leaving the towns to northern soldiery. Agriculture was disrupted; wild game reserves decimated; villages, schools, and clinics left abandoned and unstaffed. Between 1961 and 1969, in Equatoria Province alone, cultivated acreage dropped from 250,000 to 20,000 feddans. No one knows for sure how many tens of thousands may have died from starvation, disease, or the fighting itself. In light of this, it is difficult to accept the most recent population *estimate* (1970–71) for the three provinces of 4.3 million when, in 1954, the census gave a total of 2.4 million. This would imply a 4 percent annual growth rate over the intervening 17 years. Either the 1954 figure is an underestimate, or the 1970–71 figure an overestimate, but we may assume that the population in 1976 is around four million.

About 90 percent of the inhabitants are considered to be pastoralists, combining animal husbandry with subsistence agriculture. The major tribes are the Dinka, Nuer, Shilluk, and Toposa, who use the central flood plain for animal pasture, and the more sedentary Madi, Latuka, Zande, Baria, and Lukoya groups, living on higher ground to the south. The cattle population of the south is not accurately known but may be over four million head. The southern tribes cherish their beasts as status symbols even more than the westerners and offtake rates are correspondingly low—only about 33,000 are slaughtered each year. The tribes move their herds eastward and upward during the rainy season (April–November) when all pasture is under water in the flood plain (i.e., in the 8,000 km² Sudd swamp area), and westward and downward to take advantage of pasturage *(toiches)* left exposed by retreating flood waters, during the dry season (November—March). These tribes, and others not involved in animal husbandry, practice shifting cultivation and bush fallows; in 1961 about 660,000 feddans in the south were cultivated, probably an all-time record. The principal crops are sorghum, millet, maize, and groundnuts.

In the central and northern flood plain region, the soils are alluvial cracking clays, of good quality, but they have minimal agricultural use as they are flooded during the rainy season and inadequately watered during the dry. The construction of the Jonglei Canal could alter this situation. South of the flood plain, on higher ground, are acidic, lateritic soils of poorer quality than the alluvial clays but more intensively cultivated during the rainy season. There are pockets of alluvial soils along water courses as at Yei. One vast region in southeast Equatoria and Behr el-Ghazal provinces is known as the ironstone plateau. Its soils are lateritic, but the area is heavily infested with the tsetse fly (carriers of trypanosomiasis), which has made it impossible to exploit the area's considerable grazing potential, and its dependent shifting cultivation.[23]

It was evident after 1972 that the south would be dependent for some time on infusions of capital from the north to cover its recurrent budget and its investment and foreign exchange needs. In brief, while local autonomy is theroretically very extensive, because the north holds the purse strings, effective autonomy is considerably reduced.

The project which will undoubtedly have the greatest impact upon the South as a whole is the Jonglei Canal and regional development proposal. As we have seen, peace in the south after 1972, the completion of the Aswan High Dam, and both countries' growing water needs, impelled Egypt and the Sudan to finalize plans for a project less detrimental to the lifestyles of the local populations. As currently formulated, the project offers many advantages over the old. It will save about 3.9 billion m³ per year as measured at Aswan (4.6 billion m³ at Malakal), divided evenly between Egypt and the Sudan. The additional water will be vital for future sugar projects, including Renk-Gelhak and Melut in the south. There will be no tampering with the normal seasonal variations in river flow because Egypt now has the capacity to store its share over-year in Lake Nasser. Thus, only about 19 percent of the flood plain pasturage will be adversely affected by the canal. The major gains for the south reside in the possibility of irrigating some 200,000 acres of the alluvial clay soils lying west of the canal during the dry season. This acreage, if the canal is widened one day, could be increased to three million feddans. Second, the drainage effect of the canal will be beneficial to the peoples between the Behr el-Jebel and Behr el-Zeraf where land has been permanently inundated for over 12 years. Third, the canal and parallel road will allow much more rapid transit of people and goods between Juba and Malakal, a process that now takes weeks on meandering Nile steamers. The problem of vital supplies from the north, especially petrol, has been a major stumbling block on the path to southern recovery.

The south is still economically prostrate and therefore economically dependent on northern finance, expertise, and investment capital. It will be a long time before southern regional autonomy will have sound economic underpinnings. To get from here to there will require great political tact on the part of both the financier and the financee.

Over half the population of the Sudan lives in the far west and the deep south, but together they probably do not contribute more than a fifth of the country's GDP. The only truly modern sector of the economy is in the northeast, where natural resources, transportation links, government services, and port facilities are readily available. Consequently, development capital, especially commercial investment from Arab sources, will be drawn to this region and thereby reinforce its predominance. Relatively little foreign investment will go to the south and west, and what does will be tied to specific projects with high economic returns. These may, over the long term, have some spread effect, but in the short term they will not lead to balanced regional growth. Thus marginal populations will continue to abandon their overtaxed land and to throw themselves into the northeastern labor market which, because of foreign funding, will increasingly be export rather than domestic market-oriented. The government in Khartoum can try to overcome the regional development gap by diverting large amounts of local funding to the west and the south—and is in fact doing just that. But regional, as much as national, development will depend on heavy doses of foreign exchange, and Khartoum does not have and will not have any to spare for some time. One should note, however, that the AAAID has earmarked the equivalent of £S 50 million in foreign exchange for the first phase of Jonglei.

The west and the south will thus continue to remain in a quasi-colonial relationship to the northeast, supplying it at bargain prices with its modest surpluses and abundant labor. Such imbalances may in fact represent a rational evolution of the internal distribution of re-sources and factors of production. But in political terms, they are the stuff of resentment and political instability. Unrest may have to be bought off at the expense of a more economically coherent allocation of investment funds. Optimizing the costs of political expediency and the demands of rapid economic growth is the fundamental conundrum with which the northeast establishment must deal.

POLITICAL CONSTRAINTS

It probably comes as no surprise that the regional economic imbalances described above are nicely mirrored in the dynamics of domestic Sudanese politics. The south, threatened culturally and neglected economically by the North, has sought to secede. The west, deeply impregnated with militant Islam, and feeling itself both neglected by and underrepresented in Khartoum, has periodically attempted to seize power in the capital. The northwest military, bureaucratic, and commercial establishment deals with these forces through patronage or coercion, all the while feathering its own nest.

Southern dissidence, or its threat, has always been the Achilles heel of political stability in the independent Sudan. In part, the col-lapse of General Abboud's regime and the restoration of civilian, parliamentary rule was triggered by heavy rioting among Khartoum's southern population in October 1964. Elections in 1965 returned the Umma Party to power, with Muhammad Ahmad Mahgoub as PM, and the new government adopted, as had Abboud, a hard-line repressive policy toward southern demands. All this produced was a severe drain on state resources and a growing realization that a solution to the southern problem had to be found.

On May 25, 1969, the military, led by Major-General Gaafar al-Numeiry, toppled Mahgoub's government and established a Revolutionary Command Council to govern the country. Numeiry tried to apply the Nasserist formula, by which individuals, civilian and military, of all political colors were brought into the government, while at the same time, any further activities of the formal political organizations from which they came were rendered illegal. All political activity was to be monopolized by the Sudanese Socialist Union, to which adult Sudanese could belong on an individual basis. In policy terms this meant the dissolution of all political parties, although the Communist Party was tacitly tolerated. A more enlightened approach to the southern question was promised, and some attempt was made to curb the conservative religious forces, mainly through secularization of the educational system. Still, his regime rested on a coalition of what passes in the Sudan for right and left, and it was the breakup of that coalition that nearly cost Numeiry his power. It was also the impossibility of holding the coalition together that made a settlement in the south all the more imperative.

The first real confrontation came from the right, whose parties had been dissolved. Al-Hadi al-Mahdi, leader of the Ansar, calmly and defiantly withdrew with his followers and armed guard to Aba Island, where the Mahdist movement began. The regime, with Communist support, raised the gauntlet, and, in April 1970, launched a military assault upon the island. Many of the Ansar were killed and the rest scattered or arrested. Al-Hadi al-Mahdi was killed attempting to flee to Ethiopia. His successor as head of the Ansar, Sadiq-al-Mahdi, went into exile.

On the strength of a tactical alliance with the left, Numeiry accepted the risk of alienating the right. This left him and the other nationalist officers in an exposed position, for they had no political organization of their own worth the name to counter the organizational strength of the Marxists. Marxist power had to be cut down to size quickly, and the first move was to attack the brilliant veteran Abdelkhaleq Mahgoub, Secretary-General of the Communist Party. In November 1970, he was arrested and three leftist ministers dropped from the Cabinet. In February 1971, Numeiry went further and declared, as Le Monde reported on July 21, that his objective was "to crush and destroy the Sudanese Communist Party." He was professedly angered by the communists' opposition to the Sudan's adherence to the federation with Egypt and Libya.

On July 19, 1971, Hashim al-Atta, a communist officer and former minister, led a military coup d'état, put Numeiry under arrest, and proclaimed a new regime, to be founded on principles of scientific socialism. The revolution was to be built around a national democratic front allying workers, soldiers, peasants, intellectuals, and national capitalists (precisely the terminology employed since 1962 by the Arab Socialist Union in Egypt). It was hinted that the southern provinces would be granted autonomy and the incumbent Marxist Minister of Southern Affairs, Joseph Garang, would be retained in the new government. No mention was made of the Sudan's adherence to the Federation of Arab Republics.[24]

Numeiry had not been killed, and with the support of loyal army units, Sudanese troops airlifted by the Egyptians from the canal zone, and a Libyan hi-jacking of a BOAC airliner carrying exiled Sudanese Communists officers back to Khartoum, Numeiry managed to organize a counter-coup. In the subsequent purge, Numeiry wiped out nearly all the Marxist leaders in the Communist party, the labor unions, and the armed forces.

One of the victims was the erstwhile minister for Southern Affairs, Joseph Garang, but despite this ill omen, Numeiry knew he would have to seek an accommodation in the south. The fighting there had sputtered on since 1955 but became particularly intense between 1963 and 1971. Southern resistance groups had fragmented into a number of personalized factions, and it was not until 1971 that Joseph Lagu took overall command of the Anya Nya guerrillas and the newly created Southern Sudan Liberation Movement. Khartoum finally had a body and a person with which it could negotiate.

Events moved rapidly thereafter. Numeiry, isolated in Khartoum, needed a settlement in the south, and Lagu, perhaps sensing the President's vulnerability, decided that the time was ripe for hard bargaining. A neutral venue for talks was selected — Addis Ababa — and the good offices of Emperor Hailie Selassie and the World Council of Churches obtained. In February 1972, agreement was reached, and the Southern Provinces Regional Self Government Act issued. It provided for a Peoples Regional Assembly in the south and a High Executive Council. Arabic was affirmed as the national language of the Sudan, but English was granted the status of the "principal" language for the south. In legislative matters, the north retained control over defense, foreign affairs, and customs, plus overall economic and educational planning and auditing. All other fields were in the hands of the southerners. The Addis Ababa agreement itself provided for the absorption into the Sudanese armed forces of southern guerrilla fighters and for the return of over 200,000 refugees from abroad. A special southern command of the Sudanese army was created, and the now-General Joseph Lagu was put at its head.[25]

In 1972, elections were held for the Southern Assembly, and, by law, the Assembly was to recommend a chairman of the Regional High Executive Council. Instead, President Numeiry, acting as head of the Sudanese Socialist Union, nominated Abel Alier, a Dinka and his own Minister of Southern Affairs, for that post. Abel Alier was also made one of two national vice-presidents. This special relationship between Numeiry and Abel Alier has been a vital link in continued reconciliation; equal in importance to the strong link with Joseph Lagu, who has repeatedly warned that any threat to Numeiry would be a threat to reconciliation. New elections to the Southern Regional Assembly in 1978 apparently brought many representatives closely linked to the old guerrilla groups and deeply suspicious of Khartoum. Joseph Lagu replaced Abel Alier as chairman of the Southern Executive Committee. It is too early to foretell what this shift portends for the future.

One of the implications of this situation is that Numeiry's rivals may hesitate to move against him: not out of fear of him *per se*, but to prevent a new outbreak of the southern rebellion. As Albino has pointed out, a northern Sudan without the southern provinces would be ripe for absorption by her northern neighbors. The *quid pro quo* is that Numeiry will protect the evolution of regional autonomy in the south and, concomitantly, keep the Sudan from joining in any Arab unity scheme which would entail a marked diminution of southern political leverage.

The process of southern integration into the Sudan is by no means inevitable, although one wonders whether southern independence or union with Kenya, Zaire, or Uganda would be feasible or palatable alternatives. In fact, the Negroid south may have greater political weight and hopes for development in the Arab Sudan than as an independent state or a junior partner in an East African union.

THE WEST

Unlike the south, which for a time wanted to opt out of the Sudan, the west has wanted to opt in. Its resentment arises from a sense of neglect on the part of Khartoum and central government elites dominated by the north. It is an inescapable fact that, in many respects, the west is as backward as the south. With their glorious role in the Mahdist movement and a marked assertiveness about their Arab and Muslim identity, the westerners have regarded themselves as the poor cousins of a regime (or regimes) that has spent all its time and money building up the north and the east. Yet western migrants pushing east, a phenomenon that has dominated internal population movements in the Sudan for centuries, have contributed cheap labor to the big agricultural development schemes of the Northeast.

This is not to say that westerners are completely unrepresented in the establishment, and there has always been a strong contingent of western army officers. But this representation has not been sufficient to allay the regional sensibilities of the west. These in turn overlap substantially with militant Islam, and allegiance to the Ansar or Ikhwan. Predictably, the liquidation of the Ansar at Aba Island in 1970 was a bitter pill for the west, which it never did swallow.

On September 5, 1975, there was an attempted coup d'état, led by western army officers in Khartoum. The attempt failed, but Khartoum's universities were closed as the trials dragged on. A National Front, formed in 1969 and grouping the NUP, the Umma, the Muslim Brethren and occasionally some communists, was implicated in the putsch. In January and February 1976, 16 of the coup participants were executed. Qaddafi of Libya was directly accused of having instigated the movement, and it was well-known that there was considerable arms running from the Kufra oasis in Libya to Khartoum in Darfur.

Scarcely had that crisis been dissipated than the next attempt to overthrow Numeiry was launched. Upon his return from the United States, July 2, 1976, Numeiry found the airport under attack by what were later described as mercenaries. The presumed goal was to capture and kill Numeiry and seize strategic points in Khartoum. It was alleged that as this took place, Sadiq al-Mahdi was airborne over Khartoum, ready to land and claim power in the name of the Umma Party and the Muslim Brethren.

The mercenaries were described as western Sudanese, Ethiopians, Chadians, Tanzanians, and Eritreans. They had allegedly been trained in Libya and then infiltrated into Khartoum over several months. A westerner, a "Mahdist," and former Brigadier, General Muhammad Nur Saad, planned the operation. Between 300 and 700 people were killed in the action, and captured rebels exultantly declared that Aba Island had been avenged. The insurrection was put down once again with Sudanese troops airlifted from Egypt and the timely intervention of Commander Muhammad Abu al-Gassim, the Minister of Agriculture, with troops from Wad Medani.

It is said that had the plot worked, the Sudan would have moved toward union with Libya and would have, in the words of Sadiq al-Mahdi, "rectified" the Addis Ababa agreement. Soon after these events, Numeiry went to Egypt to thank Sadat, and a few days later in Saudi Arabia, Egyptian, Saudi, and Sudanese leaders agreed on collective security measures primarily against the Qaddafi menace. While it is unconfirmed, at least one source claims that 12,000 Egyptian troops have been permanently stationed in the Sudan.[26]

Part of the price of Saudi support may have been a pressuring of Numeiry to seek a compromise with his rightist enemies, who reflect a significant body of opinion within the Sudanese polity. Whatever the causes, Numeiry met secretly with Sadiq al-Mahdi at Port Sudan on July 6, 1977 and then announced steps toward "national reconciliation," including the release and amnesty of hundreds of political detainees. He agreed to work with the components of the National Front. If Sadiq al-Mahdi is to have his way, closer links with Ethiopia, even at the expense of Somalian and Eritrean ambitions, would be pursued. A similar course toward Libya would also be followed. Given his hostility to the Addis Ababa accord, one would also anticipate a hardening of northern attitudes toward the playing out of southern autonomy, with all the repercussions that that might entail. Candidates of the National Front, be it noted, carried a third of the seats in the national parliament in the elections of spring 1978.

CONCLUSION

The Sudan is a politically unstable nation surrounded by politically unstable neighbors. The instability of the one feeds into the instability of the others, and there is little the Sudan can do to insulate itself against transboundary meddling. This is so because important elements of the Sudanese population—southern, non-Muslim blacks or western Muslim pietists—welcome such meddling. Sudan's neighbors are also vulnerable in this respect, but that fact does not detract from the political volatility that characterizes this sector of the Nile basin. To the extent that regional political grievances in the Sudan are rooted in regional economic disparities, one may expect that they will be aggravated in the coming years. The northeast economic and political establishment will be the principal beneficiaries of whatever development takes place as the result of the influx of Arab capital.

It is unlikely, but not impossible, that those regional forces could pull the Sudan apart. It is highly likely, however, that neither Egypt nor Saudi Arabia would allow this to happen. Military intervention to save Numeiry and/or the union has been used before, is justified in the principles of the OAU, and finds precedent in other theaters ranging from the Congo/Zaire to Biafra and Ethiopia's Ogaden. It may be that nearly all concerned accept that something like Numeiry's careful middle-of-the-road authoritarian regime is about the best the Sudan could hope for. The alternatives revolving around the poles of secession, Marxism, and Muslim pietism would, if in power, alienate important segments of Sudanese opinion as well as some of the Sudan's neighbors. Whatever acceptance there is of Numeiry in the Sudan represents something a good deal less than consensus.

Nasser ruled in Egypt for eighteen years and died in office. Anwar Sadat has followed him for eight years without direct challenge. By contrast, over the past twenty-three years, the Sudan has known four distinct regimes, experienced two successful coups d'état and numerous attempts, and endured a sixteen-year civil war. As far as the Nile is concerned, Egypt's stability is relatively meaningless while the Sudan's instability is of incalculable importance for it is the mid- and not the downstream state. In another sense, however, Egypt and the Sudan are very similar. Whether it is a question of confrontation with Israel or of coping with the tangled skein of domestic politics, both Sadat and Numeiry have their attention fixed elsewhere than on the Nile. While no one would argue that it should be their overriding concern, it is nonetheless probable that a preoccupation with the ostensible crises of today may impede effective measures to deal with a water crisis of the near future.

8

SHORTAGE IN THE MIDST OF PLENTY

MORE THAN HALF A CENTURY AGO it was widely recognized that Egypt and the Sudan could not simultaneously expand their agricultural sectors and their use of Nile water within the confines of seasonal storage technology. The way out of the dilemma, laboriously elaborated over twenty-five years, was to move to over-year storage. Once again, the two countries are approaching the outer limits of what the existing system of seasonal and over-year storage facilities can provide. The "far future," as H. E. Hurst referred to it in 1946, is fully upon us. To explain what that statement means in its most significant ramifications requires not only detail but a careful, nonalarmist elucidation of the challenge in water management that both countries are facing.

There are a number of premises to the argument presented here. First, it is not our contention that there will inevitably be a water shortage in the Nile Valley in an absolute sense in the foreseeable future (say, to the year 2000). The Nile catchment area, and especially the Equatorial lakes, retain such vast quantities of water that the notion of shortage seems almost ludicrous. But, as must be abundantly clear by now, potential does not mean much unless one can work out and pay for a feasible delivery system. This has yet to be done, and there is not much time left to develop the Upper Nile projects before Egypt and the Sudan will find their plans for agricultural expansion sharply curtailed or perhaps at direct odds with one another.

The second premise is that while the problem is recognized by responsible technocracies, it is not seen as a matter of great urgency. A 1976 USAID survey encapsulates the prevailing view, to which we shall take exception:

> A question that the team knew it must answer was whether water or usable agricultural land is the single most limiting constraint to increased production. FAO concluded in an earlier study that water would not be a constraint at least through the year 2000. The Mininstry of Irrigation, in

studies recently summarized in newspaper stories, came to the same conclusion. Based on independent analysis and judgment, our team confirms this view.[1]

For reasons to be set out below, we believe water will become a major constraint within a decade. This is not the view of informed policy makers — thus we advance it with some trepidation — and beyond their realm the presumption is that Egypt and the Sudan have more water than they know what to do with. This perception sometimes manifests itself in frivolous but revelatory ways. When it became known in Egypt that Saudi Arabia had plans to tow icebergs from the Antarctic to supply Jeddah with fresh drinking water at a cost of $80 million per berg, an Egyptian Member of Parliament, Mustapha Kemal Murad, submitted a proposal to parliament to construct a pipeline from Lake Nasser to Saudi Arabia in order to sell the Saudis potable water at competitive rates. The Egyptian media did not question the assumption that surplus water was there to sell.* Of greater consequence, however, is the constant process of project-mongering in which various ministers incessantly indulge. Conquering the desert, making the Sinai peninsula green, or shifting Egypt's population center of gravity to the New Valley are slogans that have been floated by a number of officials, and if they receive presidential endorsement, as some have, it may mean that steps will be taken to implement them. We shall consider some of these in greater detail below, but the point here is that, for the most part, the availability of additional water supplies is taken for granted. Nor are many officials looking upstream to the Sudan where similar assumptions prevail.

The third premise is that the coming water crisis is not insoluble. We share the view of the Ministries of Irrigation and Agriculture in both Egypt and the Sudan that radically improved delivery networks, comprehensive field drains, and strict economy in the on-field use of

---

*As Saudi Arabia's Petroleum Minister Sheikh Yamani has often noted, it is easier to find oil than water in Saudi Arabia. It is possible that Egypt would realize higher profits by selling its rich neighbor water than by pouring it on its fields. It is estimated, for instance, that the project to tow icebergs to Jeddah would yield fresh water at a maximum cost of about $.50 per m^3, or 30 percent less than what it currently costs to produce desalinated seawater. See Paul Ceuzin, "Icebergs en croisière," *Science et Avenir* 366 (August 1977):792–94. This compares with about $.08 per m^3 at Aswan. See note 6. The same sort of assumption of unlimited Nile water clearly informed proposals in the Camp David negotiations between Israel and Egypt in the fall of 1978 that Egypt sell to Israel 800 million to one billion m^3 of irrigation water each year at 12¢ per m^3. See Teddy Preuss, "Peace Alone Won't Turn the Desert Green," *Fortune*, October 23, 1978.

water can significantly reduce the conveyance losses and overwatering on the part of the peasantry. Moreover, there is no question that the expeditious implementation of the Upper Nile projects could increase the average annual discharge at Aswan by 10 percent. All these measures taken in combination *could* cover foreseeable water needs in both countries—but that judgment begs a number of crucial questions.

One set of questions involves profitability and the net return on investments. If one is talking about piped irrigation systems, lined canals, sprinklers, and trickle irrigation — and Egyptian experts are talking about just that — then one has entered the domain of very high-priced technology which will maximize the efficiency of water use but at a cost that may not be justified by the value of what is produced. In many ways, Egyptian, and to a lesser extent, Sudanese policy makers must ask themselves if they are prepared to subsidize their agricultural sectors through massive infrastructural investments or whether they will insist on fairly strict benefit-cost criteria in opting for any particular project. At this time, one does not have the impression that this question has been squarely addressed; rather the argument appears to be that *at some undetermined cost* water can be conserved. The same line of reasoning applies to the Upper Nile projects. Doubtless they could yield up to 18 billion m³ to be divided equally between Egypt and the Sudan, but one is hard put to find detailed cost estimates of these projects or the period of time required to implement them. Again one must ask: does the return on downstream agricultural production warrant the upstream outlay, whatever it is, and will the upstream projects actually be implemented in time to avoid severe downstream shortages? The answers must be mixed. The return on investment in Sudanese agriculture may be sufficiently attractive to some Arab investors that projects which would benefit both the Sudan and Egypt would find funding. But, to date, that is purely conjectural and, in any case, says nothing about the time frame involved. The IBRD might be tempted for political reasons to become involved in developing the Upper Nile, but such involvement would be dependent primarily upon noneconomic considerations.

Easily as important as all the above are the unanswered questions about the social engineering implicit in water conservation. This brings us to the heart of all development challenges: the transformation of human behavior. It is all well and good to say that Egyptian peasants waste great amounts of water through ignorance or selfishness, but unless one can suggest concrete measures to change this behavior, the official campaign against the lavish use of irrigation water will remain as ineffective as those against defecation in the canals or the procreation of large families. Waste surely can be reduced, but no Egyptian policy makers have yet devised a strategy to attack the problem. Pending its elaboration, one must view with considerable skepticism the predictions that individual conservation of scarce water will become reality in the near future.

In short, one must treat with caution the official view that human behavior and the constraints of international financing can be so readily manipulated that the Nile Valley will yield optimal amounts of water within the next 10 to 15 years.

The final premise is perhaps the most controversial. Sometime in the 1980s, if Egyptian and Sudanese water needs grow apace, a new bargain on water allocation will have to be struck. If these needs do not grow rapidly, that fact will merely reflect various forms of economic stagnation. In 1979, with the IMF counseling extreme caution in the implementation of its investment plans, it was the Sudan that was paying the price of stagnation. For this and other reasons, it would at this juncture be premature to say whether this would entail the modification of the 1959 Agreement or the drafting of a new document, but one can assume with some confidence that the familiar confrontation of existing needs versus potential needs will once again make its presence felt. This time, outside arbitration will play a role. Saudi Arabia and Kuwait, with major interests in Egypt's political moderation and in the Sudan's economic profitability, may act as "honest brokers" in promoting a deal that, one suspects, would favor the Sudanese. The author of these lines would not like to stake his reputation on this premise, but it seems to have a lot going for it.

WATER SUPPLY AND DEMAND: EGYPT

The parameters of actual and potential water supply in the Nile system are far better know than those of actual and potential demand. Even so, the best estimates available on either dimension are frequently crude and not always consistent. Still, one must try to grasp the possible ranges of these parameters in order to fix in temporal and quantitative terms the point at which the two curves intersect. The danger to a layman, or to anyone, venturing into this treacherous realm is at least twofold. On the one hand, it is often impossible to make more than gross estimates of many of the components of supply and demand. On the other, the margin of water that would spell the difference between sufficiency and penury has become increasingly small. We are thus making our estimates on the basis of inadequate information.

Underlying this argument is an assumption of *ceteris paribus*. First of all, demand should not be confused with requirements. The latter may or may not be affected by a host of measures to render water use more efficient. To the extent such measures are successful, requirements will be reduced. Explicit attention to the question of waste is given further on. Demand, however, is a function of the price of water. At present, water is delivered to Egypt's fields at no cost to the cultivator. Delivery fees for non-agricultural water use are administered by the State. All of the argumentation in this chapter is premised on the assumption that these costs will not change over the next 15 to 20 years. The introduction of various pricing measures that reflect the availability of water could lead to radically altered patterns in use and hence invalidate parts of this argument. But as long as it is generally believed that supply is sufficient to accommodate almost any conceivable mix of requirements, there is little reason to expect any change in pricing.

With regard to Egypt, the data are more abundant and water requirements quantitatively more significant. At present (1976–77), the Ministry of Irrigation calculates Egypt's annual supply of Nile water as follows:[2]

Available at Aswan	55.5	billion m³
Return Flow/Drainage into Nile between Aswan and Cairo	2.3	billion m³
Reused drainage water in the Delta	2.5	billion m³
Utilization of groundwater	.350	billion m³
Total amount of water used	60.65	billion m³

These figures require little comment. First, it should be noted that as of November 1977, Egypt, at least according to the 1959 Agreement, will no longer receive the 1.5 billion m³ "loan" from the Sudan. Its effective share would thus be reduced from 57 to 55.5 billion m³. There is, in addition, some difference in opinion as to how much irrigation water actually drains back into the Nile between Aswan and Cairo. At least one source places the return flow between 3 and 4 billion m³, but it is likely that this figure will fluctuate annually with cropping patterns.[3]

To what extent can this gross supply be increased? Leaving aside improved delivery networks, drainage, and more efficient on-field use, two avenues are open. The first is to implement the Upper Nile projects. The second is to draw more heavily on Delta groundwater combined with the systematic reutilization of Delta drainage water. Let us consider the Upper Nile projects first.

These projects will be jointly undertaken by Egypt and the Sudan, and will yield an estimated 18 billion m^3 annually, to be divided equally between the two countries. However, one cannot share the optimism of the previously cited USAID survey (p. 2) to the effect that these projects will be *completed* by 1985. Only the first phase of the Jonglei Canal is nearing the implementation stage; some excavation began in fall 1977. Although approved by the presidents of both republics in winter 1974, it was nearly three years before contracts were awarded for some parts of the construction operation. It turned out that a great deal more engineering survey work was required before work could proceed, as the river had changed considerably since the last surveys were made in 1954. Meanwhile, cost estimates have continued to soar, perhaps as much as $240 million for the first phase. While the AAAID is prepared in *principle* to cover about half that amount, this is contingent on a feasible plan. For their part, Egypt and the Sudan are still groping for funds to cover the remainder. In sum, the project is not only delayed, but without adequate financing.

Although few cost and time estimates are available, there are a number of projects on the various upper Nile tributaries that could be carried out, for the most part within Sudanese territory. These would include seasonal storage dams on the Siwi, Yei, and Busseri rivers, and extensive embanking, channeling, and diversion of the Yei, Naam, Jel, Jelimar, Jur, Jeti, Pongo, Jol, and Behr el-Arab rivers. It is anticipated that all these projects in combination could yield 7 billion m^3 annually at Malakal. Similarly, projects to minimize water loss in the eastern Sobat tributaries and the Mashar marshes are being studied. The core of the plan would be to store water on the upper Baro, necessarily entailing an accord with Ethiopia as the dam and reservoir would be within its territory. In addition, a stretch of the Baro would be embanked and a diversion canal to the White Nile excavated. The net yield of this project would be 4 billion m^3 at Malakal each year. Initial cost estimates (1975 prices) are $300 million.

Finally, Egypt and the Sudan could move on to the second phase of the Jonglei Scheme. It would have three major components: (1) utilization of Lakes Victoria, Kioga, and Mobutu for over-year storage to even out the discharge of the Behr el-Jebel; (2) embankment of sections of the Behr el-Jebel and Behr el-Zeraf to increase their discharge; and (3) either the widening of the first Jonglei canal or the excavation of a parallel canal to increase their combined discharge from 20 million m³ to 43 million m³ per day.[4]

All the Upper Nile projects would give a *maximum* average annual yield *at Aswan* of 18 billion m³, half of which would be Egypt's, because of their engineering, financial, and political complexity, prudence would dictate that one not anticipate their implementation before the mid-1990s (see Map 8).

As has been the practice throughout the millennia, direct irrigation from the Nile has been supplemented by drawing water from the underground water table beneath or adjacent to areas under cultivation. Unlike the fossil groundwater deposits in the western desert of Egypt, the aquifer of the valley proper is recharged from the Nile itself or from seepage in the irrigation network. It is therefore in no sense an independent source of water.

There is doubtless considerable scope for tapping this source of fresh water, but the dynamics of its replenishment, and hence the optimal rates at which it can be pumped, are not yet fully understood. There is a great deal of water there — perhaps 150 billion m³ lying beneath the soils of Upper Egypt and another 500 billion m³ under the Delta — but only a fraction of these quantities is stored at sufficiently shallow depths to permit economic utilization. At present, about 350 million m³ are drawn annually from the Delta aquifer. Lennert Berg has estimated that the Delta water table receives about 1.5 billion m³ in recharge each year. In his view, it would be possible to lower the water table—highly desirable from a drainage point of view—by 18 billion m³ over a period of one or two decades. It could then be maintained at a specified piezometric head and tapped in strict accord with the rate of recharge. In this way, it would seem reasonable to assume that at least one billion m³ in Delta groundwater could be used annually.[5]

It might be recalled here that various experts have suggested that one way to overcome the difficulties of reconciling agricultural water needs and industrial power needs would be to release more water at Aswan than the crops actually require, and to then store it at Wadi Rayyan or in the Delta aquifer. These suggestions do not yet appear to enjoy much favor.

Far more significant quantitatively are the ambitious plans of the Ministry of Irrigation to recuperate unutilized drainage water for agricultural purposes. Once again, the target area is the Delta and adjacent reclamation sites. Of some 16 billion m³ drained off annually, only 2.5 billion m³ are currently reutilized while the rest are pumped into the northern lakes. The goal is to recuperate up to 12 billion m³ annu-

MAP 8

Upper Nile Projects

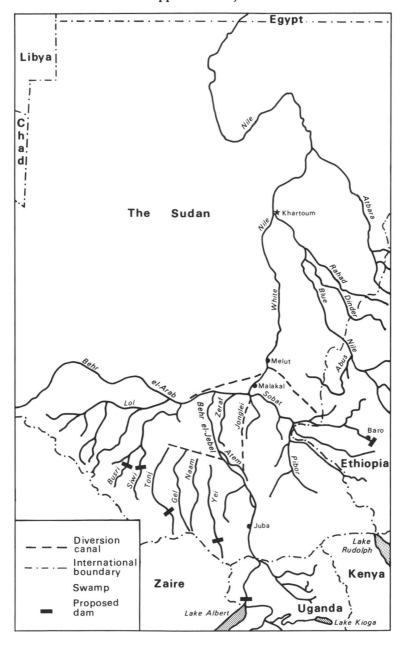

Egypt

Libya

Chad

The Sudan

Nile

★ Khartoum

Atbara

Rahad

Blue

Dinder

Nile

White

Abus

Behr

el-Arab

Lol

● Melut

● Malakal

Sobat

Zeraf

Jonglei

Behr el-Jebel

Atem

Baro

Busri

Siwi

Toni

Gel

Naam

Yei

Pibor

Ethiopia

● Juba

Lake
Rudolph

Kenya

Zaire

Lake Albert

Uganda

Lake Kioga

Diversion
canal

International
boundary

Swamp

Proposed
dam

ally. Because of the higher salt content of such water, it would then have to be mixed in varying proportions with irrigation water for application to crops of differing tolerance to salt. Rice, for instance, is relatively tolerant of high salt levels. Table 22 shows both the annual input of irrigation water into Delta agriculture and the corresponding volumes drained off. The target of 12 billion m³ is set on the assumption that by 1980, more efficient irrigation practices will reduce the amount of drainage water by at least a third, while extension of the drainage grid to nearly 1.7 million new feddans will offset this reduction by adding new sources of drainage water. The question that remains unanswered pertains to the long-range impact of this practice. As we have noted earlier, agricultural intensification throughout the Nile Valley reduces water quality through chemical runoffs and the increasing concentration of salts in the water and soil. Recirculating irrigation and drainage water surely will lead, through evapo-transpiration, to ever higher salinity levels. The process may be very gradual and partially offset by the anticipated lowering of the Delta water table, but the risks involved must be very carefully calculated.

TABLE 22

Total Amounts of Drainage and Irrigation Waters in Lower Egypt
(billions of m³)

Year	Total irrigation water	Total drainage water	% Drain./ Irrig.
1964	26.99	14.02	51.9
1965	30.05	14.38	47
1966	32.00	14.84	46.3
1967	29.17	16.02	54
1968	29.73	15.52	52.2
1969	30.24	15.94	52.6
1970	31.17	16.23	52.4
1971	32.17	16.26	50.5
1972	32.59	15.98	49.6

SOURCE: Saad el-Gendi and Osman el-Ghomry, *Re-use of Drainage Water for Irrigation Purposes*, UN Water Conference, Mar del Plata, Argentina (March 14–25, 1977), p. 5.

With this caveat in mind, we may consider what the Ministry of Irrigation believes is the potential supply of Nile water available to Egypt.

Egypt's share under the 1959 agreement	55.5 billion m³
Recuperable drainage water	12.0 billion m³
Delta groundwater	1.0 billion m³
Upper Nile Projects	9.0 billion m³
Total	77.5 billion m³

It should escape no one's notice that with the exception of the yield from the Upper Nile projects, the above figures represent considerable double-counting. The 13 billion m³ of drainage and groundwater are not really an addition to but are part of the annual share of 55.5 billion m³. They should be seen as water twice-spent.

What in the official view are Egypt's present and future needs? Current needs are estimated by Abu al-Atta in Table 23 on the basis of

TABLE 23

Ministry of Irrigation and USAID Estimates of Real Water Needs for Egypt, mid–70s
(in billions of m³)

Needs	Min. of Irrig. estimates	USAID survey
Agricultural	39.9 (11.3 mill. cropped feds)	26.0 (6.2 mill. cult. feds)
Conveyance losses	8.0	11.2
On-farm loss/waste	9.3	14.0
Domestic & indust. use	1.0	1.0
Navig. & power release	2.5	3.0
Total	60.7 billion m³	55.2 billion m³

SOURCE: Abd al-Azim Abu al-Atta, *Long-Range Planning in the Sphere of Irrigation and Drainage*, U.S. Department of Agriculture and USAID, *Egypt: Major Constraints to Increasing Agricultural Productivity* (Washington, D.C.: June 1976), p.89.

11.3 million cropped feddans. Alongside his figures we have entered USAID estimates which simply reflect the ranges that can emerge in this kind of exercise. By either estimate, on-field waste, generally attributed to overwatering, is enormous. Consideration of this phenomenon has finally brought us to the level of the irrigation inspector, the peasant, and the crop on the field. Waste is a form of double taxation on state finances, requiring large sums to dispose of it and large sums to produce it in the first place. Frequently, the question of charging the peasants for the water they use is raised, only to be dismissed as impractical or immoral. One source calculates that it costs the state two millemes for every m³ delivered to a field and the same amount for every m³ drained away. A feddan using 8000 m³ per year of which 25% is drained off would cost £E 20. The costs only of delivering water to six million feddans would approach £E 100 million.[6]

Let us turn first to the thorny question of crop-water duties. These have been calculated on the basis of field experiments, the most widely cited of which are the results of surveys carried out over the period 1948–59, that is before the High Dam era.[7] More recent figures have been advanced by I. Z. Kinawy (see Table 24), reflecting the greater profligacy in water use since 1964.[8]

Kinawy's figures warrant a few comments. His estimate for cropped acreage (10,837,000) seems closer to the mark than Abu al-Atta's 11,333,172 which is well above other published figures. If we take the average water requirement per cropped feddan of the two estimates, we find 3,819 m³ for Abu al-Atta. On a crop-by-crop basis, Kinawy consistently records higher water duties than those established 15 years earlier, e.g., 3,100 m³ for full-term Delta berseem versus 2,200 m³ in the 1950s; 1,600 m³ for Delta wheat versus 1,000 m³ in the 1950s, and so forth. Thus, if one accepts Abu al-Atta's cropped acreage figure and Kinawy's water duties, the total requirement would be 43.3 billion m³ instead of 39.9 billion m³.

Neither Kinawy, nor Abu al-Atta would deny that under any set of assumptions considerable amounts of water are wasted annually. In systemic terms, this means that the average rate of efficiency in Egyptian agricultural water use is only about 51 percent (i.e., the difference between total water delivered and that consumed in plant evapotranspiration) where it could, with better management, approach 70 percent. In other words, to meet the same plant requirements the total amount of water delivered could be reduced by several million m³.

In the past, it was common in the summer months for the tails of the lateral irrigation canals to run dry. Once the High Dam was com-

TABLE 24
Crop-Water Requirements, ARE, 1972

	DELTA			MID-EGYPT			UPPER EGYPT			TOTAL CROPPED AREA	TOTAL WATER REQUIRE-MENT
WINTER	Cropped area	Water requirement per fed. m³	Total water requirement*	Cropped area 1000 feddans	Water requirement per fed. m³	Total water requirement	Cropped area 1000 feddans	Water requirement per fed. m³	Total water requirement		
Wheat	725	1,600	1,600	217	1,700	370	297	2,100	624	1,239	2,154
Ful	135	1,350	183	153	1,470	225	77	1,600	123	365	531
Barley	73	1,400	102	6.7	1,500	10	11	1,700	19.5	91	131.5
Fennugrec	1.8	1,050	2	11.7	1,170	14	15.5	1,290	20	29	36
Lentils	—	—	—				67	1,210	81	67	81
Flax	32.5	1,070	35	.5	1,190	.6	—	—	—	33	35.6
Onions	2.5	2,250	5.5	6.5	2,500	16	22	2,700	59.5	31	81
Lupine	6	1,000	6	2.5	1,120	3	1.5	1,230	2	10	11
Chickpeas	3.5	1,020	3.5	.3	1,130	.4	6.2	1,240	7.5	10	11.4
Berseem											
Full Term	1,166	3,100	3,600	274	3,650	1,000	125	4,000	500	1,565	5,100
Temporary	903	1,910	1,730	226	2,120	480	125	2,330	292	1,254	2,502
Garlic	2.2	1,600	3.5	6.6	1,780	117	.2	1,950	.5	9	121
Vegetables	45	2,200	100	129.5	2,470	320	4.5	2,720	12	179	432
Other	11.5	1,900	22	1.5	2,110	3	16	2,320	37	29	62
SUMMER											
Cotton	1,000	2,300	3,400	334	3,900	1,300	218	4,700	1,030	1,552	5,730
Rice	1,140	8,800	10,100	6	9,920	59	—	—	—	1,146	10,159
Corn	—	—	—	92	2,800	258	392	3,080	1,210	284	1,468
Maize	1,140	2,700	3,100	322	3,000	966	69	3,300	228	1,531	4,294
Sugar Cane	12	14,760	117	25	16,400	410	165	17,800	2,940	202	3,527
Peanuts	18	3,160	57	11	3,510	39	5	3,860	19	34	115
Sesame	6	2,000	12	6	2,220	13.5	30	2,440	73	42	98.5
Vegetables	98	3,780	377.5	129	4,200	544	335	4,620	1,550	562	2,471.5
Other	60	3,420	205	18	3,800	68.5	42	4,180	175	120	448.5
Orchards	188	6,850	1,290	44.2	7,600	322	20.8	8,370	174	253	1,786
TOTAL	6,769		25,671	2,023		6,539	2,045		9,177	10,837	41,387

SOURCE: I. Z. Kinawy, "The Efficiency of Water Use in Irrigation in Egypt," Conference on Arid Lands Irrigation in Developing Countries, UNESCO, UNEP, Academy of Science, Research, and Technology, Alexandria (February 1976).

*Total water requirements in million m³.

pleted and summer water became relatively abundant, the line of least resistance followed by irrigation inspectors was to meet all the water demands of the cultivators. Under the various water rotations, the main canals are kept full while the laterals are periodically dry.* Field outlets from the laterals are under the control of individual cultivators. Those upstream tend to draw off more than their share, and the Irrigation officials must then increase the discharge in the laterals so that downstream users will have enough water. In the era of seeming abundance, the old practice of night irrigation, which minimizes waste, has begun to die out. In an earlier draft of the USAID survey, the authors summarized the situation in this manner:

> A general lack of enforcement regulations suggests that farmers manage the system more than the Irrigation Department. Unauthorized outlets exceed authorized outlets at least three times, unauthorized pumps are used, laterals and outlets on the main canals use water out of turn, turns on laterals are extended to reduce farmer complaints and farmers use water on a system more nearly approaching demand than the authorized rotation system.

In a general assessment of actual water use, Abu-Zeid concluded that while in any calendar year waste might amount to 20 percent of total water delivered, there is a seasonal inversion within this trend. Water releases at Aswan during the winter season (November–March) exceed crop requirements by 27 to 32 percent while during the summer months (May–July) releases are about 11 percent *less* than crop requirements. One might note here that an achievement of optimal water release for agricultural purposes would further detract from optimal release for the generation of power at the High Dam (see Chapter 5).

In theory, several steps could be taken to make on-field use more efficient, but their application would be extremely difficult. For instance, as mechanical pumping gradually spreads throughout the valley, a charge for water may have to be introduced. This will be technically and politically challenging. It will require the installation and maintenance of an extensive, costly metering system. Moreover, it will require an assault on the commonly held notion—more Egyptian than

---

*The three basic patterns followed are four days on, four days off for rice; seven days on, seven days off in lighter textured soils; and five days on, ten days off for the main crops of wheat, maize, cotton, etc. For a good analysis of rotations and waste see Mahmoud Abu-Zeid, "The Management of Irrigation Water in the ARE," UN Water Conference, Mar del Plata, Argentina (March 14–25, 1977).

Koranic—that water, like air, is God-given and should not be appropriated by individuals or political authorities. Pakistan has been able to overcome both obstacles, but as far as Egypt is concerned, the introduction of direct charges for water would raise a political hornets' nest.

Upgrading and expanding the corps of rural inspectors and extension agents would constitute another necessary approach to the problem. Once again, the investments would be substantial, not only for training but for raising current salary levels which provide no incentive to local officials to apply unpopular rules.

Positive measures of peasant education would also be part of the solution. Demonstrating that proper and thrifty water use increases productivity could lead to voluntary alteration of peasant habits, yet time and again it has proved difficult to communicate concepts of enlightened self-interest (for example, as noted at the outset, in bilharzia control or family planning) to illiterate peasants. This is especially true when the line official has no sense of mission and finds his target sealed off from him by a wall of suspicion, resentment, and skepticism. In short, there can be no quick, effective solution to the problem of water waste in the Egyptian countryside. Progress will come, but it will probably be a great deal slower than Egyptian policy makers would hope.

A major component of Egypt's water budget is the nonagricultural use of water in homes and industry. This component is currently and unrealistically estimated at one billion m^3 per year; moreover, for some unexplained reason, the Ministry of Irrigation implicity holds this figure steady in all its projections to the turn of the century. The mere fact that today Cairo alone consumes about 950 million m^3 per year, very little of which is returned to the Nile, should give one pause. By 1985, it is expected that Cairo's consumption will be nearly 1.5 billion m^3 each year.[9] Using per capita averages common to Africa and other developing areas, we can calculate some likely levels of domestic water consumption.

Table 25 is based on these assumptions: (1) that current water consumption is 250 liters per day per person in urban areas and 30 liters per day per person in rural areas; (2) that the total population will grow moderately to 55 million by 1990, with 55 percent urban and 45 percent rural; (3) that urban consumption may hold steady at 250 liters while rural consumption should increase modestly to 50 liters per person per day. These expectations seem conservative, but the results are nonetheless clear: household water use could, by 1990, be three and a half times the amount set aside by the Ministry of Irrigation for total

TABLE 25

Estimated Household Water Consumption, 1976–90

Year	Total population millions	Rural population millions	Water consumption bill. m³	Urban population millions	Water consumption bill. m³	Total water consumption bill. m³
1976	38	21	.230 est.	17	1.5 est.*	1.73 est.
1990	55 est.	25 est.	.812 est.	30 est.	2.7 est.	3.51 est.

*By the end of 1978 Cairo's water consumption was scheduled to rise to a rate of 1.3 billion m³ per year.

nonagricultural use. We suspect that, as now, very little of this water will be returned to the system or reused.

That leaves us with the question of industrial consumption. We must stress that Egypt's future lies in industry, which in turn requires substantial amounts of water. The bulk may consist in coolants that can be recycled if the price of water is sufficiently high. We are not able to estimate with any exactitude what Egypt's industrial water needs will be in the coming decades, but ambitious plans for petrochemicals, expanded steel and iron production, aluminum smelting, fertilizer plants, large agro-industrial projects in sugar refining, canning, bagasse, and the like, indicate a level of consumption far in excess of anything the Ministry of Irrigation is willing to contemplate. The suggestion that a good deal of water for both domestic and industrial purposes can be drawn from wells begs the question, for as we have noted, it is the Nile that recharges these wells. Very conservatively we would contend that one must expect an annual industrial demand of at least 3 billion m³ by 1990. Combined with our projected household demand, we arrive at a total nonagricultural consumption level of 6.5 billion m³ in 1990.*

*USAID, *Egypt: Major Constraints*, p. 75, estimates household/industrial consumption by the year 2000 at 4 billion m³, and Kinawy puts the figure at 4.5 billion m³. There are obviously problems of actual measurement here that must be dealt with. The bulk of the rural population does not draw its domestic water from piped sources but rather from what the Minister of Irrigation calculates as agricultural supply. So, too, does Egypt's animal population of some 9 million (including 2.1 million gamussas or buffalo, 2.1 million cattle, and 1.9 million sheep) whose per capita consumption of water is not known to the author. We have, in brief, minimized the extent of nonfield consumption of water, and it is plausible that a good proportion of the 9 billion m³ Abu al-Atta classifies as waste is in fact used for nonagricultural, or at least noncrop purposes.

We now have in hand a number of rough measures that we can combine into our own medium-term estimates of Egypt's water requirements. Once again we must specify the underlying assumptions. As regards the cultivated area, we have assumed that the net annual *loss* of agricultural land to urban sprawl will be arrested and that the cultivated surface of 5.7 million feddans in 1975 will be increased to 6.7 million feddans by the addition of 700,000 reclaimed feddans and 300,000 added to areas in which tile drains replace open field drains. In addition, we assume that cropping efficiency will be increased to 2.2 crops per year per feddan. This would yield a *cropped surface of 14.7 million feddans in the mid- and late 1980s.* We have then estimated crop-water needs according to three assumptions of efficiency: (1) 3,500 m^3 per cropped feddan, (2) 3,700 m^3 per cropped feddan, and (3) 3,800 m^3 per cropped feddan. This is the same range that we have established for the mid-1970s. We believe that it will hold in the 1980s because *possible* reductions in wastage will be traded against the water requirements of more intensive cropping. Official arguments for increased sugar cane, rice, maize, and vegetable acreage, with their relatively high water needs, would tend to reinforce this view. Finally, we believe that conveyance losses will continue to run at 15–20 percent of total agricultural supply because it will be too expensive to refurbish the old delivery system (i.e. line or cover canals, etc.), and the expansion of the cultivated surface will entail further losses. [10]

On the supply side, we have assumed that it is likely that only the Jonglei among the Upper Nile projects will have been completed. Second, we have introduced more cautious estimates of the amounts of drainage water that can be reused annually. The results presented in Table 26 are startling. If all goes according to plan—and nothing ever does anywhere—Egypt could have, despite double counting, a surplus of 15.8 billion m^3 in the late 1980s. More likely, several projects will be only partially implemented, in which case Egypt would do well to break even but might wind up with a deficit of over 5 billion m^3. In the event that projects are poorly executed or not implemented — a phenomenon with which Egypt has been all too familiar in past decades—the country could find itself with a whopping water deficit of 14.1 billion m^3. In all this we have not questioned the official credo that evaporation and seepage at Lake Nasser do not exceed 11 billion m^3 annually, whereas in Chapter 4 we argued that this figure must surely be more like 15 billion m^3. In other words, in some years actual water release at Aswan may be less than 55.5 billion m^3.

Accordingly, one must treat with substantial doubt the Irrigation

TABLE 26

Projections of Total Egyptian Water Supply
and Demand, 1986–90
(billions m³)

Supply	Optimistic	Cautious	Pessimistic
Released at Aswan	55.5	55.5	55.5
Yield from Upper Nile projects	9.0	1.9	1.9
Reused drainage water	12.0	6.0	4.0
Groundwater	1.0	1.0	1.0
Total	77.5	64.4	62.4
Demand			
Crop needs	51.4	54.4	55.8
Navigation and January closing	2.5	3.0	3.0
Conveyance losses	7.7	9.8	11.2
Industrial use	1.0	2.0	3.0
Household use		2.0	3.5
Total demand	62.6	72.1	76.5
Surplus/deficit	+14.9	−7.7	−14.1

One caveat is in order. Another "pessimistic" hypothesis not included here is that Egypt will fail to expand cultivated acreage or crop intensity. This possibility cannot be ruled out. The Plan for 1978–82 recommends that by that latter year a cropping pattern be established on *11 million cropped feddans* that would, according to our own calculations, require 43.1 billion m³ to 45.9 billion m³, according to the actual water duty for sugar cane. That is about 6 billion m³ short of our optimistic estimate above. The discrepancy can be explained by these factors: (1) the plan does not seem to allow for additional reclaimed land; (2) it is 3–5 years shy of the time period referred to here; and (3) the plan figures do not include all Egypt's crops (missing are *nili* maize, lupine, sesame, garlic, chickpeas, temporary berseem, barley, fennugrec). See ARE, Ministry of Planning, *The Five Year Plan, 1978–82*, Vol. IV: *The General Strategy for Agriculture, Irrigation, and Food Security* (Cairo: August 1977), p. 160. The inconsistencies in this document are rife. On p. 24 it is stated that the cropped surface must rise to 15,000,000 feddans, consistent with our assumption, and that that can be done with the addition of 2 million cultivated feddans.

Ministry's forecast on the basis of 11 billion cropped feddans of a potential water surplus a decade hence of 25.6 billion m³, and their conclusion that "This available supply would be sufficient for horizontal expansion into new areas ... up to four million feddans in addition to that which would rely upon groundwater in the New Valley as well as upon the rainfall and groundwater of the northwest coast which could add another 625,000 feddans."[11] To the contrary, we believe that in the coming decade Egypt should be satisfied with finding adequate water for modest expansion in the present cultivated area under more intensive cropping patterns.

Yet plans are afoot for the launching of a number of projects that would place heavy demands upon existing and future supply. Table 26 shows the Ministry of Irrigation's projections for reclamation up to the year 2000. Of the 3.2 million feddans designated, 1.1 million are to be reclaimed in the period 1976–90. Past experience, as indicated earlier, suggests that 8 to 12 years of preparation will elapse before reclaimed acreage reaches marginal levels of productivity. Many observers do not believe that there are 3 million feddans in Egypt worth reclaiming, but assuming that there are 1.1 million, we may anticipate enormous water outlays during the reclamation process itself. These range from 10 to 11,000 m^3 per feddan per year in the heavy, alluvial clays of the northern Delta to 15,000 to 20,000 m^3 per feddan in the calcareous and sandy soils along the western Delta fringe.[12] If we assume an average annual water duty per reclaimed feddan of 15,000 m^3 over the period 1980–90 on 1.1 million feddans, the yearly demand on these lands alone would be 16.5 billion m^3. This heavy water demand in the initial stages of reclamation was *not* included in the calculations of Table 25, and would of course tend to augment any potential water deficit.

The endorsement of ambitious reclamation projects is part and parcel of President Sadat's campaign, launched in spring 1976, to "conquer the desert" and to break free of "the shackles of the valley." With good cause, Sadat observed that Egypt's populace had outgrown the confines of the river valley proper and must inevitably disperse into its vast, arid hinterland. This theme appears to have been born with the sweeping plans to reconstruct the entire Suez Canal zone—cities and fields — following the October War of 1973. The hand of the then-Minister of Housing and Reconstruction, Ahmad Osman, is unmistakably present in the drive to make this area a pole for growth, attracting to it population from all over Egypt. The expansion is to be primarily urban, but hundreds of thousands of feddans have been designated for reclamation in the area between Port Said and Ismailia. The canal zone and its surrounding lands are nearly devoid of any fresh water sources and rely upon the Ismailia Canal for their needs. This canal, which already loses great amounts of water through evaporation and seepage, is to be widened to meet increased demand—but at what cost in Nile water?

The same theme was seized upon by various ministries depicting the future in terms of developing other presently waterless regions—the Red Sea coast, the northwest, the New Valley—new cities in the desert, land reclamation just about everywhere, achieving self-sufficiency in basic food production, and so forth. Nowhere discernible in any of this talk was consideration of the amount of water it would take to transfer and maintain millions of Egyptians in environments now highly unsuited for human habitation.

Projects in Egypt have a perhaps fortunate habit of dying slow and unheralded deaths. Of inevitable fascination to Egyptian planners are the great deposits of fossil water in the western desert. Nasserist policy makers envisaged upward of one million feddans blooming out in the oasis complex of Dakhla, Kharga, and Frafra. Only about 2 percent of that dream has been realized, but it still persists.

This string of oases, known as the New Valley, is underlaid by an extensive Nubian sandstone strata which holds ancient (20,000–30,000 years old) deposits of fossil water, and through which water slowly filters northward from the Erdi and Ennedi mountain ranges in the Chad basin. There may be as much as 234 billion m^3 of water locked away in this aquifer, portions of which come to the surface in the oases or in the Siwa and Qattara depressions. However, only about one percent of this water is stored within the first 150 meters below the surface. Because of the very slow rate of recharge, it may be possible to draw off only 1 billion m^3 a year without running the risk of lowering the water table drastically. For example, Libya developed 50,000 hectares at the Kufra oasis, using water from the same aquifer. In the first year's pumping, the water table dropped 10 meters. In Egypt, some experts believe the upper layers of the aquifer are already being overused and point out that at Kharga, wells 650 meters deep and more have had to be sunk. Either agricultural projects in the New Valley will have to remain on a modest scale (at 10,000 m^3 per feddan, 100,000 feddans could be cultivated annually with one billion m^3) or the water could be "mined" for a finite period, ultimately leading to the abandonment of the acreage as the area was mined out.[13]

Some Egyptian planners believe they have found a way out of this conundrum. The solution they propose reflects once again the chronic misunderstanding of Egypt's water resources. In May 1977, Egypt's top economic ministers (led by Deputy Prime Minister Dr. Abd al-Moneim al-Qaissuni) met in Paris with a consultative group of Western and Arab creditors and investors assembled by the IBRD. One of the goals of the meeting was to demonstrate to foreign sources of funding the extent of Egypt's investment potential. A number of projects were mentioned, but the Egyptian press treated one with particular fanfare. Dr. Abderrazzak Abd al-Maguid, the Minister of Planning, outlined a long-term plan for the integrated development of Southern Egypt, comprised of a horizontal strip running from the Red Sea in the east, across Aswan-Qena and Lake Nasser in the center, to the New Valley in the west. The Minister talked of mining centers, new cities, and vast agricultural potential that would permit the cultivation of three million new feddans (one million around Lake Nasser and two million in the New Valley) and the gradual transfer of five million Egyptians to the area (see Table 27).

Water, according to the economists, would come from wells in the oases and from Lake Nasser. They fastened upon the Tushka Depression project for flood control, suggested that it be permanently filled, and that a canal (they dubbed it the Kharga Canal) be excavated to draw off 8.6 billion m^3 of water to sustain the New Valley projects. The estimated cost of the canal is £E 460 million, although it is not clear if that figure includes outlays for reclamation. Whatever the case, the costs in water and money are staggering. Within days, officials of the Ministry of Irrigation, including the Minister himself, were compelled to rebut the premises of the Southern plan. Abu al-Atta stressed that Tushka would have no standing body of water, and that for decades at a time, if the reservoir did not rise above 178 meters above sea level, the depression might well remain bone dry. In his view, it was and is unjustifiable to transport Nile water to an area with great groundwater potential, and he stressed that the Ministry of Irrigation had no plans to do so. At most, in those years when excess flood waters were drawn off into the Tushka Depression, they could be piped to the New Valley to recharge the water table. Finally, it was made plain that there are not 8 billion m^3 of stored water lying about unclaimed.[14]

Whether or not the Southern strategy went back to the drawing board, other similar projects followed closely on its heels. In July 1977, President Sadat inaugurated the site for Ramadan 10 City on the road to Ismailia, the first of at least five new cities to be built in the desert. During the same month, the President visited the northwest coast where a new city is planned, as well as the reclamation of 144,000 feddans. The major existing urban center there is Marsa Matruh, currently so short of water that it must be brought in by tanker trains from Alexandria. It is proposed that the Nasser Canal which feeds the reclaimed areas along the western Delta be extended 200 kilometers to bring water to the new region. The inescapable impression created is

TABLE 27

Proposed Projects in Horizontal Expansion, 1976–2000

Zone	Total Plan Period* 1976–2000		1976–80		1981–85		1986–90		1991–95		1996–2000	
	Surface†	Cost‡	Surface	Cost	Surface	Cost	Surface	Cost	Surface	Cost	Surface	Cost
East Delta	1,335	572.85	251	153.35	257.	108.50	286	96	265	81	275	84
Central Delta	122	25.34	23	3.74	34.5	7	25.5	6.6	25	5	14	3
West Delta	293	126.1	103	48.2	48	85.2	57	25.7	50	10	35	7
Upper Egypt	112	23.8		.4		.4	32	6.5	50	10.5	30	6
Wadi Rayyan, Qattara, New Valley	1,355											
Total	3,217	748.09	377	205.69	339.5	201.10	301.5	134.8	390	106.5	354	100

SOURCE: Arab Republic of Egypt, Ministry of Irrigation, Abd al-Azim, Abu al-Atta, *Long-range Planning in the Sphere of Irrigation and Drainage* (Cairo: 1976). The Five-Year Plan, 1978–82, p. 107, using its own estimates, calls for total reclamation over the period 1978–87 of 2,093,000 feddans; 786,000 would be reclaimed up to 1983, and then 1,307,000 from 1983 to 1987, precisely the "crunch" years referred to in Table 25.

*1,117,000 feddans are to be reclaimed over the period 1976–90, corresponding roughly to the period of greatest shortage.

†Surface in 1,000 feddans.

‡Cost in millions £E.

that the government is as profligate in its spending of the nation's water resources as is the *fellah* in putting it on his fields.

Egypt cannot have it all ways. Cities in the desert, population transfers, millions of new cultivated acres, more intense use of old acres, heavy industrialization, self-sufficiency in basic foodstuffs: all bear water prices in excess of what Egypt can pay. Former Minister of Agriculture, Mustapha al-Gabali, has argued that to achieve self-sufficiency in food by the year 2000 would require a cropped area of about 22 million feddans. [15] There is simply no way to find fresh water for that kind of acreage (assuming that one could find the acres) at acceptable costs. Egypt must begin to weigh all projects in terms of their water components and to assess their final costs in full awareness that water is already a limited resource. That fact has only just begun to sink in, and many misconceived projects may be launched before it influences policy.

WATER SUPPLY AND DEMAND: THE SUDAN

Much the same process of spending water not yet earned is going on in the Sudan. We shall, in that respect, replicate the exercise carried out for Egypt. Our data are somewhat poorer but are still sufficient to determine general orders of magnitude. Part of the problem, happily for the Sudan, is that much of its agriculture is rainfed and segments of its underground water are recharged from sources independent of the Nile. We cannot treat the Sudan's water supply as a virtually closed system as in Egypt. Rather it is open-ended. But with this in mind, we may nonetheless rough out the present and future demand and supply profile for water drawn directly from the Nile.

We have already discussed the Upper Nile projects and need not go over them again. It is, however, important to note that beyond Phase I of Jonglei, the Sudan is anticipating execution of only one other project—the Machar Swamp scheme—before 1990, and that at a cost of $300 million. [16] The net water benefit to the Sudan as measured at Khartoum would be 2.4 billion m^3 from Jonglei and 2 billion m^3 from Machar. This is to be added to the Sudan's acquired right of 18.5 billion m^3 (as measured at Aswan) under the 1959 Agreement, which is in fact 20.5 billion m^3 as measured in the areas under irrigation. Real supply would thus be between 22.9 billion and 24.9 billion m^3 by the late 1980s and, assuming further progress on the Upper Nile projects, a little short of 30 billion m^3 by the turn of the century.

Acquired Right, 1959 Agreement	20.5 billion m³
Jonglei, Phase I (1984)	2.4 billion m³
Machar Swamps (1988?)	2.0 billion m³
Total	22.9–24.9 billion m³

Unlike Egypt, we have no statistic for return flow of drainage water. This is so because in the irrigated areas of the Sudan, the rudimentary artificial drains are designed only to draw off excess rainwater. Otherwise, the cultivated lands between the two Niles are allowed to drain naturally. While one must assume that some irrigation water will find its way back into the Nile, experiments at the Gezira-Managil scheme (ca. 2 million feddans) indicate that there is little waste in the on-field use of irrigation water; in fact water delivery may be somewhat below real crop-water needs.[17] Thus while there *may* be some return flow to the Sudanese Nile, there is not now any potential for reutilizing drainage water.

Calculating crop needs for the Sudan is demonstrably subject to wide margins of error. In the mid-1970s, about 4.8 million feddans were irrigated and supporting crops, or under active preparation. The per feddan water duty, according to the Ministry of Irrigation, is about 4,170 m³ per year. This is considerably less than the Egyptian average off 7–8,000 m³ annually. The difference can be explained by the fact that irrigated land in the Sudan is used much less intensively than in Egypt, with provisions for long fallows. For instance, at Gezira-Managil only about 60 percent of the land may be cropped at any one time. On this basis, one authoritative source, Saghayroun al-Zein, Sudan's Minister of Irrigation in 1977, tabulated agricultural water needs (see Table 28).

In addition to the 4.3 million feddans currently being exploited, medium term plans are to develop, in the next decade, another 2.3 million feddans (Rahad Phase II: 500,000 feddans; Seteit: 600,000; Renk-Gelhek: 400,000, etc.). By the turn of the century, a further 1.5 million feddans could be added along the Blue Nile. In projecting water demands for this acreage, official sources curiously plan for a reduction to 4,000 m³ per feddan per year in the medium term, and to 3,335 m³ over the long term. There seems little justification for such estimates.[18] By all accounts, land use will become more intensive in the coming decades, hence raising per feddan water needs. Moreover, a major shift into sugar cane and rice, as is planned, will increase crop demand considerably.

TABLE 28

Irrigated Crop Production Schemes in the Nile System

Sector	Area 1000 feddans	Water consumption millions m³
Blue Nile		
Downstream Sennar	164	976
Gezira-Managil	2,052	7,598
Pump Schemes Upstream Sennar	452	1,595
Rahad, Phase I*	300	1,139
Evaporation, Sennar Reservoir		669
White Nile		
Pump Schemes incl. Melut Asalaya, Kenana*	620	2,840
Main Nile		
Pump Schemes, downstream Khartoum	420	1,603
Atbara		
Khashm al-Girba	372	1,700
Evaporation Khashm al-Girba Reservoir		139
TOTAL	4,380	18,259

SOURCE: Saghayroun al-Zein, "The Water Resources of the Nile for Agricultural Development in Sudan," in Mohammed Obeid, ed. *Aquatic Weeds in the Sudan* NCR, ARC (Khartoum, November 1975).

*Projects still partially under execution. Note that no estimates are made for storage losses at Jebel Auliya and Roseires Reservoirs.

In an effort to approximate reality, we have worked out estimates of crop acreage and then used Kinawy's Upper Egyptian water duties to determine water needs. Our assumption is that the Sudan's hotter climate would offset the factor of seasonal rains so that Upper Egyptian water duties might be appropriate for the central Sudan.[19] Finally, we have held the water duty constant for the entire period covered by Table 29. The figures for 1975–76 seem to accord well with more aggregated Sudanese figures. Assuming that reasonable efficiency in water use has already been attained, we see no reason to reduce crop-water duties for the period 1985–86. If that hypothesis is correct,

TABLE 29

Irrigated Crop-Water Needs of the Sudan, 1975–76 and 1985–86

Crop	Irrig. Surface 1975–76 (feddans)	Crop-water req. m³ per feddan	Total water need, mill. m³	Irrig. 1000 feddans 1985–86	Total water need mill. m³
Cotton	825	4,700	3,879	905*	4,253
Sorghum	986	3,000	2,959	1,500	4,500
Wheat	707	2,100	1,484	1,010	2,121
Rice	16	9,000	147	100	900
Maize	9	3,300	3	20	660
Groundnuts	1,124	3,800	4,270	1,900	7,220
Sesame	4.5	2,440	11	6	14.0
Ful	35.8	1,600	57	50	80
Fruit & veg.	28	4,620	129	60	282
Sugar cane	42	17,800	753	400	7,120
Total	3,777.3		13,692	5,951	27,151.0

*This may be an underestimate as 450,000 feddans of cotton will be introduced at Rahad I and II alone, although wheat and rice may displace cotton acreage elsewhere. Part of the discrepancy may result from a shift from irrigated long-staple cotton to irrigated medium staple cotton. The figure of 905,000 refers only to long staple.

then we can anticipate agricultural water needs within a decade of at least 2 billion m³ and as much as 4 billion m³ in excess of likely supply.

Because sugar cane is destined to play a major role in creating this deficit, a separate word on sugar projects is warranted. Over the next ten to fifteen years a gross irrigated surface of up to 542,000 feddans will be put under cane. At any one time about 362,000 feddans will actually be planted, distributed as on Table 30.[20] In brief, by the end of the period under consideration, sugar cane may account for a third of the Sudan's agricultural water needs, and an even greater proportion of its likely supply.

Industrial and household consumption will not be of major significance in the foreseeable future. In 1973, on the basis of a clear underestimate of total population, the Sudan's inhabitants were classified as 2.6 million urban, 10.5 million rural, and 1.6 million nomadic. From the first two categories, we have been able to extract gross estimates of the

TABLE 30

Surface Proportion of Sudanese Sugar Cane

Project	Total surface, all crops	Net surface, sugar cane
Guneid (in operation)	38,500 feds.	20,000 feds.
Khashm al-Girba (in operation)	360,000 feds.	20,000 feds.
Kenana (projected)	120,000 feds.	80,000 feds.
Sennar (projected)	35,000 feds.	30,000 feds.
Hajar Asalaya (projected)	35,000 feds.	30,000 feds.
Melut (projected)	45,000 feds.	30,000 feds.
Renk-Gelhek (projected)	400,000 feds.	120,000 feds.
Seteit (projected)	600,000 feds.	60,000 feds.
Mongolla (projected)	28,000 feds.	12,000 feds.
	1,661,500 feds.	402,000 feds.

number of inhabitants who *probably* rely upon the Nile for household water. The total urban population in this respect was about 1.5 million in 1973. Using the Sudanese estimate of 150 liters per person per day, we arrive at annual urban household consumption of 83.5 million m³. Likewise, we estimate the relevant rural population to have been 4.05 million in 1973. With per capita, per day consumption of 40 liters, total annual water use by this group would thus be 59.1 million m³. Finally a very crude estimate of the consumption of the animal population that is watered directly from the Nile is about 30 million m³. The grand total is therefore 172 million m³ each year. The Sudanese population growth rate is believed to be 2.8 percent per year, and the animal population generally grows apace. In sum, we can advance a purely hypothetical figure of 100 million m³ annual consumption for industrial use, come to a total of ca. 275 million m³ of nonagricultural water consumption for the mid-1970s, double it for the mid-80s, and still come up with only 550 million m³.

We may now establish approximate estimates of total supply and demand for two points in time. The proved conveyance loss rate of the Gezira-Managil project is adopted as our guideline on Table 31.[21]

TABLE 31

Water Supply and Demand in the Sudan, 1975–76 and 1985–86
(bill. m^3)

Supply	1975–76	1985–86
Acquired rights	20.5	20.5
Jonglei, Phase I	—	+2.4
Total	20.5	22.9
Demand		
Agriculture	13.692	27.151
Conveyance loss 10%	1.369	2.715
Household & industrial	275	550
Storage Losses		
Jebel Auliya	1.000	1.000
Sennar/Roseires	.700	1.000 (after heightening of Roseires)
Khashm al-Girba	.190	.190
TOTAL	17.226	32.606
SURPLUS/DEFICIT	+3.274	−9.706

SOURCE: Figures compiled by the author.

One must, of course, treat the implications of this table with considerable caution. The entries for 1975–76 probably are not far from the mark. However, those for 1985–86 are more problematic. We *may* have maximized the potential water deficit in two ways. First, it may take longer than planned to increase the Sudan's irrigated acreage. Consequently, what we project in terms of crop needs may not become reality until the 1990s. Still, if one suspects that we are overstating the case, let it be recalled that the Arab Fund perspective calls for 9 million irrigated feddans by the year 2000 (or 36 billion m^3 at 4,000 m^3 per feddan). Second, some Upper Nile projects may come on-stream more quickly than forecast. Unlikely as that may be, if *all* were completed by 1986 the likely deficit would be reduced only from 9.7 billion to about 2.7 billion m^3.

Our tentative conclusion, as with Egypt, is that a deficit of varying magnitude is highly likely in the next decade. To emphasize this prospect we must introduce yet another factor: the Nile hyacinth. This plant, which floats in large clusters or islands in the Sudd swamps and the White Nile, was first observed in 1958 near Aba Island. In four years it had spread from Juba to the Jebel Auliya Dam. The plant reproduces exponentially and may have entered the Sudan from the Congo Basin. (It had also appeared in the Nile Delta just after the turn of the century.) By 1975, it had infested an area of some 3,000 km² in the Sudan. Its significance for our purposes is, essentially, that it increases surface evaporation rates two to three times. It is estimated that normal evaporation rates in the infested areas would be 9 billion m³ per year, whereas because of the hyacinth they are nearer 16.4 billion m³ annually. Put succinctly, "The outbreak of the water hyacinth (eichornia crassipes) in the Sudan is one of the environmental disasters of the century."[22]

Egypt has recently done battle with this plague and, through massive applications of herbicides (at an unknown ecological cost), avoided the loss of 3 billion m³ a year.* Whatever the techniques available, the results may be meager: "because of the viability of the plant, and its ability to reproduce sexually and asexually, it is believed that the best that can be hoped for is to strike a balance of control and utilization methods that will *contain the plant* and reduce its effect to manageable proportions"[23] (emphasis added).

By 1973, barges, helicopters, and airplanes had joined in the assault upon the Sudanese hyacinth in an area of 128,000 feddans. Egypt contributes directly to the small budget (£S 1 million) set aside to combat the hyacinth, and both countries are experimenting with natural predators (carp and weevils) to see if there are less ecologically destructive means to contain the plant.

As it is now, one cannot say that the hyacinth has caused an absolute decrease in the discharge of the White Nile, for most of the evapo-transpiration is taking place in the swamps where surface evaporation is enormous anyway. The real threat is further downstream. The entire stretch of the White Nile from Malakal to Jebel Auliya is partially infested by floating islands of hyacinth and papyrus. Jebel Auliya Dam, which we have noted was turned over by Egypt to full

---

*Jan Kamel, "Aquatic Weed Problems in Egypt," p. 2. 3-D herbicides are used to combat the hyacinth but already in the Sudd, through evapo-transpiration, they have caused extensive damage to tree and plant life along the swamps' habitable fringes. The hyacinth itself impedes river navigation, clogs irrigation pumps, interferes with native fishing, provides suitable environment for schistosome-bearing snails, and, through decomposition and decay, affects water quality.

Sudanese control in February 1977, is, above all else, the final barrier to the spread of the hyacinth to the Main Nile. At that, it is a frail defense. Another flood like that of 1975 might carry hyacinth islands round the dam and deliver them further downstream. Beyond that, the remarkable spread of *eichornia crassipes* around the globe has lead some experts to postulate that aquatic or migratory birds may carry seeds on their feet or in their plumage, which are then deposited in other waterways. (This theory could explain the isolated outbreak of the hyacinth in the northern Delta over 60 years ago.) The Blue Nile, which is relatively free of the plant, might in this way become infested. If the main Nile becomes infested it would simply be a question of time before the myriad *khors* of Lake Nasser/Nubia were themselves filled with hyacinth. Added to the already high rate of surface evaporation there (ca. 15 billion m^3 per year), the rapid spread of the plant could raise this figure by a third. We have not, however, assumed that such an eventuality is likely to take place; however, the potential danger of hyacinth infestation throughout the Nile Valley should not be minimized.

No attention has so far been paid to the likelihood that other riparian states will make claims upon the Nile's waters in the near future. To our knowledge, the only country contemplating projects that would reduce the discharge of the main Nile is Ethiopia. The Ethiopians surveyed the Blue Nile (or as they call it, the Abbai) system, with United States assistance, between 1957 and 1964. Included in the survey were the Atbara, Akobo, and Baro rivers. Projects have been marked out on the Blue Nile that would store water for the generation of 30 billion kWh each year and irrigate 4.6 million feddans. Similar, although smaller, projects have been earmarked for the Baro and the Taccaze, a tributary of the Atbara. Over the short term, irrigation projects on the Blue Nile, covering 225,000 feddans, have been selected, with another 71,000 on the Baro. Over the medium and long term, Ethiopian irrigation experts believe their agricultural water needs from the Blue Nile/Atbara may reach 4 billion m^3 per year. At Mar del Plata, Argentina, the Ethiopian delegation to the UN Water Conference stressed the sovereign right of any riparian state, in the absence of an international agreement, to proceed unilaterally with the development of water resources within its territory. At the same time, its delegates urged, as a general principle, basin-wide agreements to determine shares among co-riparians.[24] This is but another indication that the adequacy of the 1959 Nile Waters Agreement will come under increasing question in the near future.

The final balance sheet for the Egypto-Sudanese Nile, derived from all the foregoing analysis, registers these potential surpluses and deficits (see Table 32).

TABLE 32

Water Balances in the Egypto-Sudanese Nile, 1985–90
(bill. m³)

Country	Optimistic	Cautious	Pessimistic
Egypt	+15.8	− 6.8	−14.1
The Sudan	− 3.2	− 8.2	− 9.7
Ethiopia drawdown	− 1.0	− 2.0	− 4.0
System deficit/surplus	+11.6*	−17.0	−27.8

*Note that under the optimistic projection, the implied surplus is entirely Egyptian and could be shared with the Sudan only if Egypt agreed to reduce its drawdown at Aswan and to allow the Sudan to increase its effective share.

Once again, we stress that the deficits that may well emerge over the next decade are not inevitable. Nonetheless, in most of our calculations we have underestimated rather than overestimated the problem. While the fulfillment of expected demand throughout the system over the same time period is not beyond the realm of possibility, most evidence would suggest that it is highly unlikely.

The inescapable conclusion is that as national policy-making elites draw up and seek funding for nationally-oriented projects with heavy water demands, the Nile will be substantially overcommitted. It is our contention that this overcommitment is likely to develop *even if* all the Upper Nile projects are implemented in the next fifteen years. The implications are grave. Money, time, and expertise may be committed to developing projects now, only to find that an essential input is in short supply when the project is supposed to become self-sustaining. By that time, it will be too late to avoid substantial financial losses as well as major disruptions in development strategy.

For example, one could argue that given the ecological risks, the Jonglei project may be a mixed blessing if (1) only the first phrase is executed or if (2) it turns out that either the first phase alone or the project as a whole does not avert a major water crisis. If at the price of enormous capital outlays and ecological disruption, Egypt and the Sudan simply find that they have postponed a water shortage by some fifteen years, then it might make much better sense to pay close attention to opportunity costs *now*.

A second implication is that a new basin-wide accord on water allocation (and perhaps water quality) may have to be negotiated in the near future. The meeting of the Permanent Joint Technical Commission in June 1977 intimated steps in this direction. The task will be far from easy. The Sudan and Egypt may have to scrap some of their projected agricultural plans, and the determination of who scraps what, when, may require third party mediation. Our hunch would be that the wealthy Arab states of the peninsula, with strong political and economic stakes in both countries, will ineluctably be drawn into the role of mediator. Further, an outside assessment of the economics of the situation would probably favor the Sudanese; that is, potential might finally win out over existing needs. One must be cautious in putting forth this argument, but the agricultural future and likely rate of return on investments in the Sudan appear clearly superior to those of Egypt. As in all other facets of their relations with Egypt and the Sudan, the wealthy Arab states must tread the fine line between sound investment policies and the safeguarding of the political stability of friendly regimes. It would not be in the interests of Saudi Arabia, for instance, to so promote the development of the Sudan that it grievously damaged the Egyptian economy and thus the stability of its regime. Still, when concessions are required in the use of Nile waters, Egypt will probably be called upon to concede more than the Sudan.

One cannot help but wonder whether we are dealing here with feigned ignorance of what is developing. Could it be that Egypt and the Sudan are rushing ahead with projects that will use unavailable water in unspoken anticipation of future bargaining once the crisis is at hand? If, as in the past, great significance is attached in such bargaining to *actual* needs, then to have initiated and even populated as many projects as possible would be an intelligent tactic to insure the most favorable repartition of water in any new accord, and as matters now stand that will be a difficult challenge. The Sudanese and Ethiopians are making warlike noises at one another, although that kind of friction need not impede technical discussion of, nor policy consensus on, an equitable allocation of the Atbara–Blue Nile–Baro basins. Equally problematic would be the eventual inclusion of Kenya (hostile to Uganda), Uganda (hostile to Kenya and the Sudan), and Zaire (hostile to Ethiopia) in a new basin-wide agreement.

Two situations could obviate the otherwise looming water shortage: (1) a technological miracle of some sort (rapid, cheap implementation of the Upper Nile projects, drastic reductions in evapotranspiration through plant genetics, etc.); or (2) the stagnation of the Sudanese and Egyptian economies, both of which are carried by their agricultural sectors. The first situation is unlikely and the second undesirable. Consequently a shortage must be faced, and, in planning terms, the sooner the better. The shortage must be dealt with through the full battery of engineering, agronomic, strategic, and political instrumentalities that have always characterized interstate management of the Nile. The challenge is not new and has been met more or less successfully throughout this century. But today the stakes—economic and political—are far higher than ever before, and the margin for error far less than at any time in the past.

CONCLUSION

Prudence would dictate the avoidance of prediction, or, failing that, would urge prognostications so Delphic as to be meaningless. It is far safer to set down what has happened than what might happen. Still, there may be considerable benefit to be drawn from delineating what is probable, rather than what is possible or desirable. Policy makers, perhaps out of concern for their own sanity, dwell upon the latter two forms of forecasting. I will concentrate upon the first.

In the previous chapter it was argued that a critical shortage of varying magnitude in the Nile's waters is both possible and probable within a decade or so. It could be avoided by some of the following measures:

1. The Sudan could freeze its irrigation-based agricultural schemes at current levels and put all its energies into rainfed agriculture.

2. Egypt could delegate to the Sudan the task of agricultural production for a range of basic commodities and put most of its energies into industrialization. The Sudan, in return, could agree to barter agricultural produce against Egyptian manufactures, if need be at the expense of its own domestic industries.

3. Both countries could make dramatic breakthroughs in efficient water use by (a) re-education of their peasantries; (b) introduction of high-cost sealed water delivery systems; (c) introduction of as-yet undeveloped varieties of seeds with high yields and low water needs.

4. All projects of the Upper Nile scheme could be negotiated, funded, and completed within fifteen years, with no other riparian states making supplemental demands on Nile tributaries arising in or flowing through their territories.

Any one or some combination of all the above could avert the crisis. But the point is that none of these possibilities appears to be more than remotely probable. It would be no humiliation to be proved fundamentally wrong in this judgment, but one must summarize the reasons why such a happy eventuality is unlikely.

242

The first is that the process of resource planning in developing countries is *willfully* fragmented. On the one hand, the very fact of economic backwardness causes a widespread espousal of the need for comprehensive planning to minimize waste. On the other hand, because by definition resources are scarce in such situations, it is implicitly realized that (1) substantial segments of the population will have to be regimented in their utilization of resources or deprived of them altogether, and (2) that errors in the utilization of one resource will lead to dislocations throughout the entire economic system. The result is that the ideal of comprehensive planning is regularly violated in practice. Planners and policy makers limit their responsibility by limiting their range of vision and by retreating into narrowly defined competences. Sectoral and time horizons are constricted as far as possible. Each specialized agency seeks a closely defined mission and relies upon the information of other relevant agencies in designating targets. If the information is erroneous or not forthcoming, and if targets are missed, the blame can be shifted to other quarters. Similarly, to launch a project at time X is relatively costless, for its benefits or shortcomings will not accrue until time Y, well after its originators have passed form the scene. When the shortcomings do become apparent, the incumbent policy makers can justifiably place the blame upon their predecessors. Short of criminal neglect no one is held to account except the society itself.

All too often, bilateral and multilateral aid-granting bodies comply with this pattern of "planning" for roughly similar motives. Their *raison d'être* is to move funds, and prudent inactivity will not win their administrators any plaudits or promotions. Thus they operate with the information provided them or seek to supplement it on the strength of lightning surveys whose conclusions are — not infrequently — foregone. Here again, fragmentation of the field of analysis serves as a defense mechanism to limit responsibility for what may or will go wrong. A top-ranking official in the UN World Food Council commented on this saying, "There is a lot be be gained from not knowing what is going on." There is, then, a natural collusion between the administrators of aid programs and the formulators of programs and projects they wish to aid. Developing societies are alone held responsible for the inefficiencies engendered by this collusion.

To cite concrete examples of this phenomenon, we may note that the Ministries of Irrigation in both Egypt and the Sudan have gone on record repeatedly with the view that there is adequate water in the Nile system for all currently projected programs. In turn, national planning bodies take that view at face value and draw up projects accordingly. In some instances, they run too far with the ball, as appears to be the case with Egypt's project to introduce irrigation to three million feddans in the southwestern desert. But the assumption of adequate water supply is generally and uncritically held and crops up in the evaluations of international bodies such as the ILO/UNDP, IBRD, and USAID. When and if a shortage develops, it is unlikely that any of those in responsible positions today will be around to answer for the miscalculations that led to it.

The ultimate use and allocation of a scarce resource such as water will depend as much as anything upon considerations of a geo-political nature. That, after all, is the single most important factor explaining the decision to go ahead with the High Dam as opposed to any alternative project. Problems of national security, regional rivalries, relations with the great powers, etc., may dictate policies that wreak havoc with the rational, efficient utilization of land, water, or people. A basin-wide accord on the allocation of the Nile in light of the possibilities and real needs of all riparians would be a step toward optimal utilization, but under present circumstances, geo-political susceptibilities are such that an accord of this kind is not in the offing.

Optimal utilization would also imply a basin-wide division of labor subject to constant adjustments. Once the notion is accepted that the Nile waters are not limitless, then all those who benefit from the river must arrive at an understanding of basic priorities. The kinds of practical questions that would logically arise are indicative of the momentous political issues at stake. For example, Egypt wishes to ease population pressure in the Nile Valley by using about 10 percent of the river's average annual discharge to water the deserts and move people to them. Could a more rational use be made of this water and still achieve the demographic goal? One could instead argue that the Sudanese should retain the same amount of water in order to develop good but underexploited acreage between the two Niles or in the Sudd region, opening the new lands to Egyptian settlement. One may judge for oneself the likelihood of that kind of trade-off. Optimal utilization will fall victim to national sovereignties. Egypt and the Sudan will pursue their national economic growth strategies with little regard to one another, both proclaiming their determination to achieve, at a minimum, self-sufficiency in the production of strategic foodstuffs. It is safe to wager that neither will do so, at least not in this century, but in so endeavoring they will have overcommitted the Nile waters to projects of national autarky. It will be very difficult to stop, much less undo, the projects launched in this manner.

The final factor detracting from optimal utilization is that of the goals of those who provide external financing. The most "enlightened" of these, AFSED, has approached Sudanese agriculture as a national system, destined to produce a surplus that other deficit Arab states *may* purchase according to their means. Most aid-granting agencies are mandated to deal only with national entities (or parts thereof) although we have seen that the IBRD has been able in the past to make its grants contingent upon international accords. To date, the only international agency to finance a program involving several riparian states within the Nile system is the World Meteorological Organization, and its focus is on data-gathering, not the implementation of water utilization projects.

The attitudes of Saudi Arabia, Kuwait, the United Arab Emirates, and Qatar may be determinant in this respect. Because of their financial leverage, they may be able to impose a division of labor between Egypt and the Sudan which in turn may be distasteful to the Egyptians. To the extent that the Sudan becomes the home for substantial placements of public and private capital (in the Arabian peninsula/Gulf, the distinction is frequently obscure) with expectations of a solid economic return, the investors will probably use their weight to assure the Sudan all the water it needs to make its projects work. Similar opportunities in agriculture do not exist on the same scale in Egypt, where, in any case, past experience has tended to discourage Arab investors in all but tourism and housing. Such influence will not be exercised before a clear and present crisis in water supply has manifested itself, which may mean that Egypt will find itself burdened with a number of half-completed projects destined to die of thirst. But, if our assumptions about Saudi motivations are correct, this would not mean economic disaster for Egypt. Then, as now, deficiencies in economic performance, particularly as they relate to levels of imports and foreign exchange balances, can be covered by politically determined subventions. The goal will be to avert any kind of economic crisis that could undermine a moderate, pro-Western regime in Cairo. There is no guarantee that Saudi Arabia could bring this off successfully nor any hard indication that it has even thought about this possible dichotomy in the advantages it seeks from its two very dissimilar clients in the Nile Valley. In that sense, the scenario described above is a speculative exercise, but one that has not yet received the attention it merits.

This conclusion may smack of Murphy's Law, "Whatever can go wrong, will," but it may be advisable to anticipate the worst rather than to plan for the utopian. The factors making for poor utilization of the Nile waters apply in other countries and other regions, developed or developing, where finite natural resources are under heavy stress. A policy of internationalism in resource management is increasingly in order. Unfortunately, it tends to raise the hackles of most national elites. The acrimonious debates on the law of the sea and the codes of conduct for the use of transboundary bodies of water have amply demonstrated that its advent is not for tomorrow. Further, whatever proposals for international management of scarce resources are made, they must be as comprehensive as possible, taking into account the impact of various formulas upon questions of national security, the well-being of domestic constituencies, and the survival of political regimes. Failing that, the best-intentioned recommendations will be stillborn. The greatest challenge of all, however, is for nations that have recently acquired political sovereignty, frequently after long combat with imperialist masters, to overcome their susceptibilities and derogate some modicum of their prize in the name of regional growth. What is called for is more difficult than policies adopted out of enlightened self-interest; they must be policies adopted out of enlightened national self-sacrifice.

Between altruistic internationalism and pig-headed pursuit of national interest, are there middle-range approaches to resource crises?

Resource management in the contemporary world requires highly complex technical analyses and policies. This complexity is compounded where resources are increasingly scarce. Nowhere in the world are the highest political authorities attuned to, much less versed in, the technical considerations that would make for optimality in resource allocation and utilization. There is no reason to expect them to be so, and, to the contrary, perhaps good reason to hope that technocrats will not seize or have thrust upon them the levers of political command.

The real challenge is rather to seek those institutional means by which the technocrats may identify policy options and variable costs and benefits. These latter will be calculated in economic and resource terms. It thus remains the prerogative of national leadership to weigh the political and social costs and benefits. For example, we have paid considerable attention to the political determinants of Egypt's High Aswan Dam decision: the geo-political benefit of having the key to assured water supply within Egypt's borders. No credible cost-benefit analysis could afford to overlook this factor, no matter how difficult it might be to quantify its impact. In this sense, the geo-political return may well outweigh the more publicized economic costs. It is much the same sort of situation that prevails in military expenditures. Egypt and many other countries may reasonably justify defense outlays clearly in excess of what their economies should be asked to bear, because these arrangements allow them to bargain effectively in the international arena. Similarly, the High Dam enables Egypt to bargain with a strong hand in all matters relating to Nile water supply and to avoid dependence upon the good will of various riparians. This should be kept in mind before bemoaning the reduction in Egypt's sardine catch.

Economic and political cost-benefit analysis are not separate fields, and it is because of their interdependence that instrumentalities may be devised to link the technocrat to the politician. Obviously, if the long-term economic impact of the High Dam is to weaken the agricultural sector, the result might be to heighten Egypt's vulnerabililty to external pressure (through food imports among other things) to a degree that would outweigh the geo-political benefits mentioned above. The fact is, however, that as a rule the politically determined decision comes first and it is exceedingly difficult thereafter to nurture the informed and dispassionate debate requisite to assessing long-term costs. The political decision frequently embodies a symbolic package that is designed to catch peoples' imagination at home and abroad, to arouse the populace, to set collective goals, and thus to find in motivational terms a substitute for war. This is an atmosphere fundamentally inhospitable to the niggling of conscientious technocrats who may be seen as frontmen, witting or unwitting, for the regime's enemies. Their sincerity will be in question. This has been the case in Egypt, where the sense of national cohesion and even the consensus about national goals and leadership is far more pronounced than in many, if not most, Third World countries. But who would publicly stand up today to question the wisdom of sowing the desert with new cities or trying to make the Sinai green and populous? If this sort of debate is stifled in Egypt, then how much more so in the Sudan, where national cohesion and political consensus are either fragile or non-existent?

Yet it is certain that political elites need good technical advice, not so much to find ways to implement poorly-conceived policies, but indeed to avoid them altogether. One may dwell on the instability of developing countries, but when one looks at the Arab world, there are several regimes that have had extraordinary longevity — Egypt 27 years, Tunisia 23, Morocco 23, Algeria 14, the Sudan 10, Jordan 29 (at least), and Libya 10, as of spring 1979. Many leaders, perhaps to their own surprise, have been or will be around to reap the praise or opprobrium stemming from their development policies. They may have to live with, or like Sukarno, die politically for their mistakes. Thus, while sycophancy is a virus hard to contain, there may be a growing disposition among the highest state authorities to seek measures of immunization.

In regimes where formal checks and balances on the exercise of political power are relatively few, it will be very difficult to institutionalize procedures for expert assessment of policy costs. Legislation would not suffice. It could be written into law that every major project or development policy be subject to "impact analysis" by "independent" review boards. But, like the courts themselves, who can guarantee their independence, the representivity of their members, or their right to be highly critical or even negative? At present, no one. Moreover, the greater the economic-cum-political crisis in a country, the less leaders are willing to accept questioning of their best—albeit desparate—judgment. If we look again at the countries mentioned above, none but Egypt in the early 1960s and Algeria since 1968, have engaged in a long-term economic policy. Thus expediency and short-term survival tactics cannot be all that bad, except that structural crises deepen and require ever more artful patching to cover over the fissures.

Four avenues might be followed to promote regular procedures for bringing together and weighting the political and economic aspects of policy evaluation. Two are necessarily long-term, and depend upon a third which is crucial. This latter is, very simply, that the need for this kind of policy assessment be recognized explicitly and that a sort of code of professional conduct, political and expert, be delineated to set ground rules for the interaction and to underwrite the legitimacy of all participants. If this is established, then the other two avenues become open for travel. In the course of professional training, the would-be technocrat will have it driven home that it is both his duty and his right to speak out on policy issues, and that he is legally protected in so doing. This intersects with the second avenue, whereby precedents are set and the beginnings of a tradition established. There will always be an Abd al-Aziz Ahmad around to leap into the unknown, but in the future the outcome must be different. Would it have cost Nasser so much to have said, "We distrust Ahmad's motives, we question his competence, but the points he makes are important and we will study them and make both his and our arguments public"? Although the Jonglei Canal is not yet and, one hopes, never will be the symbol of struggle with colonial powers, one discerns in the Sudanese a willingness to entertain the possibility that the project contains serious drawbacks and that these are the legitimate subject of domestic and international debate. The Sudanese today may establish a precedent for which the Sudanese of tomorrow will be grateful.

The fourth avenue could be pursued immediately. Countries with the deepest economic crises and the most daunting challenges in resource management are nearly always those that resort most heavily to external borrowing to finance development needs. Organizations such as the IBRD have become much more attuned in recent years to the necessity of carrying out environmental (although not so often social) impact studies. This trend must be pursued in conjunction with other international creditors (in the Sudan with AFSED for example), with a view toward fostering the emergence of the professional ethic and the political acceptance of continuous policy review. It is a fine line between the benevolent nurture of the kind of interaction we espouse and direct interference in the affairs of a sovereign state. But that line is violated in so many other ways by international creditors that the added risk appears acceptable, given its potential pay-off.

This argument does not require that countries such as Egypt become liberal democracies, that materially-endowed interest groups promote elaborate legal mechanisms to defend their goals or promote their views, or that political elites surrender their preoccupations with survival and power to the clinical conclusions of economic cost-benefit analysis. Rather it aims at middle-range institutional and procedural changes and innovations that appear unavoidable (although some would still qualify them as utopian) if resource crises in the last quarter of the twentieth century are to be met, much less mastered. For Egypt and the Sudan, the greatest challenges in Nile management lie ahead. By what they jointly or separately do in the coming decade, they will either establish patterns of interaction that others would do well to avoid or set an example worthy of emulation in other river basins around the world.

APPENDIX

Analysis of Flood Records for the Natural Yield of the Main Nile at Aswan for Hydrologic Years, 1870/71–1975/76

Detailed flood records for the discharge of the main Nile over the past century lend some credence to the notion of a secular decline in the average volume of the flood. We have presented the data in two forms: first, the simple tabulations, water-year by water-year; second, as a graph with entries for each year and a least-squares regression line of best fit showing the slope of the decline. The tabular data require no comment *per se*, but the regression analysis clearly does. For both presentations, it should be kept in mind what is meant by natural yield. Until the 1920s, the natural yield of the Nile as measured at Aswan scarcely differed from the real yield. But as the Sudan began to draw off water for agricultural purposes, the natural yield statistic became a hypothetical estimate of what would have been discharged at Aswan had the Sudan not drawn off any water. Real discharge, measured upstream of the entrance to Lake Nubia/Nasser, is therefore a considerably smaller figure than that of natural yield.

Let us turn to the figure that accompanies this Appendix. The mean annual discharge for the period covered is 92.67 billion m^3 and the standard deviation about this mean is 30.7 billion m^3. We have 105 observations recorded which are plotted on the graph below. Least squares regression analysis yields a best-fitting line sloping downward from left to right at an average annual rate of decline of 228 million m^3. The rate of decline is statistically significant at the .005 level and thus cannot be attributed to chance phenomena.

Does this mean that the Nile is perhaps in a short-term secular decline in average annual discharge? For the entire period under scrutiny, the answer would have to be "yes." Yet the graph tells us visually that that conclusion should probably be modified. The overall trend is unquestionably downward, but the trough in discharge was reached in the two decades between 1915 and 1936. Since that date there has been some increase in discharge, although not to levels prevailing in the late 1800s. If we split the data into two roughly equal sections — 1870–1920 and 1920–1975 — we find that the mean discharge for the first period is 96.3 billion m^3 and for the second, 88.02 billion m^3. However, if we take ten-year means, we discover that Egypt enters the trough in the period 1901–1910 and continues thus:

10-Year Period	Average Annual Discharge
1901–10	86.3 billion m³
1911–20	82.8 billion m³
1920–30	82.3 billion m³
1930–40	85.2 billion m³
1940–50	82.4 billion m³

Thereafter, the natural yield increases somewhat to 89.3 billion m³ for the decade 1950–60 and to 91.4 billion m³ for the period 1960–70. After that point, the mean discharge declines to 86.8 billion m³ for 1971–75. In sum, while there can be no question that the discharge of the Nile has been declining in the past century, one may well ask whether the decline bottomed out in the 1940s, and whether the Nile is waxing in terms of the water it delivers downstream. It may still be a resurgence within an overall trend toward reduced yield; then again it

Natural yield of the Nile at Aswan by hydrologic year, 1870/71–1975/76

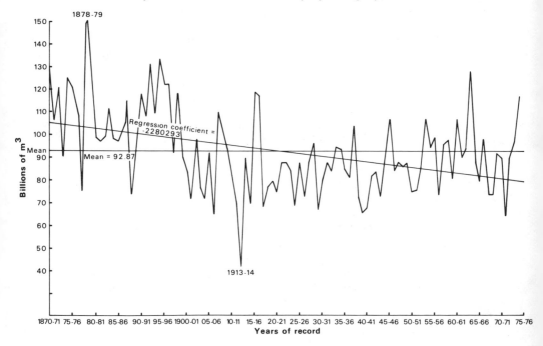

TABLE 33

Water-Year by Water-Year Natural Yield Recordings for 1870/71 –1975/76
(billions m³)

Year	Volume	Year	Volume	Year	Volume	Year	Volume
1870/71	131	1900/01	90	1930/31	68	1960/61	81
71/72	106	01/02	84	31/32	80	61/62	107
72/73	121	02/03	72	32/33	88	62/63	90
73/74	90	03/04	98	33/34	84	63/64	94
74/75	125	04/05	77	34/35	95	64/65	128
.1875/76	121	1905/06	72	1935/36	94	1965/66	88
76/77	111	06/07	92	36/37	85	66/67	80
77/78	75	07/08	66	37/38	81	67/68	98
78/79	150	08/09	110	38/39	104	68/69	74
79/80	129	09/10	102	39/40	73	69/70	74
1880/81	99	1910/11	94	1940/41	66	1970/71	92
81/82	97	11/12	81	41/42	66	71/72	90
82/83	99	12/13	70	42/43	82	72/73	65
83/84	111	13/14	42	43/44	84	73/74	90
84/85	98	14/15	90	44/45	73	74/75	97
1885/86	97	1915/16	70	1945/46	86	1975/76	117
86/87	102	16/17	119	46/47	107	(provisional)	
87/88	115	17/18	117	47/48	84		
88/89	74	18/19	69	48/49	88		
89/90	99	19/20	77	49/50	86		
1890/91	118	1920/21	80	1950/51	88		
91/92	108	21/22	75	51/52	75		
92/93	131	22/23	88	52/53	76		
93/94	109	23/24	88	53/54	86		
94/95	133	24/25	84	54/55	107		
1895/96	122	1925/26	69	1955/56	94		
96/97	122	26/27	84	56/57	99		
97/98	92	27/28	73	57/58	74		
98/99	118	28/29	84	58/59	96		
99/ 0	63	29/30	98	59/60	98		

SOURCE: Unpublished statistics, Arab Republic of Egypt, Ministry of Irrigation.

may not. Suffice it to say that the question must be considered open and that planners proceed accordingly. It is important to bear in mind that the mean discharge figure of 84 billion m^3 used in Sudano-Egyptian negotiations over the High Dam was based on the period 1900–59, bracketing the trough mentioned above, and both countries may have subsequently enjoyed Nile discharge over and above what they had anticipated.

It is of course true that 105 years out of the life of a river as ancient as the Nile is virtually insignificant. Perhaps twenty-five to fifty years from now, we shall witness a great and steady upsurge in Nile discharge; then again, perhaps we won't. The point is that the next twenty-five years are crucial to the development strategies and prospects of both the Sudan and Egypt, so that even if the phenomenon at which we are hinting is temporary, it falls, devastatingly, at a peculiarly crucial moment.

NOTES

INTRODUCTION

1. FAO, *Water for Agriculture*, E/Conf. 70/11, January 29, 1977, prepared for the UN Water Conference, Mar del Plata, Argentina, March 14–25, 1977, p.4.

2. Cited in John Waterbury and Ragaei el-Mallakh, *The Middle East in the Coming Decade* (New York: McGraw-Hill, 1978), p. 65. See also Mohammed Masmoudi, former Tunisian Minister of Foreign Affairs, who treats Egypt and the Sudan as the "hinge" of the Arab world: *Les Arabes daus la tempête* (Paris: Simeon, 1977), p. 224.

3. CAMPAS, General al-Askar, *The Population of Egypt: Results of the General Census of November 1976*, special supplement of *al-Ahram al-Iqtisadi*, May 1, 1977; in Arabic.

CHAPTER 1

Development of The River System

1. The literature on the Nile system is justifiably extensive. The classic technical account is the multivolume study directed by Hurst, Black, Phillips, and Simaika. See esp. H. E. Hurst and P. Phillips, *The Nile Basin: Vol. I, General Description of the Basin, Meteorology, Topography of the White Nile Basin* (Cairo: Ministry of Public Works, Physical Department, Government Printing Office, 1931); and H. E. Hurst, R. P. Black, and Y. M. Simaika, *Vol. VII: The Future Conservation of the Nile*, (Cairo: Publisher as above, 1946). In addition see Sir William Willcocks, *The Nile in 1904* (London, 1904); H. E. Hurst, *The Nile* (London: Constable, rev. ed. 1957); the Sudan Government, Public Relations Branch, *Sudan Almanac 1954* (Khartoum, 1954); Democratic Republic of the Sudan, Ministry of Irrigation, *Control and Use of Nile Waters in the Sudan* (Khartoum, June 1975); and the important geopolitical analysis of Gamal Hamdan, *Shakhsiyyat Misr: A Study in the Genius of a Place* (Cairo: Anglo-Egyptian Bookshop, 1970), in Arabic; Julian Rzoska, ed., *The Nile: Biology of an Ancient River* (The Hague: Dr. W. Junk, 1976).

2. From Beardsley's comment in C. S. Jarvis, "Flood-Stage Records of the River Nile," *Proceedings of the American Society of Civil Engineers* (August 1935):1046. I am grateful to Reid Bryson for calling this article to my attention.

3. Reid A. Bryson, "Climatic Modification by Air Pollution, II: The Sahelian Effect," Report 9, Institute for Environmental Studies, University of Wisconsin (August 1973); and Reid A. Bryson and Thomas Murray, *Climates of Hunger* (Madison: University

of Wisconsin Press, 1977), pp. 95–106. A prescient article that fastened on basic climatic dynamics for all the Sahel is G. T. Renna, Jr., "A Famine Zone in Africa: the Sudan," *Geographical Review* 16 (4) (1926):583–96.

4. For extensive treatment and debate of Nile records see C. S. Jarvis, "Flood-Stage Records," pp. 1012–70; and S. A. Prince Omar Toussoun, *Memoire sur l'Histoire du Nil* (Cairo: Imprimerie de l'Institut Francais, (1925), Tomes I and II, pp. 361–454.

5. Gamal Hamdan, "Evolution de l'Agriculture irriguée en Egypt," in *A History of Land Use in the Arid Regions* (Paris: UNESCO, 1961), pp. 133–61 (citation p. 136).

6. Republic of the Sudan, *Control and Use of Nile Waters*, p.7.

7. K. Butzer, "Environment and Human Ecology in Egypt during Predynastic and Early Dynastic Times," *Bulletin de la Société Géographique de l'Egypte*, 32 (1959).

8. K. Butzer, *Early Hydraulic Civilization in Egypt* (Chicago: University of Chicago Press, 1976), p. 110. Cf. Chapter 9 of this book for the latter-day manifestations of local manipulations of the irrigation system. For the general theory, Karl Wittfogel, *Oriental Despotism* (New Haven: Yale University Press 1957).

9. Robert M. C. Adams, "Historic Patterns of Mesopotamian Civilization" (pp. 1–6), and McGuire Gibson, "Violation of Fallow and Engineered Disaster in Mesopotamian Civilization" (pp. 7–20), in T. E. Downing and McGuire Gibson, eds., *Irrigation's Impact on Society*, Anthropological Papers of the University of Arizona, No. 25 (Tucson: University of Arizona Press, (1974).

10. H. E. Hurst in Jarvis, "Flood-Stage Records," p. 1037, pointed out that these practices rendered the flood readings at the Roda Nilometer at Cairo susceptible to wide error, for the initial flooding of the basins lowered the flood peak appreciably. Indeed, the release of waters 40 days later could on occasion produce a second peak as large as the first.

11. Butzer, *Early Hydraulic Civilization*, p. 48, 91–92, and 109.

12. See Hamdan, "Evolution de l'Agriculture," p. 142; D. Mackenzie Wallace, *Egypt and the Egyptian Question* (1883), esp. pp. 250–53; Raoul de Chamberet, *Enquête sur la condition du Fellah égyptien* (1909); Helen Rivlin, *The Agricultural Policy of Mohammed Ali in Egypt* (Cambridge, Mass.: Harvard University Press, 1961).

13. Mackenzie Wallace, *Egypt and the Egyptian Question*, pp. 15, 250.

14. See E. R. J. Owen, *Cotton and the Egyptian Economy: 1820–1914* (Oxford: At the University Press, 1960), p. 144, and the article he cites: J. J. Craig, "Notes on Cotton Statistics in Egypt," *l'Egypte Contemporaine*, 6 (March 1911):180–81; R. L. Tignor, *Modernization and British Colonial Rule in Egypt: 1882–1914* (Princeton University Press, 1966); 'Issam al-Dessouqi, *Large Landowners and their Role in Egyptian Society* (Cairo: New Culture Publishing House, 1975, p. 135; in Arabic); and de Chamberet, *la condition du Fellah*, p. 83.
p. 83.

15. E. W. Lane, *Manners and Customs of the Modern Egyptians* (New York: Dutton, 1966), pp. 498–503.

16. Willcocks, *The Nile in 1904*, p. 71; and Mackenzie Wallace, *Egypt and the Egyptian Question*, pp. 240–41.

17. Willcocks, cited in Jarvis, "Flood-Stage Records," p. 1045.

18. Tignor, *British Colonial Rule in Egypt*, pp. 224–25.

19. Hurst, *The Nile*, p. 286.

CHAPTER 2

Political and Economic Unity

1. Tony Barnett, "The Gezira Scheme: Production of Cotton and Reproduction of Underdevelopment," in Ivar Oxaal et al., *Beyond the Sociology of Development* (London: Routledge and Kegan Paul, 1975), pp. 183–207.

2. There is abundant literature on this very important period. On the occupation and events leading up to it, see Anouar Abdel-Malek, *Idéologie et renaissance nationale: l'Egypte moderne* (Paris: Editions Anthropos, 1960), pp. 335–479; David Landes *Bankers and Pashas* (Cambridge, Mass.: Harvard University Press, 1958); P. J. Vatikiotis, *The Modern History of Egypt* (New York: Praeger, 1969), pp. 126–164. On the European scramble for the rest of Africa, that was touched off by the British occupation of Egypt, see R. Robinson, J. Gallagher, and A. Denny, *Africa and the Victorians* (New York: St. Martin's 1961).

3. See P. M. Holt, *The Mahdist State in the Sudan* (Oxford: At the University Press, 1958); Thomas Hodgkin, "Mahdism, Messianism, and Marxism in the African Setting," in Yusuf Fadl Hassan, ed., *Sudan in Africa* (Khartoum: Khartoum University Press 1971).

4. See Harold Mac Michael, *The Anglo-Egyptian Sudan* (London: Faber and Faber, 1939), and in general on this period of history, P. M. Holt, *A Modern History of the Sudan* (London: Weidenfeld and Nicolson, 1967), and Ahmad Hamrush, *The Story of the July 23 Revolution*, Pt. III *Nasser and the Arabs* (Beirut: Mu'assassa al-Arabia lil dirasat wa li nashr, 1976), pp. 271–368.

5. See P. K. Bechtold, *Politics in the Sudan* (New York: Praeger 1976), pp. 32–34.

6. In the extensive literature on the conspiracy in Arabic and other languages, see Anouar Abdel-Malek, *Egypt: Military Society* (New York: Random House, 1968); P. J. Vatikiotis, *The Egyptian Army in Politics* (Bloomington: Indiana University Press, 1961); Ahmad Hamrush, *The Story of the July Revolution*, Parts I and II (Beirut: Arab Organization for Studies and Publishing, 1974–75); Abd al-Latif al-Baghdadi, *The Memoirs of Abd al-Latif al Baghdadi*, Part I (Cairo: The Modern Egyptian Library, 1977).

7. Ahmad Hamrush, *The Story of the July Revolution*, Part II: *Gamal Abd al-Nasser's Group* (Beirut: The Arab Organization for Studies and Publishing, 1974–75), pp. 11–12, and Ibrahim Tala't, "The Last Days of the Wafd," *Ruz al-Yussef* 2531 (December 13, 1976).

8. Hamrush, *July Revolution*, Part II: *Gamal Abd al-Nasser's Group*, p. 14.

9. By far the best account of the 1954 RCC crisis is Dr. Abd al-Aziz Ramdan, *Abd al-Nasser and the March Crisis* (Cairo: Ruz al-Yussef Press, 1976), but see also Hamrush and Baghdadi.

10. Hamrush, *July Revolution*, Part II: *Gamal Abd al-Nasser's Group*, pp. 19–25.

11. Al-Baghdadi, *The Memoirs of Abd al-Latif al Baghdadi*, Part I, pp. 273–276.

12. Holt, "Modern History," *A Modern History of the Sudan, p. 131;* and Bechtold, *Politics in the Sudan,* p. 80. Both authors refer to unnamed but allegedly sure sources in accounting for Azhari's motives.

13. Cited by Ibrahim Tala't, "The Last Days of the Wafd," *Ruz al-Yussef* 2531 (December 13, 1976).

14. Robert Tignor, *Modernization and British Colonial Rule in Egypt: 1882–1914* (Princeton: Princeton University Press 1966), p. 219.

15. Dr. Abbas Ammar, "The Unity of the Nile Valley: Its Natural Ethnographic, Cultural, and Economic Foundations," in A. Ammar, Muhammed Shafiq Ghorbal Bey, Dr. Ibrahim Nashi, and Dr. Ahmad Badawi, *Unity of the Nile Valley: Its Geographic Foundations and its Manifestations in History* (Cairo: al Amiria Printing House 1947), pp. 1–62.

16. *The Five Year Plan* 4 (Cairo: Ministry of Planning, August 1972), 36.

17. See Ahmad Yussef al-Qar'i, "Unity of the Nile Valley and Egypto-Sudanese Integration," *International Politics* 42 (Cairo: October 1975):137–142, and 'Assam Rifa'at, "The Parameters of Economic Integration with the Sudan," *al-Ahram al-Iqtisadi* 450 (May 15, 1974):22–24.

18. The agricultural project was presumably largely inspired by the *Project for Mechanized Production of Sorghum, Oil Seeds, and Fodder: Southern Funj Region, Sudan* (Khartoum: Arab Organization for Agricultural Development, June 1974). See also *al-Ahram*, November 11 and 23, 1976. For evidence that all was not proceeding smoothly at the level of implementation see Tuhani Ibrahim, "Egypto-Sudanese Integration: How Far?" *Akhbar al-Yom* (June 14, 1975).

CHAPTER 3

Water Supply and Security

1. Harold and Margaret Sprout, "Environmental Factors in the Study of International Politics," in James Rosenau, ed., *International Politics and Foreign Policy* (Glencoe: Free Press, 1961), pp. 106–19; Citations from pp. 107 and 117.

2. See R. L. Tignor, "Nationalism, Economic Planning, and Development Projects in Inter-war Egypt," *International Journal of African Historical Studies* 10 (2) (1977):185–208. MacDonald's study was issued as *Nile Control* (Cairo: Ministry of Public Works, 1920).

3. From the November 22, 1924, ultimatum cited by Harold Mac Michael, *The Anglo-Egyptian Sudan* (London: Faber and Faber, 1937).

4. Cited by A. H. Garretson, "The Nile Basin," in A. H. Garretson et al., *The Law of International Drainage Basins* (Dobbs Ferry, N.Y.: Oceana, 1967), pp. 256–97.

5. *Ibid.*, p. 267.

6. On the negotiations, see Ministry of Irrigation, *The Nile Waters Question: The Case for the Sudan; the Case for Egypt and the Sudan's Reply* (Khartoum: December 1955); K. M. Barbour, "A New Approach to the Nile Waters Problem," *International Affairs* 33 (3) July 1957: 319–30; and L.A. Fabunmi, *The Sudan in Anglo-Egyptian Relations: A Case Study in Power Politics* (London: Longmans, 1960).

7. Ministry of Irrigation, *Nile Waters Question*, p. 36.

8. *New York Times*, 2 June 1955, cited in Tareq Ismael, "The UAR and the Sudan," *Middle East Journal* 23 (1) (Winter 1969): 14–28.

9. P. K. Bechtold, *Politics in the Sudan* (New York: Praeger, 1976), p. 312.

10. *Ibid.*, pp. 196–207.

11. D. C. Watt, "The High Dam at Aswan and the Politics of Control," in Neville Rubin and William Warner, eds. *Dams in Africa* (New York: Augustus Kelley, 1968), pp.

106–217 (citation p. 124). In and of itself the notion of an authority has much to recommend it; see Barbour, "Nile Waters Problem," p. 321. The real problem in 1959 was that of its sponsor(s). In July 1977, The Permanent Joint Technical Commission, set up after 1959 between the Sudan and Egypt, recommended the establishment of a basin-wide authority for execution of projects and exchange of technical information.

12. Garretson, "The Nile Basin," p. 291.

13. Authority for Development of the Jonglei Area: Abel Alier, *Statement to the Peoples' Regional Assembly on the Proposed Jonglei Canal* (Khartoum: n.d.).

14. Sadat's speech cited in *Guardian*, May 31, 1978, and King Hassan's remarks in *Le Monde*, June 25–26, 1978. See also his interview in *Newsweek*, May 16, 1977. Typical Egyptian Fashoda-ism can be found in Abd al-Hamid al-Islambuli, "Red Menace to the Sources of the Nile: Yesterday Angola, Today Zaire, Tomorrow the Sudan," *al-Ahram*, April 18, 1977.

15. P. K. Bechtold, "New Attempts at Arab Cooperation: the Federation of Arab Republics," *Middle East Journal* 27 (2) (Spring 1973):152–72.

16. Numeiry to Eric Rouleau, *Le Monde*, February 17, 1972.

17. See the fine analysis of Yves Loiseau, "Le combat des nationalistes Erythréens," *Le Monde Diplomatique*, January 8, 1974.

18. See the interview of President Sayyid al-Barre in *al-Ahram*, May 18, 1977.

CHAPTER 4

International Hydropolitics

1. *Gamal Hamdan, "Shakhsiyyat Misr: A Study in the Genius of a Place* (Cairo: Anglo-Egyptian Bookshop, 1970), p. 254, in Arabic.

2. Cited in Tom Little, *High Dam at Aswan* (London: Methuen, 1965), p. 24.

3. See Democratic Republic of the Sudan, Executive Organ for Development Projects in the Jonglei Area, *Jonglei Project (Phase One)* (Khartoum: January 1975), p. 42; see also Abdullah Mohammed Ibrahim, "The Jonglei Development Project — 1975," *Sudan International* 1 (12–23) (May 1975); H. E. Hurst, R. P. Black, Y. Simaika, *The Nile Basin: Vol. VII, The Future Conservation of the Nile* (Cairo: Ministry of Public Works, Physical Department, Government Printing Office, 1946); M. Kassas, "Ecological Consequences of Water Development Projects," in Nicholas Polunin, ed., *The Environmental Future* (London: Macmillan, 1972), pp. 215–36; Southern Development Investigation Team, *Natural Resources and Development Potential in the Southern Provinces of the Sudan* (London: 1955); Julian Rzoska, "The Upper Nile Swamps," in J. Rzoska, ed., *The Nile: Biology of an Ancient River* (The Hague: Dr. W. Junk, 1976), pp. 197–213.

4. Jonglei Investigation Team, *The Equatorial Nile Project: Report of the Jonglei Investigation Team* (Khartoum: Sudan Government, 1954), Vol. I: *A Survey of the Area Affected*, Vol. II: *The Equatorial Nile Project*, Vol. III: *Special Investigations and Experimental Data*; Vol. IV: *Maps and Diagrams*.

5. Abdel Aziz Ahmad, "Nile Control," pp. 162–164.

6. *Ibid.*, pp. 159–63; and H. E. Hurst, *The Nile* (London: Constable, 1957).

7. Hurst, Black, and Simaika, Vol. VII, *Future Conservation of the Nile*, p. 9. It is estimated that implementation of the Jonglei, lake storage, fourth cataract, and Wadi Rayyan projects would have cost £122 million to yield about 13 billion m³, in High Dam Authority, *High Dam Project* (Cairo: Ministry of Irrigation, 1962), Pt. II.

8. Most of my account here is drawn from the fine and readable study of the late Tom Little, *High Dam at Aswan*, pp. 28–35. The substance of Daninos' own ideas appears in his "L'utilisation intégrale des eaux du bassin du Nil," *Bulletin de l'Institut d'Egypte*, R. XXX, session 1947–48.

9. H. E. Hurst, *A Short Account of the Nile Basin* (Cairo: Ministry of Public Works, Physical Department, 1944), p. 61.

10. Their arguments are contained in Hurst, Black, and Simaika, Nile Basin: Vol. IX, *The Major Nile Projects* (Cairo, 1966), esp. pp. 41–42.

11. See for instance H. E. Hurst, *The Nile* (London: Constable, 1957), p. 332, and Colonel Samir Hilmy's remarks reproduced in *The Nile Waters Question* (Khartoum: Ministry of Irrigation, December 1955), p. 36.

12. Mason and Asher, *World Bank*, p. 623.

13. I have relied in this recounting primarily upon Nutting, *Nasser*, pp. 129–46; Philippe Ghallab, *Must We Destroy the High Dam?* (Cairo: Ruz al-Yussef Press, 1974), pp. 22–49; Muhammed Heikal, *Nasser: The Cairo Documents* (London: New English Library, 1972), pp. 62–74; D. C. Watt, "The High Dam at Aswan and the Politics of Control," in Neville Rubin and William Warner, eds., *Dams in Africa* (New York: Augustus Kelley, 1968), pp. 106–27; James Dougherty, "The Aswan Decision in Perspective," *Political Science Quarterly* 74 (1) (March 1959):21–45; and Mason and Asher, *World Bank*, pp. 627–42.

14. Heikal, *Nasser*, pp. 73–74.

15. See Keith Wheelock, *Nasser's New Egypt* (London: Stevens, 1960), pp. 173–205.

16. Little, *High Dam at Aswan*, has admirably presented the story of the dam's construction, and there is no need to go over it here.

17. In the closest thing to an official review of the project, no final cost estimates were offered. See Dr. Abd al-Qadir Hatem, General Supervisor of the Specialized National Committees, *The High Dam and Its Effects*, published as a supplement to *al-Ahram al-Iqtisadi* (February 1, 1976); also Dr. Ahmad el-Feel, *et al.*, "The Application of Benefit-Cost Analysis for the Economic Evaluation of the High Dam Project in Egypt," *L'Egypte Contempraine* 65 (356) (April 1974):139–54. Their estimate included £E 283 million for the main body of the dam and £E 141 million for the power station. See also Gerhard Tintner and Abdel-Fattah Kandeel (USC), "Economic Appraisal of the Aswan High Dam: A New Approach" (unpublished ms 1970?); "Benefit-cost Analysis of the High Dam," *National Bank of Egypt Bulletin* 18 (4) (1965):267–73.

18. Cited in Ghallab, *Must We Destroy the High Dam?*, pp. 96–8.

CHAPTER 5

The Nile Stops at Aswan

1. Stewart Udall, in discussion of Mohammed Kassas, "Ecological Consequences of Water Development Projects" in Nicholas Polunin, ed., *The Environmental Future*

(London: Macmillan, 1972), p. 244.

2. Engineer Ali Fathy, *The High Dam and Its Impact* (Cairo: General Book 1976), pp. 50–51.

3. See *Bana' al-Watan* 68 (February 1, 1965).

4. See Ministry of Power, *The High Dam is Completed: 1960–70* (Aswan, 1970), pp. 12–13.

5. *Al-Ahram*, May 17, 1973; for other official views see Mohammed Abdel Rakeeb (Minister of Irrigation) General Authority for the High Dam, *The High Dam Project: its Benefits Far Outweigh Adverse Doubts and Side Effects*, 1971; "The High Dam and the Campaign against it," *al-Ahram*, December 20, 1974; and Dr. Mohammed Abd al-Qadir Hatim, General Supervisor of the Specialized National Committees, *The High Dam and its Effect* published as a supplement to *al-Ahram al-Iqtisadi*, February 1, 1975. The single best overview is Yusuf Shibl, *The Aswan High Dam* (Beirut: Arab Institute for Research and Publishing, 1971).

6. Philippe Ghallab, *Must We Destroy the High Dam?* (Cairo: Ruz al-Yussef Press 1974), pp. 79–80. Ghallab makes a leftist defense of the dam and dismisses Ahmad as a reactionary, old-regime, neo-imperialist agent whose arguments could not be taken seriously as his competence was in electrical engineering and not hydrology.

7. His letter of December 11, 1964, as well as that of his widow to President Nasser of December 1967, were reprinted in *Akhbar al-Yom*, January 31, 1976.

8. The report took the form of two papers: "Recent Developments in Nile Control" (Paper #6102) pp. 137–80; and "An Analytic Study of the Storage Losses in the Nile Basin, with Special Reference to Aswan Dam Reservoir and the High Dam Reservoir" (Paper #6370), pp. 181–200, in *Proceedings of the Institution of Civil Engineers*, 17 (October 1960).

9. Abdel Aziz Ahmad, "Storage Losses in the Nile Basin," (Paper #6370), p. 188. For the period referred to, the storage capacity was about 2.5 billion m^3, but with the raising of the dam in 1934, capacity increased to 5.6 billion m^3, although actual storage seldom exceeded 5 billion m^3.

10. See University of Michigan and Egyptian Academy of Scientific Research and Technology, *Water Quality Studies on the River Nile and Lake Nasser*, (Ann Arbor: 1975); the lower is from H. E. Hurst, R. P. Black, and Y. Simaika, *The Nile Basin, Vol. IX, The Major Nile Projects* (Cairo: Ministry of Irrigation, 1966) p. 41; Dr. Moustafa Hafez and W. K. Shenouda, The Environmental Impacts of the Aswan High Dam, UNWC E/CONF:70/TP17 (January 15, 1977), p. 4. On the *Khors* see B. Entz, "Lake Nasser and Lake Nubia" in Julian Rzoska, ed., *The Nile: Biology of an Ancient River* (The Hague: Dr. W. Junk, 1976), pp. 271–98.

11. Economic Commission for Africa, *Regional Report* (Mar del Plata, Argentina: UN Water Conference, March 14–25, 1977) E/CONF. 70/7 (January 3, 1977) p. 6. Christaan Gischler likewise argues for an estimate of 15 billion m^3 in annual evaporation of 2.5 meters per year at reservoir levels between 175 and 183 meters above sea level. See Christaan Gischler, *Present and Future Trends in Water Resources Development in the Arab States* (Cairo: UNESCO, 1976), p. 48. Despite the fact that measurements of evaporation have been made since 1964, I have seen no public presentation of any of the data in tabular form. The former Minister of Irrigation, Mohammed Abdel Rakeeb stated that total evaporation and seepage in 1971, when the reservoir level reached 165 meters, was 11.4 billion m^3. The later Specialized National Committee Report merely stated that evaporation and seepage losses remained within previous estimates — see note 5 for

sources. One may also note a general problem in statistical reporting. Ahmad citing Hurst, *et al*. (1931), uses their figure for evaporation at Aswan of 7.4 mm per day or 2.7 meters per year. When Hurst (1966) used that figure he stated that it referred to evaporation *and seepage* (p. 41) although elsewhere in the same volume he uses the same figure to refer to evaporation only.

12. Claire Sterling, "Superdams: the Perils of Progress," *The Atlantic* 229 (6) (June 1972):35–41, citation p. 37. Sterling's numerous critiques of the dam stirred Egyptian resentment. Sayyid Marei, who facilitated her study of the dam, subsequently hinted darkly that she is Jewish and possibly a Zionist agent. See his interview in *Ruz al-Yussef* #2506 (June 21, 1976).

13. Tahar Abu Wafa and Aziz Hanna Labib, "Investigations and Observations of Seepage Losses from the Aswan High Dam Reservoir," *Commission Internationale des Grands Barrages*, 10th Congress, Montreal (1970), pp. 1047–1069.

14. Kemal Hefny, *Groundwater Potentialities in ARE* (Mar del Plata, Argentina: UN Water Conference, March 14–25, 1977).

15. Ali Fathy described this process to me in a personal interview, April 3, 1975.

16. Abd al-Khaleq Shinnawi, "The Fertility of Egypt's Land in the Balance," *Broadcasting and Television* 2128 (December 27, 1975):10–11.

17. For Instance an interview, "The Return of the Flood will Solve Egypt's Problems," *Akhir Sa'a* 2095 (December 18, 1974):12–13; "I do not Demand the Destruction of the Dam; I Demand the Destruction of the High Dam Covenant," *Broadcasting and Television* 2129 (January 3, 1976).

18. Fathy, *The High Dam and Its Impact*.

19. *Ibid*., pp. 38–39.

20. "The Tushka Depression Scheme," *al-Magalla az-Zira'ia* 19 (6) (June 1977).

21. Abd al-Qadir Hatim, *High Dam and Its Effect*, p. 26.

22. Samir 'Izzat, "The Minister of Irrigation Reveals the Campaign against the Dam," *Ruz al-Yussef* 2432 (January 21, 1975):27–29. A mission from the High Dam Authority was dispatched to Moscow in June 1977 to discuss both weirs and barrages (at least one near Kom Ombo with hydroelectric capacity). The results, if any, of the mission are not now known. *Akhbar al-Yom*, June 25, 1977.

23. *Akhbar al-Yom*, November 30, 1974.

24. See Abd al-Aziz Ahmad, "Recent Developments," Paper #6102 p. 143 and Y. M. Simaika, "The Suspended Matter in the Nile," Paper No. 40, (Cairo: Physical Department, 1940).

25. See U. S. Department of Agriculture and USAID, *Egypt: Major Constraints to Increasing Agricultural Productivity* (Washington, D.C.: Foreign Agricultural Economic Report No. 20, June 1976), p. 102. Former Minister of Agriculture Mustapha Gabali (*al-Ahram*, March 18, 1975) stated that silt loss annually comprises 160,000 tons of azote, 200,000 tons phosphoric acid, and about one million tons potash. How Gabali and Abdel Rakeeb could advance such contradictory figures is a matter for conjecture. But Gabali joins Rakeeb in minimizing the significance of lost trace elements. "As for the elements of calcium potassium and magnesium, the land and the Nile contain enough for several thousand years."

26. *Akhbar al-Yom* (Decemer 14, 1974). By the end of 1976 the situation had not been alleviated. Althouh a contract had been signed with Poland in 1964 for the construction of

12 sand-brick factories, by 1974 only one was in operation. By 1975 around Cairo-Giza one feddan of top soil was selling for £E 1500 (al-Ahram, November 11, 1975). As with all other aspects of the High Dam, Egyptian experts foresaw potential problems but failed to elicit preventive policies. For instance, A. A. el-Tonberry and M. S. Abou el-Ezz, "Economics of Water Supply and Control in the Southern Region of the United Arab Republic: An Outline," International Journal of Agrarian Reform 3 (1) (January 1961):15–36, warned of silt deprivation, soil depletion, and the need for the government to begin to phase out the mud-brick kilns.

27. The expectations of improved drainage are expressed by Ragaei el-Mallakh, "Some Economic Aspects of the Aswan High Dam Project in Egypt," Land Economics 35 (1) (February 1959):15–23, esp. p. 18. A good general discussion of drainage and salinity is R. C. Reeve and M. Firemen, "Salt Problems in Relation to Irrigation," in R. M. Hagen, et al., eds. Irrigation of Agricultural Lands (Madison, Wisc.: American Society of Agronomy, 1967), pp. 988–1008.

28. Lennart Berg, "The Water Balance of the Nile Delta," Symposium on Nile Water and Lake Projects, National Research Center, Dokki, Cairo (March 1–4, 1976).

29. FAO, Near East Regional Office, Research on Crop Water Use, Salt Affected Soils and Drainage in the ARE (Rome: 1975); and USAID, Agricultural Productivity, p. 55.

30. Sayyid Marei's remarks are in The Egyptian Gazette, May 24, 1975; al-Ba'athi's in al-Musawwar, January 24, 1975, p. 33; see also former Minister of Irrigation Shinnawi, Broadcasting and Television 2128 (December 27, 1975), who claims that between 1965 and 1968 he repeatedly called Nasser's attention to the dangers of silt deprivation, but Nasser was not interested.

31. Fathy, The High Dam and Its Impact, pp. 70–73. Fathy in a related point notes that as it is now, the High Dam reservoir is like an atomic bomb hanging over Egypt's head. If the Israelis could blow up the dam, Egypt would be washed away. The Soviet experts who worked on the dam recommended that if hostilities were to break out, the reservoir should be lowered at a rate of 600 million m^3 per day. Neither in 1967 (when it may not have been necessary because of the low level of the reservoir) nor in 1973 was this advice followed.

32. Mohammed Kassas, "Impact of River Control Schemes on the Shoreline of the Nile Delta," in M. Taghi Farvar and J. P. Milton, eds., The Careless Technology (Natural History Press, 1972) pp. 179–88, citation p. 181; and G. Sestini, "Geomorphology of the Nile Delta" in Proceedings of the Seminar on Nile Delta Sedimentology, UNDP/UNESCO and Department of Geology, University of Alexandria, Alexandria (October 25–29, 1975), pp. 12–25.

33. We have already cited Berg on this problem His evaluation would seem to be confirmed by some limited experimental evidence: I. H. Elsokkaray, M. Sombol, M. I., Fahmy, "The Effect of Sea-water Intrusion on the Soil Salinity status of the Sannania Project in the Northern Coastal Area of Egypt," Beitrage zur tropischen Landswirtschaft und Voterinarmdizin 12 (1) (1974):33–39. Very much confirmed by Kemal Hefny, Ground Water Potentialities in ARE, UNWC (January 15, 1977), p. 7; Ev Nilsen, "Nile Delta Erosion: Interdisciplinary Science at Work," Bulletin of the UNESCO Field Science Office for the Arab States 2 (3) (April–June 1974):20–24.

34. Ibrahim Zaki al-Kinawy and Osman Ahmad al-Ghomry, "Some Effects of the High Dam on the Environment," unpublished manuscript of a paper prepared for the 13th Congress of Great Dams (1972), p. 5; also Hatim. High Dam and Its Effect, p. 27.

35. Gamal Hamdan, *Shakhsiyyat Masr: A Study on the Genius of a Place* (Cairo: Anglo-Egyptian Bookshop, 1970), p. 366.

36. Gabriel Saab, *The Egyptian Agrarian Reform, 1952–1962* (Oxford: At the University Press, 1967), p. 159.

37. Mohammed Hassanenin Heikal, "Le problème agraire: horizons nouveaux," in *La Voie Egyptienne vers le Socialisme* (Dar al-Ma'aref: 1965?), pp. 185–202. There were expert casters-of-doubt as to the wisdom of horizontal expansion: in 'Shakhsiyyat Misr' Gamal Hamdan argued forcefully for priority being given vertical expansion, and Wyn Owen warned against heavy investment in reclaiming poor soils at high costs: "Land and Water Use in the Egyptian High Dam Era," *Land Economics* 40 (3) (August 1964):277–93, esp. p. 289.

38. Interview with Osman Badran, Minister of Land Reclamation, *al-Ahram*, June 10, 1972. Differing figures were given by Hilal Abduallah Hilal, Director of the General Organization for Land Cultivation and Development: 345,000 feddans reached marginal levels of production; 353,000 feddans had not reached that level; 341,000 were under preparation. These are presumably gross areas including roads, dwellings, etc.; *al-Ahram al-Iqtisadi* 2416 (September 30, 1974), pp. 88–89.

39. See Ministry of Agrarian Reform and Land Reclamation, *Agrarian Reform and Land Reclamation in Ten Years* (Cairo: 1962?), p. 73; Dr. Muhammed Abou el-Dahab, "Horizontal Expansion in UAR Agriculture," Institute of National Planning (INP), Memo 820 (August 1968); and Dr. Iz al-Din Hamam Ahmad, *et al.*, "Maximum Horizontal Expansion in UAR Agriculture," Institute of National Planning, Memo No. 795 (August 1967).

40. *Soil Survey Project, United Arab Republic, Vol. I. General Report* (FAO/SF: 16/UAR) (Rome: FAO, 1966); USAID, *Agricultural Productivity*, p. 36. One may contrast this reserved position to that of Iz al-Din Hamam Ahmad, "Maximum Horizontal Expansion," who concluded in 1967 that the FAO survey indicated the existence of 2.8 million feddans capable of high production. They also mention 4 million cultivable feddans in the New Valley and a similar amount in the Sinai peninsula.

41. H. A. el-Tobgy, *Contemporary Egyptian Agriculture*, 2nd ed. (Cairo: Ford Foundation, 1976), p. 27. This figure presumably does not include the 50,000 Nubians resettled on the land at Komombo in Upper Egypt (see Map 5).

42. Amin Mohammed Amin, "Uneconomic Land Reclamation," *al-Ahram al-Iqtisadi* 477 (July 1, 1975), pp. 22–23. Some of the areas most affected have been the New Valley, a sector of at least one million cultivable feddans so it was said, where in 1975 only 20,000 were sustaining crops; Wadi Natroun essentially written off; Samalut in middle Egypt with 32,000 feddans out of production; plus large sections along the fringe of the western Delta.

43. Natural movements of the water table are a matter of some conjecture in this area. UNESCO believes that there are two "water mounds" under this area that will one day join. They exert an easterly flow but in areas a SE, SW, and westerly flow. Because the specifics of the situation are not precisely known, UNESCO advocated a careful monitoring project before taking remedial action. FAO, however, believed that whatever the areas of ignorance priority should be placed on drainage installation. Their view has apparently won the day, but no one seems to know who will pay for the drainage system.

44. Some of this information was drawn from UNESCO, *The Rising Water Table and Related Problems in the West Nubaria Project Area*, ILRI (UAR) 1973; FAO *Country Develop-*

ment Brief, February 1974, in addition to interviews with experts who shall go unnamed.

45. USAID, p. 11; for equally cautionary remarks, see Ministry of Housing and Reconstruction and the UNDP, *Suez Canal Regional Plan: June 1976* (GOPP, TAMS, DAG) (Cairo 1976), p. 72. Future reclamation sites are all Class IV except for drained lake bottom acreage where there is a major question whether the loss in fish production would not outweigh the value of agricultural gains.

46. D. Entz, *Morphometry of Lake Nasser,* Lake Nasser Development Center, Aswan (1973); University of Michigan; on Cairo's water *al-Ahram* (October 31 and December 9, 1974, and January 3, 1975); Fathy, *The High Dam and Its Impact,* pp. 54–55. The University of Michigan (Dr. Khalil Mancy) and the Egyptian Academy of Scientific Research and Technology have entered into a long-term agreement to monitor all aspects of water quality in the Egyptian Nile.

47. Ministry of Housing and Reconstruction, *Ismailia Master Plan Study: Environmental Factors* (December 1975) p. 31; see also John Elkington, "Beware the Wrath of Osiris," *New Scientist,* December 11, 1975; Carl J. George, "The Role of the Aswan High Dam in Changing the Fisheries of the Southwest Mediterranean" in Farvar and Milton, *Careless Technology,* pp. 159–78.

48. See *Ismailia Master Plan, al-Ahram,* July 22, 1975. Counterarguments in favor of reclamation are advanced by Dr. Abd al-Moneim Balba', *al-Ahram,* August 12, 1975 who contends that the advocates of fish farming have far overestimated the likely per feddan yield of fish.

49. Al-Kinawy and al-Ghomry in *Some Effects of the High Dam* talked of potential takes of 80,000–100,000 tons. See more sober studies of Dr. Abd al-Fattah Abd al Latif, "Project for Regional Planning of Aswan Governorate: Fisheries of Lake Nasser," "Concerning the Development of Lake Nasser," and "Towards Settlement of Lake Nasser Fishermen," Lake Nasser Development Center (1973–74); and Ahmad Abd al-Wahab Branih, "The Fish Wealth of Lake Nasser and the Social Aspects of its Exploitation," *al-Tali'a* 9 (3) (March 1973):45–51. On the general question of fisheries in artificial lakes, see International Council of Scientific Unions, *Man-Made Lakes as Modified Ecosystems* (Paris: 1972), esp.p. 52.

50. Sherif Hattata, *Health and Development* (Dar al-Ma'aref, 1968), p. 54; L. J. Fogel, M. Maxfield, O. Sullivan, *Epidemiologic Consequences of Schistosomiasis in Egypt* (Washington, D. C.: 1970); Henry Van Der Schalie, "Aswan Dam Revisited: the Blood Fluke Thrives," *Environment* 16 (9) (November 1974):18–26. There is no prophylactic medication against schistosomiasis.

51. An excellent early study of the problem is A. J. Dorra, "L'aménagement hydro-electrique du Barrage d'Assouan," *l'Egypte Contemporaine* 29 (n.s. 179–80) (November–December 1938):549–648; also Leon Feiner, "The Aswan Dam Development Project," *Middle East Journal* 6 (4) (Autumn 1952):464–67. The imperialist plot notion is probably valid to a certain extent, but on occasion the British behaved out of character. The British sponsored the construction of Owen Falls dam at Jinga in Uganda (1948–54) to promote Uganda's industry; see Walter Elkan and Gail Wilson, "The Impact of the Owen Falls Hydro-electric Project on the Economy of Uganda," in Neville Rubin and William Warner, eds., *Dams in Africa* (New York: Augustus Kelley, 1968), pp. 90–105. Philippe Ghallab, *Must We Destroy the High Dam?* who is a staunch believer in the imperialist plot theory unfairly associates Abdel Aziz Ahmad with it. The latter, like Adrien Daninos, was in fact an early advocate of electrification of Aswan and of indus-

trialization. See Ahmad, "Recent Developments in Nile Control" and his earlier: *Aswan Dam Hydroelectric Scheme* (Cairo: Imprimerie Nationale, 1932), and *Hydroelectric Power Development on the Nile as a Stepping Stone to the Industrialization of Egypt* (Vienna: World Energy Conference, 1938).

52. Abd al-Meguid, R. P. Burden, R. R. Revelle, Rafael Salib, W. O. Spofford, H. A. Thomas, "Notes on a Study of the Uses of the High Dam" (Aswan: Regional Planning Project, March 1966); H. Thomas and R. Revelle, "On the Efficient Use of the High Aswan Dam for Hydropower and Irrigation," *Management Science* 12 (8) (April 1966):296–311. The authors jaundice most of their argument by basing their mathematical computations on the assumption of an average annual inflow of 90 billion m^3, well above established averages and neglecting the Sudanese share of the river's discharge. Repeating the same error is Mahmud Abd al-Fadil, "Economic Development in Egypt in the New High-Dam Era," *l'Egypte Contemporaine* 65 (356) (April 1974):247–73.

53. See Hatim, *High Dam and Its Effect*, pp. 20–21; Ahmad Sultan, Minister of Electricity, "Electric Power in the ARE," special supplement to *al-Ahram al-Iqtisadi* (April 1, 1973); Salah Qalash, Deputy Minister of Electricity, "Power and the Dam," *al-Ahram*, June 26, 1976; Egypt's per capita electricity consumption is 230 kW annually as compared to 7,600 kW in the United States.

CHAPTER 6

Egypt: The Wages of Dependency

1. See the analysis of Salah 'Issa, "The Future of Democracy in Egypt," *al-Katib* 14 (162) (September 1974):9–28.

2. Robert Mabro, *The Egyptian Economy: 1952–1972* (Oxford: At the University Press, 1974), p. 127.

3. Abd al-Azim Ramadan, *Nasser and the March Crisis* (Cairo: Ruz al-Yussef Printing House, 1976), pp. 14–18 and p. 320 has adduced evidence that the RCC had no plan for a land reform before coming to power.

4. The actual distribution of the 1969 reforms are readily available. Fathy Abd al-Fatah, *The Contemporary Village Between Reform and Revolution: 1952–1970* (Cairo: Dar al-Thiqafa al-Jadida, 1975), p. 111, calculates that prior to 1969, land reform had resulted in the distribution of only 644,699 feddans to 261,439 families.

5. "Special Study on Land Use," *al-Tali'a* 8 (10) (October 1972). See also Price Planning Agency, "Distribution of Individual Income," memo No. 18 (January 1973) which claims that 2 percent of all landowners own 29 percent of all cultivated land and earn 30.4 percent of all agricultural rents (p. 6). In contrast to this rural bourgeoisie is the growing class of subsistence, sub-subsistence, and landless peasants, which must number over four million families.

6. Fawzi Habashi, "The Extent of Parasitic Incomes in the Contracting Sector," *al-Tali'a* 9 (7) (July 1973):27–31.

7. See Patrick O'Brien, *The Revolution in Egypt's Economic System* (Oxford: At the University Press 1966), p. 153.

8. Mabro, *Egyptian Economy*, p. 123.

9. Bent Hansen, "Economic Development in Egypt," in C. A. Cooper and S. S. Alexander, eds., *Economic Development and Population Growth in the Middle East* (New York: American Elsevier, 1972), pp. 22–91, esp. p. 73.

10. From *al-Ahram* (August 27, 1974).

11. Fuad Mursi, "The Public Sector and Private Investment," *al-Tali'a* 10 (2) (February 1974):16–23, esp. p. 21.

12. *Financial Times* (August 1, 1977) citing Deputy P. M. Abd al-Moneim Al-Qaissuny, p. 12; also al-Qaissuny's interview in *al-Ahram*, April 8, 1977. In summer 1977, Egypt suspended all bi-lateral agreements with the Eastern Bloc, particularly all cotton shipments to the USSR. This meant in effect that all servicing of the debt to the USSR was suspended.

13. See Essam Muntasser, *Egypt's Long-term Growth: 1976–2000 (Preliminary Projections)* Conference on Long-term Planning and Regional Integration (Cairo: INP, January 14–21, 1976).

14. For general background, see Galal Amin, *Food Supply and Economic Development: with Special Reference to Egypt* (London: Frank Cass, 1966) and Central Agency for Public Mobilization and Statistics, *Population and Development* (Cairo: June 1973), p. 245.

CHAPTER 7

The Sudan: In Quest of a Surplus

1. W. D. Hopper, "The Development of Agriculture in Developing Countries," *Scientific American* 235 (3) (September 1976):197–205, citation p. 201. For equally heady appraisals of the Sudan's role as supplier, see Dr. Ahmad Hiba, agricultural counselor to the Islamic Bank,who predicts that the Sudan will meet the food deficits of the entire Muslim world, *al-Ahram*, July 16, 1977. Erring, perhaps inadvertently, on the other side is Marion Clawson, *et al.*, *The Agricultural Potential of the Middle East* (New York: American Elsevier, 1971), who do not even include the Sudan in their study.

2. DRS, Ministry of Finance, Planning, and National Economy, *Initial Highlights of the Six Year Plan for Economic and Social Development, 1977/78–1982/83* (Khartoum: July 1976), p. 44.

3. Quoted in Ministry of Agriculture, *Food and the Sudan* (Khartoum: Khartoum University Press, 1974), p. 33.

4. The income distribution figures appeared in a 1975 ILO/UNDP survey, *Growth, Employment, and Equity: a Comprehensive Strategy for Sudan* (Geneva: ILO, October 1975) Vol. II (Technical Papers).

5. *FAO Perspective Study of Agricultural Development for the Democratic Republic of the Sudan: Land and Water Development and Use* (Rome: 1973) ESP/AGL/PS/SUD/73/6.

6. For details, see Appendix Table 4.2 in DRS, National Planning Commission, *Economic Survey 1974* (Khartoum: July 1975), p. 205. The same declines, except for sorghum, carried over to 1975–76.

7. Mohammed Hashim Awad, "The Evolution of Land Ownership in the Sudan," *Middle East Journal* 25 (Spring 1971):212–28; and A. R. C. Bolton, "Land Tenure in

Agricultural Land in the Sudan," in J. D. Tothill, ed., *Agriculture in the Sudan* (London: 1954).

8. P. Bechtold, "Politics in the Sudan," p. 76.

9. DRS, NPC (Transport and Communication Section), *Transport Statistical Bulletin 1974* (Khartoum: April 1975), p. 24.

10. World Bank Staff Working Paper No. 247, *Developing Country Foodgrain Projections for 1985* (Washington, D.C.: 1976), p. 30.

11. See Mohammed Mirghani Abdel Salam, "Agriculture in the Sudan," in Ali Mohammed al-Hassan, ed., *An Introduction to the Sudan Economy* (Khartoum: Khartoum University Press, 1976), pp. 38–75.

12. Confederation of British Industry, Market Study, *The Sudan* (London: May 1977), p. 14.

13. Arthur Gaitskell, *Gezira: A Story of Development in the Sudan* (London: 1959).

14. R. F. Wynn, "The Sudan's 10 Year Plan of Economic Development 1961–62—1970–71. An Analysis of Achievement to 1967–68," *The Journal of Developing Areas* 5 (July 1971):555–76. A general but inadequate survey is Didar Fawzi, *La République du Sudan. échec d'une expérience de décollage économique dans la voie capitaliste par une ancienne dépendance coloniale* (Algiers: SNED 1973); and Adel Bishai, *Export Performance and Economic Development in the Sudan: 1900–67* (Oxford: St. Anthony's Middle East Monographs, 1975).

15. DRS, NPC, *Economic Survey 1974*, pp. 174–75.

16. Oluwadare Aguda, "The State and the Economy in the Sudan: From a Political Scientist's Point of View," *The Journal of Developing Areas* 7 (April 1974):431–48.

17. Karl Lavrencic, "Will the Sudan Fill the Arab World's Need for Sugar," *Arab Business* 4 (June–July 1976):34–35.

18. On sugar markets see, "The Tempest in the Sugar Pot," *Fortune* (February 1977):106–20; "L'Impossible OPEP du sucre," *L'Economiste de Tiers Monde* 19 (July–August 1977):45–48; Carole Webb, "Sugar Politics in the European Communities," *Government and Opposition* 11 (4) (August 1976):464–80.

19. Sudan Sugar Corp., *Sugar for Sudan and Neighboring Countries* (Khartoum: August 1975), and "Sudan, the Sugar Explosion," *Mideast Markets* (March 3, 1975).

20. AFSED, *Basic Programme for Agricultural Development of the Sudan 1976–85: Invitation to the Founders*, unofficial BCI translation (London: 1977); and Jeswald Salacuse, "The Arab Authority for Agricultural Investment and Development," *Journal of World Trade Law* 12 (January–February 1978):56–66.

21. Matthijis de Vreede, "Deserts Advance," *Development Forum* (May 1977):8.

22. ILO/UNDP, *Growth, Employment and Equity*.

23. IBRD, *Report of a Special Mission on the Economic Development of Southern Sudan* (June 1, 1973), and Southern Development Investigation Team, *Natural Resources and Development Potential in the Southern Provinces of the Sudan* (London: 1955). This baseline study stands alone in quality and comprehensiveness. No follow-up survey of equivalent scope is yet available. Its authors believed that under prevailing cultivation techniques, the best southern soils were already maximally cultivated.

24. Eric Rouleau, "Soudan: la commune avortée," especially parts II and III, *Le Monde*, August 21–23, 1971, and "Soudan: les Colonels sans les camarades," *Le Monde*, February 16–18, 1972.

25. For the politics of the south see, Francis Mading Deng, *Dynamics of Identification* (Khartoum: Khartoum University Press, 1973); Muhammed Omar Beshir, *The Southern Sudan: Background to Conflict* (London: 1968); Oliver Albino, *The Sudan: A Southern Viewpoint* (Oxford: At the University Press, 1970); Joseph Oduhu and William Deng, *The Problem of the Southern Sudan* (Oxford: At the University Press, 1963); David McClintock, "The Southern Sudan Problem: Evolution of an Arab-African Confrontation," *Middle East Journal* 24 (4) (August 1970):466–78; John Howell, "Politics in the Southern Sudan," *African Affairs* 72 (287) (April 1973):163–78; David Roden "Regional Inequality and Rebellion in the Sudan," *Geographical Review* 64 (4) (October 1974):498–516; R. K. Badel, "The Rise and Fall of Separatism in the Southern Sudan," *African Affairs* 75 (301) (October 1976):463–74; Nelson Kasfir, "Still Keeping the Peace" (NK-1-'76), *Fieldstaff Reports*, NE Africa Series 21 (4) (1976).

26. Christophe Batsch "Le Soudan peut-il devenir le grenier du monde arabe?" *Le Monde Diplomatique* (January 1978):10. Part and parcel of the general effort to shore up Numeiry's regime was Washington's decision in December 1977 to sell the Sudan a squadron of F-5 fighters. The $80 million bill would be paid by Saudi Arabia, *New York Times*, December 23, 1977.

CHAPTER 8

Shortage in the Midst of Plenty

1. U.S. Department of Agriculture and USAID, *Egypt: Major Constraints to Increasing Agricultural Productivity*, Report No. 120 (Washington, D.C.: June 1976), p. 33. The FAO report referred to is *Egypt: Country Development Brief, Food and Agricultural Sector* (Rome: February 1974).

2. The basic document is Abd al-Azim Abu al-Atta (Minister of Irrigation), "Long-Range Planning in the Sphere of Irrigation and Drainage," presented at the Conference on Long-Range Planning and Regional Integration, Institute of National Planning, Center for Arab Economic Unity, and UNDP (January 14–21, 1976), in Arabic. Essentially the same document was published in condensed form as "Our Water Resources and the Planning of their Exploitation," *al-Magalla az-Zira'ia* 18 (5) (May 1976):21–29. The press excerpts mentioned by the USAID report *(Egypt: Major Constraints)* refer to this document. The Minister of Irrigation, in conjunction with the UNDP and the IBRD, is initiating a long-term water-monitoring and water-budgeting project which may produce the precise data that are now lacking. The project will not cover water use in the Sudan.

3. See Kemal Hefny, "Ground Water Potentialities in the A. R. E.," presented at the UN Water Conference, Mar del Plata, Argentina (March 14–25, 1977), p. 4.

4. See DRS, Executive Organ for the Development Projects in Jonglei Area, *Jonglei Project* (Phase I), Khartoum (January 1975); A. M. Khalifa and M. A. el-Nasry, "Improving the Water Yield of the River Nile by Minimizing the Losses in the Swamps," and Kemal Ali Mohamed, "The Projects for the increase of the Nile Yield with Special Reference to the Jonglei Project," both at UN Water Conference, Mar del Plata, Argentina (March 14–25, 1977), Jonglei risks provoking the same ecological outcry as the High Dam. Its potential effects on rainfall, the recharge of underground water, wildlife, etc. are not

fully known. See Oscar Mann, *The Jonglei Canal: Environmental and Social Aspects* (Nairobi: Environment Liaison Center, August 1977).

5. Lennart Berg, "The Water Balance of the Nile Delta," Symposium on Nile Water and Lake Dam Projects, Cairo, National Research Center, Dokki (March 1–4, 1976); Hefny, "Ground Water Potentialities," pp. 2–3; and USAID, "Egypt: Major Constraints," pp. 79–80.

6. Iz al-Din Kamil, *Mechanized Agriculture* (Cairo: Dar al-Thiqafa al-Jadida, 1976), p. 123. His figures are consistent with those of Arthur Peterson, "Egypt's Agricultural Dilemma," *Wisconsin Academy Review* 15 (4) (Winter 1969):2–7. Another way of calculating cost is to determine the investment necessary to *add* one m³ to existing supply. Jan Kamel puts that figure at 4 piastres (US $.075) in "Aquatic Weed Problems in Egypt," UN Water Conference, Mar del Plata, Argentina (March 14–25, 1977).

7. To calculate real crop needs accurately is very complex as these will vary with soil type, region, climate, sun exposure, irrigation intervals, and amount of fertilization. See FAO, Near East Regional Office, *Research on Crop Water Use, Salt Affected Soils, and Drainage in the ARE* (Rome, 1975). The 1948–59 surveys seemingly inform the following studies: H. A. el-Tobgy, *Contemporary Egyptian Agriculture*, 2nd ed. (Cairo, 1976) Table 17, p. 48; Marion Clawson, *et al.*, *The Agricultural Potential of the Middle East* (New York: American Elsevier, 1971), Table 4.2, p. 29; and Wyn Owen, "Land and Water Use in the Egyptian High Dam Era," *Land Economics* 40 (3) (August 1964):Table 1, p. 289.

8. I. Z. Kinawy, "The Efficiency of Water Use in Irrigation in Egypt," Conference on Arid Lands Irrigation in Developing Countries, UNESCO, UNEP, Academy of Scientific Research and Technology, Alexandria (February 1976). See also M. T. Eid *et al.*, "Preliminary Estimated Balance between Irrigation Requirements and River Resources in the UAR," *Agricultural Research Review* (Minister of Agriculture) 44 (1) (1966), which estimates crop-water needs at more than 50 billion m³ per year. The range of estimates is thus a low of 26 billion m³ advanced by USAID to a high of 50 billion m³ by Eid *et al*. A cursory inspection of a recent book on this subject yields a water duty estimate more in keeping with those of the Ministry of Irrigation. Referring to CAMPAS, *Irrigation and Water Resources Publication*, Ref. No. 3-421 (1967–68), Mustapha Ali Mursi and Ni'amit Nur al-Din come up with a figure of 35 billion m³ for 11,000 cropped acres. The source is early enough that it may have failed to take into account expanded rice acreage after the High Dam or growing profligacy in on-field use. *Irrigation of Field Crops* (Cairo: Anglo-Egyptian Bookshop, 1977), p. 218.

9. See "Also on the Banks of the Nile," *Ruz al-Yussef* 2560 (July 14, 1977).

10. The 15–20 percent figure is inferior to that of conveyance losses in irrigated areas of the United States, which probably run at 25 percent of total water delivered; see C. W. Lauritzen and P. W. Terrell, "Reducing Water Losses in Conveyance and Storage," in R. M. Hagan, *et al.*, eds., *Irrigation of Agricultural Lands* (Madison, Wisc.: American Society of Agronomy, 1967), pp. 1105–19.

11. Abu al-Atta, "Long-Range Planning," p. 15; Saad al-Din al-Hanafi of the Institute of National Planning makes the same assumptions in, "The Shape of the Egyptian Agricultural Sector to the Year 2000," Conference on Long-Range Planning and Regional Integration, INP, CAEU, UNDP, Cairo (January 12–21, 1976). Also interview with Abu al-Atta, *Ruz al-Yusef* 2596 (March 13, 1976), in which he predicts adding 2.8 million feddans with existing water supplies and another 1.5 million after completion of the Upper Nile Projects.

12. See Abd al-Moneim Balba', "Concerning Land Reclamation in Egypt," *al-Ahram al-Iqtisadi* 456 (August 15, 1976):9.

13. Abu al-Atta, "Long-Range Planning," pp. 10–11; USAID, *Egypt: Major Constraints,* pp. 79–80; A. A. el-Tonbarry and M. S. Abou el-Ezz, "Economics of Water Supply and Control in the Southern Region of the United Arab Republic: An Outline," *International Journal of Agrarian Affairs* 3 (1) (January 1961):15–36; Christaan Gischler, *Present and Future Trends in Water Resources Development in the Arab States* (Cairo: UN-ESCO, August 1976), pp. 53–66, and his "Hydrology of the Sahara," *Ecological Bulletin* (NFR Sweden) (1976):83–102; and Hefny, "Ground Water Potentialities," pp. 9–10. A UNDP-FAO survey in 1972 of 25,000 km² area comprising Kharga and Dakhla oasis felt that pumping there could be trebled to 800 Million m³ but no more. J. P. Peroncel-Hugoz, "L'Egypte cherche son avenir daus le désert," *Le Monde,* May 9, 1978.

14. A summary of the scheme appeared in *Akhbar al-Yom,* May 14, 1977, and *al-Ahram,* May 27, 1977. The Minister of Irrigation registered his rebuttal in an interview in *al-Ahram,* May 21, 1977.

15. *Al-Ahram,* February 27, 1977.

16. On this and water resources in general, see DRS, National Preparatory Committee for the UN Water Conference, *The Water Resources of the Sudan* (Khartoum, 1977), p. 6; and Abdullahi Ibrahim, *Likely Irrigated Agriculture of 2000 A.D. in the DRS,* mimeo (Khartoum, February 1977).

17. H. S. Adam and H. G. Farbrother, "Crop-Water Use in Irrigated and Rainfed Agriculture in the Democratic Republic of Sudan," UN Water Conference, Mar del Plata, Argentina (March 14–25, 1977), pp. 19–20.

18. See *Water Resources in the Sudan,* p. 5.

19. Acreage figures and crop distribution were extracted from DRS, Minister of Agriculture, *Current Agricultural Statistics,* CAS-Vol. 1 (2) (June 1976). On future acreage for main crops, figures are from *Water Resources of the Sudan,* p. 25.

20. Osman Abuzeid, "The Potential and Prospects for Sugar Production," *Sudan International* 1 (12–13) (May 1975):28–30; *The Sudan Sugar Industry,* Sudan Sugar Corporation and Cane Machinery and Engineering Company, Inc. (July 1975).

21. Adam and Farbrother, *Crop-Water Use.*

22. Staff Summary Report, *Regional Workshop on Aquatic Weed Management and Utilization in the Nile Basin* (Khartoum: NCR, Agricultural Research Council, November 24–29, 1975), p. 3; M. Obeid, "The Water Hyacinth: Eichornia Crassipes," p. 39, and J. Rzoska, "The Invasion of Eichornia Crassipes in the Sudanese White Nile," in Julian Rzoska, ed., *The Nile: Biology of an Ancient River* (The Hague: Dr. W. Junk, 1976). Based on development costs at Rahad I, Kemal Ali Mohammed " Projects for the Increase of the Nile Yield," p. 29, estimates the loss of each billion m³ at £S 12 million.

23. Staff Summary Report, *Regional Workshop on Aquatic Weed Management.*

24. The Ethiopian position and a description of its development plans are contained in "Ethiopia: I. Water Resources Development, II. The Need for Cooperation among Co-basin States," UN Water Conference, Mar del Plata, Argentina (March 14–25, 1977).

BIBLIOGRAPHY

BOOKS

Abd al-Fatah, Fathy. *The Contemporary Village between Reform and Revolution: 1952–1970*. Cairo: Dar al-Thiqafa al-Jadida, 1975; in Arabic.

Abdel-Fadil, Mahmoud. *Development, Income Distribution and Social Change in Rural Egypt 1952–1970*. Cambridge: At the University Press, 1975.

Abdel-Malek. *Egypt: Military Society*. New York: Random House, 1968. *Idéologie et renaissance nationale: l'Egypte moderne*. Paris: Ed. Anthropos, 1969.

Ahmad, Abdelaziz. *Aswan Dam Hydroelectric Scheme*. Cairo: Imp. Nationale, 1932.

———. *Hydroelectric Power Development on the Nile as a Stepping Stone to the Industrialization of Egypt*. Vienna: World Energy Conference, 1938.

Albino, A. *The Sudan: A Southern Viewpoint*. New York: Oxford University Press, 1970.

Amin, Galal. *Food Supply and Economic Development: with Special Reference to Egypt*. London: Frank Cass, 1966.

———. *The Modernization of Poverty*. The Hague: Mouton, 1975.

Ammar, A., et al. *Unity of the Nile Valley: its Geographic Foundations and its Manifestations in History*. Cairo: al-Amiria Printing House, 1947; in Arabic.

Baghdadi, Abd al-Latif al-. *The Memoirs of Abd al-Latif al-Baghdadi, Part I*. Cairo: The Modern Egyptian Library, 1977; in Arabic.

Ball, John. *Contributions to the Geography of Egypt*. Cairo: Government Press, 1939.

Balba', 'Abd al-Mon'eim. *Reclamation and Land Improvement*. 2nd ed. Alexandria: Dar al-Matbu'at al Gadida, 1976; in Arabic.

———. *Soil Fertility and Fertilization*. Alexandria: Dar al-Matbu'at al-Gadida, 1976; in Arabic.

Bechtold, Peter. *Politics in the Sudan*. New York: Praeger, 1976.

Beshir, Mohammed Omar. *The Southern Sudan: Background to Conflict*. New York: Oxford University Press, 1963.

Bishai, Adel. *Export Performance and Economic Development in the Sudan: 1900–1967*. Oxford: St. Antony's Middle East Monographs, 1975.

Bishri, Tariq al-. *The Political Movement in Egypt: 1945–1952.* Cairo: Egyptian General Book Organization, 1972; in Arabic.

Bryson, Reid and Murray, Thomas. *Climates of Hunger.* Madison, Wis.: University of Wisconsin Press, 1977.

Butzer, Karl. *Early Hydraulic Civilization in Egypt.* Chicago: University of Chicago Press, 1976.

Clawson, Marion, *et al. The Agricultural Potential of the Middle East.* New York: Elsevier, 1971.

Craig, J. I. *Egyptian Irrigation.* London: 1913.

Dekmejian, H. *Egypt under Nasser.* Albany: SUNY Press 1971.

Deng, Francis Mading. *Dynamics of Identification.* Khartoum: Khartoum University Press, 1973.

Dessuqi, 'Issam al-. *Large Landowners and their Role in Egyptian Society.* Cairo: Dar al-Thiqafa al-Gadida, 1975; in Arabic.

Downing, T. E., and Gibson Mc., eds. *Irrigation's Impact on Society.* Anthropological Papers of the University of Arizona, No. 25, Tucson: University of Arizona Press, 1974.

Fabunmi. L. A. *The Sudan in Anglo-Egyptian Relations: A Case Study in Power Politics.* London: Longmans, 1960.

Fathy, Ali. *The High Dam and its Impact.* Cairo: General Book Organization, 1976; in Arabic.

Fawzi, D. *La République du Soudan, échec d'une expérience de décollage économique dans la voie capitaliste par une ancienne dépendance coloniale.* Algiers: SNED, 1973.

Federation of Egyptian Industries. *Yearbook,* various years. Cairo; in Arabic and English.

Gaitskell, A. *Gezira: A Story of Development in the Sudan.* London: 1959.

Garretson, A. H., *et al. The Law of International Drainage Basins.* Dobbs Ferry, N.Y.: Oceana, 1967.

Ghallab, Philippe. *Must We Destroy the High Dam?* Cairo: Ruz al-Yussef Press, 1974; in Arabic.

Gritli, Ali al-. *Population and Economic Resources in Egypt.* Cairo: Matba' Masr, 1962; in Arabic.

————. *The Economic History of the Revolution 1952–1966.* Cairo: Dar al-Ma'aref, 1974; in Arabic.

Hagen, R. M.; Haise, H. R.; Edminster, T. W., eds. *Irrigation of Agricultural Lands.* Madison, Wis.: American Society of Agronomy, 1967.

Hamdan, Gamal. *Shakhsiyyat Masr: A Study in the Genius of a Place.* Cairo: Anglo-Egyptian Bookshop, 1970; in Arabic.

Hamrush, Ahmad. *The Story of the July Revolution, Parts I, II, and III.* Beirut: Arab Organization for Studies and Publishing, 1974–76; in Arabic.

Hansen, B. and Marzouk, G. *Development and Economic Policy in the UAR.* Amsterdam: North Holland, 1965.

Hassan, Ali Mohammed al-, ed. *An Introduction to the Sudan Economy.* Khartoum: Khartoum University Press, 1976.

Hassan, Yusuf Fadl, ed. *Sudan in Africa.* Khartoum: Khartoum University Press, 1971.

Hattata, Sherif. *Health and Development.* Cairo: Dar al-Ma'aref, 1968; in Arabic.

Heikal, Muhammed Hassanein. *Nasser: The Cairo Documents.* London: New English Library, 1972.

Holt, P. M. *A Modern History of the Sudan.* London: Weidenfeld & Nicolson, 1967.

————. *The Mahdist State in the Sudan.* Oxford: At the University Press, 1958.

Hurst, H. E. *The Nile.* London: Constable, rev. ed., 1957.

Landes, D. *Bankers and Pashas.* Cambridge, Mass.: Harvard University Press, 1958.

Lane, E. W. *Manners and Customs of the Modern Egyptians.* Dutton, N.Y.: Everyman's Library, 1966.

Little, Tom. *High Dam at Aswan.* London: Methuen, 1965.

Mabro, R. *The Egyptian Economy: 1952–1972.* Oxford: At the University Press, 1974.

Masmoudi, Mohamed. *Les Arabes dans la tempête.* Paris: Jean Claude Simeon, 1977.

Mason, E. S., and Asher, R. *The World Bank since Bretton Woods.* Washington, D.C.: Brookings Institution, 1970.

Mayfield, James. *Rural Politics in Nasser's Egypt.* Austin: University of Texas Press, 1971.

Mursi, Mustapha Ali, and Ni'amit, Nur al-Din. *Irrigation of Field Crops.* Cairo: Anglo-Egyptian Bookshop, 1977; in Arabic.

Nutting, Anthony. *Nasser.* London: Constable, 1972.

O'Brien, Patrick. *The Revolution in Egypt's Economic System.* Oxford: At the University Press, 1966.

Oduhu, J., and Deng, W. *The Problem of the Southern Sudan.* Oxford: At the University Press, 1963.

Owen, E. R. J. *Cotton and the Egyptian Economy: 1820–1914.* Oxford: At the University Press, 1969.

Polunin, N., ed. *The Environmental Future.* London: Macmillan, 1972.

Raanan, U. *The USSR Arms the Third World.* Cambridge, Mass.: MIT Press, 1969.

Ramadan, Abd al-Azim. *Nasser and the March Crisis,* Cairo: Ruz al-Yussef Printing House, 1976; in Arabic.

Riad, Hassan. *L'Egypte Nasserien*. Paris: Editions de Minuit, 1964.

Rivlin, Helen. *The Agricultural Policy of Mohammed Ali in Egypt*. Cambridge, Mass.: Harvard University Press, 1961.

Robinson, R.; Gallagher, J.; and Denny, A. *Africa and the Victorians*. New York: St. Martin's, 1961.

Rubin, N., and Warner, W., eds. *Dams in Africa*. New York: Augustus Kelley, 1968.

Rzoska, Julian, ed. *The Nile: Biology of an Ancient River*. The Hague: Dr. W. Junk, 1976.

Saab, G. *The Egyptian Agrarian Reform 1952–1962*. Oxford: At the University Press, 1967.

Shibl, Yussef. *The Aswan High Dam*. Beirut: Arab Institute for Research and Publication, 1971.

Tignor, Robert. *Modernization and British Colonial Rule in Egypt: 1882–1914*. Princeton, N.J.: Princeton University Press, 1966.

Tobgy, H. A. el-. *Contemporary Egyptian Agriculture*, 2nd ed. Cairo: Ford Foundation, 1976.

Udovitch, A. L., ed. *The Middle-East: Oil, Conflict and Hope*. Lexington, Mass.: Lexington Books, 1976.

Vatikiotis, P. J. *The Egyptian Army in Politics*. Bloomington, Ind.: Indiana University Press, 1961.

————. *The Modern History of Egypt*. New York: Praeger, 1969.

Wallace, Mackenzie. *Egypt and the Egyptian Question*. London: Macmillan, 1883.

Wheelock, Keith. *Nasser's New Egypt*. London: Stevens, 1960.

Willcocks, W. *The Nile in 1904*. London: 1904.

Wittfogel, Karl. *Oriental Despotism*. New Haven, Conn.: Yale University Press, 1957.

ARTICLES

Abd al-Fadil, Mahmoud. "Economic Development in Egypt in the New High Dam Era." *L'Egypte Contemporaine* 65 (356) (April 1974):247–73.

Abdel Salam, Mohammed Mirghani. "Agriculture in the Sudan." In *An Introduction to the Sudan Economy*, edited by Ali Mohammed al-Hassan. Khartoum: Khartoum University Press, 1976.

Abdulla, I. H. "The 1959 Nile Waters Agreement in Sudanese-Egyptian Relations." *Middle East Journal* 7 (3) (October 1971):329–41.

Abu Ali, Mohammed Sultan. "A Test of the Domar Model for Economic Growth with Reference to Egypt." *L'Egypte Contemporaine* 64 (352) (April 1973).

Abu al-Atta, Abd al-Azim. "Our Water Resources and the Planning of their Exploitation." *Al-Magalla az-Zira'ia* 18 (5) (May 1976):21–29; in Arabic.

Abu Wafa, Tahar, and Aziz Hanna Labib. "Investigations and Observations of Seepage Losses from the Aswan High Dam Reservoir." *Commission Internationale des Grands Barrages*, 10th Congress. Montreal (1970):1047–69.

Abuzeid, O. "The Potential and Prospects for Sugar Production." *Sudan International* 1 (12–13) (May 1975):28–30.

Adams, Robert McC. "Historic Patterns of Mesopotamian Civilization." In Downing and Gibson, eds. *Irrigation's Impact on Society*, Anthropological papers of the University of Arizona, No. 25, University of Arizona Press, Tucson (1974), pp. 1–6.

Aguda, Oluwadare. "The State and the Economy in the Sudan from a Political Scientist's Point of View." *The Journal of Developing Areas* 7 (April 1973):431–48

Ahmad, Abd al-Aziz. "Recent Development in Nile Control," paper 6102, pp. 137–180. "An Analytic Study of the Storage Losses in the Nile Basin, with Special Reference to Aswan Dam Reservoir and the High Dam Reservoir," paper 6370, pp. 181–200. *Proceedings of the Institute of Civil Engineers* (UK) 17 (October 1960).

Amin, Galal. "Income Distribution and Economic Development in the Arab World." *L'Egypte Contemporaine* 64 (352) (April 1973):5–37.

Amin, M. A. "Uneconomic Land Reclamation." *Al-Ahram al-Iqtisadi* 477 (July 1, 1975):22–23; in Arabic.

Atribi, Muhammed Subhy al-. "Bureaucratic Growth during the Last Ten Years." *Al-Tali'a* 8 (10) (October 1972):7–75.

Badel, R. K. "The Rise and Fall of Separatism in the Southern Sudan." *African Affairs* 75 (301) (October 1976):463–74.

Barbour, K. M. "A New Approach to the Nile Waters Problem." *International Affairs* 33 (3) (July 1957):319–30.

Barnett, Tony. "The Gezira Scheme: Production of Cotton and Reproduction of Underdevelopment." In *Beyond the Sociology of Development*, edited by Ivar Oxaal, *et al*. London: Routledge & Kegan Paul, 1975.

Balba', Abd al-Mon'eim. "Concerning Land Reclamation in Egypt." *Al-Ahram al-Iqtisadi* (456) (August 15, 1974).

Batsch, Christophe. "Le Soudan peut-il devenir le grenier du monde arabe?" *Le Monde Diplomatique* 25 (286) (January 1978):10–11.

Bechtold, Peter. "New Attempts at Arab Cooperation: The Federation of Arab Republics." *Middle East Journal* 27 (2) (Spring 1973):152–72.

"Benefit-Cost Analysis of the High Dam." *National Bank of Egypt Bulletin* 18 (4) (1965):266–73.

Binder, L. "Political Recruitment and Participation in Egypt." In *Political Parties and Political Development*, edited by J. LaPalombara. Princeton: Princeton University Press (1966):217–40.

Bolton, A. R. C. "Land Tenure in Agricultural Land in the Sudan." In *Agriculture in the Sudan*, edited by J. D. Tothill. London:1954.

Boularès, Habib. "La Somalie va-t-elle changer de camp?" *Jeune Afrique* (853) (May 13, 1977).

Branih, Abd al-Wahab. "The Fish Wealth of Lake Nasser and the Social Aspects of its Exploitation." *Al-Tali'a* 9 (3) (March 1973):45–51.

Butzer, Karl. "Environment and Human Ecology in Egypt during Pre-Dynastic and Early Dynastic Times." *Bulletin de la Société Géographique de l'Egypte* 32 (1959).

Ceuzin, P. "Icebergs en croisière." *Science et Avenir* (366) (August 1977):792–94.

Crowe, C. "The Gathering of the Money-Movers." *Alicia Patterson Foundation* KCC-5 (January 1976).

Daninos, Adrien. "l'Utilisation intégrale des eaux du bassin du Nil." *Bulletin de l'Institut d'Egypte* 30 (session 1947–48).

Dorra, A. J. "l'Aménagement hydro-éléctrique du Barrage d'Assouan." *L'Egypte Contemporaine* 29 (179–180) (November–December 1938):549–648.

Dougherty, J. "The Aswan Decision in Perspective." *Political Science Quarterly* 74 (1) (March 1959):21–45.

"Egypt." Supplement to *The Financial Times*, August 1, 1977.

Eid, M. T., *et al.* "Preliminary Estimated Balance between Irrigation Requirements and River Resources of the UAR." *Agricultural Research Review* (Egypt) 44 (1) (1966).

El-Feel, Ahmad, *et al.* "The Application of Benefit-Cost Analysis for the Economic Evaluation of the High Dam Project in Egypt." *L'Egypte Contemporaine* 65 (356) (April 1974):139–54.

Elkin, W. L., and G. Wilson. "The Impact of the Owen Falls Hydroelectric Project on the Economy of Uganda." In *Dams in Africa*, edited by Neville Rubin. New York: Augustus Kelley, 1968.

Elkington, J. "Beware the Wrath of Osiris." *New Scientist* (December 11, 1975).

Entz, B. "Lake Nasser and Lake Nubia." In *The Nile: Biology of an Ancient River*, edited by J. Rzoska. The Hague: Dr. W. Junk, 1976.

Elsokkary, I. H. *et al.* "The Effect of Sea Water Intrusion on the Soil Salinity Status of the Sannania Project in the Northern Coastal Area of Egypt." *Beiträge zur tropischen Landwirtschaft und Voterin armdzin* 23 (4) (1974):33–39.

Fathy, Ali. "The Return of the Flood Will Solve Egypt's Problems." *Akhir Sa'a* (2095) (December 18, 1974); in Arabic.

―――. "I Do not Demand the Destruction of the High Dam; I Demand the Destruction of the High Dam Covenant." *Broadcasting and Television* (2129) (January 3, 1976); in Arabic.

Feiner, L. "The Aswan Dam Development Project." *Middle East Journal* 6 (4) (August 1952):464–67.

Field, Michael. "Developing the Nile." *World Crops* (January–February 1973):13–14.

de Forges, M. "Irrigation et Salinité." *Options Méditerranéennes* 14 (August 1972):40–45.

Furtado, Celso. "The Concept of External Dependence on the Study of Underdevelopment." In *The Political Economy of Development and Underdevelopment*, edited by C. K. Wilber. New York: Random House, 1973.

George, C. "The Role of the Aswan High Dam in Changing the Fisheries of the Southeast Mediterranean." In *The Careless Technology*, edited by M. Taghi Farvar and J. P. Milton. Natural History Press, 1972: pp. 159–78.

Gibson, McC. "Violation of Fallow and Engineered Disaster in Mesopotamian Civilization." In *Irrigation's Impact on Society*, edited by T. E. Downing and McC. Gibson. Anthropological Papers of the University of Arizona, No. 25, University of Arizona Press (1974).

Gischler, Christaan. "Hydrology of the Sahara." *Ecological Bulletin*. NFR, Sweden (1976), pp. 83–102.

Gueyras, Jean. "La Libye trouble-fête: I; la sainte alliance contre le Colonel Kadhafi." *Le Monde*, August 13, 1977.

Habashi, Fawzi. "The Extent of Parasitic Incomes in the Contracting Sector." *Al-Tali'a* 9 (7) (July 1973):27–31; in Arabic.

Hamdan, Gamal. "Evolution de l'Agriculture en Egypte." *A History of Land Use in the Arid Regions*. Paris: UNESCO, 1961, pp. 133–161.

Hansen, B. "Economic Development in Egypt." In *Economic Development and Population Growth in the Middle East*, edited by C. A. Cooper and S. S. Alexander. New York: Elsevier, 1972.

Harik, Ilya. "The Single Party as a Subordinate Movement." *World Politics* 26 (1) (October 1973):80–105.

Heikal, Mohammed Hassanein. "Le problème agraire: horizons nouveaux." *Le Voie égyptienne vers le socialisme*. Dar al-Ma'aref, 1965.

"The High Dam and the Campaign Against It." *Al-Ahram al-Iqtisadi*, February 1, 1975; in Arabic.

Hodgkin, T. "Mahdism, Messianism, and Marxism in the African Setting." In *Sudan in Africa*, edited by Yusuf Fadl Hassan. Khartoum: Khartoum University Press, 1971.

Hopper, D. W. "The Development of Agriculture in Developing Countries." *Scientific American* 235 (3) (September 1976):197–205.

Howell, J. "Politics in the Southern Sudan." *African Affairs* 72 (287) (April 1973):163–78.

Ibrahim, Tuhani. "Egypto-Sudanese Integration: How Far?" *Akhbar al-Yom*, June 14, 1975.

Ibrahim, Abdullahi Mohammed. "The Jonglei Development Project—1975." *Sudan International* 1 (12–13) (May 1975).

Ismael, Tareq. "The UAR and the Sudan." *Middle East Journal* 27 (1) (Winter 1969):14–28.

'Issah, Salah. "The Future of Democracy in Egypt." *Al-Katib* 14 (162) (September 1974):9–28; in Arabic.

'Izzat, Samir. "The Minister of Irrigation Exposes the Campaign against the Dam." *Ruz al-Yussef* (2432) (January 20, 1975):27–29; in Arabic.

Jarvis, C. S. "Flood Stage Records of the Nile River." *Proceedings of the American Society of Civil Engineers* (August 1935).

Kandeel, Abdelfattah, and G. Tinter. "Economic Appraisal of the Aswan High Dam: A New Approach." Unpublished manuscript, 1970.

Kasfir, Nelson. "Still Keeping the Peace" (NK-1-'76) *Fieldstaff Reports*, Northeast Africa Series 21 (4) (1976).

Kassas, Mohammed. "Ecological Consequences of Water Development Projects." In *The Environmental Future*, edited by N. Polunin. London: Macmillan, 1972.

———. "Impact of River Control Schemes on the Shoreline of the Nile Delta." In *The Careless Technology*, edited by M. Taghi Farvar and J. P. Milton. Natural History Press: 1972.

Lavrencic, K. "Will the Sudan Fill the Arab World's Need for Sugar?" *Arab Business* 4 (June–July 1976):34–35; in Arabic.

Loiseau, Yves. "Le combat des nationalistes Erythréens." *Le Monde Diplomatique*, January 8, 1974.

"Lomé Dossier." *The Courrier* (31) (special issue March 1975).

Mallakh, Ragaei. "Some Economic Aspects of the Aswan High Dam Project in Egypt." *Land Economics* 35 (1) (February 1959):15–23.

McClintock, David. "The Southern Sudan Problem: Evolution of an Arab-African Confrontation." *Middle East Journal* 24 (4) (August 1970):466–78.

Moore, C. H. "Authoritarian Politics in Unincorporated Society." *Comparative Politics* 6 (2) (January 1974):193–218.

———. "The New Egyptian Technocracy: Engineers at the Interstices of Power." Paper presented at the International Political Science Association meetings, Montreal, August 19–25, 1972.

Mursi, Fu'ad. "The Public Sector and Private Investment." *Al-Tali'a* 10 (2) (February 1974):16–23; in Arabic.

Najjar, Fawzi. "Islam and Socialism in the UAR." *Journal of Contemporary History* 3 (3) (July 1968):183–99.

Nashashibi, K. "Foreign Trade and Economic Development in the UAR: A Case Study." In *Trade Patterns in the Middle East*, edited by Lee Preston. Washington, D.C.: American Enterprise Institute, 1970.

Owen, Wyn. "Land and Water Use in the Egyptian High Dam Era." *Land Economics* 40 (3) (August 1964):277–93.

Peterson, A. "Egypt's Agricultural Dilemma." *Wisconsin Academy Review* 15 (4) (Winter 1969):2–7.

Qalash, S. "Power and the Dam." *Al-Ahram*, June 26, 1976; in Arabic.

Qar'i, Ahmad Yussef al-. "Unity of the Nile Valley and Egypto-Sudanese Integration." *International Politics* (Cairo) (42) (October 1975):137–42; in Arabic.

"Red Sea Tug of War." *The Middle East* (30) (April 1977).

Reeve, R. C., M. Fireman. "Salt Problems in Relation to Irrigation." In *Irrigation of Agricultural Lands*, edited by R. M. Hagen, *et al.* Madison, Wisc.: American Society of Agronomy, 1967.

Rifa'at, 'Issam. "The Parameters of Economic Integration with the Sudan." *Al Ahram al-Iqtisadi* (450) (May 15, 1974):22–24; in Arabic.

Roden, D. "Regional Inequality and Rebellion in the Sudan." *Geographical Review* 64 (4) (October 1974):498–516.

Rouleau, Eric. "Soudan: la commune avortée," August 23, 1971, and "Les colonels sans camarades," February 16–18, 1972, *Le Monde*.

Rzoska, J. "The Invasion of *Eichornia Crassipes* in the Sudanese White Nile." In *The Nile: Biology of an Ancient River*, edited by J. Rzoska. The Hague: Dr. W. Junk, 1976.

Salacuse, Jeswald. "The Arab Authority for Agricultural Investment and Development. *Journal of World Trade Law* 12 (January–February 1978):56–66.

Sanderson, G. N. "Review Article." *Middle East Studies* 12 (1) (January 1976):108–11.

"Seminar on the Investment of Foreign and Arab Capital." *Al-Tali'a* 10 (7) (July 1974); in Arabic.

Shephard, G. "National Integration and the Southern Sudan." *The Journal of Modern African Studies* (42) (October 1966).

Shinnawi, Abd al-Khaleq. "The Fertility of Egypt's Land in the Balance." *Broadcasting and Television* (2128) (December 27, 1975):10–11; in Arabic.

Sohn, L. B. "The Stockholm Declarations on the Human Environment." *Harvard International Law Journal* 14 (1973).

"Special Study on Land Use." *Al-Tali'a* 8 (10) (October 1972); in Arabic.

Springborg, R. "Patterns of Association in the Egyptian Political Elite." In *Political Elites in the Middle East*, edited by George Lenczowski. Washington, D.C.: American Enterprise Institute, 1975.

Sterling, Claire. "Superdams: the Perils of Progress." *The Atlantic* 229 (6) (June 1972):35–41.

"Sudan: The Sugar Explosion." *Mideast Markets*, March 3, 1975.

Taha, Abdel-Rahman E. Ali. "Sudanese Development Path." In *Development Paths in Africa and China*, edited by Ukandi Damachi, *et al*. London: Macmillan, 1976.

"The Tempest in the Sugar Pot." *Fortune*, February 1977.

Thomas, H., and R. Revelle. "On the Efficient Use of the High Aswan Dam for Hydropower and Irrigation." *Management Science* 12 (8) (April 1966):296–311.

Tignor, Robert. "Nationalism, Economic Planning, and Development Projects in Interwar Egypt." *International Journal of African Historical Studies* 10 (2) (1977):185–208.

Tonberry, A. A. el-, and M. S. Abou El-ezz. "Economics of Water Supply and Control in the Southern Region of the United Arab Republic. An Outline." *International Journal of Agrarian Affairs* 3 (1) (January 1961):15–36.

"The Tushka Depression Scheme." *Al-Magalla az-Zira'ia* 19 (6) (June 1977); in Arabic.

Van Der Schalie, H. "Aswan Dam Revisited: the Blood Fluke Thrives." *Environment* 16 (9) (November 1974):18–26.

de Vreede, M. "Deserts Advance." *Development Forum* (May 1977).

Waterbury, John. "Egypt: the Wages of Dependency." In *The Middle East: Oil, Conflict and Hope*, edited by A. L. Udovitch. Lexington, Mass.: Lexington Books, 1976.

Watt, D. C. "The High Dam at Aswan and the Politics of Control." In *Dams in Africa*, edited by Neville Rubin and W. Warner. New York: Augustus Kelley, 1960.

Webb, C. "Sugar Politics in the European Communities." *Government and Opposition* 11 (4) (August 1976):464–80.

Wissa-Wassef, Cérès. "Le prolétariat et le sous-prolétariat industriel et agricole en RAU." *Orient*, 2–4ᵉ Trim. 13 (51) (1969):87–112.

Wynn, R. F. "The Sudan's Ten-Year Plan of Economic Development, 1961–62— 1970–71. An Analysis of Achievement to 1967–68." *The Journal of Developing Areas* 5 (July 1971):555–76.

PUBLICATIONS OF GOVERNMENTS AND INTERNATIONAL ORGANIZATIONS
PAPERS AND PROCEEDINGS OF CONFERENCES

AFSED. *Basic Programme for Agricultural Development in the Sudan 1976–85: An*

Invitation to the Founders. Unofficial translation, British Council of Industries. London, 1977.

Arab Organization for Agricultural Development. *Project for Mechanized Production of Sorghum, Oil Seeds, and Fodder: Southern Funj Region, Sudan.* Khartoum: 1974; in Arabic.

Arab Republic of Egypt (ARE); Central Agency for Public Mobilization and Statistics (CAPMAS). *Population and Development.* Cairo: June 1973.

—————. "The Population of Egypt: Results of the General Census of November 1976." *Al-Ahram al-Iqtisadi.* Supplement, May 1, 1977; in Arabic.

ARE, Dr. Abd al-Qadir Hatem. General Supervisor of the Specialized National Committees. *The High Dam and Its Effects,* supplement to *al-Ahram al-Iqtisadi,* February 1, 1976; in Arabic/English.

ARE, Egyptian Academy of Scientific Research and Technology, and the University of Michigan. *Water Quality Studies on the Nile River and Lake Nasser,* Ann Arbor: 1975.

ARE, Institute of National Planning, M. M. Abd al-Ra'uf, "Agricultural Mechanization in the UAR." Memo. No. 1069, July 1974; in Arabic.

ARE, Institute of National Planning, Sa'ad al-Din al-Hanafi. "The Shape of the Egyptian Agricultural Sector to the Year 2000." Paper presented at the Conference on Long Range Planning and Regional Integration, INP/CAEU/UNIDO. Cairo: January 14–21, 1976; in Arabic.

ARE, Ministry of Housing and Reconstruction/UNDP. *Suez Canal Regional Plan: June 1976* (GOPP, TAMS, DAG). Cairo: 1976.

ARE, Ministry of Irrigation. Mahmoud Abou-Zeid, *The Management of Irrigation Water in the ARE.* UN Water Conference, Mar del Plata, Argentina, March 1977.

ARE, Ministry of Irrigation, Kemal Hefny, *Ground Water Potentialities in ARE.* UN Water Conference, Mar del Plata, Argentina, March 1977.

ARE, Ministry of Irrigation, Abd al-Azim Abu al-Atta, *Long-Range Planning in the Sphere of Irrigation and Drainage.* Conference on Long-Range Planning and Regional Integration, INP/CAEU/UNIDO, Cairo, January 1976; in Arabic.

ARE, Ministry of Irrigation. Jan Kamel. *Aquatic Weed Problems in Egypt.* UN Water Conference, Mar del Plata, Argentina, March 1977.

ARE, Ministry of Irrigation. Mustafa Hafez and W. K. Shenouda, *The Environmental Impacts of the Aswan High Dam.* UN Water Conference, Mar del Plata, Argentina, March 1977.

ARE, Ministry of Planning. *The Five-Year Plan 1978–1982, Vol. I: The General Strategy for Economic and Social Development.* Cairo, August 1977. Vol. IV: *The General Strategy for Agriculture, Irrigation and Food Security,* Cairo, August 1977; in Arabic.

ARE, Ministry of Planning. Essam Muntasser. *Egypt's Long-term Growth:*

1976–2000. Conference on Long-Range Planning and Regional Integration, INP/CAEU/UNIDO Cairo, January 1976.

ARE, Price Planning Agency. "Distribution of Individual Income." Memo No. 18, January 1973; in Arabic.

Baumer, Michel. "Desertification Press Seminar." *Earthscan.* London, September 27, 1976.

Berg, L. "The Water Balance of the Nile Delta." Symposium on Nile Water and Lake Dam Projects, National Research Center, Dokki, Cairo, March 1–4, 1976.

Confederation of British Industry (Market Study). *The Sudan.* London, May 1977.

Democratic Republic of the Sudan (DRS) Ministry of Agriculture. *Food and the Sudan.* Khartoum: Khartoum University Press, 1974.

DRS, Ministry of Agriculture. *Current Agricultural Statistics.* CAS-1, (2) June 1976.

DRS, Authority for the Development of the Jonglei Area, Abel Alier. *Statement to the People's Regional Assembly on the Proposed Jonglei Canal.* Khartoum, n.d.

DRS, Executive Organ for Development Projects in the Jonglei Area. *The Jonglei Project: Phase I.* Khartoum, January 1975.

DRS, Ministry of Finance, Plan, and National Economy. *Initial Highlights of the Six Year Plan for Economic and Social Development 1977–78 — 1982–83,* Khartoum, July 1976; in Arabic.

DRS, Ministry of Irrigation, Abdullahi Ibrahim. *Likely Irrigated Agriculture of 2000 AD in the DRS.* Khartoum, February 1977.

DRS, Ministry of Irrigation, A. M. Khalifa and M. A. al-Nasry. *Improving the Water Yield of the River Nile by Minimizing the Losses in the Swamps.* UN Water Conference, Mar del Plata, Argentina, March 1977.

DRS, Ministry of Irrigation, Kemal Ali Mohammed. *The Projects for the Increase of the Nile Yield with Special Reference to the Jonglei Project.* UN Water Conference, Mar del Plata, Argentina, March 1977.

DRS, Ministry of Irrigation, H. S. Adam and H. G. Farbrother. *Crop-Water Use in Irrigated and Rainfed Agriculture in the DRS.* UN Water Conference, Mar del Plata, March 1977.

DRS, Ministry of Irrigation. *Control and Use of the Nile Waters in the Sudan.* Khartoum, June 1975.

DRS, Ministry for Southern Affairs. *A Revolution in Action: Regional Autonomy for the South.* Khartoum, n.d.

DRS, NCR, ARC, Saghayroun al-Zein. "The Water Resources of the Nile for Agricultural Development in the Sudan." In *Aquatic Weeds in the Sudan,* edited by Mohammed Obeid. Khartoum, November 1976.

——. *Staff Summary Report of Regional Workshop on Aquatic Weed Management and Utilization in the Nile Basin.* Khartoum, November 1976.

DRS, NPC. *Economic Survey 1974.* Khartoum, July 1975.

DRS, NPC, Transport and Communications Section. *Transport Statistical Bulletin 1974.* Khartoum, April 1975.

DRS, National Preparatory Committee for UN Water Conference. *The Water Resources of the Sudan.* Khartoum, 1977.

DRS, Sudan Sugar Corporation and Cane Machinery and Engineering. *The Sudan Sugar Industry.* July 1975.

DRS, Sudan Sugar Corporation. *Sugar for the Sudan and Neighboring Countries.* Khartoum, August 1975.

Entz, D. *Morphometry of Lake Nasser.* Aswan: Lake Nasser Development Center, 1973.

Ethiopia, Ministry of Irrigation. *Ethiopia: I, Water Reserves and Development; II, The Need for Cooperation among Co-Basin States.* UN Water Conference, Mar del Plata, Argentina, March 1977.

FAO, Near East Regional Office. *Research on Crop-Water Use, Salt-Affected Soils and Drainage in the ARE.* Rome, 1975.

FAO. *Egypt: Country Development Brief.* February 1974.

——. *Perspective Study of Agricultural Development for the DRS: Land and Water Development and Use.* ESP/AGL/PS/SUD/73/6 Rome, 1973.

——. *Soil Survey Project, UAR: Vol. I; General Report.* FAO/SF: 16/UAR, Rome 1966.

Fogel, L. J., et al. *Epidemiologic Consequences of Schistosomiasis in Egypt.* Washington, D.C.: USGPO, 1970.

Gischler, Christaan. *Present and Future Trends in Water Development in the Arab States.* UNESCO/ROSTAS, Cairo? August 1976.

Government of Egypt, Department of Public Works. Y. M. Simaika. *The Suspended Matter in the Nile.* Paper No. 40, Cairo, 1940.

Government of Egypt, W. E. Garstin. *Report Upon the Basin of the Upper Nile.* Cairo: Natonal Printing Department, 1904.

Government of Egypt, Ministry of Public Works, H. E. Hurst. *A Short Account of the Nile Basin.* Cairo, 1944.

Government of The Sudan, Public Relations Branch. *Sudan Almanac 1954.* Khartoum, 1954.

Government of The Sudan. *Southern Development Investigation Team, Natural Resources and Development Potential in the Southern Provinces of the Sudan.* London, 1955.

Government of The Sudan, Jonglei Investigation Team. *The Equatorial Nile Project: Report of the Jonglei Investigation Team.* Khartoum, 1954.
Vol. I: *A Survey of the Area Affected*
Vol. II: *The Equatorial Nile Project*
Vol. III: *Special Investigations and Experimental Data*
Vol. IV: *Maps and Diagrams*

Hagg, Ahmad Osman al-, and Qadi, Nagwa Ahmad al-. *The Experience of the Sudan in Planning with Regard to Arab Integration.* Seminar on Long-Range Planning and Regional Integration, INP/CAEU/UNIDO, January 1976; in Arabic.

Hurst, H. E., P. Phillips. *The Nile Basin; Vol. I: General Description of the Basin, Meteorology, Topography of the White Nile Basin.* Cairo: Government Printing Office, 1931.

Hurst, H. E.; R. P. Black; Y. M. Simaika. *The Nile Basin; Vol. II: The Future Conservation of the Nile.* Cairo: Government Printing Office, 1946.

IBRD. *Report of a Special Mission on the Economic Development of Southern Sudan.* Washington, D.C., June 1, 1973.

IBRD, Staff Working Paper No. 247. *Developing Country Foodgrain Projections for 1985.* Washington, D. C., 1976.

International Council of Scientific Unions. *Man-Made Lakes as Modified Eco-Systems.* Paris, 1972.

International Law Commission. *Work of the International Law Commission on the Law of Non-Navigational Uses of International Water Courses.* UN Water Conference, Mar del Plata, Argentina, March 1977.

Kinawy, I. Z. *The Efficiency of Water Use in Irrigation in Egypt.* Conference on Arid Lands Irrigation in Developing Countries, UNESCO/UNEP/ Academy of Scientific Research and Technology, Alexandria, February 1976.

———, and O. A. al-Ghomry. "Some Effects of the High Dam on the Environment." Ms. prepared for the 13th Congress on Great Dams, 1973.

Mann, Oscar. *The Jonglei Canal: Environmental and Social Aspects.* Nairobi: Environment Liaison Center, 1977.

Nilsen, Ev. "Nile Delta Erosion: Interdisciplinary Science at Work." *Bulletin of the UNESCO Field Science Office for the Arab States* 2 (3) (April–June 1974):20–24.

Obeid, M. "The Water Hyacinth: Eichornia Crassipes." In *Aquatic Weeds in the Sudan,* edited by M. Obeid. Khartoum, November 1976.

Okidi, Odidi, C. *Challenge to the Management of Water Resources.* Paper prepared especially for the UN Water Conference, Mar del Plata, Argentina, March 1977.

Republic of Sudan, Ministry of Irrigation. *The Nile Waters Question: The Case for Egypt and the Sudan's Reply.* Khartoum, December 1955.

Sestini, G. *Geomorphology of the Nile Delta.* Conference on Arid Lands Irrigation in Developing Countries. UNESCO/UNEP/Academy on Scientific Research and Technology, Alexandria, February 1976.

UAR, General Authority for the High Dam, Mohammed Abdel Rakeeb. *The High Dam Project: Its Benefits Far Outweigh Adverse and Side Effects.* Cairo, 1971.

UAR, CAPMAS. *Sample Survey of the Work Force in the UAR: Results of the May 1968 Round.* Ref. No. 1–222, October 1970.

UAR, Aswan Regional Plan Project, Abderrazak, Abdel-Maguid, *et al. Notes on the Study of the Uses of the High Dam.* March 1966.

UAR, Authority for the High Dam. *High Dam Project.* Part II, Cairo, 1967.

UAR, INP, Mohammed Abou al-Dahab. "Horizontal Expansion in UAR Agriculture." Memo 820, August 1968.

UAR, INP, Iz al-Din Hamam Ahmad, *et al.* "Maximum Horizontal Expansion in UAR Agriculture." Memo 795, August 1967.

UAR, Ministry of Agrarian Reform and Land Reclamation. *Agrarian Reform and Land Reclamation in Ten Years.* Cairo, 1962?.

UAR, Ministry of Power. *The High Dam is Completed: 1960–1970.* Aswan, 1970.

UN Economic Commission for Africa. *Regional Report* (Water Conference Recommendations), E/CONF. 70/7, UN Water Conference, Mar del Plata, Argentina, March 1977.

UNDP/ILO. *Growth, Employment and Equity: A Comprehensive Strategy for Sudan.* ILO, Geneva, October 1975.

UNDP/UNESCO and Department of Geology, Alexandria University. *Proceedings on the Seminar on Nile Delta Sedimentology.* Alexandria, October 25–29, 1975.

UNESCO. *The Rising Water Table and Related Problems in the West Nubaria Project Area.* ILRI, ARE, 1973.

U.S. Department of Agriculture and USAID. *Egypt: Major Constraints to Increasing Agricultural Productivity.* Washington, D.C., June 1976.

U.S. Department of Commerce, Bureau of International Commerce. *Foreign Economic Trends and their Implications for the United States: Sudan.* FET 75–055, June 1975.

INDEX

HYDROPOLITICS

of the

NILE VALLEY

was composed in 10-point VIP Palatino and leaded two points,
with display type set in Typositor Nubian
by Utica Typesetting Company, Inc.;
printed offset on acid-free Warren's Antique Cream paper stock,
Smyth-sewn and bound over 80-point binder's boards in Columbia Bayside Linen
by Maple-Vail Book Manufacturing Group, Inc.;
and published by
SYRACUSE UNIVERSITY PRESS
SYRACUSE, NEW YORK 13210